ENVIRONMENTAL ACCIDENTS

RICHARD H. GASKINS

Environmental Accidents

Personal Injury and Public Responsibility

TEMPLE UNIVERSITY PRESS   Philadelphia

Temple University Press, Philadelphia 19122
Copyright © 1989 by Temple University. All rights reserved.
Published 1989
Printed in the United States of America

The paper used in this publication meets the minimum
requirements of American National Standard for Information
Sciences—Permanence of Paper for Printed Library Materials,
ANSI Z39.48-1984

Library of Congress
Library of Congress Cataloging-in-Publication Data
Gaskins, Richard H.
Environmental accidents : personal injury and public
responsibility / Richard H. Gaskins.
p.   cm.
Bibliography: p.
Includes index.
ISBN 0-87722-609-1
1. Liability for environmental damages—United States.
2. Personal injuries—United States.   3. Accident law—United
States.   4. Accidents—United States.   I. Title.
KF1298.G37 1989
346.7303'23—dc19
[347.306323]   88-23661
                                                         CIP

For Elizabeth

Preface

Near the end of the twentieth century, the United States remains the only country in the world where the judicial system dominates public perceptions of personal injury. We still view accidents as essentially *legal* events, defined by the doctrines, institutions, and professional perspectives of the law. But this monopoly now shows signs of weakening. Over the past decade, our complex social and industrial environment has been sending out disturbing new signals, suggesting that public prosperity is counterbalanced by substantial costs in personal security. Many collective risks of modern life may well be worth taking, but we are increasingly reminded that the costs fall randomly but inevitably on an indeterminate minority of Americans.

The problem of accidents underscores the fundamental interdependence of private individuals in industrialized societies. Our collective response to personal injury should be addressed in a wider forum than the traditional judicial process can provide; it belongs at the center of national debate about public health, safety, and welfare. The chapters below introduce a social or *environmental* definition of accidents to replace the outworn legal definition

Legal concepts and procedures are ideally designed to handle only a special subset of accidents: isolated events involving two people, played out against a background of self-evident moral duties. Since these conditions are rarely found outside the abstractions of philosophers, the courts have struggled mightily to apply their traditional categories to contemporary reality. As we shall see, they are losing the struggle. The judicial system has now been stretched to the point of permanent crisis, giving rise to an unprecedented search for cures and alternatives.

Unfortunately, that search remains trapped in legal concepts. Instead of treating accidents as a *social* problem, we still see them as a special type of legal disturbance. Rather than connecting accidents with social policies on health, safety, and disability, we tinker with legal institutions and try to preserve their autonomy. Most of all, the adversarial combat of litigation has invaded the political arena, multiplying interest-group conflicts and paralyzing any prospects for effective public response. In the complex industrial environments of today, the legal definition of accidents has become a serious hazard in its own right. It needs to be assessed from an entirely new perspective.

In recent years, economic and moral concepts have gotten entangled in the legal definition of accidents. These themes too remain narrowly developed within the margins of standard legal categories. To be sure, some aspects of neoclassical economics and individualist moral theory fit neatly into the atomistic social model favored by the law; like an invisible helping hand, these theories can be used to rationalize the autonomy of legal institutions. But we have not yet begun to see what economics or moral philosophy might say about a different definition of accidents. In a concrete world of social interdependence, the problems of personal injury should invite much richer economic and moral speculation, along with fresh approaches to public policy. These will be the long-term benefits, I hope, from a new analysis of accidents.

Some central ideas in this book were formed over the past decade in discussions with my colleagues at Bryn Mawr's Graduate School of Social Work and Social Research, with its program in Law and Social Policy. I am especially indebted to Jane Kronick and William Vosburgh for their support and encouragement over many years, which began with their invitation to participate in a study of New Zealand's innovative social policy for accidents. I was challenged to reexamine many aspects of my legal training during those discussions, which also included Noel Farley, John Orbell and Miriam Vosburgh. That project received generous support from the National Science Foundation (the program on Ethics and Values in Science and Technology), along with the National Endowment for the Humanities. I should add that none of the conclusions reached then, and none contained in the present volume, represent the opinions of either organization.

Let me also thank Mary Patterson McPherson, President of Bryn Mawr College, for her warm personal support, which included encouraging me to take the sabbatical leave that launched this project.

In spring 1987 I was able to spend several weeks at the Centre for Socio-Legal Studies at Oxford University. Over many years, the multidisciplinary research staff at the Oxford Centre has made important contributions to the analysis of compensation issues. I am indebted to Donald R. Harris and members of the Centre for their many suggestions, and for helping me locate materials for a comparative survey of national compensation policies. Jane Stapleton of Balliol College was also very generous with her time.

As for the University of Chicago, where this book was written, it is impossible to praise too highly the outstanding research facilities. The staff at the D'Angelo Law Library was especially helpful in making the collection accessible, despite the disruption of major building renovations.

I am grateful to Kenneth Avio of the University of Victoria, British Columbia, for commenting thoughtfully on an early version of this manuscript—as did Jane Kronick and William Vosburgh. The reviewers for Temple University Press also gave many probing and useful suggestions. I have greatly enjoyed working with Michael Ames and his excellent staff, and am pleased to acknowledge their efforts in seeing this book through.

Chicago
September 1988

Table of Contents

Part III
Institutional Options: Recent Trends
in American Policy

ENVIRONMENTAL ACCIDENTS

Introduction

Accidents and the Environment

Accidents teach us about social interdependence. They are important and necessary reminders that plans laid out by even the most careful people quickly move beyond the narrow horizons of human vision. They are rude and sometimes catastrophic evidence that our ability to control events is fundamentally limited. Indeed, things almost never turn out exactly the way we plan them; life deviates from the most skillfully written script. After we have done our very best to anticipate the future, we can only watch—occasionally with horror—as unintended results unfold.

How much human injury, illness, and disability in modern societies can be associated with such unpredictable but inevitable turns of fate? That depends on how each society defines accidental events and organizes its response. The range of answers varies widely among countries, and varies in the same country over time. Our review of American approaches to personal injury will take us into a largely tacit and deeply ambivalent form of response. We cannot pretend that the United States has anything close to a formal social policy on accidents, but it surely has one of the most bizarre and confusing systems for responding to this major challenge faced by all complex societies.

3

Recently the American notion of accidents has been thrown into disarray by the discovery of latent dangers in our industrial environment. Given our pride in technological accomplishments, this has been an especially difficult and controversial lesson. Take that remarkable element, asbestos, which American know-how fashioned into a useful servant for many decades. Heralded as a miracle substance, it improved the performance of American battleships during World War II, insulated America's heating systems, and served as a fire retardant in countless schools and other public buildings throughout the country. We now know, however, that asbestos is an important cause of disabling and often fatal diseases that may wait twenty years to strike. Just who is susceptible and why is not entirely clear, but current evidence suggests that 200,000 persons may die from asbestos-caused diseases by the end of the century.

America's trust in its future is deeply challenged by the possibility that other materials in our environment hold the same lethal potential as asbestos. Studies cited by the U.S. Surgeon General in 1988 predict a comparable death toll from exposure to radon, a naturally occurring substance that can become trapped in today's tightly sealed, energy-efficient private homes and public buildings. Along with other nations, the United States has also acknowledged a health threat of unknown magnitude from depletion of ozone in the upper atmosphere. In addition, we face uncertain environmental costs from a global "greenhouse effect" traced to new technologies and patterns of economic development. Such examples blur the lines between accidents and disease and raise new political and social issues that may take decades to comprehend.

Meanwhile the American judicial system—to which we have always entrusted our primary institutional response to accidents—has weathered a series of highly publicized crises. Some of these episodes are explicitly tied to hazardous substances, like the asbestos cases, and the claims of Vietnam veterans exposed to dioxin in Agent Orange. But other crises such as medical malpractice and product liability also reflect the complex relation between modern technology and personal injury. Even the ongoing crisis of automobile accident liability, which spreads its costs through insurance premiums to nearly every household in the country, has its roots in technological and social patterns. In a sense to be defined more precisely in Chapter 2, all these events illustrate the critical impact of modern social environments on public health and safety. It is thus a tragic mistake to classify such problems as institutional crises for the courts. The stunning failure of judicial processes, while significant, is merely the symptom of a deeper flaw in our traditional understanding of accidental events.

The message of this book is that *environmental accidents* compel us to review our whole understanding of the social order. They illustrate in unusually graphic fashion the reality of our social interdependence, and thus the limitations of a political and legal system still bound in many ways to the individualist premises of classical liberalism. Before they have finished with us, environmental accidents will require something entirely new: a systematic public response to personal injury. In short, the United States needs to develop a more comprehensive social policy on accidents.

Some outlines for such a policy are suggested later on in this study, but more important than another abstract model is the evidence that American responses to accidents have already undergone significant change over the past two decades. The survey of American policies in Part III will show the degree to which we have already watered down traditional judicial perspectives on personal injury—except for occasions when that view still meets the strategic interests of particular groups. Of course, like everything else, public policy development is subject to unforeseen events and strange twists of fate. Our prospects for a better policy—the best one can hope for in an imperfect world— depend on developing a sharper sense of where our perilous environment seems to be leading us.

The View of Accidents in This Study

For at least a century the subject of accidents has been jealously protected by the legal profession, which dominates both its practical and theoretical dimensions. Far more than any other nation, the United States relies on its judicial structures, practicing attorneys, and law professors to organize, implement, and interpret the entire field. This monopoly of legal perspectives extends to the definition and even the pathology of the prevailing system. "Accidents" are what the courts define them to be. A "crisis" in accident policy is understood to be some failure of the judicial structure. Alternative systems are designed with judicial procedures as the constant reference point.

Owing to this esoteric structure and jargon, nonlawyers have often had trouble grasping the broader significance of accidents. A fuller definition covers a much wider range of personal injuries, illness, and disability. The "crisis of accidents" is thus more serious than high legal fees, crowded courts, or unfair treatment of plaintiffs and defendants: it refers more poignantly to our profound ignorance about the personal impact of complex social forms. It demands a full assessment of public obligations for environmental regulation and social welfare.

Curiously, our deference to the professional perspectives of lawyers seems to be enhanced when the popular press focuses attention on the more ludicrous side of litigation. When juries award six-figure sums to plaintiffs for loss of psychic powers, or when irate sports fans file suit against referees for inaccurate officiating, it somehow adds to the mystery and majesty of the law. Attorneys, hardened to the fictions of their trade, quickly lose patience with their literal-minded critics. Although occasional defenders of the legal system still help themselves to the moral vocabulary of "fault," most lawyers take an utterly pragmatic approach to their field: if it works, it doesn't really matter how outlandish it seems to the layperson. Whether something truly works, however, depends on our initial expectations. The aims of most lawyers (even ignoring the matter of professional self-interest) are too modest to represent society's broader needs for accident policy. What works for them may not be working for us.

The efforts of legal academics provide a further challenge to any simple analysis of accident policy. Ever since Oliver Wendell Holmes's pathbreaking essay more than a century ago, legal commentators have been building a formidable intellectual apparatus to support and criticize the prevailing law of accidents. For decades the doctrinal structure of judge-made law has been measured by legal scholars against a shifting background of vaguely defined social purposes, ranging from the interests of emerging industrialism (Holmes) to the social welfare of uncompensated workers (the progressives) to "optimal" accident prevention (the law-and-economics movement). Despite the impressive intellectual resources invested in these and other analyses, they have often been narrowly addressed to other legal scholars and the occasional enlightened judge. The resulting debate—both ornate and parochial—has remained largely inaccessible to outsiders. These contributions are virtually the only commentary on current accident policy, however, and we have no choice but to consider them carefully.

Since new policies relating to accidents are conceived as alternatives to litigation, we must begin our study with the judicial process to see what is alleged to be wrong. This is actually a two-stage effort, covering first the conceptual field of judicial doctrines and procedures, but also two popular frameworks imported by legal academics to support their doctrinal models: economics and ethics. Part I below does the first of these tasks, contrasting the traditional individualist concepts of common-law doctrines (Chapter 1) with an interpretation of accidents using a social or environmental model (Chapter 2). Then in Part II we examine the two major conceptual tools used to reinforce the individualist categories of law: the free-market model (Chapter 4), and analytic moral philosophy (Chapter 5). Preceding these two chapters is an analysis of major interest-group strategies in the political struggle over "tort reform"—the debate on changing the judicial process (Chapter 3).

Although Parts I and II deal with technical subjects, I have tried to make these chapters accessible to the general reader. For the rarefied theories derived from economics and moral philosophy, my intent is simply to show that neither field can rescue an accident policy centered on the judicial system. My criticisms may not satisfy partisans of either approach, but I hope they give the interested outsider some glimpse of what has gotten lost in these specialized discussions.

Analyzing interest-group politics runs a different risk of appearing to reduce objective theory to purely adversarial terms. In a field like accident policy, however, we cannot ignore the strategic value of arguments based on allegedly neutral legal doctrines, economic logic, and moral reasoning. I have thus sought to interpret the subtle alliance between major analytical positions and the interest groups that champion them. But such an exposé is not meant to replace theoretical critique, as Chapters 4 and 5 make clear.

Part III provides a survey of current American accident policies, presented as a series of four institutional strategies for modifying or replacing judicial procedures. These are arranged in order of departure from the traditional litigation model: self-reform through judicial activism (Chapter 6), legislative modification of judicial rules and procedures (Chapter 7), substitution of the federal government for one of the traditional parties in the litigation process (Chapter 8), and administrative preemption of judicial procedures (Chapter 9). Each chapter presents selected case studies of new and proposed policies for accidents associated with problematic environments: accidents involving vaccines, asbestos, Agent Orange, medical services, defective or dangerous products, toxic wastes, nuclear power, workplace injuries, and occupational diseases. The sequence of chapters is mainly an organizational device, but it may also be seen as a developmental path leading from a purely judicial policy, through step-wise departures from judicial forms, up to the point where judicial institutions cease to play any formal role.

The logical completion of this sequence does not appear until Part IV, since it has yet to be formulated in the United States as a concrete policy. Chapter 10 generalizes the basic principle of administrative compensation schemes, outlining a policy that would abandon judicial procedures for most types of personal injury. Based on a view of accidents as essentially social or environmental, this approach would exploit separate strategies for dealing with two major elements of accident policy: *compensation* and *accountability*. It would extend the reach of compensation to injuries, illnesses, and disabilities that go beyond the prevailing judicial definition of accidents; and it would expand the principle of accountability to include the interlocking behavior of individuals, groups, government agencies, and society as a whole. The concept of *public responsibility* will be used to convey the unity of both domains.

Comprehensive accident policies similar to the public responsibility model were enacted in New Zealand and briefly considered by Australia and Great Britain during the 1970s. Chapter 11 adds a comparative perspective to the American debate by exploring alternative approaches used in other industrialized Western nations.

The reader is invited to preview the overall argument of this book by scanning the brief introductions to each of the four parts. Readers with specialized interests should be able to tell which chapters to emphasize or avoid—although this book is specifically designed for nonspecialists in the legal literature on accidents.

Relation to Previous Studies

The view of accidents as social or environmental has received little attention from legal commentators, especially in the United States. But the basic themes have been developed over the past twenty-five years in works by Terence G. Ison, P. S. Atiyah, Eli P. Bernzweig, Donald R. Harris and his colleagues at the Oxford University Centre for Socio-Legal Studies, and Jane Stapleton. During the 1970s comprehensive policy models were drafted in separate government reports from New Zealand and Australia, inspired by Sir Owen Woodhouse. This book has been influenced by all these studies, and tries to apply their perspective to the unique problems of American social policy in the late twentieth century.

What is new here, in addition to my focus on American issues, is the description of accidents as "environmental." This concept is explored at length in Chapter 2, but its meaning can be summarized as the ultimately *statistical* relation between personal injuries and an expanding catalogue of environmental agents. Common law, by contrast, treats as "accidents" only those events that can be fully reduced to concrete, motivated behavior of discrete individuals—a definition so conceptually barren that for decades its proponents have had to embellish it with fictions and presumptions. In the late 1960s and early 1970s, Ison, Atiyah, and Woodhouse developed the basic outlines of an environmental model, focusing mainly on workplace and automobile accidents. But traditional legal concepts won out (except in New Zealand), and the next decade discovered new applications of economic theory and moral philosophy for strengthening the individualist perspective.

In the 1980s, however, epidemiological studies began to document the harmful effects of common substances in modern industrial environments, requiring a dramatic change in our definition of personal injury. As these overtly statistical forms of causation find halting acceptance in judicial proceedings, the traditional definition of "accident" fades into the background. The line between accidents and illness is removed, leaving the way open for a potentially endless flow of plausible judicial claims. We can now tie the argument for more comprehensive policy reform to these intriguing "toxic torts," supplementing the more subtle case based on standard workplace injuries and automobile accidents.

In the United States, new information about environmental injuries is partly the result of expanding federal regulatory policies over the past twenty years, a trend that seems hardly blunted by periods of economic retrenchment, soaring public debt, and the Reaganite attack on regulation. The new federal role in identifying, tracking, cleaning up, and setting standards for public exposure to toxic hazards brings more than increased awareness: it draws public regulatory policy directly into the causal chain of injury. If accidents broadly conceived are the random but inevitable results of social interaction, public regulation of the environment becomes a highly focused expression for an otherwise nameless force. By formalizing a concern for public safety in areas like nuclear power, toxic chemicals, vaccines and other health measures, consumer products, and agents of occupational disease, federal regulation has helped point the way to a reorientation of American accident policy.

Is It Realistic?

With so much talk here about comprehensive change, it is fair to ask about the political prospects for major policy shifts. American politics prefers incremental steps to heroic leaps, and perhaps this is all we can expect with complex issues like personal injury. Certainly nothing contained in this book will support the view that coherent or planful reform of accident policy is currently in progress. Indeed, one of the reasons for outlining a comprehensive model is to underscore the comparative aimlessness of what now passes for "tort reform."

But the conventional wisdom of incrementalism needs some qualification. The familiar instruments of accident policy may be confined to incremental change, but there are other policy fields that reflect the larger arena of social interdependence. Federal environmental regulation, social welfare entitlements, and health programs are all likely elements of some future comprehensive accident policy; and the confluence of these various streams is prefigured by their parallel movements. Ambitious regulatory programs going back more than twenty years are a sign of public initiative in areas of the environment that were long conceptualized as purely private behavior. Despite the hostile climate for regulation in the Reagan era, the mandate for environmental reform has steadily increased—even if the actual performance remains erratic. Another change over the same two decades has been the growth of public entitlement programs for persons who are ill or disabled. Here, too, important changes have prevailed despite the Reagan administration's best efforts to stop the tide. Finally, federal health initiatives have helped transform the entire field of medical services, even though specific programs have focused on discrete populations.

Politics has to deal with crises in all parts of this larger system: the scandals in EPA enforcement, the explosive growth of disability payments, the high costs of health services, and many others. But if these problems are larger versions of the specialized crises facing the judicial process, they offer better evidence of underlying social pressures. While the legal system continues to use appallingly expensive means to match up deserving plaintiffs with culpable defendants, the wider problems of public safety and personal welfare are being increasingly shifted over to the federal bureaucracy. What happens incrementally in any of these broader arenas can be quite fundamental for the more limited field of civil liability.

Incrementalism has never denied that changes accumulate over time, and that quantitative change can eventually lead to qualitative transformation. The reason for bringing new interpretive views to social policy, from time to time, is to anticipate some of these larger patterns. We should not treat a comprehensive vision of accident policy as just another political proposal, but rather as a guide for integrating gradual changes across a broad span. The gentle platitude of incrementalism should not be a barrier to such interpretive exercises.

To invoke another platitude: accidents can always happen. One of the most alarming prospects, given the political and institutional disarray of American accident policy, is the occurrence in this country of a Bhopal or a Chernobyl. In addition to widespread personal injuries, a separate casualty toll would have to be computed for those whose future health and welfare depended on prompt legal relief. Just as no one can predict how such an event would affect our country in human and environmental terms, the impact on the political process would be unprecedented. In response to catastrophic events, political action is unlikely to remain incremental; one hopes it would at least be constructive.

Sudden lurches in political mood need not wait for poisonous vapors or nuclear fallout. An equally challenging blow to incremental politics can result from cumulative discoveries about toxic substances in our everyday environment. As we learned in the Love Canal episode, a localized public health crisis can provoke national political reactions, no matter what verdict is pronounced months or years after the fact by scientific assessment. Love Canal brought critical support for the enactment of Superfund, just as the nation's momentary panic over Legionnaire's Disease forced Congress into action on the swine flu program. When public safety is on the line, the political climate can be highly volatile. But are measures adopted under extreme political conditions likely to work out over the long run? Probably not, unless in calmer times we are willing to speculate about the larger goals of accident policy.

Incrementalism may be a useful hypothesis about American political behavior, but it is not a complete public philosophy. Our survey in Part III of recent developments in American accident policy should end any nostalgia for the old pragmatist notion that incremental political change is the very embodiment of social intelligence. Despite the overall drift of American policy toward more active forms of public regulation and personal welfare, the vital coordinating perspectives are missing from public debate. The enormous pressures now being placed on judicial procedures in environmental accident cases are not the root of the problem, but they are a revealing symptom of the need for clearer public vision.

Part One

Accidents as Events: Individual and Social Frameworks

O ur first systematic look at the problem of accidents explores the differences between individual and social frameworks of interpretation. Most American policies on personal injury come under the authority of the judicial system and are expressed in the form of legal rules—the doctrines of tort law. This arcane rhetoric initially suggests a highly rationalistic order composed entirely of sovereign individuals bound together by contracts and duties, of events arranged in linear and transparent causal sequence, and of reasoning that conforms to the models of classical logic. Such a world contains very few compensable accidents, making it a hostile environment for the injured and a welcome haven for potential culprits.

It is also a world long since abandoned in the judicial implementation of legal doctrines, most of which have been functionally transformed to encompass a wider range of personal injuries. Thus American policies speak the language of traditional individualism but struggle desperately to keep pace with a more complex social environment: the world of industrial employment, powerful machines like automobiles, and toxic chemicals. As a bold and pragmatic judiciary encounters entirely new species of personal injury, however, its traditional categories are finally stretched beyond recognition. Chapter 1 charts the instrumentalist reconstruction of tort law, highlighting the most controversial doctrines that figure in the current national debate over "tort reform."

Chapter 2 approaches the problem of accidents from several non-judicial perspectives and notes the enormous challenges created by our complex social and technological environment. It uses the phrase *environmental accidents* to designate those personal injuries that can be statistically associated with hazardous substances, human behavior, organizational structures, and geographical locations—but which cannot be satisfactorily resolved into personal encounters and single-impact events. These are the injuries that systematically elude our legal categories despite creative efforts by the judicial process. Fortunately, other concepts come to our aid from public health, organizational sociology, and certain applications of economic theory.

The social or environmental approach to accidents illuminates the central weakness of policies derived from judicial practice: the vain attempt to correlate compensation of specific victims with the accountability of specific agents. This model of accidents as individualized events understates the potential public interest in both compensation and accountability, which should instead be pursued in separate policies. Both interests also need to be coordinated at a general level by legislative oversight, rather than subjected to instrumental micro-management in judicial proceedings.

Part I begins with a Prologue on the nature of accidents, previewing some of the broader interpretive issues with a few definitions and a brief historical review.

Prologue

What Is an Accident?

> *Every society embodies conflicting factors, simply be-*
> *cause it has gradually emerged from a past form and is*
> *tending toward a future one.*[1]

The Need for an Open-ended Definition

Some chance events merely happen. They may have serious and harmful effects on their victims, but they are not attributable to the careless or intentional actions of anyone, including the victims themselves. Imagine, for example, that a bolt of lightning strikes near a lone individual walking down a country road, causing temporary shock but no serious disability. The most important feature of such a "mere accident"—apart from our natural sympathy for the victim—is that nothing follows from it. There are no social implications extending into the past or the future. It neither calls for anyone to compensate the victim's losses, nor teaches us ways to prevent similar events from happening in the future.

In contrast to these "mere accidents," this study defines *accidents* as injurious events that *do* implicate other members of society, and in a number of specific ways. The two major forms of public response include relieving the victim's burden, often through some type of compensation, and holding someone (perhaps even the victim) accountable, either through punishment for the past event or through inducements for future prevention. These responses may implicate a wide network of people and organizations, up to and including society as a whole.

15

This text starts from the premise that the residual category of "mere accidents" is rapidly disappearing (if not yet confined to the proverbial bolt of lightning). A critical change has occurred with our new ability to link statistically a growing number of disabilities with harmful stimuli in the workplace, in the home, and in the general environment. These environmental accidents, thrown in with more familiar injurious events occurring in the factory and on the highways, have created unique social demands while placing increasing strain on judicial processes, legislative policies, and economic resources.

It takes some effort at first to connect instances of disease with the concept of an *accident*, as the term is commonly understood. However, even though our knowledge is highly fragmentary, we do know that an estimated 200,000 American workers may die before the end of the century from exposure to asbestos occurring over the past forty years.[2] We have also read that the Chernobyl accident may cause anywhere from 30,000 to 250,000 cancer deaths in the Soviet Union, with figures for neighboring countries still difficult to calculate.[3] The evidence is much more speculative in predicting the medical impact on Vietnam veterans of exposure to dioxin used in the infamous Agent Orange, not to mention the effects on earlier veterans from nuclear testing.

The very fact of indefinite evidence and variable estimates confounds our usual picture of an accident. With environmental injuries there is no clearly observed physical impact on the victim, and in most cases it is impossible to say precisely when the decisive exposure occurred. We cannot rely on the vivid imagery of body parts being mangled by industrial machinery or automobiles colliding in spectacular chain reactions; environmental accidents call for entirely different models and images. Nor, it turns out, do our customary procedures for responding to accidents (notably the judicial system) adjust to environmental accidents any faster than our pictorial imaginations. As scientific evidence accumulates about this vast interplay of disparate events, the social implications grow more complex, forcing us to rethink the outlines of compensation, punishment, and prevention in contexts broader than industrial injuries or highway accidents.

It is tempting to object that this definition of *accident* is too broad, that it leaves out practically nothing. And in fact, concrete policies concerning accidents—whether they deal with compensation or accountability—inevitably distinguish in some fashion between events that trigger a social response and those that do not. (Part IV of this study will explore ways of translating the notion of environmental accidents into such a policy framework.) But our main purpose throughout this book is to challenge the largely tacit definitions and assumptions of current accident policy, especially those connected with the judicial process. Notwithstanding all the modern apparatus of judicial pragmatism, welfare economics, and moral philosophy, these anachronistic categories preserve a fundamental view of events and of human interaction little changed from eighteenth-century atomism. Ad hoc accretions to these categories—laboriously developed for particular events like workplace injuries and automobile accidents—are often unable to encompass even these specialized cases, let alone serve as general criteria for designating other accidental events.

Most general definitions of accidents equivocate between conflicting elements of surprise and foreseeability. We often think of accidents as unexpected or unforeseen occurrences, as they surely are to at least *some* persons involved in them (usually the victims). But most injuries can also be anticipated by at least someone implicated in the event; indeed, common law has been rather ingenious in finding people of remote connection whom it credits with astonishing degrees of foreknowledge. Whatever the actual or constructive knowledge of individual persons, most accidents take place within organizational or statistical contexts in which the unexpected event is an everyday occurrence.[4] Under these conditions, the whole issue of surprise offers very little guidance for policies on compensation or accountability. And we beg too many questions when we build criteria like foreseeability or other imputed states of knowledge into the very definition of accidents, even though the judicial system has often found it a prudent exercise. The purpose of our open-ended definition is to escape these ad hoc solutions, sensible as they may have seemed for earlier social conflicts around specific kinds of accidents.

Likewise we will not try here to separate accidents from intentional harms. For almost any event that comes to notice, some prior human actions are obviously intentional, others clearly not, and still others of uncertain mental quality. We can, of course, create special categories of events, based on imputed mental states of key actors, and label them "intentional" or even "criminal." One can usually infer an assault and battery from an injurious encounter in a dark alley. But the event may still seem like an accident from the standpoint of the victim, as we have begun to recognize in setting up programs for crime victim counseling and compensation.[5]

In short, many common preconceptions about accidents reflect past efforts to structure the public response to injurious events in particular ways. Our premise, however, is that the appropriate form of social response may shift dramatically with changes in our environment, our social philosophies, and our institutional structures. Since the purpose here is to examine those past approaches in a critical way, we cannot simply adopt their contextual understanding of terms like *accident, injury, intent,* or *foreseeability.* In moving toward new forms of public response to qualitatively different types of events—what we are calling *environmental accidents*—these concepts would in fact prove highly misleading.[6]

Paradigm Accidents: Some Historical Reflections

In 1844, soon after the first major railroad catastrophe in Europe, a French commentator wrote this somber note on the connection between accidents and technology:

> All man-made things are subject to accidents. By a kind of compensation . . . , the more these things are perfected, the greater the gravity of the accidents that happen to them. . . . The mass of the objects they set in motion, the velocity they engender, their very power, once halted or turned from its proper objective, is transformed into a terrible agent of destruction. Steam power, while opening up new and hitherto unknown roads to man, also seems to continually put him in a position best compared to that of a man who is walking along the edge of a precipice and cannot afford a single false step.[7]

Public definitions and perceptions of accidents change over time as societies are forced to adjust to new events and social relationships. Technological innovation, especially with the spread of industrialization, has greatly accelerated these shifts in the social classification of events. By continually enlarging the scope of personal injuries beyond those easily assigned to either personal contact or natural sources, technology alternately confounds then expands our conceptual categories. Over time, perhaps the only constant is a peculiar sense of human vulnerability to forces both within and beyond social control.[8]

Each generation thus has to find its own response to new events arising from changing technologies under the thrall of an unforgiving environment. But which events are accidents, and what kind of response do they require? Social interpretation invariably lags behind events themselves, since it is restricted by the definitions, theories, and policies painfully worked out by prior generations. Changes in accident policy (if any) are usually focused on a single type of event—a paradigmatic accident—capable of commanding public attention. Such accidents define the policies and theories of a particular era, becoming the kind of event against which future perceptions are invariably tested.[9]

During the period of rapid industrialization in the United States, at the end of the nineteenth century, the injured worker emerged as the focal point of public reform, and industrial accidents became the paradigm around which a generation of progressive legal analysts went on to develop a vision of accident policy. By the mid-twentieth century a more affluent, consumer-oriented society had shifted its focus to automobile accidents—a less overtly ideological paradigm yielding a theory of accidents based on neutral techniques of cost-accounting. Finally, in the late twentieth century, as the progressive and the economic schools battle each other for conceptual and political dominance, a new set of events has begun to occupy public attention: what we are calling *environmental injuries*. Popularly associated with toxic substances that are potentially widespread in the public environment, these cases pose a serious challenge to policies, perceptions, and ways of thinking still centered on earlier paradigms. A brief overview of these historical patterns will anticipate the controversies analyzed in later chapters.

Industrial Injuries and Progressive Policy

During the period of industrialization, accident policy in both Western Europe and the United States was shaped by public concern for injuries to factory workers.[10] These accidents became the special target for liberal reform at the close of the nineteenth and beginning of the twentieth centuries. In the United States, the major policy change was the adoption of state workers' compensation statutes by most states before 1920.[11] Advocates of reform, while they may have differed over solutions, commonly agreed on certain critical social implications of workplace injuries: the impact on health and economic

security for industrial workers and their families, the general obligation of society to compensate injured workers for their losses, and the
imposition of compensation costs on industries themselves, based on a
somewhat generalized notion of their causal responsibility for the
surge in industrial accidents.[12]

In the United States progressive social critics attacked traditional
judicial rules that prevented workers from winning compensation
through the court system.[13] The common law imposed an increasing
number of evidentiary and strategic burdens on injured workers—
burdens that ignored, in the view of reformers, the unequal bargaining status between employer and employee, the coercive economic
climate that forced workers to accept unsafe working conditions, the
hardship on working families from economic loss consequent on accidental injury, and the disproportionate risks placed on workers in comparison to employers, who nonetheless stood to gain the most from the
success of industrial production.[14]

While they eventually endorsed the reform strategies of workers'
compensation schemes and campaigned for mandatory safety standards in factories, many law-trained progressives would have preferred
to see the judicial system lead the way to greater compensation benefits. Indeed, most recent commentators on workers' compensation
view the decision to bypass judicial institutions as a compromise with
employers, who thought it would be easier to limit the total costs of
compensation under a statutory regime. Over the first half of the century, legal theories about accidents nurtured this progressive idealiza-
tion of judicial institutions. Notwithstanding the New Deal infatuation
with administrative bodies, American legal thinking maintained a
strong commitment to judicial *procedures*, provided judicial *doctrines*
could be functionally altered to supply more of the compensation an
enlightened society ought to provide.[15]

Using instrumentalist language: the specific rules of common law
had to be recast to promote better working conditions and to increase
the amount of compensation for all injured persons, based on a social
welfare standard of entitlement. Although existing common law was
rejected as the ethical criterion of justifiable compensation, reformed
legal doctrines were nevertheless the preferred means for institu-
tionalizing the social response to accidents.[16]

This *progressive* approach to legal reform, long since extended beyond its original concern with industrial accidents,[17] emphasizes the
income distribution effects of uncompensated injuries, stern (if not

punitive) corrective attitudes toward corporate defendants, and the need for strict government regulation of industrial conditions. It is a value-laden approach in that it looks beyond existing common-law rules to find new standards of entitlement, which may variously emphasize the ethics of punishment or the general goals of welfare-based utilitarian social philosophy. But no matter whether defendants were thus seen as guilty parties or as deep-pocket sources of humanitarian assistance, most progressives assumed there was a close connection between accident victims and the irresponsibility of big business. This connection made it plausible to impose the costs of accidents specifically on corporations rather than on wealthy individuals at random or on society as a whole. Some progressives noted the ability of companies to distribute costs to their customers through insurance contracts, allowing prices to reflect more adequately the true social costs of production.[18]

Apart from workplace accidents, which gradually faded from the view of most lawyers behind the administrative screen of workers' compensation, the progressive theory had only sporadic effect on the bulk of accident cases until comparatively recently. Kept alive by academic critics and maverick state judges, this approach suddenly blossomed in the 1960s, when injured consumers found greatly expanded grounds for suing manufacturers of consumer products.[19] As White notes, at this point a new emphasis on wider risk distribution edged out the older progressive sentiments for using accident law as a form of retribution:

> An idea of Torts as a public law subject, concerned primarily with the adjustment of risks among members of the public so as to achieve fairer and more efficient means of compensating injured persons, was replacing an idea of Torts as a private law subject, concerned primarily with deterring and punishing blameworthy civil conduct.[20]

Automobile Accidents and Economic Theory

A second paradigmatic type of accident concerns the automobile, especially in the period following World War II when Americans increased substantially both their reliance on driving and the number of resulting personal injuries. In retrospect it seems appropriate that the decade of the "end of ideology" was a moment for analysts to concentrate on the kind of modern accident whose causes are most easily reduced to the behavior of discrete individuals.[21] The auto accident as a paradigm case involves random encounters in a mass consumer society, where social class and economic status presumably bear no relation to who becomes either perpetrator or victim.[22] Moreover, the very notion of culpability seems strained by the combined complexity and quantity of cases. Except where alcohol may be a factor (in which case criminal rather than civil penalties predominate), auto accidents can, through minor or momentary lapses of attention, happen to anyone; indeed in many instances the assignment of fault after the fact seems artificial or arbitrary.[23]

The costs of automobile accidents (including the costs of compensation ordered by the courts) are reflected in insurance premiums, which are paid not primarily by corporations or other powerful economic units but by all individuals who drive, with only minor allowance made for one's driving record. The anomic incidence of auto accidents and the resulting attenuated vision of personal responsibility seemed to draw all the more attention to risk distribution and cost considerations, including the costs associated with judicial procedures. At the broader social level, little hope was held out that automobile injuries could be significantly reduced, let alone eliminated.[24] Society would be forced to accept some level of accidental injury as the price of modern living.[25]

Since compensation awards in automobile cases were funded largely by private insurance, many states in the late 1960s debated the cost advantage of privatizing this class of accidents, removing some or all cases from formal litigation procedures.[26] In addition, many critics argued that government safety regulation (including regulation of car manufacturers) could help reduce the level of accidents,[27] but such suggestions were eventually tempered by cost-benefit criticisms of regulation. Based on new techniques in welfare economics, influential theories soon emerged suggesting that the private market system might spontaneously establish a socially optimal rate of accidents. This particular social objective presented a major challenge to the social welfare approach of earlier, progressive critics.[28]

In place of income redistribution, the economic design for accident policy emphasizes cost-benefit calculations (to be made wherever possible through unregulated markets) to help society move toward some optimal level of accidents it is prepared to afford. Under this approach, no special group of defendants may be singled out for punitive treatment; indeed the economic perspective relativizes the attribution of responsibility to the point where the victim classes favored by progressives were viewed as special-interest groups competing for scarce social resources—resources that the market might more efficiently allocate somewhere else.[29] On welfare economic principles, those the progressives called "innocent victims" have no distinctive claim to compensation, unless of course the political system decided to make a purely distributional decision in their favor. Liability rules (where not superseded entirely by private insurance) were viewed instrumentally as enabling an imperfect market system to allocate the costs of accidents in ways that minimized social expense—the combined expense of compensating victims and avoiding future accidents.

While this economic approach grew out of the controversy over automobile accident costs, it has quickly made itself more broadly applicable to other cases. Today it represents the chief theoretical alternative to progressivism as a well-developed source of prescriptions for reforming accident law. This conflict has become especially evident in recent controversies over consumer product injuries, resulting in two alternative ways of construing the social implications of such accidents. The progressive reformers stress compensation, higher levels of damages, corporate liability, some degree of administrative regulation, and vigorous judicial activism to promote the redistribution of resources to victims. The economic strategists take a very different perspective on the social implications of product injuries, emphasizing future accident prevention rather than compensation, treating economic losses and damages awards as incentives affecting future behavior, measuring regulatory proposals by cost-benefit standards, revising judicial doctrines in accordance with economic efficiency arguments, and relying on private insurance markets to address personal needs occasioned by uncertainty and risk.

Environmental Accidents and Future Policy

The chapters that follow chart the exhaustion of both the progressive and economic approaches in the face of new challenges from a much broader field of personal injuries. As the disarray in current American policy will sadly show, neither viewpoint is able to cope with what we have labeled environmental accidents. The central difficulty with these cases is their essentially statistical reality, as constructed by epidemiological research. In recent years studies have begun to correlate the onset of specific diseases with human exposure to dangerous sub-stances, human involvement in certain occupations, and human pres-ence in particular environments. We cannot, however, directly ob-serve the physical impact of such stimuli on an individual victim, whose disease could always have been caused by other factors. For example, while we know that asbestos exposure may contribute to lung cancer, only a small percentage of people developing that disease may have acquired it that way. We cannot specify precisely which lung cancer patients are in fact the victims of this type of environmental injury.[30]

The judicial process looks for specific accident victims, not statisti-cal probabilities. Using only epidemiological evidence, it cannot pro-ceed case by case and produce a plausible list of victims. Since system-atic data on court findings are scarce, we cannot say exactly how courts are actually responding to recent claims based on environmental ex-posures. Studies on asbestos claims appear to confirm that the aggre-gate results of individual court determinations bear little relation to epidemiological targets.[31] In other words, we do not know whether the courts are overcompensating or undercompensating the victims of environmentally induced illness. Some ingenious suggestions have been made for restructuring judicial procedures in response to these new challenges. But even these highly ambitious schemes fail to con-sider appropriate welfare standards for compensation. Confidence in judicial mechanisms for assigning compensation—the very center-piece of progressive policy—begins to look misplaced.

But the courts are not alone in requiring individualized evidence before responding to personal injuries. With the courts' failure to es-tablish a plausible total cost figure for environmental injuries (com-piled from damage awards in particular cases), the economic system loses critical information for performing its distinctive optimizing function. The market needs accurate data on the financial impact of accidents—not out of tenderness for the victims, but in order to pro-ject future costs of activities responsible for such accidents. Uncom-pensated injuries represent massive social costs; their accurate recog-nition by the legal system and the corresponding expense placed on relevant defendants are the primary means for bringing those costs back into market calculations.

Without this information, markets would appear to have two op-tions: either to collect relevant information from somewhere else, or simply to ignore uncompensated social costs altogether. Perhaps because the former approach would require a level of public regulation threatening the very autonomy of markets, conservative theorists seem to prefer the latter option (having held doubts all along about the existence of "negative externalities"). Either way, the capacity of markets as a central coordinating device appears to be heavily compromised in an era of environmental accidents.

These weaknesses in progressive and economic policies are just as important for older categories of accidents, but they are much easier to demonstrate in the case of environmental injuries. Our argument—that judicial and market mechanisms are incomplete without active political intervention—thus questions the basic policy strategies mapped out by progressives and economists based on earlier paradigms of personal injury. The emphasis here on the distinctive challenges of environmental accidents is meant to shift the debate out of these well-worn tracks.

Chapter 1

The Evolution of Tort Law
as Public Policy

*For all the impressive scholarly energies directed at the
unification, simplification, and ordering of tort law, the
field seems to have an inherent capacity to lapse into dis-
orderliness, inconsistencies, and complexities.*[1]

Tort Law and the Public Interest

In contrast to other industrialized nations, the United States has responded to accidents primarily through its judicial institutions. For the
past century courts have been the guiding force in American accident
policy, transforming social issues of compensation and accountability
into the doctrinal categories of tort law. Since the hundred-year history of these doctrines is the source of much specific reference and
nuance in current debates, it becomes the logical starting point for our
survey.

Even though American accident policy begins in the courts, few
observers believe it should stop there. Critics often try to enlist other
social structures—political, economic, or ethical—to remedy the
shortcomings of litigation. But these other systems have their own
weaknesses, which may explain the persistence of tort law long after
its numerous failings have entered common wisdom. The legal profession tries to keep a firm grip on its own procedures, but periodic crises
make tort law a favorite topic for media discussion. General outrage
can be mobilized fairly easily against scandalous time delays in court
proceedings, or ruinous cost increases in private liability insurance.
Public attention can also be captured by new or ominous forms of

injury, as we saw in relation to workplace injuries and automobile accidents.

One of the great mysteries about the tort system as a first line of response to accidents is the proportion of personal injuries that actually find their way into the courts. As we have seen, the answer lies partly in the choice of definitions. But whichever definition we choose, there is no reason to assume that the current judicial caseload exhausts the incidence of personal injury—even if we include cases settled prior to litigation. Nor can we automatically assume that most judicial awards approach the level treated as full compensation under current standards of civil damages. In the only major empirical study of these issues, researchers in Great Britain concluded that scarcely one accidental injury in eight results in any payment of damages.[2] Later chapters will return to this theme, but for now we should note that the legal doctrines discussed below do not automatically reach the majority of accident cases.

For the past century the standard critical perspective on tort law has been instrumentalism: understanding the law as the means to some larger social end.[3] This emphasis on the law's purpose began in 1881 with Holmes's famous treatment of "trespass and negligence," an essay that established the law of negligence as a topic for academic discussion in the United States.[4] Most later commentators have accepted the instrumental perspective, even though their interpretations of "public purpose" have varied widely from one another and from Holmes's original view. Today most critics and defenders alike measure tort law doctrines in functional terms.[5]

With instrumentalism so thoroughly entrenched in legal commentary and judicial practice, nothing about the tort system is what it first seems. Legal doctrines are formulated in declarative sentences, but lawyers and judges interpret them as conditional. Our summary below will try to clarify the inevitable rhetorical confusion of combining both modes in the same policy structure. In general, instrumentalism subverts the judicial system's traditional, mist-enshrouded image as an autonomous source of social values. No matter how logical they seem, or how tightly ordered into self-enclosed patterns, judicial doctrines must eventually relate to something *outside* the legal system. Commentators have located possible sources in community standards, in value choices taken from legislation, or (more recently) in the logic of economic efficiency. Thus it happens that ethics, politics, and economics find their way into legal analysis; instrumentalism ensures that legal rules are ultimately measured by nonjudicial standards of public choice.

The ideal of a unified social goal or common good has gradually faded over the past century of instrumental legal commentary. For the pioneers of instrumentalism, goals external to law were a fund of substantive values accessible to most educated persons, and thus also a source from which wise judges might freely borrow.[6] The first major slippage occurred in the 1920s under the skeptical influence of American legal realism, which reinterpreted the concept of public good in terms of interest-group politics—transforming collective values into the outcomes of legislative bargaining.[7] According to this view, as long as democratic rules are fully respected, these outcomes may claim neutrality in a procedural guise; but there is no other way to validate public choices. This conclusion already spells trouble for instrumental commentary on legal doctrine: exactly *which* group's interests should be decisive in shaping judicial practice? For many progressive writers after the 1920s, it was a matter of simple faith that the needs of accident victims were paramount. The declarative posture of evolving legal doctrines conveniently allowed this value preference to remain hidden beneath the surface

The concept of a public interest became still more attenuated with the rise of cost accounting and economic theory as external criteria for measuring judicial performance. Welfare economists reject the outcomes of political bargaining as a source of universal value. They treat the results of political action as irrational, in contrast to market-coordinated choices (assuming the usual "perfect" market conditions). Economic efficiency thus becomes the only available universal standard for judging social action. Accordingly, economic interpretations of tort law use efficiency as the primary basis for evaluating judicial doctrines, even though they disagree among themselves on the precise meaning of this controversial term. One commentator influenced by the Chicago school of economics defines market efficiency as "aggregate social wealth maximization,"[8] a position that insinuates substantive values associated with older slogans about the free market. Chapters 4 and 5 explore these economic and normative developments in some detail.

We have followed this tangled trail from substantive ethics to interest-group politics, all the way to welfare economics, in order to trace the shifting standards used over the past hundred years of instrumental legal criticism. Each change has taken the form of a challenge by one group of critics against another: substantive values were skeptically received as fictional distortions of interest-group politics, and politics in turn was subordinated to the ostensibly rational analysis of market-defined economic interests. Currently in America all three competing standards regularly do battle with each other. However, the emerging political and economic models—built on *procedural* criteria—indicate the growing ambivalence toward value questions in most legal debate. Both the political and economic standards are more persuasive when attacking the "bias" of other positions than they are in defending the universality of their own.

This impasse over basic value definitions comes as no surprise, a full century after instrumentalism began to shape public reflection on judicial processes. As a critical method in law, instrumentalism holds out the initial promise of demystifying existing rules by relating them to something more immediate. But over time the selection of value standards external to law is subject to changing intellectual fashions and strategic manipulation by special interest groups. Just about any legal doctrine can be soundly attacked from a variety of instrumentalist positions. At the same time, the peculiar rhetoric of law permits anyone to defend an *existing* legal doctrine without articulating an explicit instrumental premise. In other words, defenders of the status quo can always declare their "neutral" deference to the majesty of the law. And if even that fails, they can wrap themselves in the antique moral language of legal terms: "It wasn't *my* fault."

Goals of the Judicial Process: The Battleground of Legal Doctrine

What then do we expect from the judicial system as a central process for organizing the public response to accidents? Its major tasks appear to be three: (1) to identify specific compensable victims, (2) to impose those specific compensation costs on particular culpable parties, and (3) in accomplishing these two tasks, to avoid departing from previous judicially articulated rules.[9] The first two goals embody the common law's inherent individualist orientation to persons and events. They are also mutually defining, in that neither can be successfully accomplished without the other. With no culpable defendant, even the most deserving plaintiff can win nothing through the tort system; and like-

wise the most depraved defendant owes nothing unless his or her actions cause harm to a particular plaintiff. It can thus be claimed that
the judicial process simultaneously resolves the compensation and accountability interests of accident policy. However, it frequently does
so by willfully reducing or expanding one side of the equation to match
the other. We will begin describing this process in the next section.

We need first to clarify the third task, which is critical to whatever
fragile legitimacy can be credited to the judicial process. Notwithstanding the instrumentalist theories of legal commentators, the process of reasoning toward conclusions in particular cases must come
close to formal rationality. In practice these formal strictures are pragmatically adjustable within certain tolerances, but individual judges
must nonetheless reason with sufficient formalism to avoid the fatal
charge of treating individual decisions as purely distributive choices.
We can thus distinguish the instrumental perspective of the legal critic
from the task of the judge in specific cases. The legal critic's job is to
help "get the right rules" established as formal doctrines, while the
judge is charged with "getting the rules right" in rendering individual
decisions. Even the instrumentalist critics of tort law expect judges to
follow precedent; otherwise there would be no security in working
toward the gradual acceptance of new doctrines.[10]

This tension between the instrumentalism of commentators and
the formalism of judges remains a source of major conflict in both
theory and practice.[11] For everyone except judges, legal doctrines operate as somewhat ambiguous rules governing the social distribution of
resources. When the courts produce socially undesirable results, we
recommend new doctrines that will make future results more acceptable. While it would seem that legislation is the most obvious way to
replace or supersede common-law rules, judges themselves are understood to *adapt* the rules through the skillful exercise of shading and
interpreting. Indeed, most legal critics expect them to do so, while
not deviating too far from the formalist rhetoric of judicial reasoning.

Such controlled and subtle changes are greeted by progressive lib-
erals as a sign of evolutionary reform. They are attacked by political
conservatives as irresponsible policy making, and by radicals as verbal
trickery. How have tort doctrines actually changed under such ambiguous judicial stewardship? As we shall see, the history of these doctrines contains a good many surprises—defended as benign by sympathetic commentators and righteously condemned as illegitimate by
hostile critics and sore losers in litigation. Legal commentary has influ-

enced substantially the way judges construe the *true* path of precedent.[12]

In emphasizing the instrumental perspective, we should be careful to note how the discussion in this chapter differs from some other treatments found in the legal literature. We are not presenting a summary of current doctrine, which would mean freezing the law in its current state and treating it as conceptually self-contained. That is how tort law presents itself in the context of specific judicial decisions—it is, in fact, the legitimizing task mentioned above. Unlike most legal commentaries, the summary here is meant not for practitioners, but for those interested in tort law as social policy.[13]

The Progressive Agenda: Applying Formal Doctrines to Social Problems

Having noted the unusual formal constraints under which courts apply legal rules, we may start examining the fate of particular tort doctrines. Under the influence of instrumentalism, the judicial system has steadily broadened the application of legal rules, while leaving in place much of the language. In responding to new forms of injury, judges prized for their subtle craftsmanship have been able to preserve the traditional fabric of the law while boldly reshaping its use.

In the view of progressive commentators, these timely changes came at the expense of the traditional individualism and moralism widely embraced by defenders of nineteenth-century doctrines. Take, for instance, that stirring victory of doctrinal reform: the demise of *privity of contract*. This evil-sounding doctrine restricted the right of injured parties to recover damages from persons with whom they had no direct contractual relationship. Well into the twentieth century, courts used this doctrine to prevent most consumers from suing the manufacturers of defective products, unless they had somehow dealt directly with each other. Such a barrier appeared to ignore modern ways of marketing consumer products, including complex and potentially dangerous products like the automobile. The gradual erosion of this doctrine, extending over many decades, is one of the most celebrated events in the progressive chronicles of legal change.[14]

Its appeal comes at least in part from the exotic factual circumstances of key lawsuits. Perhaps best loved is the English case brought by the person who found a decomposed snail in his freshly opened bottle of ginger beer.[15] While the bottlers had no idea that Mr. Don-noghue would be the one to open this particular bottle, they certainly knew that *someone* would do so, and their traditional "duty of care" was therefore expanded to reach such "reasonably foreseeable" classes of plaintiffs. As P. S. Atiyah notes, this kind of functionalist reasoning weakens the individualist underpinnings of common law, even though it leaves doctrinal language intact. True, the structure of litigation still requires the court to find some link between plaintiffs and particular defendants, but that link can be expansively interpreted to draw a much larger group of persons into the legal framework.[16] We will re-turn to this point in Chapter 2, when we consider just how large that group needs to be in an era of environmental accidents.

We can no longer guess the established meaning of tort doctrines from their outward appearance. Opponents of doctrinal reforms often lose track of this fact; legal orthodoxy is a moving target. We cannot simply look at a concept like "duty of care" and understand it outside a historical context. Nowhere is this lesson more important than in the battle over *fault* as an element of tort liability. For nearly a century, lay critics have righteously condemned court decisions that deviate from traditional moral intuitions concerning fault. Through that entire period, however, courts have carefully distanced themselves from such intuitions, even though they have preserved much of the associ-ated language.

The battle to overcome fault marks an even greater victory for in-strumental reform than privity of contract. The usual version of this story derives from the progressive viewpoint of legal realist scholars, although alternative interpretations have recently begun to appear.[17] Since Holmes's day, we are told, we have witnessed the steady erosion of a tradition-bound, moralistic brand of tort law—secretly tailored to the interests of early capitalism, and symbolized by the complex no-tion of fault.[18] This edifying tale credits innovative judges and academ-ics with the struggle to establish more socially desirable rules, helped out on rare but important occasions by directive legislation. The suc-cess of this trend, using progressive criteria, can be measured by how much better the judicial system produces compensation for those cases deemed worthy under the standard of enlightened public inter-est.[19] Some commentators, as we shall see later on, believe that changes in common-law doctrine make very little real difference, and have argued instead for more substantial reforms.[20]

What we now generally mean by the fault doctrine is not a single legal principle but rather a series of doctrinal and strategic relationships between potential plaintiffs and defendants. It is probably better to speak of a set of doctrines that base liability on *negligence*. Taking fault or negligence from the plaintiff's point of view, the law requires an injured party to show that the defendant's behavior departed from standards identified with the *reasonably prudent person*, and that the defendant's act was the *proximate cause* of the plaintiff's injury. Frequently plaintiffs must also show that the defendant falls within a particular class of individuals deemed to owe the plaintiff a "duty" to avoid negligent behavior. This notion of the *class of permissible defendants* has likewise played a major role in the history of tort law, as we just saw in the case of privity of contract.[21]

In addition to these affirmative burdens, the successful plaintiff has to counter a number of possible defenses that may insulate the defendant from liability, even when the affirmative case is successful: most notably the twin doctrines of *assumption of risk* and *contributory negligence*. Finally, plaintiffs must navigate successfully through the shifting currents of judicial *procedure*, and they have to establish the amount of *damages* to be awarded should defendants be found liable.

The strategic balance between plaintiff and defendant comes from the interaction of all these doctrinal elements plus the practical difficulties of mounting and sustaining a lawsuit. Legal representation becomes a necessary expense for plaintiffs hoping to win compensation. Evidence about past events must be presented and defended against challenges that exploit the passage of time, fallibility of witnesses, and uncertainties over scientific facts. In addition, the complex interplay of legal doctrines, each with an esoteric history, can be mastered only by the law-trained professional.

To a great extent, the stakes for individuals and for society as a whole are invisible when tort law is viewed formally as a process for determining who, if anyone, was at fault. An openly instrumental perspective asks the more probing question, "Under what conditions is it in the public interest for plaintiffs to recover damages from defendants?"[22] For many years tort law has been changing its application of major rules according to a central value premise of progressivism: that plaintiffs should prevail more often than they do. The progressive reform agenda can be summarized by four main doctrinal trends: (1) relaxing the plaintiff's affirmative burdens, (2) requiring a wider class of persons to stand as defendants, (3) making it harder for defendants to use traditional defenses, and (4) tilting the overall strategic balance toward plaintiffs by restructuring judicial procedures. We shall look briefly at the results of each of these progressive trends, along with some alternative formulations by economic reformers.

Relaxing Plaintiffs' Affirmative Burdens

Contrary to connotation, the bundle of doctrines and practices that constitute the fault system cannot be traced directly to moral theories of culpability, like those found in criminal law. Documenting a psychological intent to cause injury has probably never been the legal criterion for proving negligence, although the defendant must be shown to have intended some act or other. Rather the law construes negligent action (somewhat paradoxically) as an unintentional harm, related in some elusive fashion (usually conveyed by the term *cause*) to an intended act of the defendant. In addition to demanding some kind of causal link between the parties, negligence law further limits the liability of defendants according to the nature of their actual performance. This quality is not to be found anywhere in the psyche, but rather in certain public features and consequences of the defendant's deliberate actions.

The plaintiff's initial burden is to prove that the defendant could reasonably have avoided an accident—in other words, that the defendant did not behave like a reasonably prudent person. While it is possible to invest these terms with moral significance (as defenders of existing doctrines sometimes do, even today), Holmes set the prevailing tone by bringing out the functional, even fictional quality of this complex standard. The reasonable-prudence test does not inquire into a defendant's state of mind, but simply measures outward conduct against community expectations of normal competence.[23]

It is easy to see why critics of Holmes's reasonable-prudence standard found his formulation useful for progressive social purposes. Based on his premise that the public interest favored entrepreneurial activity, Holmes concluded that the law should insulate such activity wherever possible from liability claims.[24] His argument opened the way for later critics to counter that the public interest was changing in line with the progressive critique of industrialism. This kind of response alters the impact of negligence doctrine without repudiating the language. In this way, pro-plaintiff changes can be grafted directly onto a doctrinal system.

Progressive writers thus interpreted the reasonable-prudence concept as a standard of social expediency, one that could adapt to evolving social definitions of acceptable behavior. Ideally, the judicial process should transfer the costs of accidents from victims to causally related defendants when (but only when) it can classify the defendants' behavior as socially undesirable. Courts and juries were thus invited to substitute new criteria of social desirability for those Holmes originally built into the reasonable-prudence standard.

Despite the ingenious flexibility of this approach, courts in the twentieth century have not applied it wholesale. The most consistent pro-plaintiff doctrinal changes have emphasized cases where defendants were engaged in such unusually hazardous activities as blasting, harnessing powerful sources of energy, or handling products like poisons—activities beneficial in some uses, but potentially quite dangerous in others.[25] In such cases, courts may stretch the reasonable-prudence test so far that it loses all restrictive meaning; what is often called *strict liability* is simply negligence doctrine minus the reasonable-prudence standard.

As commentators have pointed out, there is often little difference in practice between this new and much-maligned concept of strict liability and evolving interpretations of negligence, with their attenuation of the reasonable-prudence test.[26] This similarity eludes those lay critics who contrast strict liability with intuitive moral notions of fault. To be sure, the daily practice of courts remains murky, since even the most reform-minded judges observe the formal reasoning style of their profession: deciding individual cases with attention to distinctive facts, stressing continuities with past decisions, and disowning consequentialist logic.[27] But the general drift of doctrine is plain enough; plaintiffs nowadays find it easier to show that the defendant failed to meet prevailing legal standards of prudent behavior. The very nature of modern accidents, especially those based on inherently dangerous activities, plays a part in plaintiffs' success by raising social expectations that hazardous substances will be kept under tight control.

With the selective demise of the reasonable-prudence standard, legal attention has shifted to the equally contentious issue of the causal link between the plaintiff's injury and a particular defendant's actions.[28] As with fault, the connotation is somewhat deceiving, and most commentators now concede the irreducibly functional meaning of causation.[29] By the laws of physics, it is theoretically possible to tie almost any defendant to any known event. In order to find some practical limit to liability, courts in Holmes's day wanted to shorten the chain of potential causation: hence the doctrine of proximate cause.[30]

In general a functionalist perspective would make that chain sufficiently long or short to reach defendants in precisely those cases where liability is socially desirable.[31] If the public generally profits from entrepreneurial activity, as Holmes believed, then the rule on proximate cause should be strict enough to sever most of that activity from the complex physical events surrounding personal injuries. On the other hand, if the progressives were correct that the actions of large industry are socially responsible for creating unsafe working conditions or unsafe products—in short, that society's interests favor recovery by the plaintiff—then the causal chain should be extended farther, to reach corporate defendants (among others).[32]

A number of cases with freakish fact patterns have shown over the years just how far courts were prepared to stretch the proximate-cause doctrine. An important English case,[33] influential for American law, found a "proximate" link behind an improbable series of events, beginning with some loose boards on a ship's deck and ending with a destructive fire. The defendant's employees accidentally dislodged a wooden plank, which fell into the ship's hold, causing a spark and igniting benzine vapors from the ship's cargo. Despite an arbitrator's finding that "the causing of the spark could not reasonably have been anticipated from the falling of the board," the English Court of Appeals found there was a "direct" relationship between a negligent event (knocking the board) and the ultimate damage to the ship.

By expanding proximate cause to more remote events, such cases have blurred a possible distinction between the source of injury and the extent of injury. Once the employees dropped the fateful board, they could have been held responsible for something as small as a dent in the deck or as large as the resulting conflagration. Between these two possible termini of their actions, nature took its course; but according to the evolving meaning of proximate cause, nature becomes part of the chain of events that begins with the defendant's behavior. This expansive way of interpreting proximate cause obviously has major consequences, particularly, as Atiyah notes, with "the arrival of mechanical power and devices which were capable of killing or maiming large numbers of people in a single disaster."[34]

It may be noted briefly that recent economic theorists offer an entirely different functional interpretation of causation. According to their view, it makes little difference in assigning the costs of accidents precisely how the past is causally reconstructed. Provided we can show how it will be cost effective in the *future* to impose the costs of injury on specific actors, we do not really care how close any particular defendant once stood to an actual plaintiff in a causal chain.[35] Since the primary purpose of liability rules is to deter future accident-producing behavior that is too expensive, such incentives are effective only if the future behavior of potential plaintiffs and defendants is physically associated in some meaningful way. Not past causation, then, but *future control* gets reflected in this view of the tort system. People in some position to affect future activity are the ones on whom accident costs should fall, even if it means leaving some or all of those costs with future victims.[36]

New Categories of Defendants

While trends in the interpretation of fault and causation have improved the strategic advantage of some plaintiffs, still other changes have increased the number and types of defendants the injured person has an opportunity to sue. We already noted the addition of product manufacturers to this group with the demise of privity of contract. Another famous example of progressive expansion is the doctrine of *vicarious liability*. Common law has long recognized special instances in which some individuals are deemed to stand in the shoes of others for purposes of judging liability.[37] Thus an employer has generally been held accountable for the behavior of an employee, or of anyone acting as an agent. Through such vicarious implication in the behavior of others, parties may be found liable who would otherwise escape responsibility under the reasonable-prudence and proximate-cause tests.

Vicarious liability can be rationalized from an individualist point of view by attributing to vicarious defendants either causal or judgmental responsibility for the negligent behavior of people under their authority. This is no doubt why common law would excuse a defendant whose employee strayed beyond the expected scope of employment. But from a purely functional viewpoint, anyone seen as a socially desirable bearer of accident costs becomes a candidate for vicarious liability, regardless of actual past behavior. For example, if income redistribution is the primary social objective in responding to product injuries, a large corporation might be held vicariously liable simply because it has more money than either the victims or those workers who proximately caused any injuries. If cost-efficient accident prevention is the goal, corporations may still be best situated to compare the costs of compensating future victims against the costs of preventing employee carelessness. Vicarious liability as a doctrine thus holds appeal for both progressive and economic instrumentalists.[38]

In its usual form, vicarious liability still requires a finding that someone was at fault. As Harper, James, and Gray explain, "It does not relieve plaintiff from the need to show fault, but it is satisfied with a showing of the *servant's* fault. As to the master it is a form of strict liability . . . involving . . . assurance that claims will be paid and widely distributed."[39] As the other doctrinal components of fault continue to weaken, however, this precondition for vicarious liability obviously becomes less onerous.

The example of vicarious liability illustrates how persons or corporations may become qualified defendants because of status rather than specific interactions with the plaintiff. The defendant does not even have to foresee this kind of plaintiff, although other aspects of the fault doctrine may need to be addressed by the plaintiff seeking redress. Some commentators have argued that a sly combination of strict liability and the vicarious treatment of corporations by progressive judges has created a new doctrinal synthesis, dubbed *enterprise liability*.[40] The suggestion is that enterprise liability is virtually unlimited when applied to accidents involving manufactured products. It thus approaches *absolute liability*, the term for a conclusive legal claim that eliminates all the affirmative burdens and traditional defenses of negligence.

The concept of enterprise liability is promoted mainly by critics of progressive doctrinal reform, although the label itself can be traced to a progressive author.[41] According to Priest, the theory of enterprise liability "provides in its simplest form that business enterprises ought to be responsible for losses resulting from products they introduce into commerce." This considerably overstates both the intent and the contemporary effect of progressive reforms in weakening the traditional elements of negligence. Any current treatise on product liability law reveals large exceptions to such a blanket rule, notwithstanding all the changes of the past decades. Even more sweeping is Priest's claim that "by the mid-1950s, the theory of enterprise liability commanded almost complete support within the academic community, and it was accepted and implemented as a tool of social policy in the early 1960s, first by the courts and later by legislatures and other regulatory bodies."[42]

What Priest doubtless means is that corporate absolute liability for product accidents appears to be the logical terminus of the whole series of reforms advocated by progressive critics of fault doctrines.[43] His extensive historical commentary documents various stages in this movement, but it does not substantiate his assertion that absolute liability was the conscious goal of progressive reformers. Overstating the progressive program in this way may have a certain polemical value in arguing for the reversal of doctrinal change, especially in the context of product accidents. In Chapter 7 we will explore some recent efforts to reintroduce fault doctrines into the law of product liability.

Priest's generally balanced commentary ultimately reveals the hidden norm from which absolute liability appears most vulnerable: an individualist ethic of responsibility. Commenting on a "notorious" New Jersey asbestos decision, he objects on grounds of fairness to holding a producer liable for dangers that "could not have been scientifically known at the time of the breach." In Priest's view, this decision "seems to strain the most basic conceptions of responsibility."[44] Like many critics who question the results of progressive instrumentalism, Priest falls back on ethical intuition.

Assumption of Risk and Contributory Negligence

These two doctrinal defenses represent ways a defendant may escape liability for negligence, even when the plaintiff has prevailed on all the rules discussed above. An injured person who voluntarily or negligently assumed risks associated with an accident can thus lose an otherwise promising lawsuit, recovering nothing at all from a negligent defendant. Since historically these doctrines have limited the plaintiff's prospects for recovery, they were subjected to severe criticism by progressive reformers, and their current effect on litigation has been much altered. We no longer consider that entire groups of people, including industrial employees, assume all the risks of unsafe working conditions. Victims who share responsibility for an accident—perhaps an automobile accident—may now find their damages reduced by a proportionate amount, rather than forfeiting damages entirely.

Commentators agree that the phrase *assumption of risk* has been used to describe a heterogeneous class of situations. In the most controversial cases, this "assumption" was imputed to members of a class, but with no specific inquiry into the victim's prior understanding of actual risks or prior consent. Thus industrial employees were once prevented as a group from recovering compensation for the risks considered intrinsic to their employment, based on the capitalist nostrum that employees are rational economic men who have already weighed the risks and benefits of the work environment. In time the effects of this defense were overturned by workers' compensation legislation.[45]

Other kinds of risk assumption involving conscious choice or careless acquiescence belong to the broader concept of contributory negligence. Most striking about this concept under common law at the time of Holmes was its all-or-nothing effect: a badly injured employee might win nothing, despite a clear showing of an employer's negligence, if he or she also contributed in any degree to the accident. While it is possible to support this idea conceptually on the theory that the plaintiff's action interrupts or preempts the chain of causation, that rationale scarcely supports a blanket rule. One ad hoc judicial response has been to abandon the defense whenever the defendant had the "last clear chance" to avoid the accident, even though the plaintiff was also found negligent.[46] Considering the difficulties of forcing human action into a temporally precise causal order, however, such attempts to soften the perceived harshness of contributory negligence were highly unpredictable in their results.

The most common response to the contributory negligence rule, encouraged by the many inscrutable situations presented by automobile accidents, has been to apportion fault between plaintiff and defendant.[47] In these cases, the negligent plaintiff can still recover something, but the damages awarded are diminished by his or her share of fault. However, this solution is only as good as the fault concept itself, and it presupposes a vibrant doctrinal structure defined by the reasonable-prudence standard, proximate cause, and all the rest— concepts that are now well hedged with functionalist applications.[48] The reason for comparative negligence turns out to be not nostalgia for the doctrinal lore of fault, however, but merely its value as a strategic compromise with the all-or-nothing contributory negligence rule. A progressive critic, concerned among other things with income distribution, might continue to argue that some plaintiffs are unable to shoulder the financial burden created by a comparative negligence approach. By contrast, the economist critic, interested in the impact on future economizing behavior, tends to see comparative negligence as creating more discriminating incentives for all persons who are potentially involved in accidents, including potential victims.

Procedures and Damages

So many issues fall under these important headings that we can select here only a few with current relevance. Judicial procedures set contextual conditions for how easy or difficult the plaintiff's task will be. Some procedural battles are now history, such as eliminating certain technicalities of pleading where minor formal defects would immediately defeat the plaintiff's claim.

Perhaps the most critical role for procedure is in structuring the uncertainty potentially present in every tort claim; procedural rules determine what happens when a case lacks decisive evidence or falls between doctrinal cracks. The normal rule in civil litigation is that plaintiffs carry the burden of proof, including the responsibility both to produce sufficient evidence and to make a persuasive case in doctrinal terms. Under progressive influence, these procedural burdens have been subtly blunted, especially in recent years. Because uncertainty plays such a central role in environmental accidents, it is no surprise that these procedural innovations are under significant scrutiny and are among the judicial practices most vulnerable to legislative reversal today.

One contentious issue concerns multiple defendants. Several persons may contribute to an accidental event in proportions indiscernible to the plaintiff, or the evidence may be insufficient to show which one alone among the group caused an injury. Tort textbooks cite the case where two separate people shot the plaintiff in a hunting accident, but the physical evidence did not show clearly which person actually caused the principal harm.[49] Courts now generally hold in such cases that both people are proper defendants, with each one severally (that is, fully) liable for the entire result of their joint actions. This theory of *joint and several liability,* in effect, shifts the burden to either defendant to establish a convincing defense to the allegations.[50]

The shooting accident belongs not only in a textbook but in a museum of common-law period art. It displays the interpersonal structure of civil lawsuits as a kind of allegory of environmental accidents. (It is to modern injuries what Crusoe economics was to national economic planning.) The terms *joint* and *several* are convenient legal metaphors for the instrumentalist's chief interest: shifting the burden of proof in situations where factual evidence is insufficient to resolve an issue of causation.[51]

In a widely cited application of this approach, the California Supreme Court in 1980 allowed a group of cases to go forward against eleven drug companies—erstwhile manufacturers of DES, a fertility drug commonly used from about 1940 to 1970.[52] DES is now associated with reproductive cancers in the children of patients who took the drug, but the passage of time makes it virtually impossible for victims to identify the specific manufacturing source. The court followed the "joint and several" approach, shifting the burden to defendants to show—as if they somehow could—that their own product was not involved in specific cases. In a novel twist, the court allowed defendants to apportion liability among themselves based on each company's economic share of the former DES market. This homage to economic rationality underscores the figurative distance that separates defendants' actual behavior from the resulting injuries.

In later chapters we shall summarize current efforts to reverse the whole progressive tide in doctrinal development, through legislation if necessary. Joint and several liability often tops the list of revisionist changes, and it is not hard to see why.[53] In cases where factual evidence is not reducible to individual actions, and where injuries may have occurred well in the past—two dominant features in environmental cases—a plaintiff needs to shift the burden of proof onto someone who is still around and can afford to pay. The judicial finger in these cases points inexorably toward currently well-funded corporations, especially when it is now so easy to maneuver them into the defendant's chair under weakened fault doctrines. Of course the most popular defendants (and their insurers) feel unfairly treated, and by a strict individualistic interpretation of legal rules they are rightly alarmed. Analytic philosophers have lately come to their aid by evaluating judicial decisions according to individualized models of ethics, an example of the backlash to progressive values that will be examined more closely in Chapter 5.[54]

In the area of damages, the courts have gained a great deal of publicity for the amounts awarded in successful injury suits.[55] It is no longer unusual for juries to award million-dollar sums, although the reasons frequently have little to do with doctrinal theories under which juries receive their instructions. Judges and reviewing courts often reduce the jury's generosity, and legislation is fast spreading around the country to limit top amounts on such awards.[56]

Doctrinal changes may contribute at least indirectly to these trends by gradually altering the conceptual landscape of damages, notably by extending the notion of intangible or psychological injuries in addition to physical harm, and by highlighting punitive damages. The former category includes *pain and suffering*, while the latter is an awkward reminder that the courts' retributive function is indissolubly tied to the compensation process.

The publicity accompanying these changes creates the unfortunate impression that accident victims on the whole make out very well in the judicial system.[57] Perhaps the only comparable examples of ordinary citizens receiving such vast sums occur with public lotteries, thus confirming the judgment of some critics on the consistency and instrumental rationality of negligence cases.[58] There is little question that the public image created by these spectacular awards has affected the political climate for tort reform, inciting on the one hand public resentment that resources could be so airily tossed about by the judicial system, and on the other hand a lottery player's jealous protection of the right to keep the jackpot high against the day when his or her lucky number turns up.

Pain and suffering has an especially profound effect on cases involving latent disease, the sort of case we will examine in later chapters. Unlike more traditional types of damages, pain and suffering is not compensation for pecuniary losses like medical expenses or lost earnings from temporary or permanent disability. It is not, therefore, subject to easy rebuttal by a defendant who wishes to challenge the plaintiff's proposal for compensation, and it is similarly difficult to provide operational guidelines for juries or appellate judges in reacting to these proposals. The economic critic of tort law can point to the absence of quantitative guidelines as further reasons why the judicial process needs a dose of economic discipline.[59]

Punitive damages raise important theoretical and constitutional issues. While the concept of charging the culpable defendant with an exemplary sum has a long legal history,[60] it has lately become a major strategic issue between consumers and corporations. As consumer groups organize and take advantage of class-action procedures before the courts, punitive damages offer an irresistible temptation. The

strategy becomes especially dramatic in mass litigation like that surrounding A. H. Robins, Inc., manufacturers of the Dalkon Shield, a
contraceptive device found to have permanent harmful effects on
users. More than 330,000 women filed claims against Robins, some of
which were litigated separately, before the company went to bankruptcy court. At one point a class action involving 1,600 suits re-
quested punitive damages of over $2 billion, or eight times the com-
pany's net worth. (In 1988 the company's petition for reorganization
was approved under federal bankruptcy laws.)[61]

Although the general idea of punitive damages seems consistent
with progressive reform strategies from the era of industrial injuries, it
conflicts with the ascendent theory of risk distribution, especially as
developed by economic critics in recent years. The well-publicized
resort to this doctrine in mass litigation suits has raised the question
whether retribution properly belongs to the civil justice system at
all.[62] Beyond the self-interested outrage of modern-day tort defendants, we can identify larger social interests in finding more exacting
standards for measuring both regulation and retribution.

Still another area of tension in the progressive approach has to do
with plaintiffs receiving compensation from more than one source.
Courts are divided on whether funds from a *collateral source* (such as
disability payments from government or private insurance, or salary
and sick pay from an employer) should be deducted from the defendant's payments. If one views the essential purpose of tort law as compensation, then subtractions seem logical; if on the other hand retribution or economic disincentives are the central goal, the defendant
should have to pay the full assessment. We might even want to transfer
part of the plaintiff's award to the public collateral source, thereby
offsetting social expenditures. The collateral-source controversy is the
inevitable dilemma of a system that has collapsed two distinct policies—compensation and accountability—into one process. It is also a
proper matter to consider in any policy permitting multiple routes to
compensating accident victims, whether or not the judicial process is
involved.

As we shall see in later chapters, a revisionist interest is gaining
strength in legislatures across the country (including Congress), which
seeks to point the tort process back toward its nineteenth-century
roots in negligence. Among the four most common targets are the
doctrines covered in this section: joint and several liability, pain and
suffering, punitive damages, and the collateral-source rule.

Tensions in Doctrinal Reform

Any survey skimming quickly over a century of doctrinal change runs the risk of oversimplifying that process. There has in fact been no comprehensive reform plan developed by progressive critics of tort law, nor enough agreement among them to have allowed for one.[63] Even if there had been a more codified vision, its implementation would have depended on the cooperation of thousands of judges in hundreds of thousands of cases. As explained earlier, a judge does not take a purely functional look at each case; changes, when they do occur, are embedded in highly specific situations, varying across separate jurisdictions.

At any one moment the tort systems of all fifty states occupy distinct points along the continuum of change. About all we can safely conclude is that this continuum, viewed historically, has pointed in the direction recommended by progressive instrumentalism: (1) toward relaxing plaintiffs' burdens under the reasonable-prudence and proximate-cause tests; (2) toward expanding the general class of eligible defendants; (3) toward reducing defenses to liability; and (4) toward reforming procedures and recognizing new categories of damages. Nothing guarantees that all jurisdictions move continuously along these routes, nor even that they keep moving in the same direction. Over the past hundred years we can discern a clear progressive tendency, but in the next ten years that direction could well be reversed.

We may finish this survey with a summary of major tensions between the entire doctrinal structure of tort law and the social environment it is somehow meant to serve. These problems are not likely to disappear with further adjustments to doctrine, whether based on progressive or economic reform strategies; they are perhaps unavoidable conflicts in any society whose initial and primary response to accidents comes through the judicial process. Their resolution depends instead on finding alternatives to judicial procedures.

Individualism

The first tension is *political*: the conflict between a judicial system based on individualist models of events and responsibility, and a larger social system whose problems are not reducible to an individualist level. Common-law doctrines have been stretched and distorted in all sorts of ways by "creative judging." One effect has been to relativize our view of an "event," which becomes complex enough to implicate physically remote defendants in cases where their liability seems desirable on instrumental grounds. But it is not at all clear that this flexibility is enough to cover the statistical or probabilistic events common in environmental injuries.

Even more critical is the model of responsibility as a relationship between specific persons, a mutually defining relationship where compensating an injured plaintiff presupposes assigning responsibility to a viable defendant. The common law has expanded its individualist premises metaphorically to permit attributions of liability to persons connected by status rather than by specific action, as well as to corporate or collective defendants for actions taken under their authority. But the use of legal metaphors and fictions may have its limits; especially in the case of environmental accidents, we may want to recognize multiple and simultaneous levels of responsibility: individual, organizational, governmental, and social. This degree of complexity strains the common-law framework to the point of risking a backlash of strict ethical individualism. The political system will almost certainly need to reduce these tensions, with or without the support of ethical codes.

Efficiency

A second kind of tension is *economic*. While the judicial process addresses with increasing boldness the issues of income distribution surrounding personal injuries, it has no internal economic principle for going about its business in a cost-efficient way. On the one hand there are the costs of litigation itself—both time and money—which figure heavily in everyday life but not in legal doctrine. On the other hand, as economic theorists have pointed out, distributive decisions made by courts are not necessarily the most efficient way for society to respond to injuries. It is likely that some accidents could be avoided altogether at less cost than it takes to compensate victims, but the doctrinal structure of common law has no criterion for determining when this is so. By continually extending the grounds for compensation (as well as the amounts), courts inevitably influence market choices between prevention and compensation; but they have no way to measure the social impact of this effect.

Much of the difficulty goes back to individualism. As long as courts make compensation decisions on a case-by-case basis, there is no assurance that the resulting pattern will correspond to the way a perfect market would balance compensation and prevention. Some economic theorists nonetheless view the legal system as appropriately dealing with individual cases that fall through the cracks of a market system— the residue of market failures. But even this group urges judges to approximate market norms, putting greater emphasis on promoting future accident prevention than on the dominant progressive theme of increasing compensation. As we shall see in Chapter 4, the economist views the judicial process, at best, as a supplement to the market system in organizing future behavior. The compensation function becomes a kind of afterthought.

Values

The third source of tension is *ethical*. We have already explored ways that an instrumental view of legal doctrine comes into conflict with the nonconsequentialist ideal of case-by-case litigation. The more pressure put on doctrines to resolve the various tensions discussed here, the more likely that the judiciary will undermine its own legitimacy. In some fashion, the implicit value scheme behind instrumental legal change must be more clearly articulated with the help of political, economic, and ethical criteria.

"Getting the right rules" into the judicial process will almost certainly prove impossible for judges themselves to accomplish. In the first place, there is no common agreement about what those rules ought to be; as we shall see when we discuss proposed changes for product liability cases, the prescriptions of progressives and economists differ considerably. Both are at odds with further positions based on individualist ethics. All these approaches—which grow more coherent and self-confident along with their swelling ranks of academic partisans—will become more vigilant in challenging judicial rule changes in conflict with their own prescriptions. Judges will inevitably be less creative under this kind of scrutiny than in past decades, when progressive values and judicial activism were more politically fashionable.

The most immediate pressure for restructuring common-law rules will come from the political process, through which a variety of interest groups have already made themselves heard. In Chapter 3 we shall examine some of the alliances between academic theories and organized interest groups with personal stakes in the direction of future reform. Considering the vast amount of legislation now poised to restructure judicial rules, it is doubtful that judges and lawyers in the future will have the same free hand to shape those rules from within. In any event we should pose the question whether these efforts might be more productively devoted to finding institutional alternatives to common law for reacting to the problem of personal injury.

One wonders, in fact, why legal doctrines remain the focus for public debate in the United States when it seems apparent that the major social and economic impact of accidents falls on other programs within the larger social welfare structure. In practical terms, most accidents never enter the judicial arena; estimates cited earlier in this chapter suggest that perhaps one out of eight injury victims eventually receives damages through the courts.[64] These figures appear plausible despite the increase in civil litigation over the past twenty years; even a 100 percent increase would leave the vast majority of injury cases untouched by the courts.

The obsession of current political forces with sculpting a congenial set of judicial rules severely narrows public discussion, delaying the development of a more effective national accident policy. The possibility remains, however, that emerging environmental accidents will eventually steer the political debate away from judicial doctrines and toward a wider field of public response.

Chapter 2

The Challenge of
Environmental Accidents

*Ideas about dirt have serious political implications, as
will be evident from a moment's reflection on today's
struggles over toxic chemicals, radioactive waste, and
other environmental pollutants. A broad conception of
dirt may imply a need for a correspondingly large investment in cleaning things up.*[1]

A Broad Conception of Dirt

Systematic attention to the physical environment in relation to illness
and accidents was supplied originally by neither doctors nor tort lawyers, but by the loosely defined profession of public health. In the
nineteenth century, Starr notes, "public health was mainly concerned
with sanitary reform and affiliated more closely with engineering than
with medicine." Along with advances in bacteriology, according to
Starr, public health professionals after 1900 modified their emphasis
on environmental influences and began concentrating on human
transmission of disease. "Shifting attention from the environment to
the individual, they increasingly relied on the techniques of medicine
and personal hygiene."[2] Before long, however, environmental factors
reemerged along with improved methods of epidemiological research.
Over the past two decades, armed with new quantitative techniques
and massive supplies of data, the field has returned to Starr's "broad
conception of dirt."

The divergence of epidemiology from mainstream medicine has at
times suggested a sterile dichotomy: identifying the source of disease
with either individual pathology or factors in the larger environment.
But public health approaches illness through an *ecological* model,
which embraces multiple relations among hosts, agents, and the larger

49

environment. The concept of disease is broadly understood as a deficit in personal physiological or psychological function, caused by exchanges with environmental forces—whether human, mechanical, or chemical. While clinical medicine concentrates mainly on curing the host's illness and on isolating microorganisms as agents, public health expands both variables. It emphasizes "the host's own capacities to shape the manifestations of disorder," thus encouraging preventive measures like immunization. And it defines the disease agent in highly functional terms as "any factor, whether event, characteristic, or other definable entity, so long as it brings about change for better or worse in a health condition."[3]

As the American legal system reluctantly brings diseases into the category of injury, public health has been energetically exploring personal injuries within its ecological framework for disease.

> Approaching injury as a disease affecting susceptible groups in the population relies on an etiologic framework which attributes the physical manifestations of injury to the interaction among host, agent, and environment, a method proven successful in the prevention of infectious and communicable disease and widely used to appraise risks to health. There are several assumptions at work here. First, injury is not a random event but is invariably attributable to the complex interaction of the three factors, host, agent, and environment. Second, no one of these factors alone can be considered a sufficient cause. And third, primary prevention can only be effective when implemented at the community level.[4]

The epidemiological view of injuries does not rule out preventive strategies aimed at individual behavior, including legal sanctions, economic incentives, and public education. Unlike the individualist approaches of both the judicial and economic systems, it does not derive its strategies from a single behavioral model. But its major contribution to future accident policy comes from its definition of agents at a broader level, including environmental substances, human organizations, and geographical locations.

Borrowing from the research practice of epidemiology, we define an environmental accident as *any personal injury whose incidence is statistically linked to the presence of one or more environmental factors.* Although the most common manifestation of such injuries is disease, more familiar kinds of accidents—including workplace injuries and automobile accidents—also lend themselves to epidemiological study.[5] The ecological model uses a complex notion of causation able to handle multiple and reciprocal causes. It relies on statistical correlation to replace the mechanical and anthropomorphic metaphors favored by common law. Such metaphors, even with further instrumental expansion, cannot reach probabilistic relationships without seriously compromising their mission of aiding case-by-case adjudication.[6] As epidemiological evidence grows in public acceptance, the strain on traditional legal categories may prove insupportable.

Anxiety over environmental accidents—especially their defining feature of statistical correlation with the environment—has already begun to spread through legal circles. Variously described by legal observers as *mass torts* or *toxic torts*, a series of cases arising in the 1980s have provoked new public skepticism about the tort system and about conventional strategies for tort reform. The best-publicized injuries are those connected with asbestos litigation, which may represent a pattern for future cases as epidemiology explores the growing list of toxic materials found in the workplace.[7] Other prominent legal actions have centered on the toxic properties of dioxin (an ingredient in Agent Orange), drugs like DES and Bendectin, pesticides, various forms of radiation, and consumer products like the Dalkon Shield. Similar problems arise in litigation over adverse reactions to vaccines, including the polio and swine flu vaccines. Lawsuits based on radiation exposure anticipate questions that could emerge from a major nuclear accident, but also include alleged injuries from long-term exposure to low-level radiation. Chemical substances stored or spread across the natural environment have also joined this roster of environmental factors awaiting further investigation.

The most striking legal aspect of these cases is the complex link to disease, requiring plaintiffs to fit a new definition of *accident* into the common law doctrine of causation.[8] But equally important is the actual and potential scale of such claims, which stretch both the procedural limits of the judicial system and the financial resources of available defendants.[9] While both of these points are often mentioned in the current literature on tort law, less attention has been given to the systematic implications of environmental causation. The environmental sources of toxic tort injuries are simply graphic examples of the complex causal agents that determine the rate and incidence of other forms of personal injury, including workplace and automobile accidents. A central purpose of this book is to explore the wider policy implications of this collective, nonpersonalized approach to accidents, thereby expanding public awareness of the potential scope for personal compensation and environmental regulation.

Despite their novel conditions, toxic tort claims resurrect questions about the legal process that have long been raised by critics. Indeed, there are some signs that the emerging crisis over mass tort litigation has reawakened broader criticisms of the entire system, going beyond the usual debate over the proper evolution of judicial rules.[10] Doctrinal battles still dominate the policy arena, however. In the courts themselves, further strain is being placed on the threadbare doctrines of fault and causation, while litigants wrestle with prodigious delays and litigation costs. Judges and juries continue to expand the scope of damages—penetrating farther into the dark territory of intangible harms—and to increase compensation awards, including occasional astronomical amounts for punitive damages. As we shall see, the dominant reaction of policy-makers is to fret over these predictable symptoms and to neglect the more important environmental sources of our public malady.

In the most extensive empirical study yet made of toxic tort litigation, a recent report on asbestos has identified some major distinctions from earlier legal battles. Citing the "widespread belief that asbestos injury cases represent a new and growing class of lawsuits that pose special problems for the tort system," the report lists four specific differences:

- The injuries are medically complex—often difficult to detect, associated with multiple causative factors, and of uncertain prognosis.
- The injuries are attributed to earlier exposure to toxic substances or products that likely occurred many years before symptoms were detected.
- The circumstances of injury apply to a large group of plaintiffs.
- A relatively small number of producers and suppliers were implicated in the behavior that led to the plaintiffs' injuries.[11]

The first two points address the doctrine of causality and the temporal boundaries to the legal concept of accident. The latter two raise issues of delay and fairness caused by the number of plaintiffs, plus the limited resources available from a restricted number of defendants. We shall expand on these problems in the remainder of this chapter.

Statistical Causation and Environmental Context

The contention that accidents occur within a complex structure of social and environmental relations may stir fears of vague metaphysical forces, in contrast to the comfortable nominalism shared by the common law and many of its critics. However, the Rand study of asbestos litigation confirms some painfully real implications of toxic injuries associated with indeterminate conditions. The truth is, we face daunting uncertainties of diagnosis, etiology, and prognosis in handling these cases. Moreover, the time periods encompassed in each of these assessments seem controlled by unknown forces in the natural world, with little regard for human aspirations to gain greater technical control over accidental events.

Far from metaphysical, these complexities form a dominant reality in the late twentieth century. One might argue instead that it is the judicial system that dwells in imaginary worlds, where discrete events are governed by determinable impinging causes, which in turn are open to human cognition without temporal constraint. Pushed to its limits, this perspective presupposed by common-law categories approaches the perfect rationalism of a Leibnizian God. Its imposition on human experience requires a substantial reconstruction of events as we confront them daily.[12]

What can social or environmental categories contribute to a new public policy for personal injury? First, they provide ways to conceptualize a pattern of events defined at the probabilistic level, as depicted in current epidemiological research. Second, they increase opportunities for public control as we discover stronger correlations between personal injuries and a growing number of environmental agents. And third, they help reshape our traditional ideas about compensation and accountability. Compensation becomes part of a broader network of social responsibility for individual well-being, while corrective measures may be aimed more widely at personal, organizational, and social agents of accidental injuries.

The judicial crisis over toxic tort litigation reveals a widening gap between our incipient environmental knowledge and the individualist mode of public response. Events governing the onset of serious disease may never be definable below the level of probabilistic evidence, even as that evidence is steadily accumulated to include further natural and social agents.[13] There is a paradox to the uncertainty we are now able to display in the courtroom: diseases whose source would previously have been consigned to the mysteries of biology can now be associated with exposures to common substances and to specific environments. Without the statistical evidence of epidemiology, our ignorance would have precluded the causal hypotheses now being advanced in court by plaintiffs. Once raised, however, these theories present unique and overwhelming challenges.

When the evidence for or against a causal connection is essentially statistical in nature, the outcome of litigation can be decisively influenced by the burden of proof. Through custom that shares the same rationalistic metaphysics as the common-law view of events, the law initially assigns that burden to the plaintiff.[14] And indeed, as long as we assume that litigation can successfully use its individualist categories to reconstruct complex events occurring long ago, that burden raises few questions. But an openly instrumental judicial system can scarcely hide from itself the profound significance of assigning burdens of proof: it thereby decides who will pay the price of future environmental accidents.

The Rand study of asbestos litigation offers some preliminary evidence that courts will be sorely challenged to dispose of environmental injury claims in either a prompt or equitable fashion. Since problems of court delay and litigation costs will be discussed in a later section, our comments here are confined to the issue of causation, which in the case of asbestos-related diseases combines the twin aspects of probability and long latency periods. For asbestosis (a serious respiratory disorder) and mesothelioma (a rare cancer of the lining of the lung), the correlations with earlier asbestos exposure are about as strong as epidemiology can hope to provide. Even so, as courts make thousands of individual assessments, they must also wrestle with conflicting evidence on each plaintiff's medical condition and on the details of individual exposure. Furthermore, the claimant's statistical theory must be formally introduced and conveyed to the jury. Despite its unusually strong support for claims involving asbestosis and mesothelioma, probabilistic evidence can easily be confounded in single applications by possible intervening factors (such as whether the plaintiff used tobacco).

Most courts, it turns out, have handled the issue of causation through standard tort doctrines and procedures—rules that vary considerably across the state and federal jurisdictions covered by the report.[15] Usually the final judgment on causation is left to a jury, along with the determination of damages. As we might expect, the report documents divergent outcomes even in the same court. A Texas jury, for example, made the same massive awards to four individual plaintiffs in a consolidated trial, even though the diagnosis in one particular case had a much higher association with asbestos exposure than the others. Another example comes from Philadelphia:

> In two cases before this judge, two men had similar physical problems. They each had pleural thickening and some shortness of breath. In the case involving the man who most counsel believed to be the sicker of the two, the jury awarded $15,000. For the other plaintiff, the jury awarded $1,200,000. These results make this litigation more like roulette than jurisprudence.[16]

In addition to juries, of course, judges themselves have considerable discretion over such matters as the selection and application of legal doctrines, the kinds of evidence they will allow or require, and their formulation of jury instructions. In summary,

> As toxic tort cases become more common, the treatment of statistical evidence on causation and rules for linking specific products to injuries become large issues for the civil justice system. By failing to recast the rules of causation so that they more accurately fit the realities of latent injury cases, the courts may have contributed to the wide variation in compensation outcomes for similarly situated plaintiffs, a response that many consider inequitable.[17]

In contrast to asbestos claims, which are being litigated on a case-by-case basis, the Agent Orange cases were consolidated into one class-action suit under the direction of a highly visible federal judge, who played an almost unprecedented role in bringing the parties to settlement.[18] Here too the issue of causation became a central factor in the outcome, as the plaintiffs failed to produce epidemiological evidence on the human toxicity of dioxin. The fact that the burden of proof rested with plaintiffs assumed dominant importance as the litigation advanced, as the attorneys for both sides and the judge fully understood. The Vietnam veterans and their families had a difficult time figuring out why that burden should have counted against them rather than the defendants.

Epidemiological perspectives are relevant to more than newly discovered toxic injuries. We can find an important place for the environmental approach to events even in the prosaic, pretoxic world of automobile accidents. Atiyah supplies an interesting illustration:

> The statistician does not think so much of the individual accident and its causes, but of the probability of accidents and whatever may affect this probability. Now such things as the width of a street, its curvature or gradient, the quality of its surface, the flow of traffic and its speed, all influence the probability of an accident in a street. Such things, since they influence the probability of accidents and therefore the number of accidents, should appear in the statistical picture of factors important in accident causation. Add a foot to the width of a road and a certain number of accidents will in the long run be eliminated or provoked. When individual accidents are studied and "causes" sought it is not, in general, these factors that will be cited. Then only the unusual or abnormal are usually noticed: not the width of the road but only where it narrows suddenly, not the visibility allowed by the size and shape of the car's windows but only the obstruction caused by pennants or a dangling doll. Ignoring the normal gives rise to a tendency to ascribe most accidents to human factors such as error or carelessness, since it is usually possible to believe that there would have been no such accident if someone had acted differently. [19]

Common law restricts its focus to the actions of the parties before it, and no clear device exists for drawing environmental factors systematically into the causal vortex. Since the immediate purpose of deciding causal issues in the standard lawsuit is to assign financial responsibility, Atiyah argues, the narrow focus seems defensible. "By concentrating on the relationship between plaintiff and defendant it is understandable that the fault principle should often leave a meritorious plaintiff without compensation—if the only alternative is to burden an equally innocent defendant with the loss . . . and no attention is paid to the possibility of the loss being borne by society itself, or some larger section of society."[20]

Judicial trends toward strict liability, vicarious liability, and even enterprise liability do not substantially change this conclusion. Of course, some defendants who are found liable—notably product manufacturers—may have had no direct personal involvement in the accidental event, but they are nonetheless precisely defined legal personalities. Obviously the law has been broadening its search for accountability, but its terms are still too narrow. Forcing vicarious or corporate defendants into common-law categories, moreover, invites the sort of backlash we have seen from individualist ethical schemes, while it oversimplifies the complexity of environmental forces.

Perhaps one reason we try to personalize or otherwise confine our causal understanding of events may be our desire to focus on matters over which we have some control. This was suggested by the philosopher R. G. Collingwood, who observed that "for any given person the cause of a given thing is that one of its conditions which he is able to produce or prevent."[21] This position was recently elaborated by a psychologist investigating how ordinary people perceive causation in accidents:

> We can expect different causes for an accident to be assigned by the driver (his driving), the county surveyor (the road), and the vehicle manufacturer (the car design). When each is threatened with sanctions, however, one might expect a shift in orientation to a defensive one and a consequent shift in perceived cause. The victim interested in compensation might attribute responsibility to the most likely source.[22]

The zero-sum relation between the parties to litigation guarantees the adversarial approach to causation that we see in the courts. Depending on who has been placed in the defendant's seat, the plaintiff may tailor his or her causal theory accordingly, but always with the goal of bringing responsibility down to the level of the defendant's behavior. The defendant must join this narrow issue, using only those arguments and defenses encompassed by prevailing legal doctrines; a defense built on the ecological model of events will not defeat a claim based on negligence or strict liability. In other words, the defendant must show in traditional legal terms that the plaintiff's case somehow fails to capture the underlying event, or else that the plaintiff was also negligent. Each side has a strong incentive to portray complex events as a simplified drama featuring the individual behavior of the other.[23]

The judicial process is thus unable to move beyond its traditional individualist notions of causation and accountability to reach the distinctively *environmental* level of events. We have defined these environmental factors in terms borrowed from epidemiology, which investigates the statistical connections between personal injuries and a broad set of causal agents, including natural substances, human behavior, and geographical locations. The ecological model of events stresses the multiple and reciprocal relations among hosts, agents, and the larger environment; and while this model leaves room for individuals themselves to influence events, it draws systematic attention to the social context in which individuals carry out their actions. Events may embrace individual actions but cannot be fully reduced to those terms.

Apart from the field of public health, similar theories of contextual or collective action have been worked out by some branches of sociology and economics. Our interest in these methods is to find new vocabularies and concepts for a more comprehensive public policy for personal injuries. As we shall see in Part IV, environmental models expand both our basic conception of accidents and the potential scope of public policy. Given the practical orientation of epidemiological methods, identifying a causal source is in fact the same thing as formulating a possible course of social response. If certain organizational and environmental factors represent conditions that we are "able to produce or prevent," we need to engage them through a more comprehensive policy than we can create out of common-law tools.[24]

We do not have to make an exclusive choice among analytical levels of events, so long as we can find appropriate ways to respond on each level. Using epidemiological data as a broad index of causation does not put an end to individual accountability through judicial procedures. Thus in response to the slogan "Guns don't kill people; people kill people," we are entitled to sidestep the dichotomy and to ask whether societies with easy access to handguns have a relatively high incidence of violent homicides. We can also prosecute the person who pulls the trigger.[25]

"System Accidents": A Sociological View

The role of contextual factors in ordinary accidents has been noted by various commentators, but their importance is easier to explain for the kinds of accidents we are calling *environmental*. A useful conceptual treatment of these matters comes from sociologist Charles Perrow, based on his investigations into the 1979 nuclear accident at Pennsylvania's Three Mile Island power plant.[26] Perrow has expanded that analysis to include the "catastrophic potential" of several high-risk technologies, whose systematic complexities make large-scale accidents "inevitable, even 'normal.'"[27]

In the tangled litigation that followed the accident at Three Mile Island, all parties suing each other (those with alleged injuries, the utility in charge of the plant, and those who designed and manufactured the equipment) tried to reduce the event to a level of individual culpability—"a seemingly endless story of incompetence, dishonesty, and cover-ups."[28] Although Perrow's study found a number of personal decisions and actions that might be questioned after the fact, he presents the far more chilling prospect that even exemplary behavior by all concerned will not prevent future accidents of this sort, with consequences potentially far more serious. Moreover, "for most of the systems we shall consider . . . , neither better organization nor technological innovations appear to make them any less prone to system accidents." Indeed most organizational or technological steps designed to promote future safety simply add to the "interactive complexity" of systems, thereby increasing the opportunities for accidents to occur.

> The argument is basically very simple. We start with a plant, airplane, ship, biology laboratory, or other setting with a lot of components (parts, procedures, operators). Then we need two or more failures among components that interact in some unexpected way. No one dreamed that when X failed, Y would also be out of order and the two failures would interact so as to both start a fire and silence the fire alarm. Furthermore, no one can figure out the interaction at the time and thus know what to do. The problem is just something that never occurred to the designers. Next time they will put in an extra alarm system and a fire suppressor, but who knows, that might just allow three more unexpected interactions among inevitable failures. This interacting tendency is a characteristic of a system, not of a part or an operator."[29]

Perrow's argument is no diatribe against technology, whose legitimate presence in our society he fully acknowledges.[30] It is instead a careful analytical treatment of the interactive elements in complex systems (found in social systems as well as technology), plus a series of illustrations of how large-scale system accidents can occur in fields like nuclear power, petrochemical production, aircraft and marine transportation, and other high-risk activities. These accidents share a number of common features:

- The level of damages is potentially catastrophic, out of any proportion to the causal or personal responsibility that may be assigned to any single event or person.
- The consequences are especially grave for "innocent bystanders" (those with no contractual or commercial relationship to the activity) and to members of future generations.
- Seemingly innocent or "banal" initiating causes, by chance coincidence with equally mundane events, can interact in completely unforeseen ways.
- These interactions (for which Perrow supplies abundant examples in more than a dozen areas of "high-risk technology") are by definition not open to anticipation or simple correction.
- And when such events are "tightly coupled," they leave human operators little time to react.
- In many instances these "system interactions" involve malfunctioning or poorly understood "engineered safety devices," on which operators and procedures have relied.
- Because these interactions are unplanned and unforeseen, they have not entered into any risk-benefit calculus.[31]

The boundaries between interactive systems and the distinct events or components within those systems are necessarily flexible. While Perrow defines these terms broadly enough to cover quite ordinary events (including accidents that occur in the workplace, on the highways, or in the home), his main focus is on industrial "transformation" processes: recombinant DNA technology, chemical plants, nuclear power production, nuclear weapons, and some aspects of space missions.[32] In these fields, raw materials are not merely fabricated or assembled but are chemically transformed in processes highly susceptible to trial and error, unexpected feedback loops, and novel interactions with complex safety mechanisms and control devices.

The petrochemical industry, for example, which has both more mature technology and more experienced management than the nuclear power industry, must cope with the daily threat of fires and explosions. Despite the industry's comparatively strong safety record for workplace injuries, Perrow concludes, the fact that a "very mature operation has to be shut down for repairs about 30 percent more frequently than expected, generally from major equipment failures,"[33] suggests that system accidents are endemic in volatile technological processes. His review of major accidents in Texas City, Flixborough (England), and Pocatello (Idaho), illustrates how potentially massive damages can result from an unforeseen sequence of "prosaic, trivial" events.[34]

As Perrow notes, "The possibility of many unintended interactions is recognized by designers, so they introduce buffers and other safety devices to prevent some kinds of interactions."

> Imagine a chemical plant where gas is expected to flow from tank A to tank B, because the pressure is kept higher in tank A than in tank B. Various things go into tank A besides the basic gas—reagents, purifiers, "inerting" gases, and so on. Then the gas flows to B, where additional substances are piped in to alter that mixture even further. This is quite straightforward and linear.
>
> But there is a danger that it might become nonlinear. A feedback loop could occur if pressure declined in tank A because of a failure there or elsewhere, and the now-modifed gas in tank B flowed back into A. This could create problems; it might even be dangerous. The engineers are aware of this, so they design a butterfly valve to be placed between the two tanks to prevent reverse flow. An engineered safety device (ESD) is installed to keep the system as linear as possible (in this case, flowing in one direction.) But valves can fail, especially rarely used ones. If the pressure in tank A were to fall and the butterfly valve to fail, the feedback loop would open again, and the operators might not expect the interaction.[35]

This example follows the same pattern Perrow applied to the Three Mile Island accident. When water began leaking through a faulty seal, an "engineered safety device" shut down the steam-driven turbine. However, another safety device (designed to relieve pressure inside the chamber that housed the reactor core) failed to close properly, and warning lights that might have alerted personnel to this danger likewise malfunctioned. "Safety systems, such as warning lights, are necessary, but they have the potential for deception. If there had been no light assuring them the valve had closed, the operators would have taken other steps to check the status of the valve, as operators did in a similar accident at another plant a year and a half before."[36]

We need not follow all the details of this much-studied event, which in Perrow's view illustrates the characteristic "banality and triviality behind most catastrophes."[37] The interpretation of such accidents as the unforeseen "interaction of multiple failures" explains Perrow's central conclusion that system accidents are both *inevitable* and *normal*. Especially in technologically complex, transformative processes, accidents are inevitable because no systematic strategy can prevent them; specially designed safety devices may only contribute to the complexity of the system.[38] By calling such accidents *normal*, Perrow does not mean they are necessarily frequent, but that "it is an inherent property of the system to occasionally experience this interaction."[39] In fact, accidents of this sort are everyday occurrences, but only rarely (and by further coincidences) will they lead to catastrophic results.

Other sociologists dealing with both catastrophic events and complex human organizations have provided studies consistent with Perrow's theory of system accidents.[40] The concept can be generalized to a broader level than high-risk technologies, although Perrow's transformative processes offer intuitively compelling illustrations of how the entire "catastrophic" event can be analytically greater than the sum of its parts. By contrast, epidemiological research cannot be used to explain single and idiosyncratic events, but it likewise explores fields that resist simple analysis into linear causal relationships.

Like epidemiological findings, the model of system accidents can also help explain why environmental accidents offer insuperable challenges to courts of law. Where complex events cannot be plausibly reduced to demonstrable causal relationships, knowledge of which could be held by (or attributed to) discrete individuals, the courts have difficulty finding grounds for assigning both accountability and compensation. If they nonetheless do so by importing presumptions and manipulating burdens of proof, they end up concentrating responsibility on only those defendants who happen to fall within their jurisdiction. This pattern for handling environmental accidents has practical results that may slowly undermine our society's reliance on judicial processes.

Costs and Delay in Judicial Proceedings

The amount of damages at issue in most environmental cases ensures public attention to mass litigation, just as the occasional multimillion-dollar jury award to individual plaintiffs will command newspaper headlines. Much of the attention goes to the relatively recent surge in awards for intangible losses and punitive damages.[41] (Large jury awards are often reduced by the trial judge or appellate court, but such reductions are considerably less newsworthy than the original award.)

Any trend toward inflation of awards for comparable injuries deserves attention, particularly when the increase is due to new categories of loss. We should remember, however, that damages in tort cases are conceived by the law as redistributions of losses already sustained. The primary loss is incurred at the time of the accident, not the moment of judgment in the lawsuit; litigation either shifts all or part of that loss to the defendant, or it leaves the loss on the plaintiff. (In making this observation we are obviously putting aside the separate category of punitive damages, as well as ignoring popular skepticism about the authenticity of pain and suffering as a form of loss.)

Damages from toxic torts place special demands on the judicial process for several reasons. These are individual claims based on allegations of statistical links between injuries and environmental sources. No matter how clear the scientific evidence, however, courts face a logical gap between class probability and single instances; they must therefore be willing to infer causation across that gap before the plaintiff can win. Assuming this process is repeated for hundreds or thousands of cases, there is no applicable "law of large numbers" that can match aggregate litigation results with relevant base probability figures. Ten percent of lung-cancer victims may have contracted their disease from asbestos, but the total number of victims winning compensation could turn out to be a greater or smaller proportion of the potential pool. Besides, epidemiology cannot supply the probability figure that would help most: the likelihood that a specific victim's illness can be traced to a specific source. Most epidemiological research measures the probability that exposure to some substance will eventually lead to illness—a piece of information much more useful for accident prevention than for compensation.

As we noted earlier in the discussion of asbestos cases, outcomes in individual cases depend, in part, on how individual courts assign the

burden of proof, compounded by the uncertainties of jury decision
making. Assuming a low-probability relation between some injury and
an alleged source, it may be impossible for any claimants to win—
although some proportion may well have suffered uncompensated accidental injuries. Similarly, if proof burdens are shifted systematically
to defendants in high-probability instances, it is possible that nearly all
claimants will receive payments, even though some unknown proportion might not have derived their illness from the source in question.
As one commentator sums it up, "To resort to presumptions whenever
evidence is absent is to invite major systematic errors. . . . This inability to identify individual victims and match them with individual
wrongdoers, or even classes of wrongdoers, with a reasonable degree
of credibility presents a dilemma for the tort system, regardless of
what theory is used to determine liability."[42]

Of course, even when courts might succeed in collectively attributing to defendants the exact number of injury cases predicted on the
basis of their collective behavior, we have no guarantee that defendants could afford to pay full compensation. Again, the asbestos industry furnishes our best-researched example; citing other studies, the
Rand team reports that "estimates of future costs range between $4
billion and $87 billion." The widely publicized bankruptcy case involv-
ing Johns-Manville Corporation, the largest manufacturer of asbestos,
is the predictable result of claims filed throughout the 1970s (estimated at 30,000) and expected through the rest of the century (between
200,000 and 450,000).[43] In 1985, the manufacturers of the Dalkon
Shield contraceptive device took the same step after paying out $520
million to settle a mere 10,000 out of some 330,000 claims from wom-
en in all fifty states and seventy foreign countries.[44] Whether the anticipated claims actually rendered these companies insolvent, or simply provided them an economic incentive to seek relief from escalating
claims, is a matter of current controversy.[45] It seems likely, however,
that some defendant corporations can expect to face ruinous expenses
from toxic tort actions.

Estimates are hard to find for the costs of cleaning up hazardous
waste disposal sites across the United States, but much publicity was
given to the quantity of sites during recent debate over reauthorization
of the Superfund Act.[46] While EPA has spoken of some 2,000 sites
requiring cleanup, the Office of Technology Assessment (OTA) has
published a more credible estimate of 10,000 sites, with 8,000 more

ready to join the list soon.[47] For just the 10,000 sites, OTA has predicted a federal cleanup effort costing $100 billion over the next fifty years. All such figures are difficult to assess, given our imperfect state of knowledge about environmental hazards; but over the past decade the only revisions to these estimates have been increases—often dramatic ones. And as one writer has commented, "The greatest risk may be presented by releases from sites the contents and location of which are unknown."[48]

Whatever cost estimates we accept, the financial burdens on plaintiffs and defendants alike are dramatically increased by the costs of deciding claims through the judicial system. The high administrative costs of litigation have frequently been contrasted with those of other programs supplying compensation to injured or disabled persons, and there is every reason to suppose that those costs will remain relatively high for toxic torts. One Rand study estimates the costs of defending asbestos claims at 45 percent of every dollar paid in compensation. This contrasts with other product liability cases (35 percent), malpractice (27 percent), and automobile accident cases (5 percent).[49] Plaintiffs' costs were not documented in the report, but other estimates have put the total costs of litigating asbestos claims between 67 and 80 percent of every compensation dollar.[50] From the standpoint of legal doctrine, the costs of running the judicial process are invisible; only the instrumentalist critic notes the effect of time delays and costs on the willingness of parties to involve themselves in the process at all.

Time delays in disposing of claims represent added costs of the judicial process, especially noticeable in toxic tort cases. The Rand study of asbestos claims reaching the courts in the mid 1980s analyzed the disposition of over 23,000 claims in ten courts, both state and federal. Although delays were partly caused by strategies followed by plaintiffs' attorneys, the record is disappointing. "Across the 10 courts we studied, only a small proportion of cases reach full disposition at the same pace as that of other civil cases; a larger proportion obtain partial settlements, reaching full disposition only after a four- to five-year wait or even longer after filing. Finally, in a few courts the rate of disposition is so low that it is impossible to predict when current asbestos cases will reach disposition." Awards, when made, are equally difficult to predict, given the complex variables in litigation. "The variation in outcome from one asbestos victim to another, all of whose lives have been similarly disrupted, is a much more complex problem. By relying on private settlements and lay juries that need not account for their decisions, the American tort system places a low priority on consistency across cases."[51]

Social Costs and "Positional" Goods: An Economic View

Epidemiological evidence connecting environmental factors with disease and other injuries opens up a new world of unanticipated social costs. These conditions present a parallel challenge to economic processes, to whatever extent markets are expected to organize social responses to accidents. The economic and judicial burdens are closely connected; indeed the two processes are intertwined in a society that expects its economic sector to gain information about the incidence and value of unanticipated costs directly from the judicial process. That happens presumably when the courts impose compensation costs on organizations or activities based on their association with accidents, enabling future prices of goods and services to reflect more closely their true social costs. If environmental accidents make the courts' job harder, they consequently create problems for a market system waiting for information about these elusive costs.

We can mention several implications for the economy that result from our fragmentary, probabilistic understanding of environmental accidents. Taking probability first, the market would appear to assimilate statistical information more easily than the judicial process. When the market seeks associations between accidents and accountable organizations or activities, it does not demand a physical model centered on mechanical causation; it wants rather an indication that someone (or some group) is in a position to control or prevent such accidents in the future—should prevention turn out to be less costly than paying further compensation. Statistical evidence in itself does not change matters from an economic perspective. For example, if we suppose that asbestos causes serious injuries for 40 percent of insulation workers exposed to it, that fact should send a signal to the insulation industry about how much they might spend on prevention. They do not have to know precisely which 40 percent will suffer, as was true in the judicial process when it came time to determine compensation. The problem here is logistical: how to send that signal to the insulation industry in a way that compels attention, if not via the judicial process.

The challenge to the economic system becomes more significant, however, when we consider that epidemiological research is highly fragmentary; its preliminary explorations cannot be taken as accurate information about future causation. Some economists—including many influenced by the Chicago school, who have devoted much attention to accident problems—believe that unregulated markets can respond to risk and uncertainty (along with everything else) in a more socially efficient way than other signaling mechanisms, especially the political process. We shall investigate some of those arguments in Chapter 4; for now let us simply note the more widely accepted position of E. J. Mishan:

> The postwar cornucopia of drugs and synthetics about whose consequences, singly or in combination, we know next to nothing, now runs into many thousands. And although the probability of some genetic or ecological calamity in the production or use of any one of them might be very small indeed, as the number of such products continues to multiply, the resulting risk of some such calamity actually occurring increases to a point beyond which society is in grave peril. In these circumstances, measuring social gains against social costs with the aid of market prices is no longer that of a routine exercise in allocation economics. Indeed, any hope of translating these sorts of risk into money values that can somehow be internalized into the economic system is to be dismissed as chimerical. The nature of many of the risks we are courting can be dealt with only at the highest political level and following considerable public debate.

And in more summary terms, "the social problem is that of somehow adjusting the economic system to the existence of our dangerous state of ignorance until we know more."[52]

Despite its recent advances, epidemiology over the long term may simply compound our economic ignorance by continuing to discover significant but weak correlations across a growing range of activities. As some previous correlations grow stronger, new ones will continue to crowd in. It is the rate of growth in our knowledge of the environment (an unpredictable rate at that) which makes the social costs of environmental accidents difficult to capture in market systems. We know just enough to suspect the existence of widespread social costs, but not enough to weave them securely into the market fabric. For those who respond that the economy can simply wait until our knowledge deepens sufficiently to exert real influence on the market, we can once again turn to Mishan: "Bearing in mind the costs of unearthing relevant information, the effect of such conservative advice is to put the burden of expense and proof on the antipollution faction."[53] We cannot accept the old lawyer's trick of assigning to an opponent the burden of proof on this issue; some nonmarket public response to the reality of environmental risk will have to be made.

Borrowing terms used in the 1970s by Fred Hirsch, we can summarize the economic consequences of environmental injuries from a slightly different angle. Building on the concept of negative externalities, Hirsch drew attention to the *positional* nature of certain scarce goods in modern society. "Social scarcity . . . expresses the idea that the good things of life are restricted not only by physical limitations of producing more of them but also by absorptive limits on their use. Where the social environment has a restricted capacity for extending use without quality deterioration, it imposes social limits to consumption."[54] Hirsch treats at length the examples of higher education, leadership positions in closed hierarchies, and access to uncrowded suburban land as positional goods.

Under conditions where future injuries and illness are known to have a statistical relation to activities that flourish and expand in a modern society, we may say that safety and health become progressively more "scarce" in Hirsch's sense. In addition, going beyond Hirsch's own applications, we have noted an odious random quality to the actual distribution of these unwanted social costs, even when the probable extent of aggregate damage may be reliably known in advance.

To illustrate Hirsch's point in the context of public health, we might consider the federal government's 1976 swine flu immunization program.[55] This was a response to a purported national emergency: to immunize Americans against an expected epidemic of a dangerous strain of human influenza. It was the largest mass immunization program in American history, and besides carrying out a public health initiative it taught us, tragically, something about the harmful side effects of influenza vaccine. In retrospect we know that swine flu vaccine, even when properly made and administered, is statistically correlated with the often fatal paralytic disease called Guillain-Barré Syndrome. When 40 million people voluntary accepted doses of this vaccine in 1976, however, that link was not known—or at least it was insufficiently observed to fall within the side effects of which patients were informed. In large part because of the federal government's unusual vicarious liability for these injuries,[56] itself an artifact of the unprecedented scale of the entire effort, a pattern of association between the vaccine and this rare disease was eventually recognized. The physiological evidence has since been investigated, although the medical profession is still unable to say exactly who will develop Guillain-Barré from flu vaccine.

This example illustrates Hirsch's notion of positional goods: the demand for vaccine was (ironically) aimed at promoting individual health, but the satisfaction of that demand on a massive scale produced unanticipated costs. It makes no difference on Hirsch's theory that the demand for vaccine was registered through the political process (in fact, many believe it was engineered by President Ford for political purposes). The basic concept still holds: in seeking the aggregate good of mass vaccination, society incurred an unanticipated cost in severe personal injuries—perhaps 400 people seriously disabled or killed by Guillain-Barré.[57] To be more precise, *these specific people* incurred the cost, while the benefits of inoculation were distributed across the remaining 40 million who took the vaccine. Hirsch sums up the resulting social paradox: "What individuals want and what individually they can get, society cannot get; and society has to find some means for determining how the difference should be reconciled. This problem is a fundamental one for all social organizations predicated on fulfilling the wants of the individual."[58]

This application of Hirsch's theory departs in some ways from his own examples. Although the swine flu case presented the paradox of a health program that caused serious personal injuries, a collective impact on health and safety may result from any other initiative expressed through market or political processes. Under conditions where we do not know the strength of the correlation between personal injury and some particular activity, it is impossible for rational individuals to anticipate the extent of resulting harm, let alone its precise distribution. Thus no person contemplating either market or political action can properly take into account the collective effects on public health of his or her own action, although there may be a statistical basis for linking broadly defined activities with adverse effects. The problem for individual action can only rarely be mitigated by epidemiological findings, since most correlations with specified activities are well under 100 percent, and the impact on an affected population is seldom universal.

What can we learn from Hirsch's view of social costs and positional goods? First, people acting separately may be unable to avoid endangering individual health and safety, either their own or that of others. Such limits will occur whenever market or political choices collectively constrain the individual in ways that cannot be subject to economic control. Second, these limits appear to grow as market activity expands. Thus the pursuit of individual preferences under any prevailing state of technology creates the conditions under which individuals are less able to ensure their future health and safety.

Third, the distributional consequences of increased hazards in the environment are statistically random. By contrast, in the cases considered by Hirsch, various strategies exist for deciding who shall prevail in the pursuit of scarce positional goods—such as auction bidding or imposing bureaucratic burdens on competing candidates. These devices provide rational, if not always socially desirable, methods of distributing scarce commodities, but they are no help in the case of environmentally related disease and injury. Although individuals may take some mitigating steps to reduce the impact of risk (such as purchasing individual insurance), our understanding of environmental dangers is too fragmentary to say with any confidence whether risks have been adequately covered. Fourth, and at the core of Hirsch's concept, economic growth cannot be expected to ease the scarcity of, or mollify the demand for, health and safety; indeed, everything suggests that combined risks of personal injury would increase under conditions of economic growth.

Epidemiology thus offers a perspective on causation and responsibility that challenges the deepest individualist assumptions of our law, our politics, and our economy. It represents a diffuse level of causation that cannot, in most cases, be reduced further either to identify an individual perpetrator or to predict an individual victim. As more afflictions in society come under epidemiological scrutiny, we are gradually finding ways to depict a social network of events that cannot be reduced to the individualist categories of economy, state, or legal system.

A Social Perspective on Personal Injury

Our review of environmental accidents tends to support long-standing arguments that the judicial process for handling personal injury has serious difficulties. It is possible to see this new type of accident as creating one more crisis for tort law, which someday may finally succumb to its well-chronicled maladies. In Part II we shall consider the major remedies prescribed by politicians, economists, and exponents of ethical systems for keeping the judicial process functioning—and even for assuming some of its burdens, should the latest crisis prove terminal.

By focusing attention on resuscitating tort law, however, we risk ignoring the much broader social dimensions of personal-injury problems. Awareness of environmental accidents reminds us that accidents are a far more pervasive social problem than we are hardened to believe. Even a fully functioning judicial system probably misses most ordinary accidents, as defined in its own narrow terms. In the end, the central problem is not the current failure of tort law to do its job. Rather it is our selection of judicial processes as our first line of response to a complex set of social problems.

Before environmental injuries raised new questions about the very nature of accidents, we seem to have allowed the judicial process to define the relevant social issues and the primary modes of response. Public discussion sticks to such issues as whether we should move toward no-fault compensation, strict liability, or even enterprise liability. We debate whether to compensate accident victims who lose out in the judicial system—because of onerous doctrines, burdens of proof, or simply the costs of time-consuming procedures. These questions are important—they are in fact at the center of current American debate—but they are dominated by the judicial system's own limited terms. We were in the habit, before environmental injuries intruded, of defining accidents as those injuries that an ideal judicial system would compensate. Accountability had become an enlightened vision of civil liability. We were expecting the creativity of economists and politicans to clarify that ideal judicial system, or to help carry out that enlightened vision through remedial procedures.

The most important lesson from environmental accidents is that compensation issues and accountability issues are, and will remain, more complex than the judicial vision can encompass—even in a healthy judicial regime. The claims for compensation far outstrip the occasions on which a fiscally solvent person or corporation can be steered into the defendant's spot; we see this clearly in the growth of Social Security programs, particularly for health care and disability support. Likewise the need for more rigorous accountability applies to several layers of society: not just to those individuals or deep-pocket corporations who qualify as civil defendants, but to organizations of all sorts, governmental agencies, and even the electorate as a whole. Responding to environmental injuries gives us an opportunity to rediscover these missing components of a comprehensive public response to accidents.

The assertion that most accidents, in fact, never reach the judicial process in any form requires more attention. Commentators on tort-law reform generally ignore this possibility, or they may assume that potential parties settle out of court on the basis of judicial guidelines. But recent evidence from Great Britain suggests that few accident claims may enter the judicial arena, let alone receive compensation adequate to offset losses. A British survey published in 1984 shows that 85 percent of 1,202 accident victims in the research sample never even filed claims.[59] The failure of accident victims of all kinds to take on the legal system was caused in part by the costs, delays, and technical eligibility criteria discussed earlier. But even more fundamental barriers emerge from the study: "The vast majority of victims either never considered the question of claiming compensation, or if they did so, failed to take any positive steps to make a definite claim." Among the explanations for this failure are the tendency not to associate an accident with possible fault-based compensation, the further tendency not to seek legal advice unless urged to do so by friends or workplace associates, problems of obtaining evidence, and fear of legal costs.[60]

> The accident victims who do succeed in obtaining damages for their injuries are a strange group. They are not necessarily the most seriously injured, nor those who have suffered the greatest losses. They are not the people who have suffered the most prevalent types of accident, nor are they necessarily those who blamed some third party for the accident. They are not the people with most wealth and influence. But they do appear to have an important advantage in that they have access to advice about claiming and often receive this advice without soliciting it. Road and work accident victims are more likely to be involved in formal or semiformal procedures for reporting the accidents and for dealing with

the aftermath. Victims of accidents elsewhere are unlikely to become involved in any procedure which is not initiated by them.

Even when an accident victim decided to bring suit and was ultimately successful in gaining a settlement or damages, the level of compensation was generally inadequate to cover economic losses, particularly for relatively serious disability causing prolonged absence from work. "The average delay between the date of the accident and actual receipt of damages was a little over nineteen months." The more serious cases also experienced the longer delays. For residual support, and in most instances for any support at all, disabled persons in the survey relied much more heavily on the state-run sick pay and social security schemes, rather than the tort system.[61] Britain has a more extensive network of programs to support the temporarily and long-term disabled than does the United States, but there is comparable evidence that the American social welfare structure, such as it is, plays an equally vital role in compensating injured persons.[62]

In the American context, when we look beyond traditional kinds of accidents to environmental injuries, judicial processes may play a very modest role. In the case of occupational diseases, where victims often have the option of filing workers' compensation claims, even that process is seldom used; its legalistic definition of accident still bars many instances of disease.[63] What remains is the "safety net" of public social welfare programs and private pension funds.

A 1980 Department of Labor study, involving 700,000 workers with severe occupational disabilities derived from a variety of toxic sources, reported that three-quarters of their population had received payments from social welfare programs. Of this group, over half (53 percent) received benefits from Social Security Disability Insurance (SSDI), about one-fifth (21 percent) received support from pensions, somewhat fewer (17 percent) received veterans' benefits, and about the same number (16 percent) were covered by Supplemental Security Income (SSI), the federal income support program. Only 5 percent were successful in winning workers' compensation benefits, and only a negligible number, if any, recovered damages in tort actions.[64]

Irving Selikoff's research on workers injured by asbestos provides another source of data on the fate of environmental accident victims. One might suppose, Selikoff says, that workers in asbestos-related industry represent the best case, "inasmuch as asbestos has been so widely accepted as a virulent occupational health hazard. Asbestos must be thought of as among the best understood hazards of the work-place." His study of injured insulation workers revealed surprisingly little support from either public or private sources:

> The most striking characteristics seem to be the lack of usage of these various support schemes. Over 40 percent of these workers received neither Social Security benefits (old age or disability) nor a pension at the time of their deaths. For those who stopped work-ing due to their terminal illness (84 percent of the cohort), two of every three did not file a disability claim for workers' compensa-tion. Even among those disabled for over two years or more, such claims did not materialize for over one-half of the workers. Where there was a surviving widow, death claims were filed by less than one-half of the cohort.[65]

Based on what we know about asbestos injury claims now flooding the courts, with the inherent uncertainties and predictable costs of litiga-tion, it seems highly doubtful that the judicial system can suddenly take command of these difficult social problems.

Instead of searching for ways to modify judicial processes to be-come marginally more expeditious, we should instead look for entirely different institutional structures for responding to injuries of all kinds. Some of the proposals discussed in Part III may point toward creative alternatives, but it is striking how deeply indebted these programs remain to judicial concepts. Organizational, governmental, and socie-tal responsibility are usually dealt with (if at all) by analogy with civil liability. The definition of worthy victims still seems to depend on simultaneously recognizing a specific culpable source of injury (espe-cially a well-funded source). Many of these proposals indicate sensible directions, but they do not yet constitute a secure platform for a com-prehensive accident policy. As we will show in Part IV, a comprehen-sive accident policy would have to abandon the common law fantasy of a single, neutral mechanism for resolving the issues of both compensa-tion and accountability.

Part Two

Reinforcing Individualism:

Interest-Group Politics,

Economic Theory,

and Moral Philosophy

S ocial reactions to new forms of personal injury pass through a volatile political structure, in which groups defined by their adversarial roles in the judicial process struggle mightily to control the future direction of legal doctrines. In this climate public responsibility is lost in the Hobbesian battle of diverse interest groups—whose strength, paradoxically, may be the *result* of rugged individualism enshrined in current policies, rather than the source. Chapter 3 surveys these competing interests and analyzes their role in current national debate.

Behind the political struggle we note the growing strategic importance of analytical theory—much of it derived from welfare economics—used to criticize and redirect the instrumental development of tort doctrines. While Chapter 3 covers the rhetorical dimensions of economic arguments and the rejoinder from advocates of legal rights, the remainder of Part II explores relevant perspectives from economic theory and moral philosophy. Over the past two decades academic lawyers have borrowed heavily from both disciplines, hoping to find new intellectual resources to guide the future evolution of legal doctrine. These borrowings have been selective and even opportunistic, and their dominant effect (whether intended or not) has been to reinforce the individualist framework of judicial practice.

Chapter 4 analyzes the march of economic theory into legal territory, based on the the writings of Guido Calabresi and others. Calabresi himself (unlike many who apply his arguments) treats the market process as one more tool in the hands of instrumental policy planners, whose separate attention to matters of distribution and social justice he never doubts. This relatively balanced formal program observes the normal cautions raised by mainstream economists upon venturing into the dismal practice of public policy. But Calabresi's treatment of market rationality seems to have answered the prayers of lawyers searching for apolitical, self-justifying institutions to prop up the judicial process. The uncanny parallel between self-regulating market models and self-regulating legal procedures has offered a glittering invitation to see the two as mutually supporting structures, bypassing the less orderly systems of politics.

The conceptual individualism shared by tort law and neoclassical economic theory virtually ensures that welfare economics will be used to reclaim tort doctrines from their instrumental use in pursuit of progressive values. Chapter 5 criticizes this normative extension of economic theory in the works of Richard Posner. It also examines strong individualist premises found in recent moral philosophy, notably in analytical schools identified with the anti-instrumentalist tradition of deontology. Moral theory no more compels a public philosophy of individualism than does economic theory, when carefully considered. Nonetheless, most of those applying moral philosophy to the problem of accidents celebrate the traditional individualism of early tort law. The same tendency is likewise present in efforts to steer the instrumental movement of tort doctrines by using common-sense standards of morality.

Chapter 3

Tort Law and the Politics of Pluralism

> *Our present system is a mess. Manufacturing and innovation are being inhibited; liability insurance and litigation costs continue to drive up product prices; domestic and international trade is stifled; injured plaintiffs must wait years for recovery, most of which goes to the lawyers; and thousands of small businesses—indeed, entire industries— are being driven out of business each year. As it stands now, the only truly redeeming grace of the present system is that it provides a very good living for more lawyers than we could otherwise accommodate.*[1]

Goals of the Political System: Patchwork or Replacement?

When judicial procedures are perceived to break down, Americans look to the political system for a remedy. Early in this century, the crisis over industrial accidents was resolved by replacing the negligence system with new state programs for workers' compensation, administered by special tribunals operating under legislative standards. This episode, however, turns out to be the major exception to a more moderate pattern of political response. American legislation has generally taken the limited approach of patching up the doctrines and procedures of tort law, while retaining that process as society's primary framework for handling personal injuries.

Other nations have taken bolder political action, although only New Zealand has actually replaced the entire negligence system with a legislative entitlement program for all cases of "personal injury by accident."[2] During the 1970s other countries considered similar action but stopped short of abolishing the judicial role. In Britain, for example, a Royal Commission recommended extending the workers' compensation model to automobile accidents, as well as offering new or existing social welfare entitlements to certain other classes of accident victims.

77

The tort system, so imagined the Commission, was rapidly becoming a "junior partner" to the social welfare system in meeting the needs of accident victims, and would likely wither away without the dramatic step of abolition.[3] More will be said in Chapter 11 about these policy debates in other countries.

Considering the comparatively modest remedial goals of American policy, it remains a perennial mystery to outraged Senators that the political system appears so helpless in addressing the obvious failings of tort law. Symptomatic was the fate of proposed federal product liability legislation in 1986, when a minority on the Senate floor blocked a carefully crafted plan to impose unprecedented federal guidelines on state tort law.[4] Given the powerful interests at stake—including those of consumers, manufacturers, and the legal profession itself—it is perhaps not surprising that even remedial action has been difficult. It is often said that pluralist democracies face dilemmas in reaching political solutions to major distributive conflicts,[5] and the political reform of tort law seems to demonstrate just that point. This chapter will examine some of the current barriers to effective political response, while Chapters 6 to 9 will analyze in detail major substantive proposals for altering or replacing the tort system.

The goals of political intervention can be viewed both as supporting the tort system and as independently serving the general interests of accident policy. Recalling the discussion in Chapter 1, the judicial process attempts (1) to identify compensable victims, (2) to impose the costs of compensation on culpable parties, and (3) to do so under general legal standards. By regulating those legal standards, legislatures can directly assist the judicial process in accomplishing its specific tasks, clarifying the doctrines and procedures under which plaintiffs and defendants resolve their differences. For example, by stipulating strict liability for manufacturers of such inherently dangerous products as drugs, poisons, or explosives, the legislature can try to reduce uncertainties in case-by-case judicial interpretation. Legislatures can likewise mandate rules of comparative negligence to replace the harsh common-law doctrine of contributory negligence, in addition to rules governing procedures and damages.

It is also important to formulate goals for political intervention in broader terms, whether or not common-law processes turn out to be appropriate means for accomplishing social purposes. In responding to personal injuries, the political system may address either the victim's interest in compensation, or the society's interest in accountability, or both. Unlike the judicial process, however, it can pursue each of these areas independently, without confining compensation to specific instances where culpable, well-funded defendants are identified. Similarly, its options for accountability are much broader than imposing compensation costs for past actions; it may choose to pursue retribution (commonly through criminal processes) or prevention (either through command regulation or economic incentives). In developing and implementing policies for both compensation and accountability, legislatures must also observe an additional standard: to conduct their operations in accordance with correct legislative procedures, including the rules of administrative procedure and constitutional due process.

Even though most accident-related reforms now being considered by state and federal legislatures follow the narrower approach of remedying perceived defects in the judicial process, the broader goals of political intervention deserve greater attention from the press and the public. Legislation assists the courts for purposes that are external to the common law itself, whether or not those purposes are clearly labeled. As we saw in Chapter 1, the law of torts is not a single body of static doctrines—notwithstanding judicial rhetoric; it is rather in a state of constant flux, and any attempt to organize it or to direct its content requires a secure sense of instrumental purpose or direction. In other words, legislatures tinker with the tort system for reasons that deserve robust political debate.

This much would have been understood by progressive critics of tort law throughout the past century. They were accustomed to instrumental arguments, especially when invoking political action. But we must also acknowledge the growing importance in accident policy of other arguments couched in terms of legal rights. We now commonly find nonconsequentialist positions that assume or postulate certain rights and responsibilities that ought to guide public policies on compensation and accountability.[6] This idiom does not, however, alter the instrumental character of political intervention, but simply defines the goals of intervention as protecting rights or imposing responsibilities that may be erroneously treated by the judiciary. Political action remains instrumental, in other words, even when the goals of such action are to establish, clarify, extend, or even leave untouched the nonconsequentialist rules of a common law system. In Chapter 5 we will say more about the role of rights-based concepts in shaping the public response to personal injury.

Responsive Capacities of the Political System

Accidents focus a society's attention on issues of distributive justice, both in rectifying past events and in preventing future injuries. Environmental accidents sharpen that focus in a number of significant ways. By placing additional strain on judicial processes, they force us to reexamine the instrumental values imbedded in prevailing legal rules; we cannot simply rely on tort law to reach results that are correct by definition. Second, their statistical nature directs our attention to levels of accountability that are systematically ignored by the individualist bias of common law: specifically the actions of groups, organizations, government agencies, and society as a whole. Lastly, environmental accidents suggest a vast but unknown scale of social costs tied to complex events, justifying review of our standard reliance on civil liability and market forces to finance either compensation or future protection.

Under pressure from the threat of future environmental accidents, the political systems in all industrialized nations will eventually have to devise new and independent policies on both compensation and accountability. They will need to decide, for example, how to respond to groups like the American asbestos workers, whose personal losses may be largely uncompensated because of time and doctrinal barriers in the tort system. There will be other groups like the Agent Orange veterans, whose physical complaints are imperfectly correlated with specific exposure to known toxic substances. And there will be incidents like the swine flu episode, where future government-sponsored initiatives lead to unforeseen injuries. Nations will have to contemplate nuclear accidents on the scale of Chernobyl or even greater, along with other possibly catastrophic contamination of the environment. Because all these cases, for separate reasons, cannot be dealt with through standard judicial proceedings, they will inevitably end up as political issues requiring specific action on compensation.

On the equally important problem of accountability, environmental accidents will necessarily increase the public's desire to estimate and internalize more of the social costs of modern industrial development. Governments will have to deal more directly with whole industries rather than individual companies, with problems spread out over many years rather than discrete episodes, and with standards governing acceptable risk from a growing list of hazardous substances in our working and living environments. A more comprehensive approach to regulation—whether based on administrative commands or economic incentives—will play an important role in any general policy on accountability. Large private organizations and government agencies will themselves have to be included in such a policy, given their deci-, sive roles in determining future environmental conditions. Finally, although assigning costs does not have to correlate in every case with a decision to compensate victims, both compensation and prevention will have to be financed in some fashion.

Explicit policies along such lines raise questions of distributive justice that are among the most difficult issues contemporary societies can face. They cannot simply be delegated to the common law for adjudication, since the issue is often the very fairness of how those procedures have operated in the past. As we saw in Chapter 1, the tort system rests implicitly on a set of values extrinsic to that system, displacing the final criteria of distributive justice onto other spheres. Nor can distributive conflicts be resolved under market-based standards of social efficiency, since those standards explicitly exclude issues of wealth distribution. The economic system transforms problems of public policy into technical tasks for the market by ignoring questions of social distribution. Notwithstanding the limitations of judicial and economic structures, contemporary discussions of accident policy show a remarkable tendency to remain within these restricted frameworks, leaving untouched the most difficult social issues surrounding personal injuries.

We are forced to conclude that political processes themselves may arouse even more suspicion than the parallel structures of law and economics, based on apparent skepticism that the "dilemmas of pluralist democracy" allow a society to resolve its differences fairly in the political arena. Paradoxically, it is the openness of political conflict over the distribution of resources that fuels such skepticism: where social issues are reduced to a struggle between competing interest groups, there appears to be no way to satisfy one group except at the expense of another. If all that matters is the electoral strength or lobbying skill of each competing group, then the political system offers little hope of resolving conflicts on terms acceptable to all. This uncomfortable situation explains, perhaps, why the political process remains the forum for debate over accident policy while the *content* of that debate tries valiantly to incorporate the more universal rhetoric of law, economics, or ethics. The place where we bring our social conflicts seems too impoverished to provide satisfying solutions without reference to these other systems.

Such impoverishment need not be traced to the very nature of political life. Rather, our current system may be rendered helpless to deal with accident problems because the public agenda has been largely restricted to "micromanaging" the rules of tort law. Unless that agenda is opened up to include the basic principles of accident policy, there is no chance for getting beyond the level of interest-group conflict. As Robert Dahl has argued, despite the inevitable conflicts of complex democratic societies, it is conceivable that diverse interests may reach some political consensus on certain "regulative structures and principles."[7] This suggests how we might ultimately describe the larger political challenge of personal injury, and in the conclusion to this chapter we will review some conditions for meeting that challenge.

Meanwhile, far from approaching consensus, the multitude of voices confronting the tort system has only intensified under the special challenges of environmental accidents. As the law recognizes new categories of potential accident victims and oversees increasing compensation costs and procedural frictions, there is a lot more to be shouted about. Today, as in the past, a lawsuit calls forth a conflict-centered, adversarial interpretation of events, even when the natural world deals more in bottomless probabilities. Plaintiffs and defendants are expected to place sharp outlines around amorphous situations, and to lay special stress on their opposing interpretations of uncertainties. This heightening of conflict is natural in the "forensic lottery," where by definition winning requires that others should lose. Those others can now be quite far removed from accident-producing events, according to the latest developments in strict and vicarious liability. Insurance carriers have always shared the stakes of adversaries to a suit, and more recently so do federal, state, and municipal governments. It is often pointed out that corporations pass the costs of tort claims through to consumers, so that we all, in a sense, become interested parties to accident litigation.[8]

In addition, wherever the remnants of negligence theory still cover the expanding torso of civil liability, parties collide over measuring the defendant's performance according to legal standards of care, foresight, and prudence. A negligence suit requires the plaintiff to portray the defendant as deviating from some operational standard of acceptable behavior. Under these conditions both sides have a stake in stereotyping the behavior of the other, magnifying relatively minor peccadillos into epic misdeeds—playing on the prejudices of judge or jury to win a victory against the heartless corporation, or to deny damages to the hypochondriacal worker. The interest-group model of politics is thus well matched by the "fight theory" of adjudication.[9]

The Politics of Tort Reform

At the most fundamental level, the battle in tort cases comes down to plaintiffs against defendants. What remains is to fill in these general classifications with groups typically found on either end of a lawsuit: for plaintiffs, these would include consumers and employees; for defendants, product manufacturers, other employers, and numerous surrogates under theories of vicarious liability.

The most elaborate position statements on tort reform are put forward, as we might expect, by business groups, major labor unions, and consumer-oriented organizations. By far the most numerous lobbyists are connected with major American corporations and industrial trade associations.[10] These groups regularly square off against each other, as happened in recent congressional hearings on product liability legislation. Taking the manufacturers' position in those battles were, among many others, the Product Liability Alliance, the National Machine Tool Builders Association, the American Textile Machinery Association, the Machinery and Allied Products Institute, and the Chemical Manufacturers Association. Labor interests were represented by the AFL-CIO, while consumer groups were led by the Consumer Federation of America, Consumers' Union, and Ralph Nader's Public Citizen/Congress Watch.[11]

Among the plaintiff groups making submissions to this Senate committee was DES Action, a national organization specializing in one category of product liability plaintiff: the offspring of mothers who took the pregnancy drug DES.[12] It is now quite common for plaintiff groups in class-action tort cases to form associations strengthening their cause in both judicial and legislative forums. Among currently active groups are the National Association of Atomic Veterans, National Committee for Radiation Victims, White Lung Association, and

Agent Orange Veterans Association. Attorneys representing asbestos claimants around the country are themselves organized as the Asbestos Litigation Group.

But the list grows longer. In the numerically largest class of accident cases, for example, drivers of automobiles may find themselves on either side of the table; where fault is an issue, parties often counterclaim and thus have a taste of both adversarial postures. In cases involving professional malpractice, the defendant's slot is generally filled not by a corporation but by private practitioners and nonprofit institutions, such as hospitals. The corresponding professional associations thus also take interested positions on the proper direction of tort law, including the American Medical Association and comparable organizations for health administrators, accountants, and many others. With the decline of civil legal immunity for charitable organizations and for state and local government, new groups enter the ranks of defendants, including private social welfare agencies, universities, and municipalities. In the recent protest wave over liability insurance premium increases, legislators have heard "a cry for help . . . from doctors, manufacturers, day-care providers, [and] municipal governments,"[13] surely an unusual coalition.

This elementary description of interests requires expansion in at least two directions. First, the institutional frameworks for adjudicating and financing tort claims create distinctive interests for both the legal profession and the insurance industry. While the lawyer's interest is avowedly derived from the client (whether plaintiff or defendant), everyone knows that a portion of the bar earns its livelihood by representing personal-injury plaintiffs. They have not hesitated to use their formidable advocacy skills on issues of tort-law reform. The most outspoken organization is the American Trial Lawyers' Association, but the much larger American Bar Association has been a powerful force opposing almost all attempts to change the current system.[14] The widespread use of contingency fees, in which the plaintiff's attorney charges a percentage of any eventual award in lieu of hourly payment, is sometimes said to reinforce the attorney's common interest with the client, as in many cases it clearly does.[15] But the growing criticisms of this practice raise several broader considerations, such as the inflating effect on damages, the bias toward representing dramatic but procedurally uncomplicated cases,[16] and the fixation on judicial processes of compensation rather than administrative or no-fault schemes.

The second group, the insurance industry, has long been a recognized player in the financial system that underwrites the shift in accident costs from plaintiffs to defendants. It was widely assumed by the progressive/instrumentalist critics of tort law that corporate defendants would insure themselves against losses, and indeed this financial route was usually deemed desirable as a way of spreading the costs of compensation as widely as possible across industries and to the entire economy.[17] For them the theoretical possibility of calibrating premiums to a company's or industry's accident record held more promise than the tort system for deterring corporate misconduct, since actual tort damages are usually determined as much by the extent of a particular victim's injuries as by the defendant's actions.[18] It is now widely understood in automobile accident cases that the true defendant, from a financial point of view, is the nominal defendant's insurance company. Many tort critics preferred insurance, seen as a commodity subject to market forces, to government programs socializing risk or regulating productive activity. Insurers' interests are thus in some sense derived from those of defendants: they coincide on reducing damages awards, maintaining doctrinal barriers to greater liability, and strengthening procedural defenses.

In addition, however, insurers frequently conflict with their clients in interpreting benefit coverage. These differences have been magnified over the past twenty years by the judicial expansion of liability rules, by epidemiological theories that spawn new categories of plaintiffs, and by the enlarged time horizons accompanying environmental accidents. For example, insurance companies have found they can better predict (and reduce) their costs if they limit pollution coverage to only those claims actually filed during a specified period, rather than covering claims based on all events that happened during that same period. Abraham discusses this shift from "occurrence" coverage to "claims-made" policies as one of the industry's self-interested strategies.[19] Finally, the insurance industry has had to keep an eye on public regulation, particularly in times when the "crisis" in tort law has been blamed on excessive premium increases.[20] Speaking publicly for the industry on tort law issues are such groups as the American Insurance Association, the Alliance of American Insurers, and the Insurance Information Institute.

But this catalogue is still not complete. Some of the most forceful positions on accident policies now come from relatively young lobbying groups speaking for the public as a whole through both legislative advocacy and class-action litigation.[21] Several studies have analyzed this movement under the label of *public interest liberalism,* an outgrowth of political activism by the 1960s moderate left.[22] Groups like Common Cause, Friends of the Earth, Consumer Federation of America, and Ralph Nader's Public Citizen increased greatly in number and size after 1968, joining revivified older organizations like the Sierra Club to represent points of view they felt were being excluded by the corporate-dominated market and weak public regulatory agencies. McCann has chronicled how these groups mobilized public support for environmental and consumer causes, presenting themselves as "correcting the imbalance" created by the power of large industrial organizations (seen as the sources of pollution and consumer manipulation), not only in the legislative and judicial arenas but in the public media.[23] A notable increase in environmental and consumer-oriented legislation since the mid 1960s has accompanied the rise of this movement, as have continued trends in common law favorable to plaintiffs.

Since the election of Ronald Reagan in 1980, however, the fortunes of these organizations have faltered along with popular support for environmental and consumer regulation. Impersonating the structure and strategies of the liberal public-interest organizations are a number of ideologically opposed groups, often specializing in environmental issues. The appearance of such conservative public-interest lobbies raises awkward questions about any group's aspirations to represent the *general* public rather than some special subset within the public. All such organizations now contribute heavily to the fractious debate on environmental and consumer concerns, including the role of tort law in the larger process of responding to personal injury. According to McCann's analysis, their current strongly adversarial posture was in fact presaged by their initial attraction to judicial reform strategies, such as class action suits and procedural challenges to administrative action.[24]

All these groups and organizations, beginning with classes of plaintiffs and defendants, expanding along with newly recognized members of each class as part of the growth of tort-law doctrine, extending to supporting players within the judicial structure such as negligence lawyers and insurers, and ending with broad public-interest organizations with their transparent political commitments—all these bodies reinforce the impression that tort-law reform is the classic battleground for a pluralist society's conflicting interest groups. As we shall see, the plurality of voices is very real, and it helps explain both the complexity and variety of proposals now before that elusive abstraction—the public—to change the way our society responds to personal injury.

Political Strategies: The Role of General Interests

The Hobbesian world just described remains somewhat veiled in the actual political debate over tort law, first by the noninstrumental concepts of legal rights, and second by reference to general interests that seem to elevate an advocate's position beyond pure self-regard. On the first point, the impersonal rhetoric of common law is especially attractive to those whose interests are already well served by prevailing tort doctrines. Consumers do not need the legislature's help, in many instances, to enjoy as plaintiffs the advantages that flow from recent trends toward strict liability; they can stand on their rights and try to protect them from erosion. But the common law is complex enough, as we have noted, to provide at least potential comfort for opposing groups. Since much of what passes as strict liability of corporations is actually premised on creative extensions of negligence doctrine, corporate interests may appear simply to be calling judges home to the central concepts of fault. We may sense a widespread reaction against judicial activism on numerous legal fronts in our society, in civil liability cases no less than in constitutional interpretation.[25]

More difficult to penetrate than the strategic language of rights are the generalized interests that dominate the arguments of most political lobbyists. No person or group enters the fray of democratic pluralism baldly asserting its desire for someone else's resources; there is usually a higher principle (or several) to which each group attaches its claims. In the context of accident debate, the three most common general interests are *compensation* of victims, *regulation* of dangerous conduct, and promoting economic *efficiency*. We need to understand each of these concepts if we are to interpret even the most transparent conflicts on the issue of tort-law reform. Our approach will be first to explain each concept briefly, and second to illustrate its use within the current national debate over product liability legislation.

Although all three of these general interests serve a clear strategic function in political discussion, each one nonetheless strives to legitimize its social impact by importing some theory of the public interest. The best indication of this ambition to universalize is the practice of using one or more general interests to balance the others—a technique that has been developed most extensively by economic tort theorists who use the market system as their balancing mechanism. Despite criticisms we shall raise about this and other academic theories, it is important to stress their common purpose: to raise the Hobbesian debate to more discursive levels, thereby allowing the political discussion to go forward. We shall conclude, however, that this putative general level of discourse wears thin under pressure from group interests just below the surface. In the debate on product liability rules, each general perspective remains hostage to competing strategic interests, lending support to the short-term advantages of prominent interest groups.

Compensation

At first glance it is unclear why compensation carries any pretense of being a general interest of society rather than the special interest of accident victims. It was one of the progressive critics' ambitions for tort law, however, that through liberalized compensation rules the courts would strengthen the regulation of dangerous practices in industry, leading to both safer environments and more efficient allocation of social costs. Built into the common law process of awarding compensation is always a corresponding burden placed on some party held civilly liable, and that burden represents an incentive for modifying future activity, both by that defendant and by others engaged in similar efforts.

Each of the three general-interest concepts contains some internal tensions overlooked by both academic and strategic partisans. In the case of compensation, the greatest difficulty is in defining the limits of a compensable person or event. Its apparently boundless scope weakens the ability of a general compensation principle to serve as a fulcrum for balancing the competing interests of regulation and efficiency. (Those concepts, rather, help supply the missing limits to compensation.) It is simple to argue that enlarging the general sphere of compensation has a direct impact on regulation of dangerous behavior by promoting the internalizing of social costs, but we never know when society has had enough of these desirable effects. Compensation defines a direction for policy but not a stopping point.

Ironically the definitional problems with *compensation* are only increased by the success of instrumentalist tort criticism in loosening the criteria of classic negligence liability: the classification of viable defendants, the causal link between parties, failure of the defendant to exercise due care, plus various aspects of the plaintiff's performance. Difficult as these traditional criteria were to justify, especially when attacked incrementally, they did provide some stability and limit to the concept of compensability. To be eligible for compensation, the victim had to clear these hurdles. Being pragmatic lawyers, the instrumentalists were content to point out that some of these hurdles were too high, but they seldom addressed the more general issue whether there ought to be any hurdles at all, and who was entitled to run the race.

The need to limit compensation is no purely academic matter in a judicial system that still imposes compensation costs on specific individuals and organizations. As long as those limits are unclear, a correspondingly indeterminate number of potential defendants will discover personal interests in narrowing that definition. In any given tort case, of course, the defendant's argument has to focus on doctrinal issues, but we can expect alert defendants to ask the legislature whether there are not at least *some* misfortunes in the universe for which they can be excused. Put in the affirmative, legislatures will continually be invited to place limits on the scope of liability in response to the uncontrolled growth of compensation interests.

Regulation

The goals of regulation are external to the common law but easily related to larger social interests. Rather than permitting personal injuries to occur, it seems reasonable to try to prevent accidents at their source whenever possible. Legislation to control accidents by regulating their most notorious sources is yet another part of the progressive/instrumentalist legacy, one that reached its height between 1965 and 1980 in a series of laws seeking to promote greater safety in the workplace, the marketplace, and the environment. But the goal of regulating unsafe behavior has its own boundary difficulties.[26] Exactly how much prevention is desirable? Indeed, how much is even possible?

As was true for compensation, the question of limits is inevitably raised by groups who stand to lose heavily under a regime of expanding regulation. There are times, it is alleged, when the cure is worse than the affliction. Regulation carries a price, whether monetary costs like the expense of purchasing safety devices for workers, or legal/procedural costs like the intrusion on employers from enforcement of safety standards. The costs might also fall on workers whose employment becomes expendable under increased costs of safety measures. Regulation promotes long-term safety, but it sharpens short-term conflict. In our legal-administrative structure, regulations are bureaucratically enforced standards, and since the mid 1960s those standards have placed increasing monetary and procedural burdens on employers and producers.[27] Conflicts over regulation are often registered in the political system as questions about the proper degree of protection: does a producer have to reduce all risk of injury from an artificial sweetener? Does a workplace have to eliminate all risk of disability from potentially toxic chemicals?

A further complication comes from scientific uncertainty about the effects of toxic substances and whether it is even possible to determine a safe degree of exposure.[28] Over the years increasingly demanding regulatory standards have been required for exposure to asbestos, as new evidence points to the toxic effects of fibers too small to be detected by earlier measurements.[29] This problem arises even as asbestos is being literally stirred up by efforts to remove it from schools and other public buildings. New standards for contractors removing asbestos would seem to require still more knowledge than we now possess of the long-term consequences of exposure to very small particles. Yet the extent of regulation must be decided now, and in all such cases where somewhat arbitrary lines must be drawn, there are parties with adverse interests, backed by powerful lobbies, waiting to wage battle over any legal territory, however small.

Efficiency

As long as the topic was automobiles, the costs of expanding liability did not fall heavily on any organized interest group. Consumers as a whole could even be said to find common cause in turning to insurance-backed no-fault schemes for handling automobile accident claims.[30] After the "fall of the citadel,"[31] however, the corporate sector became vitally interested in raising the questions of how much compensation is enough and how much regulation is too much. By itself the allocational logic of economic theory provides no simple answers, but it supplies a language for formulating these questions in a rigorous way. Even though it may be advanced most passionately by business lobbyists, the general interest in economic efficiency purports to balance the other two interests: an efficient allocation of productive resources is said to result only when compensation and regulation are brought into satisfactory relation to other elements of social welfare.

A recent fashion has developed for deriving substantive policy criteria from aggregate consumer preferences, allowing the *market* to determine "how much is enough" in the pursuit of compensation and regulation. This approach seems to have strong theoretical appeal as well as strategic value in political debate. It assumes that in the market process, consumer preferences are spontaneously coordinated to yield a collective or public interest, one that does not rely on the political process to choose among competing group interests.[32] The market mechanism becomes an alternative to politics for defining the common good: no adjustments are required for lack of political representation of certain factions, for procedural biases, for undue political power, or for the vagaries of enforcement. Most important, the differences that lead to stalemate among political factions can be effectively split down the middle through the algebraic formulations of economic theory.

There is still much room for debate even among the theoretical proponents of economic efficiency. One question is whether the existing market, without corrective regulation of economic power, guarantees of minimum income, or effective controls on fraud and deception, can offer itself as the actual embodiment of collective welfare. Past generations of welfare economists, although deeply committed to the analytical power of the efficiency concept, were confident that unregulated economic institutions could not deliver on that promise, and some economic tort theorists evidently agree. For them, the interest of economic efficiency is subordinate both logically and operationally; market signals become important only within an established framework of political judgments.[33] Others challenge this conclusion on essentially moral grounds, arguing that decisions made through political processes have, in most cases, less legitimacy than those made through existing markets, and holding further that interest group pressures should not preempt the spontaneous decisions of individual economic actors.[34]

Product Liability Legislation:
Competing Strategies in Action

The Efficiency Strategy

We have seen that the efficiency concept aspires to broad value neutrality, based on the postulate that the market will aggregate individual interests more impartially than either the common law or the political process. In the debate over product liability law, a great many
reform proposals are based more or less openly on appeals to this general interest, even though in most cases their clear effect would be to
reverse dramatically the pro-plaintiff drift in judicial and regulatory
policy over the past twenty years. Efficiency is oriented toward the
notion of limits, and its strategic appearance in the product liability
debate is usually on behalf of highly restrictive limits—down to the
logical extreme of eliminating both compensation and regulation
altogether.

The following proposals on product liability policy are frequently
defended by appeal to general interests of efficiency:

1. Placing restrictions on strict liability principles, requiring that
   an accident caused by a defective product should have been
   foreseeable and preventable with the exercise of due care (i.e.,
   the traditional negligence standard).
2. Preserving defenses to negligence liability, specifically those
   that place a duty of care on the consumer or provide some other
   source of consumer responsibility (e.g., contributory negligence, assumption of risk, modification or departure from
   ordinary-use defense).
3. In design defect cases, permitting the manufacturer to use the
   "state of the art" defense (a principle limiting the duty of manufacturers to exert unusual efforts to anticipate injurious uses of
   a product).
4. Limiting damages awarded at trial by restricting or eliminating
   punitive damages (a self-declared regulatory device) and by restricting or eliminating pain and suffering recovery (often an
   outlet for the punitive impulses of juries and regulatory impulses of judges).
5. Promoting certainty in the planning for liability awards by standardizing rules of liability and damages, setting time periods

within which claims can be brought, allowing manufacturers to use legislative or administrative quality standards as defenses.

6. Permitting manufacturers and consumers to bargain over liability, either through price adjustments or by substituting insurance or arbitration for tort-law remedies.[35]

How is it that the short-term interests of product manufacturers are here generalized to represent the good for society as a whole? The simplest argument in their favor is that legal burdens currently placed on defendant manufacturers result in aggregate overinvestment in accident compensation or prevention costs. More is being spent than market forces can justify, thus society is obtaining more of some goods (compensation and safety) than it collectively desires, and correspondingly less of other goods.

Compensation and Regulation Strategies

These two interests may be combined for purposes of clarifying competing policy models, but they are not entirely interchangeable. Compensation looks to the past and deals with personal injuries that have already occurred; regulation seeks to avoid future injuries. There are circumstances, however, where proponents of regulation have resisted judicial rules on compensation for fear that society was attempting to "purchase" future injuries in advance. Rather than accept injuries as inevitable, the advocates of regulation believe that society should invest in preventing accidents in the first place. That difference aside, however, in the context of product liability debate we generally see these two interests pursued simultaneously by consumer groups and other environmental public interest organizations.

Our second list of proposals illustrates these combined interests of compensation and regulation:

1. Requiring manufacturers to institute product safety programs, either through tax incentives, subsidies under insurance schemes, or under threat of penalty.
2. Continuing the work of the Consumer Product Safety Commission in setting regulatory standards for product safety, perhaps increasing the power of the CPSC to remove products from the

market, to levy penalties, or to seek equitable relief in the courts.

3. Supporting through legislation those aspects of tort doctrine that strengthen compensation and enhance the investment in product safety (e.g., strict liability, punitive damages).

4. Requiring manufacturers or others to contribute to a compensation fund for victims of product injuries, most of whom would be unable to collect sufficient compensation through litigation.

5. Overcoming barriers to compensation allegedly caused by the "transaction costs" of private bargaining, private insurance, or tort litigation, namely through special arbitration panels or legislative compensation schemes.[36]

As these proposals suggest, compensating past injuries is expected also to establish incentives for the future prevention of accidents. By encouraging the expansion of damages, notably through liberal allowances for intangible harms (including pain and suffering) and self-declared punitive awards, courts can presumably advance this general purpose, while also enriching individual claimants (along with their attorneys). For these broader incentives to have their intended effect, however, several conditions must be present. The actual relevance of any past injury to the prevention of future harm depends on the assumption that accidental events are foreseeable, controllable, and therefore preventable; all that stands in the way of their prevention is the need for a proper economic signal.[37]

Strategic Compromise: Federal Product Liability Legislation

The 1986 Senate proposal for product liability reform offers a revealing blend of strategies we have discussed, in a classic instance of political bargaining among lobbyists for manufacturers and consumers.[38] The essense of the proposal was to create *two* possible forums for handling product-injury claims. Injured persons could choose to enter an administrative compensation scheme that consolidated many features of strict liability, but curtailed damages to the extent of *real economic loss* (eliminating pain and suffering and punitive damages). Alternatively, injured consumers could take their chances in a full judicial forum, but one in which doctrines were modified to become less favorable to their interests. Most striking of all, the bill would have federalized certain doctrines and procedures, requiring all state courts to adopt uniform judicial standards in product liability suits.

Strategically, even this formally structured compromise seems weighted toward business interests. Producers' lobbying groups sometimes attempt to drive a wedge between regulation and compensation by seizing on proposals similar to items 4 and 5 in our second list just presented. From an efficiency point of view, where the only stated consideration is to minimize aggregate costs associated with accidents, the issue is whether safety measures imposed by regulation turn out to be more expensive than compensation. Heeding cost signals alone, it is preferable to compensate a small number of people for their injuries than to undertake more expensive preventive action. The same perspective on the part of a single manufacturer could lead that company to pay liability claims rather than follow a more pervasive program of government regulation.

Choosing compensation payments instead of regulation would be especially attractive to manufacturers if, as part of a package, they could reduce overall compensation costs (damages plus legal expenses). Defendant manufacturers as a group thus have good reasons to strike a bargain with plaintiffs in order to bypass the formal tort system, paying less than the courts might require while sparing the plaintiffs the delays and risks of litigation. Depending on how eager plaintiffs are to settle out of court, they could well agree to be compensated at more modest levels than the courts might grant. The certainty of at least some award could easily seem more attractive than facing the risks and delays of tort law.

The self-interest of manufacturers is thus simultaneously served by (1) restoring traditional tort doctrines (to make that route as formidable as possible for plaintiffs), (2) keeping the rewards of the tort system low by limiting damages, especially pain and suffering and punitive damages, and (3) encouraging alternative mechanisms for settling liability claims at levels of compensation lower than the courts provide. On balance, it is possible that arbitration and even state-administered compensation schemes could be cheaper for defendants than the present tort system. Such programs might also reduce public pressure for more rigorous enforcement of safety regulation or strengthening tort remedies. Compensation and efficiency can thus be combined to make a strategic end run around regulation and the tort system itself.

These fairly elaborate strategic considerations were clearly at work in the federal product liability proposal. Ingenious lawmakers thus found a basis for interest-group compromise within the uncontrolled dynamics of judicial processes. According to Senator Danforth, then chairman of the Senate Committee on Commerce, Science, and Transportation, the bill offered both plaintiffs' and defendants' lobbies something better than the current system.[39] Both would find greater uniformity of treatment across the country: consumers would have a quicker route to recovering economic losses; manufacturers would get surcease from expanding damages claims and, perhaps, liability insurance premiums. The whole system was designed to cost less money on balance, provided fewer claims were litigated and thus legal costs (including contingent fees for attorneys) were reduced.

At hearings held in early 1986, major lobbyists were invited to comment on the bill. In fact, most of these groups had evidently worked closely with the committee staff over a period of time to help draft the statutory language.[40] Publicly, each side declined to express complete satisfaction with the proposal, suggesting that still greater value would lie in making the administrative scheme more favorable for plaintiffs (the position of consumer lobbyists) or in building more barriers to recovery into the tort system (manufacturer lobbyists). Consumer lobbyists were further worried that manufacturers could maneuver claims too easily into formal litigation; manufacturer lobbyists worried that their opportunities for doing precisely that were too restricted. Throughout the drafting process, Senator Danforth's concern clearly had been to search for a political compromise between these polar interests:

> It seems to me that if we are going to develop something, it has to be a combination of a claims system and tort reform. We have tried each of the others separately, and there are not the votes there, so forget it. It is going to be a combination or there is not going to be anything.[41]

He shows particular impatience with witnesses and legal academics who withhold support for the general concept of the legislation because the balance of interests was not quite to their liking:

> First of all, I totally, I just absolutely do not accept the fact that the status quo is the only thing that is predictable and good . . . I think that it is always going to be possible for endless panels of law

professors to come here and say, "Oh, gee, well we just can't have this."[42]

Throughout this shadow boxing, both sides put forward their positions as striving for balance among the goals of compensation, regulation, and efficiency.[43] For example, a lobbyist representing consumers, the U.S. Public Interest Research Group, in opposing certain burdens placed on plaintiffs in the tort law stage (title III of the bill), advances quickly to the interests of general safety and market efficiency:

> We fear that title III with its rules shifted dramatically in favor of the manufacturer would undermine these important goals. Title III's restrictive negligent [sic] standard would make it much more difficult for plaintiffs to prevail in product liability suits. Facing fewer successful lawsuits, manufacturers may succumb to competitive pressures to cut corners and reduce safety expenditures.[44]

For their part, manufacturers stressed that their microeconomic contributions to social and economic health were threatened by tort damages and insurance premiums. They insisted they want to maintain, even improve, compensation, but at a socially more acceptable price.

In the end, this painstaking effort seemed to have a chance: it was a politically ingenious attempt to restructure tort law processes to provide separate forums, one biased toward each of the adversarial groups—something for everybody. The only difficulty was that one powerful interest group was left out of the bargain: the lawyers.[45] Representatives from the American Bar Association would commit themselves to nothing stronger than "further study" of the administrative portion of the scheme. On the Senate floor, during the closing moments of the Ninety-ninth Congress, Senator Danforth was outmaneuvered by Senator Hollings, champion of the negligence bar's interests. Although a procedural motion to advance the bill passed by a vote of 84–13, the majority leadership dropped the measure under pressure from Senator Hollings's threat to filibuster. Action in the One Hundredth Congress was affected by the shift in Senate control to the Democrats, which allowed Senator Hollings to replace Senator Danforth as chairman of the Commerce Committee.[46]

Conclusion: Politics and Public Responsibility

The above analysis is likely to disappoint nearly everyone involved in the debate over tort reform—litigating parties, pressure groups, and academic commentators. For those prepared to reduce social and political issues to conflicting personal interests, any talk about collective or general interests will invite great skepticism. On the other hand, advocates of efficiency and other general theories will feel that their positions have been unfairly relativized by association with diverse political strategies. These concerns reflect both sides of the troubling pluralism in current American debate: that it *remains* pluralistic, despite high aspirations for universality, and that this pluralism is nonetheless *troubling*.

The special history of tort law, with its slow evolution through mainly judicial stewardship, has helped solidify this adversarial confrontation of competing interests. It has helped consolidate pressure groups who will gain or lose at the margin, no matter which way reform tends. The general interests of compensation, regulation, and efficiency, far from reducing this complexity, recreate it at a different level. We should be sympathetic with any theoretical or practical efforts to contain political relativism, but we cannot ignore how the proliferation of incompatible general interest theories has reinforced that very multiplicity.

The problems of reconciling political interests on some basis other than relative power causes some analysts to reject any special status for political decision making as an expression of social values or aspirations. Interest-group politics can thus be assigned a place alongside common-law adjudication and market exchange as alternative systems for generating constrained public responses to important social issues.[47] Each process appears to furnish not a social policy but a social *mechanism*, out of which public decisions emerge as spontaneous products. The public interest is reflected in each process only in *procedural* terms: the results of judges deciding individual cases, of political bodies responding to pressure groups, or of the market coordinating individual exchange decisions. Each process becomes a surrogate for something greater—a public we seem to require but cannot conceptualize.

The social problems of personal injuries, especially in an age of environmental accidents, are too complex to be reduced to a single institutional process. If an adequate public response is to emerge at all, the political system will need to transcend its pluralistic bargaining procedure and respond on a different level altogether. Following Dahl's suggestion, we might identify this level with "regulative structures and procedures," matters on which a pluralist society may hope to reach consensus. The ability of a society to respond to personal injuries on this level is the literal meaning of *public responsibility* as that term will be used in Chapter 10.

Compensation and accountability are the two central themes of any social policy on personal injury, both of which at the very least need to be freed from their narrow judicial context. A stronger public awareness of the full extent of personal-injury problems will emerge only when the American debate shifts from simply patching up the judicial process to adopting more comprehensive alternative procedures. For such a shift to be politically effective, it must be manifest in concrete policies understood by the public, and not left on the level of theory or speculation.

Chapters 6 to 9 postulate a four-stage movement in American accident policy, based on existing or proposed reforms, that may indicate a growing public ability to engage the level of regulative structures and principles. These four basic types of reform strategy, which represent a gradual movement away from judicial frameworks, may at first add still more confusion to an already fragmented political scene. But their longer-term direction provides some hope that more comprehensive policies might yet emerge out of current debate. The four stages are:

1. Policies for judicial self-reform of tort law (Chapter 6).
2. Policies for legislative modification of tort law (Chapter 7).
3. Policies for treating "the public" as surrogates for either plaintiffs or defendants under tort rules (Chapter 8).
4. Policies suspending tort rules for particular classes of injuries, and substituting alternative procedures for compensation and accountability (Chapter 9).

To whatever extent American accident policy is actually moving in the direction postulated by this formula, the critical remaining step is to generalize the approach in stage four to cover more than selective classes of accidental injury. In Part IV, we will outline such a comprehensive accident policy that has liberated itself from judicial frameworks. Under this kind of policy, a new configuration of judicial, political, and economic decision-making mechanisms would necessarily take form, reflecting new institutional ground rules for expressing the social response to accidents.

Any political consensus on such a new approach depends not only on the clarification of policy goals but also on our ability to institutionalize those goals in ways that promote public acceptance. Dahl is very clear that the demands placed on citizens in pluralist democracy should not require them to be philosophers:

> A people guided in public life by their commitments to certain general principles and structures can cope daily with ambiguities and inconsistencies that a philosopher would make into a career. A political consensus is not a philosophical treatise but part of a political culture into which most people . . . are more or less adequately socialized. Consequently, to require a consensus on regulative principles and structures does not mean that citizens must be competent theorists or philosophers.[48]

This chapter has shown how a political culture that draws its leading themes from tort law is in a poor position to reach consensus on general principles for responding to personal injury. While we must remain cautious in predicting future political consensus on policies that are still evolving, the evidence in Chapters 6 to 9 suggests at least one tortuous route toward a new set of principles for accident policy in the United States. That route follows the gradual recognition of a dominant public role in what up to now has been treated as a private-law problem.

Chapter 4

The Economic Approach to Accidents

There is now no ground on which the economist, qua economist, may challenge the allocation decisions reached by the political process. He may, of course, always draw attention to the economic consequences of the course of action to be adopted and give his opinion that, on balance, they are favorable or unfavorable. What he cannot do, however, is to pronounce the politically determined allocation to be good or bad by reference to an independent economic criterion. Put otherwise, he may no longer judge the allocation to be "economically efficient" or "economically inefficient" by reference to a criterion that transcends current expressions of political opinion.[1]

Political Dilemmas and Market Solutions

In the 1960s, a growing number of legal academics began to question the progressive commentators' easy acceptance of redistributive social goals for the tort system. The implicit relativism of interest-group political theory encouraged their discomfort. So did the value indeterminacy increasingly found in lawsuits over automobile injuries, in which the roles of plaintiffs and defendants bore no clear relationship to social or economic status.

Maintaining an instrumentalist view of tort law, these critics[2] saw two possible alternatives: (1) a proliferation of conflicting policies favored by opposing groups, and (2) a reduction of policy disputes to technical terms (borrowed from recent trends in welfare economics) that preserved universal interests, but on a strictly theoretical plane. In choosing the latter approach, academic lawyers developed a powerful analytical tool that has since radically transformed the idiom of most academic tort-law criticism. Its cost, however, has been a perilous abstraction from the important policy questions surrounding personal injuries. Nor has this formidable academic enterprise moderated policy conflicts among multiple-interest groups. As we saw in Chapter 3, the newly minted goal of economic efficiency can itself be used strategically by political forces, mocking the universality intended by its theoretical partisans.

There is at least one sense in which economic critics have continued the tradition of progressive writers: by accepting legal instrumentalism, they recognized that the judicial system draws its final legitimacy from outside the doctrinal structure of common law. For both groups, furthermore, the political process was viewed as an unstable ally to the judicial process, given its central focus on expediency and value conflict. As legal academics, after all, both groups inherited a certain respect for the unique integrity and independence of the judicial function, despite the tensions of instrumentalism. They also inherited the anxiety about legitimacy from legal realism, which questioned how and whether the judicial process could avoid disintegration under pressure from competing social and political forces. The progressive writers were caught off balance by these issues, producing somewhat wistful speculation that the judiciary enjoyed special contact with the community values of their day,[3] or that judicial declarations of principles (if cautiously made) might lure other branches of government out of complacency on such divisive issues as race discrimination.[4]

The economic critics pioneered an entirely different brand of instrumentalism—rather than dwelling on the ineffable qualities of judicial craftsmanship, or the complexities of judicial interaction with other governmental branches, or the consequences of interest-group domination of the judicial system. Instead, they sought more rigorous support for the judicial project in the equally problematic power of the market system, using its complex logic as a foundation for common-law doctrines.[5] To varying degrees, the proponents of this approach have ignored the political system in forging a direct relationship between judicial doctrines and market structures. The policy implications of their work, however, require cautious interpretation, based on our overall assessment of market systems. As one woeful result of this approach, the debate over tort reform (already so complex that non-lawyers have difficulty separating legal myth from social reality) has acquired yet another barrier to comprehension—thick with economic formulae, welfare-economic jargon, and subtle ideologies of market supremacy.

Given the current dominance of economic perspectives in American academic legal discussion, we face the awesome prospect of summarizing the leading arguments as clearly as possible. Fortunately we may concentrate on the seminal expositions found in works by Guido Calabresi and Richard Posner, who in separate ways have largely defined the significant research programs now being energetically pursued in the law review literature.[6] It is regrettable that this work has received scarce criticism by mainstream scholarship in economics or political science. Much of it has been produced by lawyers or by economists teaching in law schools, while most of the critical reaction has come from ethical theorists opposed to the overt utilitarian deployment of welfare economics.[7] Leaving the ethical issues to Chapter 5, we shall concentrate in this chapter on more practical difficulties of connecting judicial systems and market systems. The special problems posed by environmental accidents will be used to challenge the claim that market systems can, in the end, spare society the need to develop its political institutions as the primary system for organizing policies on compensation and accountability.

Applying Welfare Economics to Accidents

The rapid advance of economic theories of tort law over the past decade testifies to important weaknesses in the progressive approach, which it has now largely replaced in academic circles.[8] Putting aside ritual support for the ethical and distributive goals of the preceding generation, Calabresi, Posner, and their progeny have further separated the instrumental analysis of tort law from ethics by interposing a purportedly neutral calculus of social interests. This economic idiom applies rigorous formal techniques to the question that progressive reformers answered on faith: how can the public interest be defined objectively, *apart from* the political or other special-interest perspectives of distinct social groups?

Another way of posing this central question of welfare economics is to ask, Under what conditions (more narrowly, under what changes in the status quo) are individuals made "better off," as seen from their own personal perspectives? The narrow focus of this question is the key to the apparent breakthrough made by welfare economics: if there should be policies that benefit at least one person while penalizing no one, such actions (but those actions alone) meet a distinctly nonpartisan, nonparticularistic definition of social welfare.[9] By contrast, policies requiring interest-group compromise—policies that are "zero sum" for some pairs of individuals—can never be proved desirable from a *universal* point of view.[10] Using its narrow criteria, welfare economics hopes to qualify a policy for universal assent on theoretical grounds alone. As we shall see, however, the element in welfare economics that eludes partisanship also isolates that analysis from the full range of issues and institutions that yield actual policies serving any partisan society.

In a classic essay, the economist Francis M. Bator described the development of modern welfare economics as "an attempt to sort out ethics from science, and allocative efficiency from particular modes of social organization."[11] In other words, welfare economics is the science of allocative efficiency. In even plainer terms, it calculates how to get the most out of what we have, where the definition of *most* and the supply of available resources are both taken as givens.

For example, the definition of *most* may be expressed on a scale measuring quantity of physical output. If there are ways of combining a fixed supply of resources to yield more of some products without diminishing the output of others, then the simple imperative to maximize total output dictates a clear course of action. The same principle can be applied to the process of voluntary exchange. Here, the subjective preferences of all people are maximized under the coordinating constraints of a market system. At the point where voluntary exchange is exhausted, according to this model, individuals have each attained the maximum anticipated satisfaction from exchange consistent with the protection of others from any decline in anticipated satisfaction.[12] The logic of both productive efficiency and exchange efficiency is thus the same: both are examples of allocative efficiency.

An efficient allocational result can occur only within a context of stable factors. In productive efficiency, for example, the supply of resources must be taken as given, and for exchange we must assume that individuals come supplied with systems of ordered preferences covering all possible exchange outcomes. Also excluded from the calculation are the distribution of wealth from which individuals begin to exchange and the framework of legal, social, and political rules governing exchange.[13] Most important, no ethical import follows automatically from this constrained maximization of "welfare" unless all background factors are also assigned ethical weight. As E. J. Mishan concluded, "In principle an optimum allocation of resources is neither actually nor potentially superior on welfare grounds to a nonoptimum allocation of resources."[14]

In his pioneering volume, Calabresi used a variation on exchange efficiency to describe analytically how legal rules can help reduce accident costs. They do so in two ways: by preventing some accidents from occurring, but also by allowing accidents to occur whenever their prevention would cost more than their anticipated harm.[15] An optimal allocation of resources calls for lowering accident costs to the level dictated by individual preferences, as expressed through the market. This suggests a legal framework that holds people responsible for preventing accidents only when the cost of prevention is lower than the probable cost of injury. The bottom line for guiding the judicial system is this: if net resources can be saved by preventing accidents, the standard of allocative efficiency requires prevention; otherwise it is more efficient to allow the accident to occur.

Several difficulties with this approach are immediately apparent, arising from a series of key assumptions:

1. That the costs associated with an accident's occurrence or prevention are determinable in advance and can be objectively expressed—if not by the market, then by some shadow price system based on the market.
2. That the relevant cost of an accident is the *anticipated* cost as expressed by the market or a quasi-market, rather than the cost viewed after an accident's occurrence.
3. That these costs can all be considered separately from how the rate and incidence of accidents affect the distribution of income.

But the most heroic assumption of all is one Calabresi scrupulously avoids, even though it is sometimes treated casually in law-and-economics literature. This is the assumption that a community's welfare (either economic welfare or welfare in some larger sense) is a direct function of reducing costs as defined by the model.[16] Welfare economic theory is clear that the leap from allocative efficiency to economic welfare transcends the analytics of maximization.[17] As Bator notes, such a move is "intrinsically ascientific."[18] In order to draw conclusions for legal policy from economic analysis, as most lawyers are understandably eager to do, some attention must be paid to the logical gap between strict efficiency and welfare. Since Calabresi's model carefully highlights this problem, we need to take a closer look at his theory.

Three Calabresian Abstractions:
The Theory of General Deterrence

Calabresi's singular accomplishment in *The Costs of Accidents* was to reduce the accident-policy debate to precisely those questions that modern welfare economics is prepared to answer. The careful qualifications in his text come from this emphasis on analytical reduction. Calabresi was fully aware that actual policy recommendations derived from analytical reasoning require complex empirical and normative assumptions. To the extent his own writings speak to policy issues, they do so primarily in a hypothetical mode.[19]

Calabresi's book is built on three major abstractions or reductions, all designed to transform the policy debate into economic terms. First, he separates the concept of justice from cost reduction as goals of accident policy;[20] second, within the category of cost reduction, he then distinguishes "primary" and "secondary" costs, or what may loosely be considered allocative efficiency and distributional issues.[21] The first two steps, taken together, effectively separate the economist's notion of efficiency from both ethical and economic senses of welfare. Third, within the category of primary-cost reduction, he distinguishes between the market system and other social institutions for defining and achieving primary-cost reduction, or between general deterrence and specific deterrence, respectively.[22] We can summarize these steps in the accompanying figure.

Separating justice from cost reduction is the fundamental first step in employing the tools of economic analysis. Apart from this self-evident purpose, however, Calabresi gives no further reasons for accept-

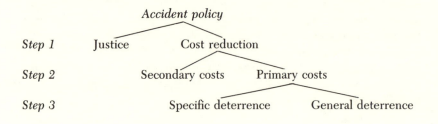

	Accident policy		
Step 1	Justice	Cost reduction	
Step 2		Secondary costs	Primary costs
Step 3		Specific deterrence	General deterrence

ing the distinction. He does note that justice is "by far the harder of the two goals to analyze"—so hard, in fact, that he never comes back for more than a spectator's view.[23] Much criticism has been leveled against economic concepts for abandoning justice,[24] but to part company on that basis is simply to disown the fundamental project of welfare economics. A valid controversy does arise when market structures are linked directly to utilitarian ethics, as in Posner's work, leaving no clear legitimate role for politics. We shall sketch out Posner's general approach in later sections of this chapter, but will leave the ethical controversy to Chapter 5.

There is at least one important difference between Calabresi's strategy and the treatment of moral issues in earlier periods of instrumental legal criticism. Holmes, for example, used utilitarian principles to separate the putative moral aspects of the fault system from social interests, treating the latter as the true idiom of normative discussion. He put moral concepts aside, not because they were too difficult or required special attention, but because to him they were false or distorted approaches to justice. The progressive tradition followed Holmes in identifying justice with the proper arrangement of social interests, conceived as having both distributive and aggregative dimensions. This position takes issue with Holmes, of course, by holding that industry and the market system cannot bring about a just configuration of utility, without some judicial initiative and political guidance.

Calabresi's first abstraction thus breaks with glib progressive assumptions about social goals, reflecting the growing sophistication of welfare economics in developing its own "value-free" technique.[25] Early welfare economists had identified their methods more closely with utilitarian normative goals, and for a period there developed a close connection between the formal treatment of utility maximization across society and the recommendation of social policies.[26] The case for progressive taxation, for example, was built on this use of welfare economics. But with the collapse of the Benthamite approach to utility—after welfare economists concluded that utilities of separate individuals should not be compared as cardinal sums—any broad normative ambitions were shattered, at least as far as economic analysis was concerned. Justice and economics went their separate ways.[27]

Apart from reflecting this critical turn in welfare economics, does Calabresi's separation of justice and cost reduction serve any useful purpose? By allowing that justice is not so much a separate goal as a higher-order view on cost reduction ("a veto or constraint on what can be done to achieve cost reduction"[28]), Calabresi suggests that the distinction has only provisional importance. He obviously concedes that policy discussions take place in a wider forum, one from which questions of justice are not banished, where the concepts of *cost* and *reduction* will somehow be reunited with independent normative concerns.[29] If this is indeed his position, it would follow that the price of staying with reductive terms is to isolate economic analysis from policy debate. Implementing Calabresi's analysis thus presumes a more complex institutional forum for public-policy discussion, one in which market actions are ultimately subordinated to political guidance. But Calabresi never suggests how this reunion can productively occur, given his largely residual and negative characterization of political action.

While the distinction between justice and cost reduction is by now a standard move to initiate formal economic reasoning, Calabresi's next abstraction is more problematic. His distinction between primary and secondary costs corresponds in some respects to the standard economic distinction between allocative efficiency and distribution of wealth.[30] But the full meaning of *secondary* costs is somewhat murky; it appears to designate unspecified *social* costs of maldistribution, brought on by the catastrophic effects of accidents on particular individuals.[31] The implications are perhaps best seen in contrast to Calabresi's companion concept of *primary*-cost reduction, or formal allocative efficiency. As stated earlier, Calabresi's concept of efficiency is based on standard assumptions about the restricted nature of costs: they must be removed from the subjective, *ex post*, and distributional contexts in which they are actually experienced. It is likely that the primary-secondary distinction in Calabresi's model is simply meant to isolate a sense of cost that can successfully enter the formal calculus of efficiency. Secondary costs are everything else, including the problems of who feels the cost, what to do when actual cost turns out to be more than anticipated, and how intensely a cost is felt by particular individuals.

The only part of this concept of secondary costs explored by Calabresi is its distributional aspect. Harking back to an older style of welfare economics, Calabresi invokes the image of the "deep pocket" for the policy of shifting accident losses from relatively impoverished victims to wealthier defendants. This shift is not necessarily motivated by compassion for accident victims, but reflects an earlier willingness of welfare economists to make interpersonal comparisons of utility. "[The deep pocket notion] holds that secondary losses can be reduced most by placing them on the categories of people least likely to suffer substantial social or economic dislocations as a result of bearing them, usually thought to be wealthy."[32]

The deep-pocket strategy is only one of many possible bridges leading from the abstract concept of primary costs back to a broader economic (and ultimately ethical) context. Other routes might include an institutional process for deriving "the" cost of an accident from the multitude of individual and collective perspectives in a given society, or some method for addressing the gap between anticipated (*ex ante*) and actual (*ex post*) accident costs. Secondary costs thus turn out to be not a separate technical category but a higher-order perspective for appraising the reductive concept of primary costs. Just as Calabresi characterized justice as not so much a goal as "a veto or constraint on what can be done to achieve cost reduction,"[33] we might now say that the secondary *aspect* of costs is likewise a set of constraints, the repository of economic, political, and ultimately ethical concerns excluded by fiat from the formal concept of primary costs. They are, accordingly, the irreducible context in which analytical terms must eventually be rejoined with the issues and institutions of actual policy debate.

But primary-cost reduction is clearly the true analytical goal of Calabresi's book, and indeed it is this topic that best represents his theoretical contribution. Primary costs are the economic costs of accidents—freed from subjectivity and expressable in some real or constructive price system. They are *anticipated* costs of either preventing an accident or of allowing it to occur, not actual costs. Reduced to this level, the problem of accidents becomes a matter for simple subtraction: whenever prevention is expected to cost more than the anticipated damage from certain accidents, then (primary) costs are minimized by allowing precisely these accidents to occur, while preventing all others.[34]

Calabresi's third abstraction is a kind of footnote to the notion of primary cost, but has received more attention than any other single aspect of his work.[35] This is a simple distinction between two possible institutional modes for defining primary costs—once again, a distinction better seen as a reduction. *General deterrence* is the formal market approach to defining primary costs, *specific deterrence* is a residual category of nonmarket processes, although it includes principally government regulatory policy.[36]

To appreciate the scope of this last abstraction, we must hold in mind the entire reductive scheme. Both general and specific deterrence are alternative ways to define *primary* costs—not costs as such, and not costs that bear any direct ethical significance. It may turn out that regulatory policies or other nonmarket mechanisms are superior to the market for identifying other kinds of costs (such as *ex post* costs, or intensely felt personal costs), and also for serving some more robust sense of justice. Given Calabresi's reductive model, such nonmarket processes would be essential for establishing actual policies. If, however, our focus is restricted to building a theoretical system, then the neoclassical equilibrium concept is the obvious analytical model for minimizing primary costs—the invisible hand of general deterrence.

To summarize, Calabresi's three abstractions can be seen as successive reductions of ordinary policy problems encountered in the field of personal injury. With each step Calabresi trims away the values, distributional economic concepts, and social institutions that exceed the analytical scope of allocative efficiency. The first abstraction leaves behind the question of justice—the entire normative framework within which economic choices are ultimately debated by active human beings. What remains is a technical concept of costs that already points toward a nonperspectival species of value. It also leans inexorably toward the idealized market process and consumer sovereignty for generating social choices, although other formal models (explored by recent public-choice theory) can also generate political outcomes that are value free in precisely the same sense.[37]

Calabresi's second abstraction overlaps with the first, focusing on the analytical concept of cost as something removed from the actual economic experience of single individuals. In practical terms, this turns the whole thrust of analysis away from traditional progressive desires to use accident law to compensate individual victims. To the extent compensation mitigates "social dislocations" (a political dimension of cost that may also have normative implications), it is set aside to leave room for the more abstract economic treatment of primary costs.

Lastly, Calabresi's third abstraction abandons what is by now seen as a subjective, emotive, political (in the worst sense), ultimately irrational approach to primary-cost reduction—namely political regulation.[38] This leaves him with the price system as the only universal, logically maneuverable, analytically clean process for handling primary costs. Throughout this sequence of reductions, an implicit methodological premise assigns the virtues of objectivity, universality, and rationality to the calculus of allocative efficiency. The simple corollary is that all other aspects of accident policy admit only irrational or strategic response. This is small encouragement when it comes time to try to recapture some of the territory vacated by Calabresi in his reductions. That territory must, nonetheless, be reentered if we are to address questions of policy as they occur in the world of concrete action—whether or not we are able to bring the tools of economic analysis back with us.

Calabresi and other writers influenced by economic models end up with a peculiar theory about social action. One finds in their work liberal use of metaphors of social or collective agency, usually focused on the activity of social decision making. In many cases, that actually means the spontaneous operation of market processes, responding to assumed supplies of resources, personal preference schedules, and technological conditions. Social decision making, or choice, is thus a metaphor for the aggregate set of individual bargains struck under these assumed conditions.[39] Individuals are viewed as carrying out their predetermined preference schemes, ignorant of the eventual outcomes of their behavior, and using solely those personal resources available under the prevailing distribution of wealth. According to this theory, society is continually responding—and responding *correctly*—to changes in underlying factual conditions. We must remind ourselves, however, that this is a matter of definition rather than an empirically testable assertion.[40] We shall come back to this point in the conclusion to this chapter, contrasting the formal economic theory of social action to our own concern about the social response to problems of personal injuries.

Applying the Economic Formula

What does such a formidable analytical structure have to do with options facing the tort system, not to mention the larger issues of social response to accidental injuries? The most significant role has been to support the judicial system in either modifying or retaining its current doctrinal structure. For legal academics (who are trained, after all, to see accidents as naturally falling within the judicial ambit), economic theory supplies a nonpolitical rationale for the doctrinal system. This is as close as any legal instrumentalist will ever come to resting the legitimacy of doctrines on a purely neutral foundation. Indeed, any alternative foundation in interest-group politics is highly distressing to the legal mind schooled in formalism and a commitment to objectivity, as we know from the vigorous debate now taking place in the legal academy between economic theorists and the neo-Marxist Critical Legal Studies movement.[41]

Economic theory has been called upon in the past two decades to clarify the specific choice confronting courts between using traditional negligence and strict liability standards in accident litigation. We are already conceding the instrumentalist view to describe the courts as having a choice at all, since the ideology of the common law was rather that judges apply *existing* rules to new cases. But if we believe that doctrinal rules are being changed—and changed often—such movements have to rely on something outside the judicial structure. Welfare economics wants to provide that criterion while respecting the legal system's commitment to impartial decision making. The fact that specific interest groups have much to gain or lose from sudden shifts in liability rules does not ruffle this approach, since the narrow technical goal of allocative efficiency is compatible with wide shifts in wealth or income distribution.[42]

In Calabresi's formal categories, many readers found justification for continuing the judicial trend toward strict liability, based on the hypothesis that defendants were often best situated to make the critical judgment for allocative efficiency: to decide whether the anticipated costs of accident prevention exceed the anticipated costs of future accidents.[43] For corporate defendants in product-liability suits, for example, one could argue that their knowledge of expected risks and of risk management techniques far outdistanced the diverse and imperfect knowledge of consumers. Some critics were disconcerted who assumed that either common-law logic or ethical considerations (these new rules were, after all, no-fault doctrines) should determine judicial decisions. Borrowing something from Holmes, Calabresi countered that ethical considerations had long ceased to control legal doctrine, despite the apparent connotations of *fault*.[44] Legal doctrine was only a transparent facade for an essentially social process, the true business of which was to maximize social utility.

Other writers influenced by economic theories of the Chicago school used similar methods to reach slightly different conclusions. Richard Posner's first major contribution to this discussion emphasized the opposite side of the liability coin from Calabresi: he showed how traditional negligence rules could be justified on welfare economic grounds, notwithstanding the progressive critics' desire to mobilize the tort system to redistribute income from wealthy and/or culpable defendants to worthy victims.[45] While he agreed with Calabresi's rejection of an overt ethical framework for guiding the court's choice of liability rules, he pointedly suggested that courts could appropriately resist popular or political sympathy for accident victims.

Almost twenty years later, as the courts have moved ever farther from negligence rules, Posner eccentrically maintains that judges not only should, but *do* base their choice of liability rules on economic reasoning—whatever that choice turns out to be. Even if negligence was a rational economic standard up to 1970, Posner is not ready to deny that strict liability might take its place—if that is what the courts decide.[46] This astonishingly passive acceptance of judicial decisions as uniquely determined by economic logic (based, Posner insists, on historical and empirical research) has grown increasingly anomolous, and the source of some frustration to his conservative colleagues.

What allows welfare economics to convert traditional legal questions into economic calculations? We can isolate several interlocking assumptions:

1. Human judgments can be construed as calculations (explicit or implicit).
2. Human relationships can be construed as bargains (explicit or implicit).
3. The sole object of accident policy is future deterrence of inefficient accidents.
4. The future will resemble the past.
5. Those categories of accident causation singled out by the courts in past cases are a sufficient indication of future activities to be considered in making cost-reducing judgments.
6. The damages actually awarded by courts in past cases are a sufficient indication of future accident losses, against which future defendants can compare the *ex ante* costs of future prevention.

A number of distinct calculations are to be governed by these principles:

1. The potential injurer's choice of whether to allow or prevent possible injury.

2. The potential victim's choice of whether to receive or evade possible injury.
3. The judge's (or policy maker's) choice of a liability standard to apply after an injury occurs.

Assuming an injurer makes judgments about future risky activity, his or her calculation will compare the cost of prevention to the cost of compensation, should the accident actually occur. Knowledge of probabilities about future events must also be imputed. The anticipated cost of compensation varies widely, depending on the likelihood that courts will apply either strict liability or negligence rules to the injurer's decision. The injurer must know *which* activities will be reviewed, since there are potentially infinite steps that might be taken to prevent future accidents; thus past court decisions serve to delimit future behavior requiring economic scrutiny. Finally, as every economic man or woman knows, the purpose of any decision is to select the cheaper alternative, once relevant costs are taken into account.

The judge's (or policy maker's) role is slightly different. Under Posner's theory any liability rule (even a rule of "no liability") is adequate that would impose the costs of prevention on whichever party can avoid the accident more cheaply. In complex product liability suits this could mean strict liability for the manufacturer, but for everyday cases where consumers need merely abide by ordinary prudence, "no liability" is often the cheaper rule. Where both parties need to make calculations (and this would seem to apply to most traditional accident cases, in Posner's view), negligence rules are the best guarantee that proper economic calculations will be made.

To reach the heart of this elaborate theory, we must remember the single purpose for accident-compensation mechanisms in the first place: to deter future uneconomic behavior. It is not to prevent accidents as such, but only those accidents for which costs are more expensive than their cure. Borrowing yet another economic concept, *optimal* deterrence becomes the central goal of accident policy.[47] Compensation of injured parties is entirely incidental to this purpose; all that is needed is some assurance that courts will apply economic sanctions to future injuries under similar conditions. Other social interests are not necessarily abandoned, but they must be taken up by social institutions other than the market system interacting with tort law, and thus they are consigned to the dark forces of politics.

The Judicial Link Between Market
Deterrence and Optimal Deterrence

The analytical systems developed by Calabresi and Posner have
proved strangely impervious to criticism, given their self-proclaimed
removal from ordinary conceptions of justice, from the competing
aims of the political process, and even from the traditional judicial role
of compensating accident victims. Most critics hope to salvage one or
more of these alternative goals, but it is an easy mistake to criticize
welfare economics for failing to deliver something it has never promised. This section will take the economic theory of accidents on its own
terms, focusing on the model of market (or general) deterrence and its
shadowy assumptions about the role of judicial processes. We will begin to draw out institutional implications of economic theory as a guide
to accident policy, beginning with its inability to prescribe ways for
transforming the goal of allocational efficiency into a social policy of
optimal deterrence.

Economic writers tend to skirt the question of why judicial institutions should play any role whatsoever in a system dominated by the
market. Why is another institutional structure even useful in achieving
the goal of allocative efficiency, whether that other structure is the
judiciary or the legislature?[48] The theory of general deterrence, as we
saw, was defined specifically to exclude any legislative role, notably
public regulation carried out through fines or other penalties. Why
does the same exclusion not extend to the judiciary, which dramatically alters the costs of activity throughout our society by its peculiar
mission of compensating worthy victims out of someone else's pocket?

Calabresi's analysis invokes the theory of market failure, a long-
standing interest of welfare economists, built on the logical possibility
that market institutions may fail in their task of achieving allocative
efficiency.[49] This concern is an important adjunct to the theory of allocative efficiency, providing purely economic criteria for challenging
the economic outcomes of unregulated market systems. But what are
these criteria, who is competent to wield them, and through which
institutions (besides existing markets) are we to launch corrective
action?

Consider the common example of social costs linked to environmental pollution—typically costs that no one has bargained for. These
costs would escape the optimal deterrence calculus unless some intervening institution (the political system or the courts) imposes them on

an appropriate party—preferably on the person best situated to make the key economic choice between prevention or compensation. A much-cited article by the economist Ronald H. Coase, which appeared about the same time as Calabresi's initial publication, supplied a popular rationale for supplementing market institutions to preserve economic goals. His theory of "transaction costs" suggests that economic bargaining is itself an expensive process, and thus some unknown number of real events with economic consequences will remain outside the market process, unless other institutions step in.[50]

Coase's argument implies that the measurement of such *external* or *social* costs is not fully in the hands of the market, any more than their correction can be assumed to rest with market processes alone. At the very least, environmental accidents would appear to raise the spectre of social costs on an unprecedented scale. Based on our analysis in earlier chapters, we can press the point here whether *judicial* institutions are competent either to identify these costs or to transfer them to economically appropriate parties. Just how good would judicial processes have to be to ensure an economically efficient response to environmental accidents? Basically they would have to supply enough information to let the market anticipate and internalize the costs of future accident prevention. In other words, the law would have to *commercialize* certain relationships that otherwise avoid market definition, thus permitting future decisions by potential injurers and victims to be treated as economic calculations.

But can the judicial system be expected to send forward proper signals to people in positions to prevent future accidents, especially those accidents we can predict only on the fragmentary evidence of epidemiology? Which activities and economic choices will prove central in the future control of accidents, and how high must incentives be set in order to commercialize future decisions in the manner presupposed by general deterrence? These questions are completely unanswerable within the analytical structure of welfare economics. They are intrinsically noneconomic questions because they address the prior ground rules under which markets actually operate. And, as it happens, the courts are a highly questionable source of information for converting market deterrence into optimal deterrence.[51]

Let us briefly revisit the judicial process, ignoring compensation issues and concentrating solely on how well the courts set future incentives for accident deterrence. Several characteristics of judicial systems would appear to limit their ability to promote optimal deterrence: (1) their focus on past behavior, (2) their reduction of events to action by specific parties to the lawsuit, (3) their emphasis on case-by-case examination of facts, (4) their failure to recognize probabilistic causation, (5) their unpredictable pattern of doctrinal change, and (6) their traditional exclusion of certain kinds of defendants, most notably the federal government.

Decisions by courts, whatever liability rules they may adopt for various categories of accidents, will at best influence future deterrence in a selective fashion. Their future impact seems limited to events that: (1) appear sufficiently like past adjudicated cases, (2) can be fully attributed to individual interaction, (3) can be broken down into discrete instances, as opposed to systematic or aggregate behavior, (4) are defined by nonprobabilistic causation, (5) can be predicted to fall under future trends in doctrine, and (6) involve potential injurers who fall under court jurisdiction. If optimal deterrence is defined by reference to sanctions actually imposed by the courts, it will thus exclude most of the events identified with environmental injuries.[52]

Even when events come within the courts' purview, they may send confusing economic signals. Future economic choices must rely on the actual outcomes of adversarial bargaining, which are influenced by the costs of litigation, the self-interest of attorneys, and other pressures on parties to settle out of court. The impact of liability insurance on the economic magnitude of court-induced incentives is yet another subject of contention, with theorists disagreeing on the insurance industry's ability to set premium structures that accurately track the course of judicial damages awards.[53]

Finally, we can doubt the courts' ability to cure their own procedural ailments, for reasons to be discussed in Chapter 6. There we consider a series of cases where courts have responded poorly to mass environmental injuries, despite the variety of techniques at their disposal: new doctrinal creativity (vaccine injuries), fundamental restructuring of the judicial process to eliminate case-by-case deliberation (mass accidents generally), class action suits and other procedural devices (asbestos cases), and managerial judging (the Agent Orange cases). Those sections present an extended argument that courts lack the capacity to achieve even the modest performance presupposed by optimal deterrence goals, especially in cases involving environmental injuries.

Calabresi echoes many of these doubts, roundly criticizing the fault system (reflecting the state of tort debate in the 1960s) as a device for correcting market failures to achieve allocative efficiency.[54] His criticisms of the judicial process point to the same problems we have noted with contemporary litigation over environmental accidents: case-by-case adjudication, the individualistic model of discrete events and personal accountability, the inability to recognize probabilistic causation, and the high process costs of litigation. But Calabresi also provides strong criticisms of market intervention by *political* institutions (considering now only the purpose of allocative efficiency, or primary-cost avoidance), as we saw earlier in his skeptical treatment of specific deterrence. He is left in the unhappy position of the theorist who has discovered how to remedy the market's failure to achieve allocative efficiency, but with no apparent institutional means for putting those principles into effect.

Was it a mere accident that Calabresi chose to conceptualize the principles of "perfect" market intervention as a set of idealized tort rules? These rules would presumably replace the fault system with a new group of doctrines, including a heavier emphasis on strict liability than the courts had adopted by 1970. Implicit in this model of perfect rules is the further postulate of perfect judicial administration, or the assurance that optimal rules would always be applied to achieve optimal results. That means that compensation costs would always be imposed on individual defendants (or denied to individual plaintiffs) in a way that established *correct* incentives for all future actors who are in a position to make maximizing decisions. Considering the need to reach perfection in both rules and implementation, the judicial process seems ill suited to correct market failures that cause actual deterrence to diverge from economically optimal deterrence. Even if we could wave the invisible hand and achieve the welfare economist's vision of perfect liability rules, we would have to trust judicial stewardship of common law to apply those rules faithfully to particular situations. This takes us finally to the theory of Richard Posner, who seems prepared to discover both perfect tort rules and perfect judicial administration actually at work in the contemporary judicial process.

As explained earlier, economic theories of tort law grew out of disenchantment with the idea that either legal logic or political oversight could justify the judicial method of handling accident cases. Legal logic is not overtly instrumental, and politics is unable to transcend the conflicting interests of diverse groups. In a curious twist, however, Posner has turned the tables and insisted that judicial institutions can and do provide legitimacy to the market system. The inspiration for this stunning surmise is the neoconservative critique of political institutions as correctives for market failure. Among theorists influenced by the Chicago school of economics, Posner's distinction is to match the presumption of political failure with a theory of judicial perfectibility (if not, indeed, perfection). His writings have evoked strong reactions, even from those sympathetic to the methods of welfare economics, on exactly this point.[55]

Posner defends what he calls a *positive* economic theory of tort law, which for many critics falls into a trap of circular logic. The circle looks like this. On the one hand, judicial doctrines require the support of market economic principles to rationalize their use. (Both Calabresi and Posner have shown analytically how that support can be provided, especially with respect to the judicial selection of liability rules.) On the other hand, it appears that fallible market systems presuppose the ideal functioning of judicial institutions before they can lend that support, even in theoretical terms. Posner defends both positions, arguing that judicial procedures can and do provide reciprocal support to the market by commercializing those human relationships for which the transaction costs of bargaining are too high.[56] But do courts perform this reciprocal service well or badly? Posner believes they do so with unparalleled success *because* they make use of economic reasoning.

Central to Posner's position is his belief that the positive economic theory of law (the theory that judges do in fact rely on economic reasoning in reaching common-law decisions, and moreover have done so for at least a century) can be verified in its own right. Notwithstanding Posner's spirited empirical defense of its scientific status, most critics have dismissed his theory as inherently untestable.[57] Based on his recent comprehensive restatement of the positive theory applied to tort law, one could argue that it is more a theory about rationality than about the legal process or legal history. Moreover, it appears that Posner commands nearly a dozen techniques for explaining away evidence contrary to his theory.

Conclusion: Levels of Deterrence
in Environmental Accidents

The abstractions of economic theory are now powerful enough to generate whole volumes of mathematical formulae modeling the intricate structures of tort law. But as the structure becomes more elegant it seems to have less to say about accident policy designed by standard legislative processes. The law-and-economics field appears to be settling into a permanent specialty for academic pursuit, as it deserves to be. It will continue to supply sophisticated prescriptions for rules of liability as means to the end of allocative efficiency, choices that are far too intricate and technical to be digested by lawmakers within the political system.[58]

It is even less likely that the judiciary will be in a position to hearken to economists and fine-tune their doctrines, unless we believe, along with Posner, that common-law judges are already in pre-established harmony with the logic of economic efficiency. In any case, time may be running out for judges to dominate the selection of liability rules; legislation is already poised to preempt many of their choices. Opinions of economic theorists will, of course, be sought by legislative committees eager to further the public interest through tort reform, but political patience is entirely too short to wade through the infinite qualifications of abstract theory. Law-and-economics will probably play some strategic role in future policy development, but in ways likely to make its proponents cringe.

In this chapter, however, we certainly have not traveled the distance with economic theory in order to bid it farewell. We must try to summarize what is useful in the formal clarification of allocational goals, and make some effort to reconnect those goals with other economic objectives and ultimately with normative concerns. Efficient cost reduction is a weighty element in a more general social policy of accountability, one of substantial importance should society free itself from its deep reliance on traditional judicial rules to deal with compensation and accountability.

The economic theory of accidents has drawn important attention to the problems of who in our society is in a position to reduce future risks, and on what occasions. To the extent we are able to identify those situations, there is every reason to examine methods of establishing incentives to influence individual behavior at critical junctures—including economic incentives. It is unfortunate, however, that the interest in prevention has been so closely identified with the judicial process as the main source of information about how and when future risks can be affected. The fact that lawyers have spearheaded the law-and-economics movement is probably the reason tort law plays such a dominant role in the economic theory of social risk reduction. No doubt the apolitical mystique and individualism of common law have recommended it to partisans of current welfare-economic methods.

A broader theory of optimal deterrence should not assume that either the current tort system, or even some ideally modified judicial process, will generate spontaneously a definitive list of opportunities for risk reduction.[59] Based on growing epidemiological evidence about the unintended collective effects of individual behavior, we have the means to identify new decision points where the choice between preventing or allowing future accidents must be made, often under conditions of great uncertainty. Some of these occasions call for economic incentives, but others may require criminal penalties, community organization and education, or broader structural policies pursued across the society.

A useful analogy may be found in the epidemiological approach to the social problem of coronary heart disease (CHD), the leading cause of death in the United States since 1950.[60] Most of the preventive steps taken by American health professions have centered on individual treatment, often by encouraging persons at risk of CHD to give up smoking, to get more exercise, to combat hypertension, and to control levels of serum cholesterol in the blood. Beneficial medical results have been achieved for particular patients through these efforts, but the cost of providing medical attention on a one-to-one level is high. Such treatment can help an individual at risk of CHD minimize the risk, but it does nothing to prevent others in society from falling into high-risk categories. As Syme and Guralnik conclude,

> While these [medical] programs seem reasonable and useful, it may be that no matter how energetic we are in developing preventive programs, these efforts cannot hope to have an impact on the distribution of disease in the community as long as they are based on this one-to-one medical model.

Two further types of intervention are mentioned by these authors: a public health model emphasizing community education, and an ecological model, involving structural changes in community life that control directly the risk factors for disease. The advantage of public health initiatives is that they "affect very large numbers of people in the community at a fraction of the cost of . . . one-to-one programs." But the authors hold out greater promise for an ecological model:

> In this approach, no direct effort is made to change individual behavior or health status. This approach has been used to lower highway fatalities. Thus, it has been argued that it is more cost-effec-

tive in reducing highway fatalities to (a) build safer cars, (b) build safer highways, and (c) lower speed limits than it is to educate drivers, one at a time, in safer driving techniques. Similarly, it may be more useful to change the cost and availability of healthful foods than it is to educate people about better nutrition. The same argument could be made for having less accessible and more expensive cigarettes.

Several general points about disease prevention can be concluded from this example. First, there is no reason to view each of these intervention levels as excluding the others. Distinct populations will be reached by pursuing all levels at once. Second, individuals stand at various removes from the dangers of CHD: some are already rated as being high risk, others may be moving into that category on the basis of inadequate knowledge, and probably the greatest number are statistically certain to enter that group unless their environment undergoes structural changes. Third, structural approaches make no direct appeals to individual rationality or behavioral responses; they are likely, however, to have a greater impact on the eventual distribution of CHD in the United States than either of the other two methods.

Deterrence in personal injury cases can be approached in much the same way as prevention in disease. While the judicial system, with its one-to-one association of accident victims and defendants, reacts to at least a small portion of personal injuries present in society, it is short-sighted to base a policy of deterrence on only one model of events. In the United States, automobile accidents are the leading cause of death for all persons between the ages of one and thirty-four—which is almost half the average lifespan.[61] Such accidents cost an estimated $35 billion annually. We can identify at least three possible levels of deterrence that might lessen this toll, following the disease example. First, deterrence focused on external behavior modification of individuals can operate through direct manipulation of the penalties imposed on drivers actually involved in accidents. Such penalties could in theory be administered by the private judicial process (torts), by the public judicial process (criminal law), by administrative bureaucracies (motor vehicles departments of state government), or by special administrative tribunals such as those set up under workers' compensation legislation.

Other opportunities for reducing risk exist on at least two additional levels.[62] Public education is focused on the individual, but is directed toward cognitive rather than purely behavioral change. According to Baker, "Educational approaches, while an essential component of injury control, are likely to protect only the small minority of people who are both well informed and highly motivated to take the necessary precautions." Moreover, injury research has established that "groups of people who are at greatest risk of serious injury—such as male teenagers, the elderly, young children, people in low income areas, and those who consume excessive amounts of alcohol—tend to be less likely than other people to take steps to protect themselves against injury."[63] Under these circumstances, the strategy of changing the environment in which people live holds the greatest promise for reducing the risks associated with automobile accidents.

Many of the steps recommended by public-safety experts are familiar targets of federal regulatory action: seat belts, air bags, and rear window lights for cars, along with such other measures as fire-safe cigarettes and limiting the sale of handguns. As it stands now, the tort system fails to acknowledge these opportunities for collective intervention because (among other reasons) it recognizes sovereign immunity, or the doctrine that the state cannot ordinarily be a defendant in a civil suit for damages. Individuals and public-interest groups sometimes try to enlist the judiciary in furthering regulatory objectives, using administrative-procedures statutes against the state and strict liability doctrines against product manufacturers. But most opportunities for environmental modification on behalf of safety exist beyond the jurisdiction of courts. The pressure to increase federal regulatory responsibility is thus likely to continue. As public attention is drawn to epidemiological research on personal injuries, the impetus for risk reduction may continue to shift from private action and the tort system to public regulation and social accountability. Even in controlling conventional accidents, such a change would seem useful. As Baker points out:

> Three major injury producing hazards come under the federal jurisdiction of the Department of Treasury: firearms, which are second only to motor vehicles in the number of injury deaths they cause; cigarettes, the ignition source in almost half of all fatal house fires; and alcohol, which is involved in roughly half of all fatal crashes, homicides, and adult drownings, and in substantial proportions of most other types of injury events.[64]

Opposition to these collective actions are often based on ethical and economic considerations. For the moment we can wrap ourselves in the immunity from ethical criticism claimed by economic theory, deferring that subject to the next chapter. That leaves economic criticism, which generally takes the position that market forces do not support public safety measures, a normative argument that cannot be objectively derived from the value-free models of economic theory. The most serious limitation of this position, beyond its hidden ethical elements, is the assumption that individual decisions are the only reliable indicators of economic value. As Mishan has argued, this "individualist maxim" is one of the basic elements in contemporary welfare economic theory. That maxim supposes that "the 'objective' data of the economist are the choices or subjective valuations of the individual members of society and nothing more."

> The acceptance . . . by the economist of allocative propositions as prescriptive ones entails a belief that in the last resort there is an ethical consensus in favor of [this maxim]. And it should be manifest that this consensus cannot be derived from individual welfare functions, no matter how elaborated. On the contrary, the acceptance of individual welfare functions as relevant data in any prescriptive statement is conditional upon this ethical consensus.[65]

We will finally part company with the welfare economist, then, if we take seriously the approach to accident deterrence based on the environmental model of causation investigated by modern epidemiology. The point of difference lies not with the technical theory of economics, but with the suppressed "individualist maxim" as described by Mishan. More will have to be said about ethical individualism and its relation to accident problems in the following chapter. But we should note here precisely what this maxim *costs* welfare economists who hope to develop socially useful theories of optimal cost reduction. The usual welfare economic optimum holds solely within a domain defined by postulated individual preferences. Optimal deterrence, under these constraints, will cover only those situations where risk reduction is achieved through individual behavior modification using economic incentives. This individualist focus, almost certainly, is the hidden source of the peculiar and complex alliance between ideal market structures and an idealized tort law. While such a combination may provide one important strategy for reducing accident risks, it systematically ignores the arguably more cost-effective methods of community education and environmental modification.

Chapter 5

Normative Frameworks for Accident Policy

> *By picturing our wishes as fulfilled, dreams are after all leading us into the future. But this future, which the dreamer pictures as the present, has been moulded by his indestructible wish into a perfect likeness of the past.*[1]

Moral Dimensions of Accident Policy

The logic of economic efficiency, when pressed into serving public policy analysis, takes its marching orders from ethics. As Mishan has suggested, there seems to be a suppressed ethical principle—the individualist maxim—that sets the rhythm to which modern economic imperialism advances. Both the marchers and the spectators seem unaware of this underlying beat, amid the swell of familiar anthems and the spectacle of bodies in motion. The parade must come to a stop before we can reflect on who establishes the rhythm, and on what authority.

Identifying the framework assumptions of market institutions may be compared to similar assessments of judicial procedures and interest-group politics. All three processes appear to have an internal, self-regulating side in addition to an external aspect, from which critical judgments first become possible. Each system presents itself as self-sufficient; but when we tear ourselves away from the oddly satisfying illusions of circular logic, we eventually find a larger normative context in which markets, courts, and legislatures all do their work. In the end one cannot isolate economic, legal, or political analysis from normative issues.

In the judicial system—our primary social process for responding to personal injuries—these framework issues have been pursued for over a century by a succession of sociological jurisprudes, progressive critics, legal realists, and others adopting instrumentalism as their external perspective. The pretense of law as an autonomous system of rules, as Levi says, "has long been under attack,"[2] and nowhere has it been repudiated more completely than in the field of accidents. But efforts to supplement legal formalism have not been very fruitful, starting with the progressives' ambiguous political theories, which wavered between consensus and conflict models. Nor, as we saw above, have recent economic theories managed to bring the unruly elements of tort law into the neutral framework of neoclassical equilibrium models.

Professional unease with ethical analysis may be the central reason that critics have looked wishfully toward enlightened judges, political bargaining, and market systems to define public values. According to the philosophical assumptions that have dominated most twentieth-century scholarship, ethics is simply not a topic for scientific study.[3] This view reached its height in popular versions of logical positivism, which characterized ethical judgments as essentially products of the emotions.[4] At least until the past twenty years, positivist attitudes toward ethics have accompanied an aggressive scientific posture in the natural and social sciences. A somewhat more benign approach entered with meta-ethical analysis of ordinary language, which restricted itself to "therapeutic" treatment of intellectual aches and pains allegedly brought on by illicit invasion of value terms into factual discussion.[5]

While rejecting any direct appeal to ethics, some writers nonetheless acknowledged the contextual nature of their fields by toning down claims to disciplinary autonomy or completeness. Herbert Simon's work on "bounded rationality" in economic models can be seen as shifting to other fields the burden of clarifying the contextual boundaries of formal economics.[6] A similar strategy was used by Lindblom and Cohen in their effort to relieve policy research from the duty of guiding social problem solving.[7] Even some professional philosophers, including specialists in ethics, have modestly abandoned the search for "foundations," interpreting the interest in frameworks as but the latest symptom in their discipline's longstanding terminal illness.[8]

These self-protective postures make sense for academic specialists, who must somehow get on with their work. But it is not quite that simple in the area of social policy, where framework issues are not just axioms or postulates of theoretical models, but rather the practical goals and purposes of living institutions. If we hope to find appropriate public goals to direct the judicial process, the legislature, or market systems, it does not help to learn that each of these processes has been captured in a self-regulating model by the cunning of virtuoso scholars. It does not help, for example, to know that legal philosophers have devised a model of ideal judging that dissolves the legitimacy problems of the court system,[9] or that social theorists have idealized the autonomous functioning of American political institutions,[10] or that market advocates have used neoclassical models to define away the problems of market failure.[11]

But the search for social-policy goals remains an obscure task, one that can easily dissolve into battles among adversarial interest groups. We have seen in earlier chapters the divisive political context in which personal injury policies are now considered, and later chapters will explore the details of fierce controversies over consumer and occupational injuries, nuclear and hazardous waste accidents, plus many other environmental injuries. These issues have now breached the autonomy of the judicial system and have moved noisily toward center stage within the political arena. However mesmerizing its appeal to academics, economic analysis was not able to bring this mob back under the orderly control of value-free theory. The jargon of efficiency has instead become the source of new slogans in the current debate, just as the rhetoric of legal rights has been adopted by those hoping to preserve a congenial system of judicial activism.

We must, at this juncture, examine still one more attempt to rescue traditional accident policy from its fractious state—this time by moral philosophy. It is perhaps inevitable that this field too has become highly ambitious and oracular, given the vacuum created by the retreating claims of science to value-free autonomy. Moral philosophy as a special field of putative expertise responds also to the paradoxical hope in our society that questions of goals and values can be compartmentalized from other pursuits, and thereby made rigorous and definitive. We find this wish in cases where society's customary values have been most widely challenged, as in legal disputes over the custody of children, and over medical decisions involving the elderly, the disabled, and other dependent people. As the courts have failed to impose harmony, the public has looked hopefully toward new specialists in ethics to rescue us from value conflicts.[12] While most practitioners in the growing field of practical ethics are appropriately modest in their prescriptions, they are increasingly caught between unrealistic public expectations and the soaring theoretical ambitions of moral philosophers.

In the idiom of this new academic movement, we shall "take seriously"[13] the possible contributions of moral philosophy to a social policy for personal injury. Accidents have long been associated in popular opinion with the moralistic language of fault, even though the legal system has largely followed Holmes's lead in emptying those words of their customary connotation. (Holmes substituted the more subtle ethical viewpoint of utilitarianism, which up until the past decade dominated the moral perceptions of legal analysts.) But the wider public still evaluates the results of judicial decisions by popular standards of fairness, and such opinions should not be ignored in fashioning a new policy on accidents.

Is it "fair" to hold accountable the producer of building materials used to construct a highway toll booth, when a drunken driver (ignoring all warning signs) smashes into the barrier, killing himself in the process? On the other hand, is it "fair" *not* to hold someone accountable for slow-moving occupational diseases like asbestosis, which are affecting an increasing number of industrial workers? And what if those workers also smoked? Although discussions of basic fairness are generally filtered through a thick prism of self-interest and adversarial behavior, we must find some appropriate way to build ethical considerations into a comprehensive approach to personal injury. As this chapter examines a series of false hopes raised by current uses of moral philosophy, we will nonetheless work toward an ethical concept of *public responsibility*, one that can eventually find its way into a larger policy on accidents.

Tort Law and Common Sense Morality

As personal injuries from environmental sources impress themselves on the general public, judgments by ordinary people about common fairness are inevitable. But there is little evidence that people attribute responsibility or grant a right to compensation in uniform ways. Recent psychological studies suggest, on the contrary, that perceptions of causation and responsibility are influenced by numerous personal and social factors,[14] and that consequently they may vary considerably from person to person. It is even likely that the legal system itself, which fosters highly artificial distinctions among types of accidents, is a determining influence on common perceptions of fairness.

A survey by researchers at Oxford University asked more than 1,000 accident victims to describe the causal source of their injury, as well as how they would assign responsibility (if any) to make compensation. In general, respondents tended to locate the source of injury in either discrete events or in more abstract contextual factors, depending (respectively) on whether the accident occurred on the road or in the workplace. Road injuries, which in Britain have long been compensated on the basis of personal fault, tended to elicit interpretations such as "He pulled out in front of me without looking." By contrast, work injuries, which are handled on a no-fault basis, evoked such explanations as "They sent two men to do a three-man job." Finally, where accidents occurred in the home and there was no obvious defendant, or where the costs to personal or work relationships in bringing suit might be very great, "accidents tend to be seen as 'just accidents.'"[15]

In an earlier literature review on attribution of cause and responsibility, Lloyd-Bostock concluded that "adequate (or 'correct') explanation and responsibility attribution are [largely] a function of why the question arises and where the sequence is leading."[16]

> We can expect different causes for an accident to be assigned by the driver (his driving), the county surveyor (the road), and the vehicle manufacturer (the car design). When each is threatened with sanctions, however, one might expect a shift in orientation to a defensive one and a consequent shift in perceived cause. The victim interested in compensation might attribute responsibility to the most likely source.[17]

The environmental accident presents special challenges to ordinary perceptions. In his study of the nuclear accident at Three Mile Island, sociologist Charles Perrow identified multiple levels of attribution, including human failure, equipment failure, and faulty plant design. The builders of the reactor, Babcock and Wilcox, blamed the plant operators for the accident. The operators blamed the equipment (a faulty valve) and sued Babcock and Wilcox. A group of design experts hired by the Nuclear Regulatory Commission blamed the design of the plant system. The President's commission investigating the accident blamed all of the above, but primarily the operators. Perrow observes that these differences in attribution inevitably reflect the multiple perspectives inherent in complex events. As mentioned in Chapter 2, he suggests a synoptic concept of the "system accident" (also called, somewhat ironically, "normal accident"), which combats our reductive tendencies to explain events in terms of our own immediate involvement: "The cause of the accident is to be found in the complexity of the system. That is, each of the failures—design, equipment, operators, procedures, or environment—was trivial by itself. Such failures are expected to occur since nothing is perfect, and we normally take little notice of them."[18]

Other research on disaster inquiries in Britain has shown that the residual impact of organizational environments is typically ignored in the aftermath of complex accidents. Often led by lawyers accustomed to assigning causes to individual behavior, such investigations select variously among the dozens of discrete personal decisions reconstructed after each incident, thus personalizing accidents to satisfy public appeals for remedial action. However, as sociologist Dingwall notes: "Disasters in the twentieth century are rarely the result of genuinely unforeseeable events. They are more usually predictable outcomes of the way complex organisations *have* to operate, if decision-makers are not to be overloaded with information or paralysed by uncertainty."[19]

Not surprisingly (in fact, the sociologists would predict it) these theories of attribution worked out by psychologists and sociologists are at odds with approaches taken by some philosophers. In the past decade it has become common for philosophers to lift complex situations from legal settings and to ponder, using techniques of verbal clarification and moral intuition, the fairness of possible legal outcomes. This is an attempt to find order and coherence in moral judgments, whatever diversity might be empirically documented in the views of ordinary people. There is some irony in how this pursuit now freely abstracts from the common views of real individuals, reaching some higher ("deontological") level of insight, when the movement from which it arose wanted simply to use ordinary language as a means of bringing philosophical abstractions down to earth. A brief example of recent moral philosophy will illustrate the contrast for our purposes.

In a widely read essay,[20] Judith Jarvis Thomson has questioned the

California Supreme Court's opinion in Sindell v. Abbott Laboratories.[21] This was the decision dividing among several defendant drug companies the costs of compensating successful DES plaintiffs, based on each company's economic share of the DES market. Plaintiffs thus did not have to demonstrate that a specific company's product caused their individual injuries. Thomson makes no pretense of evaluating the decision on the basis of legal precedent or utilitarian sentiment. Her conclusions, after some thirty pages of hypothetical examples and careful analytical distinctions, turn on her cultivated intuitions that (1) "we (ideally) wish liability to be imposed only on those who actually caused the injury," and (2) "we also are reluctant to attribute causality unless we can see the evidence of it as causally connected with the injury."[22]

This style of argument is but one more curious wrinkle in the academic commentary on tort law. "We" are obviously not the people surveyed in the Oxford report, nor the subjects of experimental study in Kahneman, Slovik, and Tversky's work. As political theorist Michael Sandel has argued, recent moral philosophy has defined a perspective utterly different from that of the empirical observer immersed in everyday life, a perspective purified of social and political distractions.[23] While this approach certainly answers popular demand for a technology to settle moral issues outside the political arena, Sandel and others have questioned its purported neutrality.[24] The conclusion in Thomson's essay certainly suggests a privileged position for world views populated by discrete individuals, atomistic events, and concrete evidence—at least when it comes to dealing with injuries and compensation. The resemblance of that cosmos to common law orthodoxy is striking, to say the least. But do the results of such arguments merely *reflect* the status quo in law (in this case, a superseded stage of common law), or do they provide independent grounds for steering the law toward the considered intuitions of ethical experts—assuming these experts manage to iron out their differences?[25]

Before drawing conclusions about the precise normative relationship between legal rules and the concepts of moral philosophers, we should note the earlier attempt by H. L. A. Hart and Anthony Honoré to correlate common-law rules with the morality of "common sense."[26] This study hails from an earlier period of analytic philosophy, one in which ordinary language was used to deflate false abstractions allegedly created by philosophers, who are in the habit of taking lan-

guage "on holiday" from its common routine.[27] Hart and Honoré's
massive study is sometimes understood as arguing in favor of specific
common-law rules *because* they reflect the same distinctions as ordinary language.[28] Such an interpretation is possible but not the central
point of their argument, which was rather to defend the general diversity of common-law rules (including some rules that went beyond the
highly individualized world of traditional negligence) from the *a priori*
objections of philosophical and legal critics.

This more general aim was consistent with the original antireduc-
tionist program of Oxford analytic philosophy.[29] Some other philosophers—influenced perhaps by Hume, Mill, or twentieth-century logical positivism—had wanted to reduce legal causality to a small
number of basic principles. The study of ordinary language was able to
show, however, that the diverse meanings found in everyday law are
matched by linguistic distinctions which "we" all recognize. Ordinary
language, with its infinitely shaded meanings, was thus used to justify
a dispersion of legal principles into dozens of distinct categories: such
proliferating uses were at least plausible in law because they are recognized in daily life. Moreover (the argument continued) the courts were
actually trying, though sometimes by circuitous means, to extend their
concepts to the degree of richness found in everyday speech. In retrospect we might want to question this general argument, but it is
clearly different from the efforts of contemporary moral philosophy to
curb the law's expansion.

The common-sense view of morality contained in the ordinary language studied by Hart and Honoré occupies a curious position halfway
between the views investigated by modern psychology and sociology,
on the one hand, and the detached perspective of the latest moral
philosophy. Hart was accustomed to viewing his work as "descriptive
sociology," but critics have decried the lack of empirical research or
sociologically based theory:

> One basic problem with both Hart's analysis of legal concepts and
> his moral arguments is his insensitivity to the need for empirical
> information and his consequent failure to utilize empirical science.
> Even when he does see this need he usually makes no effort to
> obtain the relevant data. As is the case with many Oxford analysts
> Hart seems to think that one can have knowledge of the workings
> of ordinary legal language by sitting in one's armchair. . . . For

example, in his analysis of legal rights in his Inaugural Lecture Hart makes what seem to be empirical claims about the use of legal language without any empirical evidence to back them up.[30]

In 1985 Hart and Honoré issued their second edition of *Causation in the Law*, some twenty-six years after the original printing. Although their lengthy preface deals with a variety of criticisms, regrettably they "are not concerned with the methodological basis of their claims about common sense causal notions; nor do they attempt to justify their particular common sense causal claims as either empirical hypotheses about ordinary usage or policies about causal attribution."[31]

Hart would not have needed to leave his North Oxford armchair to consult with Dr. Lloyd-Bostock, whose research raises serious questions about Hart and Honoré's work. In responding to a recent moral philosopher's objection to using psychological evidence to challenge legal rules, she argues against the "equally dangerous and oversimple view that [empirical evidence] has, and in principle can have, no relevance whatsoever."[32] While Hart's inattention to empirical evidence may have been due to mere inadvertence and his socialization into Oxford-style philosophy, recent moral philosophers have consciously widened the gulf between ethical analysis and social science.

In summary, we cannot (at least by casual observation) discover a natural harmony between ordinary conceptions of morality and the rules of tort law. Why then should we indulge analytic philosophy's tedious dissection of language, if our interest is in finding a more critical stance toward modern accident law? In the paragraph concluding their preface to the second edition of *Causation in the Law*, Hart and Honoré somewhat modestly venture the hope that a view of morality such as they find in tort law will reinforce modern values emphasizing individual dignity.

The idea that individuals are primarily responsible for the harm which their actions are sufficient to produce . . . is important, not only to law and morality, but to . . . the individual's sense of himself as a separate person whose character is manifested in such actions. . . . This sense of respect for ourselves and others as distinct persons would be much weakened, if not dissolved, if we could not think of ourselves as separate authors of the changes we make in the world. . . . [T]he allocation and apportionment of responsibility for the changes which human action brings about would in that case be inherently a matter of dispute; there would be nothing that we could unequivocally claim to be *our doing*.[33]

This statement offers a surprising solution to the normative tension between common-sense morality and tort law; it seems that traditional tort law lends support to a desirable moral point of view, not the other way around. Tort law does so, moreover, by sanctifying a form of rugged individualism that would foreclose major changes in accident policy in response to environmental injuries.

Individualist Norms in Positive Economics

Moral philosophy's focus on the abstract individual—the presumptive source of its stake in traditional negligence law—shares an intriguing number of assumptions with current welfare-economic theory. Both reduce complex events to concrete interpersonal transactions, and both assume that human intentions and desires find common unity in the autonomous will of individual persons. In analyzing this affinity here, we seek to isolate the individualist component of economics and ethics, treating it (however widely accepted) as only one option within both fields. The result may suggest broader uses of economics and ethics applicable to the special problems of environmental injuries.

Given the voluble polemics between economists and moral philosophers, this deeper affinity may seem puzzling. Most economists distinguish between positive and normative theory, taking their own discipline as explicitly removing itself from direct traffic with value questions. Ethics is what lies beyond that great divide between science and nonscience—with economics representing the analytical here and now. In Chapter 4 we saw how Calabresi scrupulously narrowed the theme of accident policy to "primary cost reduction," a species of allocational efficiency separate from other economic questions (such as income distribution and *ex post* calculations), and separate too from the broader concept of justice. His institutional corollary was the principle of general deterrence, or the pursuit of efficiency through the market rather than politics. Like ethics, politics was understood as a residual category or privitive: all institutional forces that do not operate on the resource-allocation model.

But it is also true that neoclassical economic theory, from its earliest days, enjoyed a fraternal relationship with utilitarianism, the ethical doctrine that society's good ultimately lies in maximizing utility, pleasure, or some substitute concept.[34] Indeed the first generation of welfare economists thought that economics could provide rigorous backing for policies designed to maximize collective social utility, including the progressive income tax and public regulation of negative externalities in industry. The same notion of social utility inspired progressive critics of the tort system, who freely invoked the public interest as their motive for guiding doctrinal reform. Throughout this period, they made an important distinction between the scientifically based ethics of instrumentalism and what they saw as traditional or noninstrumentalist ethics, otherwise derided as "formalism," or morality abstracted from its living social context.[35]

By the 1930s, however, economists began to back away from their alliance with social utilitarianism. Conceptually this occurred under growing skepticism that the economist (or anyone else) could compare the utilities of two or more people in common terms; a "new" welfare economics was soon born that eschewed such interpersonal comparisons. Individuals became utilitarian monads, and the domain of values recognized by economics was scaled down to reflect each individual's inscrutable and unchallengeable autonomy.[36] The resulting shift in normative perspective is difficult to exaggerate. John Stuart Mill anticipated this change in his influential essay *On Liberty* (one of the earliest revisions of social utilitarianism), when he declared that a person's "own mode of laying out his existence is the best, not because it is the best in itself, but because it is his own mode."[37] In other words, values are manifested as individual *choices*, beyond which the social critic is unable to penetrate. Accordingly, everything left for economists to say about value for the society as a whole fell under the strictures of the Pareto principle and Arrow's "impossibility theorem," both rapidly elaborated in the literature.[38]

This new welfare economics was decisively shaped by neo-Kantian epistemology, and more specifically by the rise of logical positivism in the 1930s, with its notorious noncognitive (or "emotivist") interpretation of value statements.[39] What made this school of welfare economics *new* was the position that judgments about group utility are inscrutable, unverifiable, and thus nonscientific; and such pejorative terms condemned the social utilitarian approach as incurably "ethical."[40]

Economics still managed to conserve a special alliance with preferred normative principles, but it confined itself to the more limited notions of consumer sovereignty and Pareto efficiency.[41]

Looking back on these intellectual developments, there now appear to be two major tenets shared by positive economics and moral philosophy: (1) a rigid dichotomy between means and ends, facts and values, instrumental and intrinsic good, and empirical and transempirical uses of human reason (all built on neo-Kantian foundations), and (2) a projection of the individual into the center of this strange dichotomous universe, inhabiting both worlds at the same time—indeed the function of this abstract self is to hold them together.[42] *Positive* economics and *deontological* ethics (to use the honorifics each has chosen) merely look at this universe from opposite sides of the divide. They are, in every way, two sides of the same coin.

This slender point of contact has allowed a few economists, using techniques and distinctions found in moral philosophy, to propose alternative ways of construing the individual utilities that form the basic elements of economic reasoning. In the process they have illuminated several key assumptions—we can call them normative biases—that economists frequently introduce when applying their abstract models to ordinary events. These assumptions derive from the two principles of consumer sovereignty and Pareto efficiency, concepts that, because of their close relationship to monadic individualism, can be easily shielded by the new welfare economics from the usual prohibitions against normative analysis. These concepts move imperceptibly but with impunity between the purportedly scientific statements of formal theory and economists' recommendations for public policy.

To take one example, the concept of *utility* starts as a simple variable in economic theory, lending itself readily to algebraic manipulation. But there are a lot of questions we can ask about this term, borrowing from current moral philosophy; depending on what definition we choose, the consequences for public policy can be radically affected. We know that utility is assumed to be maximized, but what else can we say about it? Is it a state of well-being, an assertion of choice, or both? If well-being, does it depend solely on personal consumption, or on other achievements as well? And whose well-being is desired— only that of the assumed monadic agent, or possibly that of others in society? Finally, given the basic content of each agent's goals, should that content be reinterpreted in certain social contexts, in response to strategic problems of coordinating individual interests?[43]

Accompanying these definitional problems is the question of measuring or certifying the content of maximized utility. Is the market system, even in theory, the best indicator of individual preferences? May we distinguish between preferences that are determined *in response to* prevailing market forces, rather than being entirely independent of the market? (The same question can be asked about social and cultural influences on preference formation.) To what extent are initial preferences influenced by the preexisting distribution of income? If an individual always knows best about his or her preferences, precisely *when* in relation to exchange does he or she know it? Are there any reasons why retrospective assessment of preferences by third parties is less reliable than that of first parties?[44]

We cannot go into the many answers economists and others have recently offered to these speculations. But we can point to the impact different answers might have on policy prescriptions for efficiently ordered economic systems. The indefatigable American law-and-economics literature, including that on tort law and accident problems generally, significantly fails to take these variations into account. Much of that literature (most notably Posner's writings) relies instead on assumptions about individual utility commonly associated with the Chicago school.[45] Posner, for example, while declaring that "economic theory is a system of deductive logic,"[46] offers the following definition of key normative terms that serve as major premises for his economic portrait of common law: "'Efficiency' means exploiting economic resources in such a way that . . . human satisfaction *as measured by aggregate consumer willingness to pay* for goods and services . . . is maximized."[47]

Some critics have reacted by staking out moral positions in strict opposition to Posner. In his widely cited article, George Fletcher assailed the economists from across the broad divide between ethics and science—between "reciprocity" and "reasonableness" as the basis of tort law, or (in plainer terms) between deontology and instrumentalism.[48] But a self-declared positive theorist like Posner seems well insulated against such attacks, since he is prepared to let normative theorists do whatever it is they like to do. Fletcher's criticism misses the central problem at the heart of positive economics itself: the essentially normative character of basic terms that serve as axioms or premises for formal theory. So long as these terms are reserved for purely *a priori* use, their normative aspects are suppressed and thus inconsequential for theory. But the moment theorems are generated for policy discussions, these normative qualities deeply influence the resulting recommendations.

In the literature applying economic theory to everyday events like personal injury, most writers have avoided airing their normative borrowings from utilitarian monadology. Wary of more speculative possibilities, they tend to identify these unmoved movers of their formal universe with ordinary people—or what is often admitted to be one *aspect* of an ordinary person's life. That piece of awkwardness behind them, the law-and-economics writers proceed *as if* our lives were like a marketplace, attended by people engaged in mutual exchange based on predetermined preferences. The fact that this model lacks all realism is not supposed to matter, however, if results derived from it can ultimately be validated against common experience. This is the epistemological basis for positive economics, as announced at mid-century by Milton Friedman and followed dutifully to this day by Posner and most other exponents of the economic approach to tort law.[49]

Is this "scientific" approach ultimately successful? Part of the answer depends on how we limit the topic of accidents. The "economic man" of this positive model, like the "common man" of ordinary language philosophy, has a special devotion to the tort system as a social process for handling accidents. The common law is attractive primarily because it limits the scope of the "accident problem" to the quite narrow function of patching up incidental cracks in an otherwise solid market system. Judicially administered liability rules can be easily integrated with formal economic analysis if they are used to correct one kind of market failure (high transaction costs), while they appear to place almost no political demands on social institutions.

What empirical evidence supports the view that this is all there is to the problems of personal injury? To the extent that human relations can be construed on a market analogy—the normative step closely associated with the Chicago school—what we ordinarily call accidents are variously explained away on mainly *a priori* grounds: (1) as differences between *ex ante* and *ex post* evaluations of a transaction, (2) as cases of imperfect information (for which the remedy lies in ironing out wrinkles in the market for information), (3) as events demonstrating the various "appetites for risk" held by individuals, and (4) as "stochastic" departures from the general equilibrium conditions that prevail across the society as a whole.[50] In brief, barring high transaction costs (for which the solution is an optimally designed tort system), accidents do not intrude on the world of economic men, even though there are doubtless many disappointed ambitions and cruel turns of fate to occupy life's brief interludes of noncalculation.

The two major themes of accident policy used throughout this book—compensation and accountability—are replaced under this economic-normative approach by the insurance market and by the deterrence function of tort law, respectively. While it may still happen that damages are charged to losing defendants in civil cases, the amounts awarded are not designed to measure lost utility (as we might expect of compensation); their sole purpose is to provide incentives for future accident deterrence. If some people in this society happen to be risk averse (and thus sensitive to the potential gap between *ex ante* and *ex post* utility), their solution as sovereign consumers is to buy first-party insurance (more poignantly, they should already have bought it).[51]

The mechanism of deterrence is thus the central policy link between the individualism of the common law and market economics. In both realms human activity is divided into discrete parts, each with its own price. Those prices are assumed to be the determining forces in future behavior, and people (both potential defendants and plaintiffs) are assumed to be fully cognizant of all cost-effective accident prevention measures. To this end, a properly designed tort system uses its sharp definitions of events (all within the capacity of human control in the future) to set prices for future market exchanges that might otherwise fail because of high transaction costs.

In Chapter 4 we discussed the limitations of the optimal deterrence model in dealing with environmental injuries. This section has tried to point out certain normative assumptions behind that model, assumptions that dovetail with the common law's traditional individualism. This discovery raises the possibility that economic logic, when combined with different assumptions about individuals and their preferences, could point social policy in other directions.[52] In particular, if preferences are distinguished from their market manifestations and are also seen as environmentally shaped, the whole problem of deterrence shifts from behavior modification to environmental control. A policy of primary-cost reduction based on these new assumptions would look entirely different from anything suggested so far in the law-and-economics literature. It would surely come much closer to satisfying the demands of personal injury policy in an age of environmental accidents.

Judicial Frameworks and Interpersonal Morality

The preceding sections of this chapter have closed off two possible shortcuts to a normative assessment of tort law. As we saw, some defenders of that system seek moral grounding by either appealing to common sense or by relying on the normative standards embedded in free-market economics. Moreover, most such arguments are confined to the topic of doctrinal options within common law, especially the choice between traditional negligence and strict liability standards. But even within these limited options for a social policy on accidents, it seems doubtful that moral reasoning can easily supply the foundations that have eluded legal, political, and economic approaches.

For more ambitious normative theories we must look to contemporary moral philosophy in its noninstrumental or deontological form. Like much recent economic theory, moral philosophy has been narrowly deployed on behalf of the most deeply individualist aspects of common law, and it has been even more insular than economics in ignoring institutional alternatives to the judicial process.[53] If instrumental approaches to law (including the economic variety) were once part of a revolt against formalism, deontological moral philosophy marks the counterrevolution.[54] Although its immediate targets in the field of accident law have been economic theories—the products of unashamed functionalism—its criticisms apply more widely to all advocates of doctrinal change who take seriously the consequences of judicial actions. We will try to show, however, that moral philosophy by no means compels us to accept the legal status quo, or to plot the return to some imagined preinstrumental state of common-law bliss.

As with economic theory, current fashions in moral philosophy strongly favor individualism, often in virulent forms. Sometimes the individualist bias is expressly tied to social-policy objectives, as in Richard Epstein's libertarian theory of strict (but also highly restricted) liability.[55] In other cases it simply reflects the conventional liberal tradition of social philosophy, one predisposed to defining social obligations as voluntary relations between atomistic individuals, with a lingering distrust of social or state involvement in private relations.[56] But moral philosophy is capable of supporting a wide span of social philosophies, including those putting greater stress on community obligations and values. One of the attractions of John Rawls's theory of justice (perhaps the best-known product of contemporary moral philosophy) is its ability to accommodate a range of social visions both left and right of center.[57]

A central theme throughout this book has been the growing significance of environmental injuries. Such events, we have suggested, may eventually undermine the view that accidents in contemporary society are strictly interpersonal events requiring private-law solutions. Perhaps as awareness of environmental accidents spreads, we will begin to see a richer selection of normative arguments, both deontological and instrumental, that consider moral obligations beyond the dyadic framework of common law. The concluding section of this chapter will speculate on possible forms such arguments could take.

Although it is dangerous to generalize about the common man's view of morality, it is safe enough to observe that popular opinion raises serious questions about the fairness of recent judicial trends in tort law, particularly the drift toward various types of no-fault liability. In most cases, however, moral questions are mixed with procedural issues endemic to the judicial system. Courts have stirred great controversy over the proper treatment of defendants by continually stretching negligence rules governing the reasonable-prudence and proximate-cause standards. Because such changes generally come as a surprise to the litigants, the problem of fairness is inseparable from reservations about judicial activism; and popular reactions are invariably prefaced by the procedural question, why is it the *courts'* business to impose these new burdens on defendants? Because our society assigns most issues of compensation and liability to the judicial process, it is unusual to hear fairness issues discussed altogether separately from that procedural context.

Yet the basic structure of the judicial process may present fairness issues too restrictively. Seen from a social perspective, as Atiyah has pointed out, the fault principle contains the moral anomaly that accident victims receive compensation only when the law can identify a culpable defendant; otherwise they are left to bear the loss themselves, whether or not an accident was their fault.

The whole essence of the fault system involves different treatment for the person who causes loss and for the victim of that loss. To treat fault as a necessary condition of legal liability—"no liability without fault"—means that a person who causes loss without fault should not be required to pay for it. But it also and necessarily means that the person to whom the loss is caused will have to bear

the burden himself. We have therefore a different rule for plaintiff
and defendant; the plaintiff, but not the defendant, must bear the
burden of loss or injury caused without his fault.[58]

In other words, the moral framework of common law embraces only
that subset of accident cases where the victim's injury can be attributed to a specific, culpable defendant. What strikes us as "just"
within this limited context may, however, appear entirely different in a
larger universe where we look also to the relation "between the victim
and society, or . . . between the person who caused the loss [but without 'fault'] and society."[59]

Although the progressive critics of tort law were troubled by this
narrow moral scope of common law, they nonetheless expected judicial institutions to identify and organize the wider public dimensions
of personal injuries. As reformers they were less audacious than their
economist critics, who seem prepared to reduce the courts' role to that
of junior partner in support of market processes. For their part, however, the progressives assumed that the tort system had already been
fundamentally altered by the growth of private insurance. The availability of liability insurance not only eroded any remaining punitive
goals of the fault system, in their view, but it also softened the burdens
being loaded onto defendants, especially corporations. Private insurance enabled defendants to distribute their losses over a defined risk
pool, and thus most costs could be passed on to consumers in the
marketplace. In the final instance, society as a whole might become
the ultimate insurer. A clear summary of this philosophy can be found
in Harper, James, and Gray:

> Human failures in a machine age cause a large and fairly regu-
> lar . . . toll of life, limb, and property. The most important aspect
> of these failures is not their moral quality; frequently they involve
> little or nothing in the way of personal moral shortcoming. The
> really important problems they pose are, rather, those of accident
> prevention and concern for the welfare of the victims. . . .
> [Losses] fall initially on people who as a class can ill afford them,
> and this fact brings great hardship on the victims themselves and
> causes unfortunate repercussions to society as a whole. Human-
> itarian objectives of society can best be met by finding ways to deal
> with accident loss that will ordinarily assure accident victims sub-
> stantial compensation to cover at least their economic loss, and will

distribute the losses involved over society as a whole or some very large segment of it. Such a basis for administering losses is what we have called social insurance.[60]

The past two decades have produced undeniable complications for this approach. Among other problems, the burdens placed on defendants in product-liability suits have not been easily shifted through insurance. Costs of insurance increased sharply during the early 1970s and again in the 1980s, and in some instances insurance coverage has been completely unavailable.[61] Those who are disadvantaged by such effects, most notably the corporate community, have obvious incentives to curse the winds of doctrinal change that have brought them at least short-term misfortune. In general, judicial creativity is almost certainly too weak as an institutional strategy for organizing an appropriate social response to personal injury. As environmental accidents begin to tax the judicial system with time and cost demands, alternative strategies are slowly emerging out of the political system.

It is not at all surprising, however, that newly burdened defendants formulate their protests within the narrow terms of private law, dwelling on the normative issues of judicial activism and the morality of no-fault liability. They simply ignore the broader social context, in which victims who are themselves without fault cover their own losses. This narrower argument likewise emerges in studies that treat the personal injury problem as a "tort crisis." Many such works reflect corporate interests, as for example in the 1986 *Report of the United States Attorney General's Tort Policy Working Group*. In commenting on a "veritable explosion of tort liability" in the preceding decade, that report specifically notes two contributing factors:

1. The movement toward no-fault liability, which increasingly results in companies and individuals being found liable even in the absence of any wrongdoing on their part.
2. The undermining of causation through a variety of questionable practices and doctrines which shift liability to "deep pocket" defendants even though they did not cause the underlying injury or had only a limited or tangential involvement.[62]

These criticisms echo traditional views that wrongdoing and causation are necessary elements in judicial findings of liability, although it is unclear whether the reasons are essentially moral or merely based on what the courts traditionally have done. A similar ambiguity appears in the writings of academic commentators, such as the following remark on an asbestos case by a critic of enterprise liability:

> In *Beshada*, the Court held an asbestos manufacturer in breach of its duty to warn of product dangers, though the court conceded that the dangers could not have been known scientifically at the time of the breach. The notion of liability for breach of a duty with which it was impossible to comply seems to strain the most basic conceptions of responsibility.[63]

Although it is possible to read such criticisms as confined to the procedural objection that the *courts* should not use instrumental or distributive reasoning in reaching liability decisions, a stronger message is almost certainly intended. Implicit in the Reagan administration's legislative drive to reverse judicial-doctrinal trends was the belief that they are inherently unwise policy. Likewise Priest's objection seems to apply quite apart from the issue of judicial activism, alluding instead to some general notion of "responsibility" (presumably a combination of culpability and causation) as a moral condition for liability.

For all the weight placed on the putative moral elements of civil liability—culpability and causation—we find little explicit justification for them in either popular or academic literature. If these positions command the almost self-evident agreement implied in statements such as those we have just discussed, we might suppose that definitive justifications have long been available. But any attempt to rest this moral vision on common sense runs into severe difficulties, as we saw earlier in this chapter. To the extent we encounter such beliefs among ordinary people, we cannot rule out that they are in part conditioned by the judicial system itself, and by our society's history of confining accident problems to that system. Nor can we, by linking these positions to economic efficiency, get around the need to make an affirmative moral case.[64]

As long as society's reactions to personal injury are dominated by the judicial process, moral issues can be mooted indirectly by: (1) postulating a judicial golden age in which fault principles presumably contained moral elements of causation and culpability, and (2) placing a burden of proof on judicial interpreters to show that current doctrines were derived from earlier rules by noninstrumental reasoning. This gambit was explored in some detail in Chapter 1, and all that needs repeating here is that point one, as an historical premise, was vigorously disputed by the progressive tort critics, and that point two is really a controversy about judicial method and the legitimacy of judicial decisions, from which no affirmative conclusions about substantive moral principles can be drawn. We are left, therefore, with only the small but intense academic debate about civil liability that deals openly with moral reasoning—to which we now turn.

Moral Philosophy—Individualist and Communitarian

Earlier we pointed out that positive economics and moral philosophy, although partly defined by their stark opposition to each other on the question of instrumentalism, are nonetheless two sides of the same coin. Their common currency is the neo-Kantian view that moral issues transcend the capacities of scientific inquiry—an epistemology that can be used either to open new space for ethical speculation or to dismiss ethics as sheer nonsense. Paradoxically this gap between *ought* and *is* (reflected by economics in its cautious distinction between normative and positive) insulates the *ought* from empirical review and thus creates breathing room for moral philosophy. Provided someone comes forward with a plausible method, philosophy can thus claim virtually exclusive jurisdiction over questions of justice defined at this dizzying level.

The ideas that may inhabit this space are potentially unlimited. They range from libertarian viewpoints to social ideals based on concepts of community.[65] Philosophers have been extraordinarily imaginative in repopulating this realm previously vacated under attack from logical positivism; but the difficulty now is the sheer variety of species. In response to this brilliant display of indestructible but mutually incompatible moral ideals, some philosophers have modestly suggested that moral philosophy may be better suited for analytical criticism than for founding new ethical systems.[66] More important, any moral reasoning likely to assist public policy will need to find a closer relationship to instrumental thinking than deontology can offer.

In evaluating the academic debate about accident law, therefore, we should not confuse the dominance of individualist positions with the discipline of moral philosophy itelf. So far the perspective of deontology has best served the rhetorical needs of legal commentators advocating a society in which traditional common-law rules exhaust the social obligations between individuals. But nothing would prevent a deontological theory that centered on the injustice of allowing the suffering of "innocent" and uncompensated accident victims, or on the justice of holding accountable those persons and organizations whose actions bear a statistical relationship to future accidents. Nor is there any philosophical necessity to anchoring both compensation and accountability to the same underlying events, nor in using the judicial process exclusively in handling accident cases. Moral philosophy cannot rule out any of these positions, nor can it settle differences between rival social philosophies.

Both the strengths and limits of moral philosophy are apparent in attempts by Fletcher, Epstein, and Weinrib to build the individualist social philosophy of common law into an impregnable structure.[67] By donning the armor of moral philosophy, these writers seem eager to defend common law from an entire century of instrumental meddling by progressive critics, creative judges, and efficiency-minded economists. Their respective goals are similar despite their choice of different moral touchstones within the common law. Fletcher wanted to reclaim the territory lost to strict liability by restoring the undisputed sovereignty of negligence, placing it beyond instrumentalist attack. Epstein projected a moral ideal for tort law based on strict liability; for him even negligence law was too broad since its imprecise standards (mainly the reasonable-prudence and proximate-cause doctrines) invited judges to extend liability beyond a limited number of strictly interpersonal encounters. Finally, Weinrib reduced the ideal scope of civil liability rules even further by limiting their coverage to violations ("takings") of legal rights, a position that Epstein has also apparently embraced.[68]

Although they found it relatively easy to seize the rhetorical high ground, none of these writers makes a decisive case for his particular moral apotheosis of common law. By directing themselves to ongoing controversies within the legal academy, they have restricted their analysis to the parochial debate over judicial liability rules. At one point Fletcher wondered aloud whether broader institutional choices might be possible, but abandoned the thought in a tantalizing footnote. Fletcher thus concedes that his article "has the limited concern of assessing problems of fairness within a litigation scheme. There is growing skepticism whether one-to-one litigation is the appropriate vehicle for optimizing accidents and compensating victims."[69]

Both Fletcher and Epstein also wanted to show that their respective moral principles squared with selected judicial case law—a style of legal scholarship that differs sharply from the hypothetical dialectics of moral philosophy. The difference is apparent in Jules Coleman's philosophical assessment of their arguments, which tries to show analytically that single normative concepts are unable to cover all the fundamental patterns of tort law. Coleman presents a series of hypothetical situations where the traditional concept of negligence would arguably reach different conclusions from any of these moral principles, including the principles of "wrongfulness" of the defendant's action, causation, the "reciprocal risk" relationship between parties, and the violation of legal rights.[70] Legal academics always seem on firmer ground when they can pick and choose actual legal precedents to be explained in terms of abstract principles. Coleman's work suggests this enterprise is misguided, and that traditional tort rules cannot finally be reduced to single moral concepts or a list of causal paradigms.

We may further conclude from Coleman's analysis that Fletcher, Epstein, and Weinrib have not *derived* their moral interpretations from the common law traditions they embrace; rather they have *imposed* their moral philosophies (independently selected) on the legal system. Their conclusions will thus appeal only to partisans of staunchly individualist social philosophies. Opponents of such views will reject these interpretations of the legal system for the same reasons they reject libertarian social philosophy—whatever those reasons happen to be.

By now deontological analysis of civil liability has become a distinct academic field, whose subject matter is generically known as *corrective justice*.[71] This term—borrowed from Aristotle's *Nicomachean Ethics*, where it supplements the broader category of distributive justice[72]—appropriately fixes the narrow approach to justice favored by the individualist critics of modern tort law. There is considerable irony in the fact that "corrective" justice is a mere formalistic detour within one of the great teleological ethical systems. For Aristotle, the good life for separate individuals was unthinkable outside the good community, which he identified with the Greek city-state: "It is evident that the state is a creature of nature, and that man is by nature a political animal. And he who by nature and not by mere accident is without a state, is either above humanity or below it."[73] An Aristotelian perspective on justice invites us to take seriously man's utter dependence on a favorable social environment for fulfilling his moral and intellectual goals. We thus return to that environment for concluding remarks on normative frameworks.

Conclusion: From Morality to Public Responsibility

Izhak England's rather harsh judgment on recent torts scholarship seems especially apt for these attempts to restore the negligence system using deontological moral theory.

> The response of modern American scholarship to the crisis in tort law . . . constitute[s] a desperate scholarly rearguard action to preserve a traditional system of individualism in a changing world. . . . The universal trends in accident law point in another direction: ideas of distributive justice have become dominant in a more and more collectivist society.[74]

This is not to say that deontological theory is inherently reactionary, but its strategic use in the current academic debate on accident law has consistently been to defend some historically superseded state of common law. Coming down from the lofty regions of timeless moral reasoning, we need to consider alternative moral principles that respond more directly to the contemporary challenge of personal injuries in technologically advanced societies. Returning to instrumental considerations does not mean renouncing serious concern with moral principles, as exponents of deontology sometimes imply. But it does permit us to anchor public-policy proposals in the timely concerns being registered throughout our legal system. As Robert Goodin has argued:

> Where instrumental rationality is banned, we are deprived of the only mechanism for choosing means to translate our morally laudable intentions into morally desirable outcomes. Even those who deny that the consequences of our actions are everything, ethically speaking, would usually not go so far as to assert that the consequences are utterly devoid of moral significance. For this reason, the repudiation of instrumental rationality as the basis for seriously held moral principles is simply implausible.[75]

On the other hand, we can also agree with Goodin that it is a mistake to represent "moral principles as just another argument tacked onto an ordinary utility function. . . . Moral principles can be seen as something special only so long as . . . people refuse to trade them off for egoistic advantage."[76]

Let us then attempt to reverse the rhetorical flow found in much of moral philosophy. Instead of drawing conclusions about the kind of world in which we live by consulting moral intuitions embalmed in tort law, we can start out from conditions in our current social environment. A later inference to moral principles need not be entirely strategic, but rather may call for revising or reinterpreting moral principles from the past in light of changed circumstances.

We have maintained throughout this study that the contemporary world of accidents is much changed from the circumstances that produced the nineteenth-century common law of torts. We can no longer rely on either the visual imagery of traumatic impact or the moral tradition of discrete interpersonal duties to organize an adequate public response to accidents. Epidemiological knowledge suggests that there is a statistically inevitable toll of personal injuries in our society that can be correlated (to varying degrees) with the presence of potentially hazardous substances, with the development of new technologies, and with the basic social and economic conditions under which people live.

We cannot document exactly which personal injuries are due to specific sources, except in such rare circumstances as an illness like mesothelioma, for which the only known cause is exposure to asbestos. But even in that case, it is obviously not the *substance* itself that deserves blame for personal injury, but the entire social context in which that substance was used. While creative tort doctrines reach as far as the possible carelessness of manufacturers who used asbestos products, a more comprehensive policy on accidents would implicate other contextual forces. These might include the private and public demand for the beneficial qualities of asbestos, contemporary organizational norms for manufacturers' assessments of product toxicity, and government policies on procurement, product testing, and the supervision of labor conditions.

This web of complex causation points to a level of social relations that challenge our tort-conditioned ideas about personal injuries. Rather than a society of sovereign individuals dealing at arm's length, we live in a highly interdependent world of persons and organizations. Some of those organizations, though nominally private, are large-scale enterprises with public functions. Moreover, the level of technology available to modern enterprise represents a qualitatively new degree of complexity, providing the basis for Perrow's model of "system accidents."[77] These are, in fact, the combined effects of organizational and technological complexity, in which both behavioral structures and natural substances play interactive parts. Finally, any society struggling to manage this complexity will surely possess a mixed economy, one in which both public regulation and private initiative define production and safety goals, acting through both political and market institutions.

In response to this challenging environment, several cultural factors bring considerable urgency to the problem of accidents. Along with a generally rising standard of living, persons in our society develop more demanding expectations about reducing risk and promoting security.[78] We cannot dryly assume that the current private market for first-party insurance is the ultimate expression of those expectations, though admittedly there are limits to other ways of measuring the concern for security. Adding to the random incidence of accidental injury is our deep uncertainty about the sources of most accidents. This uncertainty makes it intrinsically difficult to draw a line between organic illness and accidental injury, a distinction on which our legal and social welfare systems have previously been based.[79] Uncertainty also confounds our general assumptions about accountability and deterrence, through which we express our collective ambitions to improve personal security in the future.

Tort law has provided one structure for carrying out the social process of attributing responsibility, but the adequacy of that system is limited by its individualist traditions. It insists on a well-founded judgment of causal responsibility before it will concede that an accidental loss has occurred—creating intolerable pressures on courts to re-adjust mutually the boundaries of concepts like causation, reasonable prudence, and injury. As we shall see in the next four chapters, judicial creativity quickly reaches its limits in personal injury cases based on environmental accidents. Alternatives to the tort system are inevitable for an age of environmental accidents, even though their precise form is difficult to predict.

Four alternative institutional models will be reviewed in succeeding chapters, providing a continuum reaching from exclusive judicial management to the complete legislative preemption of common law:

1. Judicial self-reform.
2. Legislative review of judicial doctrines.
3. The substitution of government for either plaintiffs or defendants in private litigation.
4. Legislative compensation programs for discrete classes of accident victims.

These models of reform are all currently under discussion in the United States for numerous types of accidents, as we shall examine in a series of case studies. In Part IV, however, we will argue that such changes, taken together, indicate the need for a more fundamental shift to comprehensive policies dealing separately with accountability and compensation.

The moral principles supporting this tendency toward comprehensive revision of accident policy can be briefly suggested here, although there is no claim that they are derived from common sense, economic rationality, or socially detached moral philosophy. The central term to be used in Chapter 10 is *public responsibility*, which is intended to emphasize several themes. The term *public* is meant to underscore a departure from the exclusive individualist and private conventions of tort law, at least in its nonprogressive mode. This does not imply that responsibility for all misfortunes in society is placed on some social abstraction; surely we can retain any workable theory of attribution that discriminates among the activities of individuals, organizations, government agencies, and the society as a whole. The division of responsibility among these levels may take different forms within separate policies of accountability and compensation, reflecting a mixture of objectives that include accident deterrence, economic efficiency, and distributive social welfare, as well as any purely symbolic purposes society may wish to pursue.

Responsibility thus covers an extensive range of obligations, compatible with an unlimited number of institutional strategies. What can be conveyed in a single term, however, is the residual obligation of a society as a whole to see that policies are, in fact, developed that respond to the formidable challenge of environmental accidents. *Responsibility* here stands for the obligation to see that an adequate response is made, and my conclusion is that only the public as a whole, acting through its political institutions, will be capable of crafting that response. The reference to political institutions raises painful questions about the quality of response we can expect in an age of pluralism; some of those questions were dealt with in Chapter 3. As a society, I believe, we have no choice but to improve those institutions as much as possible.

There is a considerable leap between the hundreds of accident policies now under consideration in this country and a truly comprehensive policy with separate components for accountability and compensation. But the alternative to trying such a leap is to continue reworking the tired themes of individualism, based on increasingly unrealistic axioms about socially disembodied selves. Sandel's conclusions about contemporary liberal-political theory capture the apparent hopelessness of that direction:

> By putting the self beyond the reach of politics, [liberalism] makes human agency an article of faith rather than an object of continuing attention and concern, a premise of politics rather than its precarious achievement. This misses the pathos of politics and also its most inspiring possibilities. It overlooks the danger that when politics goes badly, not only disappointments but also dislocations are likely to result. And it forgets the possibility that when politics goes well, we can know a good in common that we cannot know alone.[80]

Part Three

Institutional Options: Recent

Trends in American Policy

Although most American policies maintain their basic orientation to judicial *concepts*, they have all moved away from exclusive reliance on traditional judicial *procedures*. The public response to environmental accidents has greatly accelerated this trend, raising expectations for more creative judicial management of litigation, legislative oversight of the judicial process, a larger role for the federal government, and institutional alternatives to tort law. Part III surveys these various responses to a growing backlog of accidents involving vaccines, asbestos, Agent Orange, medical services, defective or dangerous products, toxic wastes, nuclear power, workplace injuries, and occupational diseases. Our first impression records a series of unplanned, even chaotic efforts to reform tort law; but closer examination reveals a consistent trend toward fuller recognition of public responsibility for personal injury.

The discussion is organized around four basic kinds of institutional change, which may be seen as steps toward separating accident policy from its traditional control by the courts. These stages occupy successive points along a continuum leading from exclusive reliance on traditional litigation, up to the complete abandonment of judicial procedures. As American accident policies travel erratically down this path, they seem to be pushed by special circumstances rather than attracted by the logical end point of their journey. In dozens of separate efforts to cope with the complexities of specific environmental accidents, a bewildering variety of remedies have been proposed or adopted in the familiar American spirit of incrementalism. But the ultimate direction of change is now discernible, if not yet inevitable.

Chapter 6 examines options for reform within the judicial system itself, led by activist judges using various discretionary devices. These include further instrumental development of liability doctrines, consolidation of claims in order to reach collective aspects of causation and accountability, special procedures for expediting litigation and informal bargaining, and heroic judicial management of mass litigation. (The case examples include vaccine injuries, asbestos claims, and the Agent Orange settlement.) Those advocating greater judicial initiative hope to protect the courts' autonomy from political oversight, but they acknowledge in varying ways that the price may be the cherished case-by-case process of adjudication.

Judicial self-reform seems to encounter serious limitations in handling environmental accidents both fairly and efficiently. Those affected by these limits include not only dissatisfied victims but defendant groups required to bear new costs, which are periodically magnified by soaring insurance premiums. The failure of courts to prevent such crises has produced calls for broad legislative review of judicial doctrines and procedures. Such proposals (known under the slogan of "tort reform") have already been approved in some states, but Chapter 7 explores the emerging congressional consensus on federalized standards for product-liability litigation. All these proposals seek, in various ways, to reverse the progressive trends favored by activist judges. Ironically, they are helping to institutionalize the instrumentalist view of tort law: that doctrines are essentially means to public ends. By firmly placing the explicit review of judicial goals on the political agenda, these reform efforts take a significant step toward fuller debate on the scope of public responsibility.

Thus far the analysis of Part III traces the decline of two central features in the traditional judicial model: case-by-case adjudication and judicial autonomy. Chapter 8 considers further policy developments that undermine the private status of the parties to litigation, in special cases where the federal government has been substituted for either the plaintiff or the defendant. Examples include the swine flu vaccination program, Superfund cost-recovery litigation, and the federal government's program for structuring nuclear liability. To some extent the trend toward government liability reflects the current fashion for privatizing public regulation. Over the long run, however, casting the federal government as a litigant will more likely institutionalize various forms of public responsibility. The experience so far with government litigation reveals the high cost and inefficiency of using judicial procedures to accomplish some essential public goals: ensuring personal compensation, enforcing public and private accountability, and regulating the larger environment in which accidents occur.

Finally, Chapter 9 turns to programs that seek to abolish judicial procedures for particular kinds of accidents. The concept goes all the way back to workers' compensation, but more recent policies have been passed or proposed for dealing with occupational diseases (especially asbestos and black-lung diseases), personal injuries from hazardous wastes, and injuries caused by federally sponsored vaccines and other public health initiatives. Despite its status as the nonjudicial paradigm, workers' compensation illustrates the potential weaknesses of specialized administrative schemes. Like the judicial system itself, these programs have difficulty operationalizing sharply defined standards of eligibility, accountability, causation, and damages. The leading symptom of these problems is the resurgence of litigation over boundary disputes within statutory programs. On the other hand, when administrative programs loosen their criteria to allow more generalized application, they invariably move toward broader social-welfare models.

There is no cunning of reason which guarantees that U. S. policy will move down the developmental path mapped out in Part III. Nor is there any basis for predicting what will happen as future policies grow to occupy more points along this continuum, although some possibilities will be raised in Part IV. We may conclude from this survey, however, that environmental accidents are hastening the search for alternatives to traditional litigation. Solutions proposed by all competing groups agree on this point; they disagree only on what the specific alternatives should be.

Chapter 6

Judicial Self-Reform

> *The law of torts is entering a new era. . . . The question of the day is whether courts will have the wisdom to accelerate the process and save the tort system from collapse. If they do not take immediate action, we can expect regressive legislation at the federal level. Those who believe that tort law has served the country well, must realize that the time for creative constraint has arrived.*[1]

Can Creative Judging Reform the Tort System?

In response to environmental accidents, a controversy has arisen over whether "creative judging" can help cure the tort system of its maladies. Despite doubts about how well the system actually works, very few critics seem eager to dispense entirely with judicial processes; indeed a significant number want to preserve and strengthen the judicial function. Throughout our history, courts have played an unusually dominant role within the legal structure precisely because their piecemeal, decentralized approach has appealed to many Americans. The judicial system's conceptual incrementalism and even its procedural inefficiencies are often seen as virtues; the latter serving as self-correcting safeguards, the former as barriers to ideological political forces. During the early Warren Court period, progressive social critics awarded the courts subtle praise as modest and perspicacious institutions for introducing major value changes into American society.[2] This chapter explores several contemporary reforms, based on this perennially optimistic vision of the judicial process, designed to meet the extraordinary challenges now facing the tort system.

Most recent proposals for creative judging call for substantial departures from traditional judicial structures. It is now commonly acknowledged that claims like those from exposure to asbestos and other toxic agents cannot be adequately managed on a single-case basis.[3] Defenders of the judicial system, however, recommend novel solutions that would allow the courts to regain control over individual claims. Judicial processes may not be perfect, but to many they are superior to programs imposed by legislation. Behind these suggestions we sense a fear that legislative guidance could upset the judiciary's delicate system of internal balances, its relative freedom from mass political forces, its role in facilitating private interpersonal transactions, and its resistance to doctrinaire policy positions.[4]

In the passage cited at the beginning of this chapter, one advocate of creative judging imagines rescuing the courts, using contradictory images of acceleration and constraint. Whatever the tort system is destined to accomplish, it apparently needs to be pushed along in order to save itself from destruction. "Creative constraint" invites comparison with "deliberate speed," another oxymoron expressing the complex faith many Americans place in their judicial servants.

Although most of this chapter emphasizes structural changes in the very process of adjudication, we should not forget that the court system—however structured—operates with legal doctrines as its basic conceptual vocabulary. For several decades, and especially in the past twenty-five years, court-initiated changes in legal doctrine have embodied the judiciary's desire to shape tort law, and to make it more responsive to new social priorities. Since it is precisely these doctrinal creations that are now widely blamed for leading the tort system toward its own destruction, we should preface our treatment of future restructuring with an example of the dilemmas resulting from the creativity of the recent past.

Vaccine Injuries and the Duty to Warn

The most dramatic experiments in reform-by-doctrine during the past several decades have concerned injuries from manufactured products—injuries befalling either consumers or workers. Often described by the inexact label of *strict liability*, these doctrinal changes have, in fact, resulted from intricate elaboration of several concepts, generally easing the demands on plaintiffs under the fault system and expanding the legal duties of manufacturers.[5]

Before the 1960s, manufacturers could usually avoid civil liability whenever their products passed through mediating stages of commerce (retailers, wholesalers) on their path toward the injured user. With the fall of this older rule requiring "privity of contract," manufacturers entered en masse the circle of permissible defendants. About the same time, courts started drawing on contract law to find implied warranties of product safety in many standard sales agreements. The courts also expanded the reasonable-prudence test under negligence rules, holding manufacturers accountable for selecting a reasonably safe product design and for warning consumers of possible dangers from ordinary and extraordinary product use.[6]

Put together, these creative extensions from traditional negligence doctrine pass imperceptibly into the territory of strict liability, leaving markedly fewer ways for defendant corporations to escape responsibility.[7] Commentators now see these changes as having come together around 1964 with the adoption of §402A of the *Restatement (Second) of Torts*, a doctrinal synthesis presaged by opinions from the California Supreme Court as well as academic commentary.[8] Employing this new doctrinal model, state courts entered an unparalleled period of creativity, reaching the point as early as 1970 where the impact on defendants could fairly be labeled a "crisis."[9]

The judicial treatment of vaccine injuries during this period illustrates several dilemmas occasioned by these dramatic changes. By extending the drug manufacturers' *duty to warn* patients about possible serious vaccine side effects, creative judges during the late 1960s and early 1970s made it possible for at least some victims to win substantial damages. The duty to warn evolved through several stages: (1) instead of being allowed to communicate their warnings simply to physicans, drug companies were sometimes held accountable if their message failed to reach the vaccine patient; (2) even in cases where the risk of injury was incalculably small, courts sometimes presumed that patients would have found some way to avoid the danger had they been duly warned; (3) even direct warnings were continually faulted for esoteric language or obscure meaning.[10]

These court decisions had important consequences that are fairly simple to document, given the special qualities of vaccines as products. Although vaccines have proved highly effective in eradicating diseases like smallpox, polio, and measles, they also cause a small but statistically predictable number of serious injuries, even when properly administered. These injuries accompany the product's intended use—so clearly beneficial to society as a whole that we seem to accept harmful effects as the inescapable price of promoting public health. In the case of most other products, by contrast, consumer injuries are commonly attributed to unanticipated uses or careless consumer behavior, to negligent design or production, or to other deviations from appropriate standards. Thus even toxic materials like asbestos, whose latent health effects were at one time virtually unknown, raise the question whether manufacturers should have researched more diligently, or whether they could have found substitutes with less harmful effects from the beginning.

For most products, it is virtually impossible to say how many accidents are caused by carelessness or lack of diligence, and how many are inevitable occurrences where no one has done anything wrong. Theoretically the distinction is critical, since only the former accidents might be reduced by a regime of sanctions or incentives motivating people to take greater care.[11] The special distinction of vaccines as products is to draw attention to *unavoidable* personal injuries as the inevitable result of social choices—both economic and political choices. Injuries caused by most products doubtless share these traits to some degree, but the point is easily overlooked by those who concentrate on deterrence issues, and who thus magnify the extent of controllable harms.

Vaccine injuries were obvious candidates for creative tort reform as conceived by progressive critics of negligence doctrine.[12] By means of the duty-to-warn doctrine as it developed during the 1970s, severe losses that inevitably fall on a few innocent victims were redistributed to the larger society. The drug industry seemed to be ideally situated for loss shifting: increasing the cost of each dose by a modest amount would finance actual compensation costs, and allowing the industry to purchase liability insurance could further spread the risk of unforeseen future costs.

Such a formula for shifting losses emerged incrementally (but with breathtaking speed, by judicial standards) in a series of cases granting compensation to polio victims.[13] These decisions capture the judicial philosophy behind expanding product-liability doctrines; notice was being served via the costs imposed on drug manufacturers that society was expected to pay for personal injuries that are the inevitable by-products of new medical technology.

What appears to have gone wrong after this outburst of judicial creativity? All the elements of the product-liability "crisis" are quite clearly etched in the specific crises that befell the sale of vaccines. Drug producers and their insurers simply failed to respond as expected to doctrinal change: instead of absorbing and redistributing compensation costs, they tended to halt production. Their withdrawal from the vaccine business caused a critical shortage of vaccine supplies, at the same time that public health authorities were trying to build confidence in mass-immunization programs.[14] Manufacturers and their insurers maintain that the uncertainty of future civil liability, a necessary result of incremental policy making by the judiciary, makes it impossible to predict profitable sales or actuarially sound insurance premiums.[15] Rather than increase prices to reflect the greatest possible exposure to liability, drug companies have turned to more profitable products, and insurers have balked at underwriting policies for new products.

During the swine-flu episode in 1976 these reactions threatened to block the most ambitious public-health campaign in United States history. It was only after the federal government assumed all liability for duty-to-warn suits—an unprecedented gesture—that the drug industry and its insurers agreed to furnish the 40 million doses of swine-flu vaccine distributed between October and December. In the end, of course, their prudence was vindicated. A sudden occurrence of the paralytic disease, Guillain-Barré Syndrome, came as an unforeseen side effect of the flu vaccine.[16] It is now estimated that at least 1 out of every 100,000 who received swine-flu vaccine, or about 400 persons, contracted a serious form of this deadly disease.[17] Ten years after the incident, the federal government had paid out over $86 million in response to some 4,000 swine-flu injury claims.[18]

When the drug and insurance industries complain of future legal uncertainties, they fear that courts will further increase their burden to the level of strict or even absolute liability.[19] Indeed, while the duty-to-warn doctrine often puts a manufacturer in the position where even reasonable prudence will not provide a defense—the standard meaning of strict liability—courts have shown willingness to go even farther. In a much debated New Jersey case, for example, the largest manufacturer of asbestos was held accountable for failing to warn industrial workers about health dangers of asbestos exposure, at a time when such dangers may not have even been known. To some commentators this constitutes *absolute* liability, defined rather pungently by one writer: "As soon as the product is distributed, the manufacturer is christened as the product user's guardian angel forever."

> As matters currently stand, the pitfalls [of liability exposure] not only appear infinite in quantity, but perhaps more seriously, they are hidden because the courts are not giving the manufacturer sufficient guidelines from which to take precautions and promote safety. In essence, the dilemma posed by the attitude of our judiciary might justifiably be characterized as "counter-evolutionary" because its ultimate effect will be a reluctance by manufacturers to invest more time and funds in product safety since liability is a *fait accompli*.[20]

A sequel to swine flu is the recent debate over pertussis vaccine, one component of the diphtheria-pertussis-tetanus (DPT) inoculations recommended or required for most of America's schoolchildren.[21] For pertussis vaccine a predictable range of serious injuries has been documented by several research studies, leading many parents to oppose inoculation for their children. Even as this avoidance causes worry for public-health reasons, manufacturers have responded by limiting production, and by 1985 there was only one active American producer of DPT vaccine left.[22] Congress took a harder look at proposals to modify the compensation burdens on drug companies, agreeing in the closing days of the Ninety-Ninth Congress to preempt some aspects of state tort law governing injuries from DPT and several other childhood-disease vaccines.[23]

Among the changes is the new requirement that victims first seek limited damages under an administrative-claims process, one in which the traditional burden of establishing causation is essentially dropped. Should claimants be dissatisfied with the outcome, they can seek broader damages under tort law but may not base their claim on the duty-to-warn doctrine.[24] As Twersky predicted, the failure of courts to keep their doctrinal reforms under control has invited an intrusion by the legislature. We shall see in Chapter 7 that Congress has come close to mandating a whole new system of rules and procedures for all product-liability claims, a system heavily shaped by political lobbying of major interest groups. It is precisely this sort of political solution that partisans of judicial creativity hope to avoid.

It should not be assumed that courts are monolithic in applying duty-to-warn rules, let alone in their continual expansion. As we might expect from case-by-case adjudication, separate courts lean in opposite directions on very similar points. Although one of the early polio cases was quick to assume that the plaintiff's disease was caused by vaccine rather than an epidemic then active in Texas, other cases have turned on the opposite assumption.[25] Similarly, some courts have rejected the presumption that a clear warning about the statistically small danger of vaccine-induced injury would have caused the patient to avoid that risk.[26]

As a means for increasing liability, the duty-to-warn doctrine has at least one major drawback: it must continually expand with repeated use. Either a manufacturer can avoid liability the next time around by meeting the court's terms for proper warning, or the requirements will have to stiffen. In reality some of each occurs, leading to fragmentation of the intended policy: individual losses are therefore not uniformly redistributed, and manufacturers view the system as deeply capricious.[27]

The pertussis battle was simply a trial run for the next major public health campaign: deployment of an effective AIDS vaccine. Once such a vaccine is developed and approved for use, the pressure to distribute it widely (if not to require it) will be irresistible.[28] What about the inevitable side effects? Will manufacturers slow production until the federal government once again modifies the tort system? If so, the administrative and legal tasks may prove to be as difficult as the medical challenge.

Federal willingness to assume control of the liability process is simply an extension of government dominance in the whole process of vaccine use: federal research money supports most of the basic and epidemiological studies at the development stage; clinical testing and production licensing are governed by federal regulations; and federal agencies actually purchase more than half the country's vaccine supply for distribution to state and local health programs. Federal responsibility to compensate the inevitable victims created by an essential public-health campaign seems a surprisingly small step. Considering the scrutiny that will surely be given the afflictions of all who receive a future AIDS vaccine, a flood of accident claims is highly predictable, and it could "make swine flu look like a picnic," in the words of one researcher.[29] As the recent federal action on childhood vaccines makes clear, many groups now agree that the judicial system provides inadequate means for responding to vaccine injuries. The only question is whether this class of injuries is a minor exception, or whether it indicates the main direction for future product liability rulings.

A "Public Law Vision": Judging Probabilistic Evidence

If legal doctrines like the duty to warn were once the expected means for reforming the tort system from within, they are now generally viewed as part of what has to be constrained. The environmental-accident cases have elicited new approaches to creative judging, inviting courts to become more active in streamlining the processing of claims, appraising causal connections in mass-exposure cases, and setting damages for entire classes of plaintiffs.

In an influential article, David Rosenberg has urged far-reaching changes in judicial procedure as the only means for rescuing the tort system from what he views as a "catastrophe."

> Tort doctrine has responded vigorously to the distinctive features of twentieth-century social life. . . . The tort system's private law process, however, reflects a disaggregative conception of the causes and consequences of accidents: it treats all cases as if they arose from unrelated, stochastic, factually unique, and temporally and physically immediate interactions between individuals.[30]

In contrast to the "starkly individualistic terms" of traditional common-law adjudication, Rosenberg prescribes a number of procedural changes enabling courts to deal with mass claims characterized by probabilistic causation, wholesale classes of plaintiffs with similar case histories, and indeterminate future consequences of toxic exposure. His article is especially important for suggesting how fundamentally the judicial process would have to change if it is to deal adequately with such cases. Rosenberg states these conditions so forcefully, in fact, as to invite skepticism that appropriate changes are even possible.

Rosenberg's most fundamental suggestion is that courts abandon the pursuit of individualized justice based on specific factual inquiry into the causal connection between plaintiff and defendant. The whole notion of injury must accordingly be redefined to mean present exposure to the *risk* of future injury, understanding that later injuries will actually occur in only a limited, sometimes statistically predictable number of cases. Liability placed on defendants would be calculated collectively, based on statistical evidence of the aggregate "excess disease risk" attributable to the defendant's activity. This way of measuring liability has now become known as the *proportional liability rule.*[31]

No individual plaintiff would thus be forced to carry the burden of proof on the matter of causation in a particular case; instead statistical evidence on the defendant's role in raising disease risks beyond their background levels would establish the probable number of future harms deemed to be caused by the defendant, and would thereby determine the appropriate financial penalty. Finally, damages would be averaged out over all exposed persons and defined by schedules, as in insurance-claims systems. All claims would be consolidated in compulsory class-action suits, with evidence on individual claimants heard under nonadversarial conditions.[32]

Such a revolutionary vision contrasts substantially with the traditional procedures of tort law. Plaintiffs would include all those persons subjected to the risk of later injury from present toxic exposures, whether or not the injury develops, and despite the certain knowledge that a large portion of eventual injuries would be caused by background factors and not by the defendant's actions. Defendants would face a single lawsuit designed to determine the collective impact of their behavior on the plaintiff class. Damages would be averaged over the entire class, but would be limited in the aggregate to an amount representing full compensation for the proportion of injuries caused by the defendant, as determined by epidemiological evidence.

It is worth reflecting on the ultimate purpose of such grandiose reorganization of the judicial structure, assuming it could even be accomplished. We find here the leading clue to Rosenberg's "vision": his instrumentalist's definition of how the public good would be enhanced by a new judicial strategy. In the fashion of economic critics, Rosenberg assumes that the proper purpose of tort law is future accident prevention, not redistribution of wealth to achieve full compensation for past personal injuries. (Compensation is presumably a separate project for either the political process or private-insurance contracts; at any rate it is not an achievable or describable goal of tort law.[33]) Rosenberg's argument thus boils down to asserting that his new structural model would allow the judicial system to achieve the broad social goal of promoting optimal accident prevention, while leaving the impact on personal compensation completely outside his consideration.

By limiting his discussion to accident prevention, Rosenberg addresses the chief policy goal of many current tort theorists. But he ignores the progressive concern with adequate compensation, consigning this purpose to the political process, to whatever extent he envisions any social response. Although his restructured tort system would still award damages, the amounts would be mere by-products of the optimal deterrence scheme. These awards are adequate only to the task of promoting general productive efficiency, and they are almost certainly inadequate to meet the most serious social-welfare needs of people whose "excess risk" ripens into permanent incapacity. Rosenberg makes no comment on what sort of collective responsibility governs the political response to these welfare needs; he simply adopts the special angle on welfare popularized by economic instrumentalists.

Other commentators have wondered whether Rosenberg's scheme is a plausible means to achieve even the specific social goal of accident prevention. Some have questioned the impact of liability judgments on personal and corporate decisions to prevent accidents, as we saw earlier in Chapter 4.[34] Rosenberg himself worries that market imperfections could "distort" the impact of tort law, leading to either more or less deterrence than is socially optimal.[35] The concept of optimality presupposes a defined institutional framework. For free-market theorists, the economic system (although still a managed system in many respects) generates that framework spontaneously; for others, guidance on the rules of market exchange derive from political institutions—primarily legislation and regulation. Rosenberg admits that "without legislative guidance and administrative assistance," courts under his plan might not be able to adjust for inevitable market distortions.[36] Thus tort law, restructured according to this collective vision, may turn out to be only one ingredient in achieving even the limited welfare goal of optimal deterrence.

Rosenberg's article is best understood as a brief for maintaining the judicial system's involvement in accident cases, addressed to those academic colleagues who share his interest in developing the theory of market-guided deterrence. Even for that limited purpose, according to Rosenberg, the structure of adjudication needs to undergo radical changes; otherwise the flood of toxic-tort claims "will likely consume hundreds of millions of dollars' worth of public and private resources."[37] The tort system must be changed, in other words, both to do a better job of deterring accidents, and to do it more cheaply than case-by-case adjudication. The kinds of interests he elevates to controlling importance are "intrinsically collective," applying to all potential victims of toxic exposure.[38] Rosenberg's vision thus does *not* serve people who ultimately develop personal injuries from toxic encounters, but only those of us who manage to avoid future exposures altogether, thanks to the deterring impact of a creative judiciary.

It is this restricted vision of collective welfare that leads Rosenberg to apply the concept of *public law*, a term used more commonly in recent times to convey the collective impact of civil-rights adjudication on persons not directly represented in an actual lawsuit.[39] The same idea was used some years earlier by the progressive tort critic Leon Green: "My thesis can be expressed in a sentence. 'We the People' are a party to every lawsuit and it is our interest that weighs most heavily in its determination."[40] Unlike Rosenberg, Green and his contemporaries were confident that traditionally structured judicial processes would permit doctrinal reform to catch up with public needs. Judges and juries "have built within themselves our desires and interests." Green preferred the judicial process to legislation because judges are insulated from mass political pressure, and they can move quickly once an appropriate case comes along for extending old doctrines to current social needs.[41]

Rosenberg's public law shares this preference for judge-led reform, but it also contains some revealing contrasts to Green's position. Most important, his public interest is defined as optimal future-accident prevention, not adequate compensation for those who need or deserve it.[42] This revisionist statement of public purpose derives from economic theories of the past twenty years. Rosenberg illuminates those theories by showing how our older ideal of justice in the individual case is likely to frustrate society's attempt to find that optimal level of deterrence. To be sure, he believes that the courts are no better than the market for assigning costs of toxic exposure to specific events or persons. But they can help the market overcome its deficiencies by issuing clear information about harms statistically associated with hazardous activities. More important, they can impose penalities on producers in strict proportion to this statistical knowledge. To do these things effectively, according to Rosenberg, courts must deal exclusively with aggregated classes of plaintiffs, with injuries defined as future risks, with probabilistic causation, and with damages averaged out over competing claimants.[43]

An obvious response is, Why bother with such basic alterations of . judicial processes if the decisions critical for meeting public goals require such synoptic vision? Several commentators have argued that judges and juries should not be expected to make the change to toxic-tort problems—that their strengths and predilections lie rather with case-by-case analysis.[44] Rosenberg does not provide a clear rejoinder. His article has more the rhetorical structure of a hypothetical argument: *if* the judicial system can adapt to toxic-tort situations, *this* is what it would have to do.

Rosenberg's defense appears to rest partly on finding greater deficiencies in legislative or administrative solutions to tort crises. He worries that political influences on legislators and agencies would make them less objective promoters of optimal accident prevention—his exclusive public goal.[45] One appeal of the economic approach is its studied avoidance of politically determined welfare criteria, leading to its substitution of the market's invisible hand to define optimal aggregate levels of accident-producing activity. Rosenberg would rather see judges and juries supplementing the market in this endeavor (assuming, as he does, that the market needs guidance), based on scientific data rather than political value choices. As we saw in Chapter 4, however, it is doubtful that we can rely on either the judicial process or the political system to operate in a value-free manner. Rosenberg may be simply assuming the best about courts and the worst about legislatures, when, in fact, neither institution can insulate its decisions from their distributive impact and political consequences.

More convincing is Rosenberg's suggestion that legislatures have thus far been too timid in challenging traditional judicial approaches to accidents. "Legislatures continue to rely on the tort system for a substantial measure of deterrence and compensation in the mass exposure area. In effect, legislatures have declined the invitation to formulate a comprehensive administrative solution—in part because, at least for the foreseeable future, such a solution seems politically infeasible."[46] One wonders why courts would not encounter similar opposition should they ever pursue reforms as radical as Rosenberg's proposals. Administrative systems, at least, have the potential capacity to accomplish Rosenberg's goals, and he concludes that "an ideal system might very well employ a mix of regulation and tort liability."[47]

But there may also be special problems with mixed institutional systems. Most current proposals for hybrid structures can be interpreted as major accommodations to powerful interest groups. Under the proposed federal product-liability law, for example, the judicial structure is largely preserved, in accordance with the interests of producers and lawyers, while administrative structures are expected to tilt the whole process somewhat toward the compensation interests of consumers. Rosenberg may be right that legislation of this sort compromises too heavily by relying on the tort system to implement its constrained vision of public welfare. Chapter 8 will explore this possibility at greater length, while Chapters 9 and 10 will investigate the potential for separating administrative processes from the tort system altogether.

Streamlining Mass Claims: Asbestos

The asbestos cases constitute the largest single block of environmental-accident claims now entering the tort system.[48] We see them as a block because they are linked to a single substance for which the toxic properties have been impressively documented by epidemiological research. Contact with asbestos is thus the unifying element in a widely dispersed set of personal illnesses associated mainly with certain industrial settings, but also with public exposure in the wider environment. We do not know, of course, how many other materials in the environment may someday provide a similar connecting thread among otherwise disparate illnesses, disability, and death. Information released by the U.S. Surgeon General in 1988 suggests that radon contamination in private homes may pose a public health threat comparable to asbestos. The Occupational Safety and Health Administration currently lists more than 200 chemicals as suspected carcinogens present in the workplace.

Although asbestos cases are only a small percentage of all civil litigation before the courts, their importance is hard to exaggerate. Above all they allow us to predict future paralysis for the judicial process in the event of further epidemiological revelations on the same order. Estimates of asbestos mortality indicate that approximately 200,000 related deaths will occur in this country before the end of the century.[49] But we can conservatively expect eight times that number, based on current projections for all occupational disease.[50] With even one or two more discoveries comparable to that of asbestos, the limitations of judicial procedures would become impossible to ignore.

The glacial progress of asbestos claims passing into the legal system has been documented by the Rand Corporation study mentioned in Chapter 2. In summarizing their survey of state and federal courts, the authors report that:

> Across the 10 courts we studied, only a small proportion of cases reach full disposition at the same pace as that of other civil cases; a larger proportion obtain partial settlements, reaching full disposition only after a four- to five-year wait or even longer after filing. Finally, in a few courts the rate of disposition is so low that it is impossible to predict when current asbestos cases will reach disposition.[51]

Philadelphia Common Pleas Judge Richard B. Klein, reporting in late 1986 on one of the most troubled jurisdictions, predicts even more congestion in the future. Although his court had increased its rate of processing asbestos claims to its highest level ever, "The bad news is that cases are still being filed twice as fast as they are being disposed. At the present rate, someone filing a lawsuit today will not have their case heard until the 21st Century."[52]

Along with time delays, the costs of asbestos litigation reflect the complexities of processing an estimated 50,000 claims, each one naming an average of twenty defendants.[53] In a study completed in 1982, just as several defendants filed for corporate reorganization under federal bankruptcy laws, Rand found that the total legal costs of plaintiffs and defendants were 70 percent more than what plaintiffs received in actual compensation. For every $1.00 going to plaintiffs, an additional $.71 went to their attorneys and $1.00 was spent by defendants.[54] These estimates do not include the taxpayers' costs of protracted court proceedings.

From the perspective of judicial self-management, how might courts introduce procedural reforms to expedite asbestos claims? Why, for example, has there been apparently little use of class actions and a long list of other consolidating techniques? After examining that issue we will take a brief look at two recent developments affecting asbestos litigation. The first was an experiment in private mediation sponsored by asbestos defendants and their insurers, designed to resolve claims outside normal litigation. The second is the bankruptcy proceeding involving Johns-Manville and several other asbestos defendants.

The Rand study offers several reasons why class actions have played a surprisingly small role in asbestos litigation. During the 1970s, when plaintiffs began winning individual cases against asbestos manufacturers by using relatively novel theories of liability and by slowly eliciting evidence about manufacturers' knowledge of asbestos hazards, "uncertainty about the ultimate outcomes of specific substantive disputes probably discouraged parties on both sides from seeking definitive judgments on key issues for large blocks of cases." As litigation began to build in the 1980s, "attorneys on both sides have established well-developed routines and incentives for continuing to litigate common substantive issues on a case-by-case basis."[55] In short, the self-interest of plaintiffs and defendants has discouraged the judicial system from using its most powerful techniques for better management of cases.

The parties' strategic concerns are filtered through the distorting prism of future doctrinal shifts, attorney self-interest, and judicial behavior. Most plaintiff and defendant attorneys have avoided class actions for oddly complementary reasons. Plaintiff attorneys did not want to risk definitive foreclosure of evolving legal doctrines that place stricter burdens on asbestos manufacturers. Not only have doctrines changed, but so has our factual understanding of asbestos health effects:

> When would it have been appropriate to try causation and liability issues for the class, or preclude litigation of these issues for individual cases? With the introduction of new medical evidence, the strength of the plaintiff's case has clearly improved over time. Continuing wide-ranging discovery has produced new evidence on liability against different defendants.[56]

Defendants likewise were reluctant to stake their entire position on single rulings, and most of them further wished to avoid association with the largest deep-pocket defendant, Johns-Manville.

There was little financial incentive for attorneys on either side to speed up litigation, once the basic investment in gathering information and preparing a legal case had been made; repetitive litigation became a way to keep the meter running. Since jury awards are generally much higher than settlements,[57] plaintiffs' attorneys (paid by contingency fee) encouraged litigation, relying on their cumulative expertise in handling asbestos claims. Personal injury attorneys, unlike civil-rights lawyers, take a "traditionally negative posture" toward class actions,[58] being concerned not only about fees but also about maintaining control over legal strategy.[59] At the same time, the high costs of preparing asbestos cases meant that claims gravitated toward larger firms, who in turn were reluctant to split eventual fees with colleagues entering the field at a later time. Defendants' attorneys also had reasons to maintain case-by-case litigation, since their position, once prepared, remained relatively constant in contrast to the factual burdens on individual plaintiffs. The incentive for defendants to consolidate usually does not arise until after liability has been established, when all that remains is to determine damages.[60]

Judges surveyed for the Rand study felt generally that "their asbestos cases [did not meet] the prerequisites for a class action," whether or not attorneys for either side had raised the issue.[61] However, in cooperation with attorneys, judges would sometimes accept informal consolidation methods for specific cases. For example, one federal judge in Texas charged a single jury with the issue of defendants' liability in a group of some thirty cases. When the jury found liability and began assessing damages for individual plaintiffs, the defendants were motivated to settle them all.[62] Such arrangements have occurred in many jurisdictions but are not formally supervised or subject to appellate review. They clearly rely on situational circumstances that are difficult to generalize. As the Rand study concludes, "the fact that these informal understandings depend on the relationships between specific judges and attorneys . . . illustrates their inherent weakness as mechanisms for reducing litigation. As the specific participants change, so may the informal understandings about the set of issues that are 'settled.'"[63]

In theory, courts have broad options for streamlining the disposition of civil cases, of which formal class-action suits are perhaps the best known. Class actions are common in many situations, serving in recent years as tools of the public-interest law movement to bring organized pressure against private sources of environmental damage, and against public bureaucracies allegedly violating civil rights of plaintiffs.[64] In the field of personal injury, however, considering the common law's highly individualized construction of events and responsibility, the courts (when asked) have generally found insufficient similarity of claims to allow formal approval of a class action. Their reasons recall the comments made in 1966 by a special advisory committee to the Supreme Court, which noted that

> a "mass accident" resulting in injuries to numerous persons is ordinarily inappropriate for a class action because of the likelihood that significant questions, not only of damages, but of liability and defenses to liability would be present, affecting the individuals in different ways. In these circumstances an action conducted nominally as a class action would degenerate in practice into multiple lawsuits separately tried.[65]

Besides the factual diversity of cases, environmental accidents often present procedural diversity as well.[66] Potential members of a class generally do not all fall under the jurisdiction of a single state, their claims may have been initiated at widely different times, and those claims may differ substantially on their merits. All these conditions are barriers to formal certification of class actions, notwithstanding the common link to a single substance as an alleged cause of injury.

In addition to class actions, other tools for standardizing litigation present similar practical and technical difficulties to the judicial system, increasing in proportion to the number of potential plaintiffs and defendants. These include the use of test cases, consolidation and joinder of similar parties, mandatory use of precedent in cases involving the same parties (using technical doctrines of *res judicata* and collateral estoppel), multidistrict litigation for claims in federal courts, court-approved settlements, judicial notice of medical facts, and other devices familiar to attorneys.[67]

Whenever a court is invited or tempted to streamline litigation by standardizing one or more elements across cases, either party with a strategic incentive not to cooperate can generally block judicial action by asserting claims requiring individualized findings. By insisting on specific determinations of medical causation, for example, asbestos defendants can require every plaintiff to undergo the expense and delay of providing medical testimony based on personal and statistical data. So far most courts have not been willing to use judicial notice or offensive collateral estoppel to obviate such complex factual burdens on plaintiffs. To do so would require the court to place instrumental goals of procedural efficiency above the individual rights intrinsic to the judicial system.

Considering the enormous legal costs of environmental injury suits, the goal of streamlining the handling of legal claims would appear to be indisputable. Indeed, most commentators on tort policy agree that consolidating entire cases, or at least the central issues of causation and damages, is socially preferable to continued case-by-case adjudication of environmental-injury claims. They agree on this goal, despite differences on whether to achieve it by judicial initiatives, legislative action, or administrative preemption. These options are simply various means toward the same end: to break the common-law pattern of individualized proceedings. According to Francis McGovern:

> The traditional view of litigation as an individualistic, rights-based adjudicatory system dedicated to the compensation of victims . . . in an adversary setting is being challenged by a view of the legal process as a mechanism to further the collective interests of society by centralizing rule making and inquisitorial fact finding to maximize utility.[68]

Although proponents of judicial self-reform have suggested numerous ways creative judging might further these collective interests, the inertia of common law has proved surprisingly strong in the area of environmental accidents. The norm of individualized justice exists on a completely different plane from collective or instrumental purposes, and it continually reasserts its dominance. As long as the very logic of liability presupposes a specific relation between an injured plaintiff and an accountable defendant, lawsuits can generalize only at the risk of undermining their procedural legitimacy. Even in cases involving strict liability, the plaintiff must show a causal connection between the injury and actions by (or imputed to) the defendant.[69] In environmental cases, as we know, that link is intrinsically difficult to prove. Further questions about comparative negligence of the plaintiff and of third parties are raised by complex causal forces in most environmental accidents. Finally, to whatever extent traditional negligence doctrines are restored in the near future, the number of individualized issues in the typical injury suit can only increase.

Political pressure on courts can discourage judicial creativity, further inhibiting their use of formal techniques for consolidating legal questions. For example, many states have recently approved legislation to limit joint and several liability, a leading doctrinal method for combining multiple defendants in a single action. Under this doctrine each defendant can be held responsible for the entire amount of damages, if other defendants are unavailable or unable to contribute.[70] The novel technique used in Sindell v. Abbott Laboratories is likewise a popular target for legislative control.[71] In that case a California plaintiff who could not identify the actual source of her mother's DES prescription was allowed to sue and collect damages from a group of former drug manufacturers and distributers, with the damages apportioned according to each defendant's respective share of the DES market. Even though this approach has been rejected by other courts, the California case is widely cited as a premise for legislative regulation of courts' procedural powers, under both state and federal proposals.[72]

By 1982, in an effort to avert both legislative intervention and judicial paralysis, asbestos defendants and their insurers conceived the ill-fated Asbestos Claims Facility (ACF) as a way to settle claims outside the clogged judicial channels. Although the experiment quickly became the captive project of defendants, its original intent was influenced by the popular U. S. movement for privately organized mediation, sometimes known as *alternative dispute resolution*. The Dean of the Yale Law School, Harry Wellington, was invited to bring the major parties together in a demonstration of group bargaining outside the institutional confines of politics or courts. As Wellington idealistically noted, the project was designed to divert "all but a handful of cases" from litigation.[73] Although technically a rejection of judicial institutions, such attempts at private dispute resolution express the "creative constraint" favored by many advocates of judicial procedures. They are meant to provide a fresh start for individual justice, beyond the inhibiting pressures of legal formalism and uncompromising adversaries.

As with many noble experiments, however, ACF turned out to be a costly failure from the standpoint of all interested groups. Although ACF did oversee the settlement of some 7,000 claims during the years 1982 to 1987, it was gradually overwhelmed by an even greater volume of new claims, added to a backlog of 28,000. Based on limited information released by ACF, it appears that new settlements were both time-consuming and expensive. Administrative costs for the first 5,200 settlements averaged $70,000 per case, or more than double what Johns-Manville and other defendants had spent before 1982. ACF was unable to publish general guidelines for streamlining negotiations until March 1987, and in May 1988 it announced an end to formal operations within six months.[74]

ACF spent most of its six years embroiled in ferocious disputes between asbestos defendants and their insurers over who should pay for awards and processing costs. By 1987, after several major players chose to go separate ways, a fragile agreement on financing was reached by thirty-five asbestos defendants and sixteen insurers.[75] This agreement confirmed the steady drift of the facility toward serving the adversarial interests of its corporate sponsors; after 1987 it became the sole agent of defendants for bargaining with asbestos claimants, exercising exclusive authority over settlements. Even earlier, in the words of the Rand study, ACF became "a device to coordinate the defense side of asbestos claims."[76] Whenever settlement negotiations with individual plaintiffs reached an impasse, ACF was authorized to represent its members in litigation.

For plaintiffs, the invitation to resolve disputes outside the normal judicial channels quickly lost any initial attraction. As mentioned earlier, plaintiffs' attorneys found their interests best served by extending cases through the trial stage, preferably allowing juries to make decisions on compensatory and punitive damages. Their view of ACF gradually hardened: "All we have seen is that the defense legal team has now been made leaner and meaner, and the asbestos manufacturers have assumed a full litigation posture."[77] Whatever their practical needs, claimants who had already invested years in litigation could scarcely afford to sacrifice their chance for spectacular damages; nor could their attorneys.

ACF fell short of its goal to settle claims more quickly, humanely, and cheaply than litigation. There are no indications that plaintiffs were treated more generously in settlement negotiations, following the lengthy delays required for getting ACF established. Ironically, this project for circumventing litigation actually increased adversarial conflict, as ACF became a strategic vehicle for asbestos defendants and their insurers. In addition, the experiment seemed to inspire new forms of litigation that sharpened differences between defendants and claimants, and within the defendant group itself. In 1987 a group of claimants filed an antitrust suit against ACF, which, if successful, would have reopened all settlements and exposed the defendants to triple damages. Meanwhile, disputes among the defendants themselves culminated in a major suit against ACF, which became one of the reasons for its demise. Although a new claims facility could still emerge, each defendant began handling its own legal negotiations soon after the termination announcement was made.[78]

Even if ACF had worked the way its originators intended, we must remember that it first appeared more than a decade after litigation had already produced mountains of factual evidence on the asbestos industry and on asbestos-related diseases. During this time, legal doctrines were actively extended by the judiciary, helping to create a favorable strategic climate for growing legions of claimants. As the Rand report notes:

> In this context, coordinated negotiations primarily involve how much a claim is worth rather than whether it is compensable. In future mass litigation marked by uncertainty over whether claimants can make their cases stick at trial, a claims facility may not be workable, at least not until the potential gains of plaintiffs and defendants, as well as the relative burdens of defendants, have been established through sufficient experience with ordinary litigation.[79]

Private mediation alternatives to litigation thus face a major dilemma in mass injury cases. They cannot arrive on the scene until the courts have enabled a bloc of plaintiffs to overcome the enormous strategic disadvantages of the single claimant relying on probabilistic evidence. Once that bloc has been created, however, mediation loses its attractions for many plaintiffs and their attorneys, for whom litigation remains a goal worth waiting for. The heightened stakes for defendants and their insurers, meanwhile, raise the cost of compromise high enough to encourage internecine litigation over financing. All of these effects contributed to the downfall of ACF.

The fragmentation of interests among defendants was evident at the very inception of ACF, as several asbestos companies decided to pursue a different experiment involving federal bankruptcy laws. This was the strategy followed in 1982 by the largest asbestos defendant, Johns-Manville Corporation. Over the same period when ACF struggled to provide voluntary alternatives to litigation, the bankruptcy court was designing a somewhat comparable, but mandatory, settlement procedure for suits against Johns-Manville. As part of the reorganization plan approved in 1986 and granted at least initial support by an appeals court in 1988, claimants were required to enter into settlement negotiations with Johns-Manville, although they could eventually opt for other forms of mediation, arbitration, or litigation.[80]

The advantage to Johns-Manville—in addition to a six-year moratorium on liability payments—was an apparent outside limit on future liability, backed by the enforcement power of the bankruptcy court. The actual dollar amount in a special Asbestos Health Trust will depend on several variables: funds from Johns-Manville's insurers, the fluctuating value of Johns-Manville stock and other assets, and future profits of the reorganized company. In 1988 the parties estimated that $1.35 billion would be required to compensate approximately 52,000 claimants with an average award of $26,000—a process likely to extend over the next ten years, according to the appeals court.[81]

At least two important factors remained uncertain, however. The litigation option could eventually raise the level of awards beyond the expected average figure, if settlement offers prove unacceptable to claimants. Under the funding formula guaranteed by the court, this would not jeopardize current assets of the company, but would simply extend the period during which Johns-Manville must contribute up to 20 percent of corporate profits. Second, the mandatory settlement procedure was upheld by the appeals court for only those claimants who brought actions prior to 1982. The appeals court specifically declined to rule on the bankruptcy court's power to bar *later* asbestos claimants from initiating lawsuits outside the reorganization agreement.[82] It will clearly take several more years of litigation to test whether these future claims can actually be contained within the bankruptcy court's restrictions.

No systematic study is available to tell us what has happened to victims of asbestos-caused disease over the past fifteen years, while mass litigation choked the judicial process and defendants searched desperately for alternative procedures. The initial impact from Johns-Manville's 1982 action, according to the Rand study, was further "delay and confusion" in the handling of claims that included Johns-Manville as a defendant:

> The bankruptcy filings automatically stayed litigation against the debtor corporations, and the co-defendants argued that the litigation should be stayed against them as well. Appellate courts in every jurisdiction ultimately decided against the non-bankrupt defendants. In the interim, however, *all* cases were initially stayed in all courts for various periods of time.[83]

One immediate effect was an apparent reduction in the settlement value of claims against other defendants, possibly by as much as 30 percent.[84] For claims against Johns-Manville, as already noted, the moratorium on liability lasted for six years. Judicially-inspired alternatives to standard litigation—whatever else one might say about them—are evidently generous with individual claimants' time while the legal system tries to place some limit on defendants' liability.

Some advocates of creative judging, in addition to corporate defendants, have welcomed the new role of bankruptcy courts as a constructive development. Indeed, for David Rosenberg the very broad powers of bankruptcy judges bear an uncanny resemblance to methods he has suggested for the entire tort system.

> The centralized, collective, judicially managed bankruptcy proceedings demonstrate how the tort system's conventional, case-by-case process can be improved. The transaction costs of the case-by-case process are needless. . . . Much of the cost, however, can be eliminated by restructuring the tort system along the managerial and procedural lines followed by the bankruptcy courts. Claims would have to be tried as class actions, in which the particular as well as the common substantive issues would be decided on the basis of sampling and averaging techniques, and damages would be awarded according to specified schedules. Courts would also have to set aside funds to cover future claims.[85]

This was not an accurate forecast of how the Johns-Manville case would end, however. While it is certainly possible that bankruptcy judges can limit the future liability of major corporate defendants, they seem ill-prepared to expedite compensation. In the Johns-Manville case, claims must still be settled or litigated on an individual basis, but now under conditions where defendants have weaker incentives to negotiate in good faith. If nothing else, the passage of time during the moratorium has increased their strategic advantage.

Even though the results have not been so favorable for claimants as the above quotation intimates, the Johns-Manville case nonetheless provides a semblance of Rosenberg's "public-law vision" in actual practice. There is little question that broader judicial powers available under the bankruptcy laws give the judge much of the flexibility that Rosenberg seemed to favor. And as we noted, his primary concern had little to do with compensating victims, but was rather to find an expeditious method of assigning an economically efficient limit to the defendant's liability for environmental accidents. At this point, however, the "vision" becomes an apparition. Nothing in the Johns-Manville case suggests that the trust fund allocation for asbestos injuries represents an economically astute signal for guiding future market decisions on accident prevention.

That fund was the product of heated bargaining among multiple interest groups, shaped by a full decade of litigation under existing common-law rules and procedures. Its precise value, furthermore, depends on the outcome of negotiations between Johns-Manville and its insurers, the fluctuating market worth of various financial assets, and the ongoing health of the reorganized Johns-Manville Corporation. As for future deterrence, companies looking to this complex court agreement will need to project each of these factors onto their own circumstances. We are thus left with a kind of procedural black box, from which no clear signal has emerged for defining a socially optimal rate of investment in accident prevention.

The Heroic Judge: Agent Orange

A bold centrifugal force seems to propel environmental-accident cases away from any coherent nucleus of autonomous rules or self-controlling procedures. As seen by outside observers, the universe of asbestos litigation took on a maddening disorder. Cases quickly ramified beyond the capacity of individual courts to handle claims in a timely way, largely because the issues in each case were ill suited to judicial determination. Once that trend developed, courts were further hampered by inadequate procedural tools for simplifying complexity and controlling quantity. The techniques of doctrinal creativity, class-action suits, and collective findings on issues of facts or damages—all of which may work well enough in other legal contexts—were unable here to reestablish judicial order. Even the novel uses of bankruptcy proceedings and informal dispute settlement have so far only stimulated further litigation.

Judicial systems placed under such difficult circumstances seem to require corrective forces of heroic proportions, something more than doctrines, procedures, and other formal trappings. In these instances judicial self-management sometimes craves action in the guise of courageous judges: it needs individuals who can penetrate the haze of self-serving behavior generated by diverse parties and their lawyers. It needs judges who can cut through procedural forests and doctrinal undergrowth, catching sight once again of fundamental issues, refusing to let them slip away under pressures of time, expense, and adversarial rancor. For those who desperately want the judicial system to regain control over complex litigation, the call eventually goes out for judges themselves to transcend their unassuming common-law roles.[86] Neither fusty logicians nor dreamy philosophers, but practical, tough bargainers are needed to defy the kind of disintegrative patterns seen in the asbestos cases.

The Agent Orange litigation provides us with a clear example of such a judge at the top of his form.[87] Under his control all claims arising from the experiences of up to 2.4 million Vietnam soldiers and their families were successfully held together in a single federal court. Despite a slow beginning to the case, within six months of its reassignment to District Judge Jack B. Weinstein a settlement was reached without trial, binding all defendants and nearly all plaintiffs, including some 240,000 eventual claimants.[88] The settlement amount of $180 million plus interest was, at the time, the largest reached in an environmental-accident case. Approximately 300 additional plaintiffs outside the settlement were in turn handled as a group, costing the court only one more year before all claims were adjudicated. Finally, despite some fifty appeals on highly complex grounds, a single appellate court has sustained all of Judge Weinstein's decisions that effectively bar further trials of past or future claims. By declining to hear any further appeals, the U.S. Supreme Court in 1988 cleared the way for disbursement of funds.[89]

The conditions that enabled such extraordinary control over mass tort litigation are not difficult to find, nor are they likely to be repeated. The essential element was Judge Weinstein's willingness to reject plaintiffs' entire legal argument on grounds that precluded jury trials. This single fact permitted him to coax plaintiffs into a mass settlement, to gain the cooperation of defendants, to cut off plaintiffs who opted out of the class action, and, most important, to insulate most of his decisions from timely appellate review.[90] After the Court of Appeals' sweeping approval of these methods, Judge Weinstein's approach stands as an effective but wildly idiosyncratic formula by which environmental-injury litigation can be brought under judicial stewardship. Paradoxically, this orderliness was obtained at the price of abandoning the central fact-finding processes of trials, leaving the judge

unparalleled discretion to broker a settlement based on his independent views on facts and law. The result also depended on the defendants' willingness to settle these cases based on a realistic assessment
of their nuisance value.

Along with these judicial heroics, the Agent Orange cases offer a
number of distinctive factual and legal aspects. Agent Orange was a
powerful herbicide used by U.S. military forces to defoliate battle
areas in Southeast Asia during the Vietnam war. Its key ingredient was
dioxin, a chemical shown to have toxic effects in animal experiments,
but whose impact on humans is highly controversial. At the time of
litigation, no epidemiological or clinical evidence seemed to connect
dioxin to the cancers and genetic injuries experienced by many of the
veterans who sought compensation—nothing, at least, on the order of
Irving Selikoff's research connecting asbestos with lung cancer, mesothelioma, and asbestosis. Asbestos had been used in quantity since the
1930s, and evidence of diseases with latencies of more than twenty
years had accumulated well before litigation gained strength in the
early 1970s. By contrast, the Agent Orange cases were all dispatched
within twenty years after the first burst of military exposure. Clinical
and epidemiological testing was fostered by the litigation itself, but so
far has not yielded any significant statistical connection between dioxin and the cancers, genetic defects, and other ailments alleged by
veterans.[91]

Manufacturers of Agent Orange worked under contract with the
U.S. military, a fact the Court of Appeals would later use to absolve
them completely of liability to veterans and their families, whatever
the true toxic impact of dioxin. The seven companies involved had
little if anything to do with the way Agent Orange was handled or
stored, or with its military deployment; the use of Agent Orange on
the battlefield was guided by national security interests quite obviously beyond the control of chemical companies. The U.S. government was itself immune from liability, and it was also able to resist
claims for indemnification from the Agent Orange defendants following the settlement agreement.[92] Thus the original litigation over
health effects of Agent Orange could be launched only as a product-
liability case against private parties, even though its symbolic importance had much more to do with the treatment of Vietnam soldiers by
the U.S. government. The judicial system was thus able to hear the
complaint only by analogy with a line of cases going back to the snail in
the bottle of ginger beer.

The litigation began slowly in 1978, as a number of veterans suffering unusual illnesses learned through veterans' organizations about suspected toxic properties of Agent Orange. Schuck provides a full account of the spirit in which claimants first approached the courts: the judicial system was broadly expected to redress a sense of abandonment many returning veterans felt by the late 1970s, abandonment by traditional veterans' groups, the Veterans Administration, and society as a whole.[93] From a legal point of view, cases were initially filed with the expectation of building a unified class of plaintiffs. Attorneys supporting the litigation helped spread the word across the country, hoping to consolidate enough claims to justify the expense of collecting scientific data, extracting information on dioxin health effects from chemical companies and the U.S. government, and publicizing the legal action to reach as many veterans as possible.

Procedurally the cases fell together rather easily. The district court in New York gained jurisdiction over all claims filed anywhere in the country under a federal process known as multidistrict litigation. A class action was also loosely approved, based on the common question of whether Agent Orange was capable of causing plaintiffs' injuries, as well as on other issues raised by relationships between both parties and the U.S. government (with plaintiffs, their military service, and with defendants, government contracts). Unlike asbestos litigation, which sprang up in multiple jurisdictions and produced some early victories for claimants, the Agent Orange cases began in the same place, moved along on the same schedule, and approached each substantive legal issue as a bloc. Seven defendants, meanwhile, were successfully joined in the litigation, despite wide variations in their market share, their knowledge about dioxin health issues, and the dioxin concentrations in their respective products.[94]

The normal procedure under multidistrict litigation is for parties to hold a single trial to determine common legal questions, after which cases are referred to local federal courts across the country for individual findings on liability and damages. It was widely assumed that juries at either stage of this process might have supported the plaintiffs, whose scientific evidence on causation was nonetheless certain to be hotly contested. Thus the only sure way to avoid proliferation of litigation was to keep the case out of the jury's hands from the very beginning.[95] A pretrial settlement between the parties, one binding on as many class members as possible, could neatly avoid the combined centrifugal legal effects of new doctrinal rulings, scattered cases awarding vast damages (including punitive damages), attorneys' preferences for case-by-case litigation, and appealable decisions about applicable legal rules.

When Judge Weinstein entered the case in late 1983, he set his considerable talents to work negotiating just such an agreement. The ingenuity and single-mindedness with which he wrested that settlement are well described in Schuck's book,[96] so we need cover here only the most important points. Weinstein countered the natural tendency for delays by giving the parties a firm trial date that left only six months for collecting documents, depositions, information about plaintiff-class members, and other vital information. He then hired professional mediators to push both sides, despite their internal frictions, toward his vision of a settlement. Fairly early his mediators sensed they were making progress, and thus Weinstein dramatically summoned the parties to attend separate conferences with him on the eve of trial, treating the whole matter like labor-management negotiations.

To the defendants, Weinstein emphasized the risk of facing a jury trial on the central question of causation.[97] No matter how weak the scientific evidence against Agent Orange might be, a jury decision for the plaintiffs was clearly not impossible. Even nominal damages against such a large class (by then almost 100,000 people were listed in the Agent Orange Registry) could quickly reach hundreds of millions of dollars, on top of astronomical legal costs. It thus became thinkable that defendants should settle for an amount roughly equal to their prospective legal costs, provided they could gain assurances that all future legal proceedings against them would be barred.

To plaintiffs Weinstein was practically dictatorial.[98] He let their attorneys know his personal view that their scientific case was essentially without merit, and he even broadly suggested he might enter judgment against them (as he would have the power to do) notwithstanding a favorable jury verdict. He made sure they knew that the defendants were prepared to settle for around $180 million, and allowed them to contemplate the gamble that they could lose it all, plus additional legal expenses, by proceeding to trial. Weinstein also had wide discretion over the awarding of attorneys' fees and knew that plaintiffs' attorneys had advanced their own funds to help finance the whole action.

Weinstein further enhanced his discretionary powers by avoiding any definitive pretrial rulings, thus precluding possible appeals on such legal matters as the liability of the U.S. government. But the settlement itself was his strongest insulation from appellate review. Following the agreement, reached at 3:00 A.M. on the morning the trial had been scheduled to begin, Weinstein spent several months conducting a further inquiry to certify the "fairness" of the settlement that he himself had virtually written.[99] The appellate court would be interested only in seeing that some very broad standard of fairness was achieved. "So much respect is accorded the opinion of the trial court in these matters that this court will intervene in a judicially approved settlement only when objectors to that settlement have made a clear showing that the District Court has abused its discretion."[100]

While defendants congratulated their attorneys and felt they had purchased their protection from future lawsuits for around "ten cents on the dollar,"[101] veterans groups were stunned and hurt by the negotiated end to what they had anticipated as their day in court. The fractious ranks of plaintiffs' attorneys traded recriminations, becoming embroiled in new disputes about the precise distribution formula they would need to propose to Judge Weinstein. But such divisiveness could have no impact on future litigation of claims, once the settlement was signed and the appeals court found nothing amiss.

From the standpoint of keeping the lid on litigation, Weinstein's accomplishment was (and remains) unparalleled. But other than conserving the resources of the judicial system, what criteria might properly be applied to measure the appropriateness of his solution?[102] As Weinstein himself emphasized, the lack of clear scientific evidence linking dioxin to the long litany of veterans' complaints made their case without merit, from a *legal* point of view.[103] Thus we might overlook the inadequacy of the $180 million (plus interest) settlement, which upon disbursement would be broken up into awards of no more than $12,000 for disability and about $3,400 for death benefits—figures no asbestos plaintiff would reasonably accept. Unless the plaintiffs can carry their burden of proof on causation, defendants owe them nothing whatsoever under the obligations of tort law. Rather than opening the door to years of costly litigation, leading to the same inconsistent and lurching results seen in the asbestos cases, Weinstein might rightly feel that this was about all the veterans as a group could expect to get out of their fragile case. After all, as he noted, "'the government must be considered the source of ultimate protection whether or not' causation was ultimately proved, because of its responsibility for the Vietnam war and for the disproportionate burdens it had obliged the veterans and their families to bear."[104]

Schuck and others raise important objections to Weinstein's approach, both in coercing the parties into settlement, and in his questionable rulings against those plaintiffs who opted out of the original class action and against family members trying to win damages from either the chemical corporations or the U.S. government.[105] Indeed, from a judicial standpoint we can certainly fault the judge's methods in these latter cases, which were decided summarily against all plaintiffs on grounds that precluded a trial on the factual issues of causation. Weinstein characterized plaintiffs' proposed evidence in these cases as insufficient or unconvincing—dubious grounds indeed for resolving a case on pure judicial authority prior to any trial. The Court of Appeals carefully avoided reviewing Judge Weinstein's rulings on these matters, choosing to uphold his decision on the separate grounds that plaintiffs would be barred, for legal reasons, from recovering against either the armed forces or military contractors.[106] One could argue that at least the military-contractor defense issue should have been put before a jury, but the appeals court advised great caution in liability actions related to the military. Both the liberal Judge Weinstein and the conservative Judge Winter on the Court of Appeals thus found common ground in keeping this whole matter from entering the unpredictable world of trials, juries, and damages.

Conclusion: Dilemmas of Judicial Self-Regulation

The intellectual drift in tort-law criticism over the past twenty years has been toward economic instrumentalism, replacing the progressive critics' emphasis on redistribution with the ostensibly more neutral values of efficiency. This trend has been reinforced politically by the coalescing of corporate interests in slowing the judicial trend toward strict liability doctrines in product-injury cases. The vaccine experience shows how market distortions can result from expanding liability rules, and also how the political leverage of producers and their insurers can win selective relief from tort law through federal intervention.

Environmental accidents have added substantial new doubts about the judicial system's ability to operate efficiently. Massive administrative costs incurred in the decade-long asbestos litigation suggest that a preoccupation with individual justice may undermine the system's very capacity to function. The large number of related cases also reveals a disturbingly erratic pattern of damages flowing from trials and settlements. The costs of litigation for corporate defendants have already provoked several well-publicized bankruptcies, leaving open the question of how future large-scale compensation should be funded. Disputes between asbestos defendants and their private insurers have underlined the problems of providing stable financing for uncertain but expanding categories of compensable injuries.

Above all, the asbestos cases sharpen the conflict between instrumental measures of tort law and the internal mystique of individual justice. Despite the high costs of environmental-injury litigation, a generalized social concern with conserving resources is foreign to the case-by-case value framework of judicial action. As Judith Resnick points out, even though litigation may seem expensive at an aggregate level, we can always ask the question, Expensive for whom?

> Both parties have higher litigation expenses if a case goes to trial. On the other hand, when plaintiff recovers more at trial than defendant offered at settlement and the difference is greater than the various costs of litigation, trial has become profitable for plaintiff— and much more "expensive" for defendant. [107]

The economic costs of litigation can easily become elements in the strategic battle between the parties (and among their attorneys), regulated only by the judicial system's internal ideal of individual justice. By definition, that ideal has no instrumental value reducible to monetary terms.

Looking to the judicial system to supply its own solution to this dilemma between internal and instrumental values, there seems little hope that creative judging alone will prove effective. Many of the customary aggregative tools, such as class actions and managerial judging, are more at home in civil-rights law, where the social purposes of litigation flow directly from procedural values internal to judicial processes. But no such natural harmony promotes coherence in mass-accident suits, where self-interest of both the individual victim and the defendant may diverge from an independent social interest in reducing litigation costs.

If either heroic judging or judicial restructuring were nonetheless powerful enough to hold down litigation costs in environmental-accident cases, it could spell the defeat of individual justice. This is our conclusion from both Judge Weinstein's resolution of Agent Orange claims and Rosenberg's proposal for collectivized judicial proceedings. Both are useful demonstrations of the degree to which common-law principles must be suspended to keep mass accident cases from proliferating beyond judicial control. They are also dramatic examples of Twerski's paradoxical notion of creative constraint—in which preserving judicial authority from external encroachment becomes virtually an end in itself.

Both Weinstein's managerial tour de force and Rosenberg's theoretical exercises suggest that, at best, only limited collective goals can be served by strengthened judicial procedures, even after individualized judging has been abandoned. Merely preserving judicial autonomy by reducing litigation costs is perhaps all that can be hoped for. Observed from any broader perspective, the Agent Orange settlement is an opaque precedent for future mass-accident cases. Because of unresolved doubts about dioxin health effects, it is difficult to interpret the $180 million in that settlement as either a just form of compensating victims or an efficient imposition of costs on producers. Neither compensation nor accountability concerns were accomplished by consolidating these proceedings, nor would any more have been accomplished through individualized litigation. All that stands out from this case is a new set of bargaining dynamics that plaintiffs and defendants will have to keep in mind for future battles.

Rosenberg's approach, meanwhile, abandons any claim to providing a social response to compensation needs. His treatment of accountability is limited to reconstructing the judicial process consistent with general deterrence theory. But general deterrence leaves too much to the imagination: it presupposes that society already has an effective political and distributive economic framework. It is therefore not a sufficient goal on which to base a strategy of social engineering, even if, as a practical matter, judicial institutions could be rebuilt according to Rosenberg's design.

Since political institutions must eventually become an integral part of any social policy for compensation and accountability, how fiercely should we fight to preserve the front-line role of judicial processes in accidental injury cases? Rosenberg's initial answer, as we saw, was based on the fear that political institutions are more likely to be influenced by short-term strategic conflicts of interested parties. But the judicial process is likewise open to substantial internal pressures; even if we could find a way to curb individual lawsuits, the larger dynamics of litigation are neither impersonal nor mechanical. The kinds of strategic conflicts Rosenberg projects in political settings would remain present in the skillful manipulation of judicial procedures to block outcomes unfavorable to either side, or in attempts to sway the judge's discretionary powers. Even with a judge of such unparalleled brilliance and integrity as Judge Weinstein, the managerial role can make no greater claim to objectivity than what we find in conflict-ridden political processes.

More recently, Rosenberg has offered a different rationale for preserving the judicial system as the primary response to accidental injury. Commenting on the asbestos litigation, he endorses Paul Brodeur's praise for tort law as a means of uncovering corporate disregard for adverse health effects: "Brodeur's narrative establishes successfully . . . that the tort system emerged as *the* uniquely effective and indispensable means of exposing and defeating the asbestos conspiracy, providing compensation to victims, and deterring future malfeasance."

> The tort system was and remains the only institution capable of bringing justice to diseased workers. . . . It is impossible to deny the relative virtues of the tort system: it operates on the basis of private incentives largely immune to political control and financial co-optation; it hunts for every useful scrap of material evidence; it calls upon the opinions of the most knowledgable experts rather than relying on bureaucratic time-servers; and it values human life beyond monetary losses.
>
> The adversarial process performs a valuable function in allowing individual victims—and the public, vicariously—an opportunity to confront large social institutions, express moral indignation, and achieve clear-cut vindication of rights.[108]

A comparable report card for the Agent Orange litigation would come up with entirely different marks. The fact that scientific evidence has not linked dioxin to disease in the manner of early asbestos research does not change matters, since we are not entitled to draw any conclusion whatsoever from negative medical findings. The tort system had almost nothing to do with continued investigation of dioxin toxicity once the Agent Orange litigation was settled. We should remember that asbestos cases were being litigated without success as early as the 1930s. It was only when Irving Selikoff's research became available by the late 1960s, coinciding with the peak of judicial doctrinal activism, that plaintiffs began to win a few victories.[109] After more than fifteen years of confused judicial stewardship, the asbestos cases now seem a long way from accomplishing goals of compensation and accountability, for which Rosenberg gives the tort system full marks.

Rosenberg's last paragraph (cited above) provides an important insight into contemporary sentiment for judicial self-management; these remarks borrow the rhetoric of civil-rights battles against insensitive bureaucracies. And indeed Rosenberg is correct when he says that some current legislation is animated by a "powerful movement, financed by industry, to dismantle the tort system."[110] But unlike civil-rights litigation, where judicial institutions are sometimes deemed to have special expertise in defining intangible procedural values, there is every reason to fear that continued judicial mismanagement of accidental injuries will only quicken the pace of legislative intervention.

Tort law is too weak to control its own administrative costs without undermining the traditional core values of individual justice. As for instrumental goals of compensation and accountability, even tort law's best efforts to view problems collectively would require considerable support from political institutions. The threat is not political involvement as such, but politics forced through the individualizing categories of tort law, motivating the parties for still further strategic maneuvering within the judicial structure. After looking at this type of legislation in Chapter 7, we will go on to discuss other political solutions that depart more radically from the judicial perspective on accidental injury.

Chapter 7

Tort Law Under Legislative Review

Legislation unquestionably generates legislation . . . , and only time and opportunity can decide whether its offspring will bring it honor or shame. Once begin the dance of legislation, and you must struggle through its mazes as best you can to its breathless end,—if any end there be.[1]

Can Statutory Oversight Make the Crisis Disappear?

Hand wringing over the "tort crisis" has assumed the same ritual function in the United States as complaining about "the mess in Washington." Most people, in fact, seem to allow that the judicial system handles accident cases poorly, but there is little agreement on the criteria of good performance. Lobbyists and attorneys for plaintiff groups, for example, maintain that even the latest tort doctrines stifle worthy compensation claims. They strongly oppose legislation to limit plaintiffs' new-found rights to compensation, and they deflect blame onto the insurance industry for increasing liability insurance costs.[2]

    Quite another view of the crisis has been gathering strength since the early 1970s among professional groups, business corporations, and their insurers—all in response to liability patterns for medical malpractice and product injuries.[3] Some defendants still join with plaintiffs' attorneys in blaming the insurance industry for overreacting to judicial trends, a charge with some plausibility despite strong industry denials.[4] By the mid 1980s, however, defendants were impressively united in seeking unprecedented legislative intervention in state judicial systems. Their battle cry of "tort reform" supplies a deceptively neutral label for what has become a major political campaign.[5] The

191

proposed statutory changes—some already enacted by the states themselves, others awaiting possible federal action—represent an historic challenge to tort law's virtual autonomy as well as its dominant tendency over the past century. What has been accurately perceived (and frequently overstated[6]) as a pro-plaintiff drift in common-law doctrines and procedures would yield to legislation seeking to halt or even reverse that trend.

Political movements often feed ambitious hopes for statutory solutions, but the eventual results of product-liability reform will probably fail to satisfy defendants seeking relief from unpalatable judicial rulings. The desire to return to a simpler life before liability became a burden is understandable for those who feel mistreated by the judicial process, but waving the statutory wand will not make it come true. As we shall argue, there is little prospect for reducing the costs or the inconsistencies now identified with accident litigation, so long as courts remain the chosen process of administration—no matter which liability rules are favored. Imposing negligence standards as part of a statutory regime would invite particular confusion, given the long tradition of judicial creativity in construing doctrinal language. Under pressure of growing liability claims, especially those stemming from environmental accidents, the campaign to fine-tune tort law by legislation may only magnify its intrinsic weaknesses, hastening the eventual call for more fundamental changes.

Statutory oversight of tort law is perhaps long overdue. Over the past century, every other field of common law has been invaded by legislation, in accord with the instrumentalist spirit of our age.[7] Only the political resistance of trial lawyers has held it back, and even that is beginning to weaken. The crisis over product liability can thus be seen as an opportunity for change that seems destined to occur. And even though new legislation almost surely will heighten the immediate agonies of that crisis, it may also point the way to more radical solutions. Once judicial *doctrines* are placed under legislative scrutiny, it is only a matter of time before the entire judicial *process* is measured against alternative systems. As we will see, both political bargaining and constitutional issues play a role in shifting the reform focus from doctrines to processes, but it is mainly the unavoidable costs and inequities of the judicial system that bring it under sharper scrutiny.

We will begin by reviewing state efforts to control certain remedial powers of courts—the first tentative steps in a legislative dance, the developing variations of which are traced in succeeding sections and chapters. Moving to the federal level, we shall explore the prospects for more unified and far-reaching changes as foretold in tort-reform bills debated by Congress. It is here we encounter growing doubts about the judicial system's capacity to meet the diverse expectations of interest groups, culminating in recent drafts proposing a special claims procedure as an alternative to litigation.[8] That debate provides the occasion for a broader look at two-tiered procedures offering parties a choice between settlement and litigation.

Most proponents of procedural options assume that a stable equilibrium can be reached between tort litigation and some administrative alternative. We will end by questioning that assumption, arguing that the internal dynamics of both processes would direct the energies and resources of litigants back toward the judicial process. Nevertheless, once the political system takes responsibility for the outcomes of accident litigation—the basic premise of current tort reform—its stake in more efficient procedures may eventually cause a shift back to administrative schemes. As we shall explore more fully in Chapters 8 and 9, the special pressures of environmental injuries will only accelerate that search for institutional alternatives to judicial procedures.

Tort Reform at the State Level: Controlling Judicial Creativity

A wave of tort-reform sentiment in the mid 1970s produced significant state legislation responding to medical malpractice issues.[9] The approach differed from that used in earlier "crises" of the tort system, which saw the creation of workers' compensation schemes[10] and no-fault automobile accident plans.[11] From an institutional standpoint those earlier programs seem more ambitious than current proposals: they suspended tort jurisdiction over certain types of accidents and substituted entirely new administrative procedures (workers' compensation) or mandatory first-person insurance requirements (no-fault automobile plans). But beyond making these selective exclusions, legislatures took no role in dictating liability doctrines or remedies used by courts in cases still under their jurisdiction. By contrast, recent proposals have sought to conserve the basic tort system by placing its rule structure under direct statutory authority. What initially looks like incremental change may thus prove more radical than prior legislation by reaching to the very foundations of the tort system.[12]

The recent trend toward legislative control draws inspiration from popular theories about the nature of the current tort crisis. Where earlier crises focused on either victim compensation or administrative costs of the tort system, the latest debate highlights excessive burdens placed on defendants, particularly the high costs of insurance. Eli Bernzweig noted this pattern in the legislative response to medical malpractice during the 1970s, which gave more emphasis to trimming tort doctrines than to improving the quality of medical services. The problem of uncompensated medical injuries had been clearly documented in 1973 by a federal government study, which urged the states both to regulate the quality of health care and to consider more effective compensation remedies than those provided under tort law.[13] However, "when the legislative onslaught began, very few states saw fit to address the basic problem of health system quality controls."[14] Bernzweig cites Paul Starr's analysis of how organized interest groups can exploit the sudden appearance of a "tort crisis":

> A crisis can be a truly marvelous mechanism for the withdrawal or suspension of established rights, and the acquisition and legitimation of new privileges. . . . Some groups are better positioned than others to promote their conception of events and to enlarge their discomforts into social concerns. This is the case with the malpractice crisis. It is the malpractice problems of physicians and insurers, rather than those of patients, that now constitute a crisis. This is a reflection not so much of the relative seriousness of their difficulties as of their relative power to turn private into public troubles.[15]

From a political standpoint, the malpractice episode alerted tort critics to the possible decline of trial lawyers' traditional dominance in state legislatures, opening the way for broader statutory action. During the 1970s more than forty states passed medical malpractice laws modifying some aspect of tort remedies or procedures, including statutory limits on damages, shorter statutes of limitations, limits to the collateral-source rule, regulation of contingent fees, limits on punitive damages awards, and the mandatory use of arbitration or screening panels.[16] By the 1980s the field of product liability seemed poised for these and stronger interventions, including a doctrinal retreat from strict liability to the traditional fault system.

Tort law faces not only a statutory challenge, but the further prospect that change will be imposed at the federal level. The Reagan administration and sizable blocs in Congress have supported broad legislation to preempt much of state common law, relying on the supremacy clause of the U.S. Constitution. Although tort-reform forces narrowly lost a major Senate battle in 1986,[17] the momentum in favor of federal action has gained impressive strength. It is also at the federal level that we can expect the most ambitious proposals for alternatives to the judicial process.

Certainly, those groups who feel themselves badly treated by judicial activism over the past two decades have little to lose by shifting their energies to the legislature, where their legal-defense budgets can doubtless be put to more effective use. Their announced objective is to put an end to the legal uncertainty created by innovative judicial decisions, an effect allegedly magnified as the insurance industry continually adjusts premium costs.[18] But relieving uncertainty is not the primary goal; we could, after all, put an end to uncertainty by consolidating the pro-plaintiff trends of the past two decades. So far that idea has not received much attention from reform advocates, whose true interests lie in reducing the financial burdens on defendants.

Three distinct legislative strategies have been advanced for meeting this goal. The first, now being actively pursued by the states, seeks to control the courts' remedial powers and to revise statutes of limitations. The most common limits on remedies respond to the notorious court initiatives of the 1970s: they seek limits on damages for pain and suffering (along with other forms of noneconomic loss), restrictions on punitive damages, an end to joint and several liability (the deep-pocket rule that makes any one defendant liable for harm caused by multiple actors), and the strengthening of the collateral source rule (which reduces the plaintiff's damages when payments are received from other sources, like workers' compensation or social security).[19] Two other reform strategies are best seen in connection with federal legislation, and will be discussed later on in this chapter: statutory revision of liability doctrines (the return to fault) and administrative alternatives to the judicial process.

No one can predict how effective any of these strategies may be. Most reformers obviously expect that restrictions on the courts' remedial powers will reduce the number and size of compensation awards, thereby reducing the financial burdens on defendants. But other forces beyond the control of legislation could counteract such results; the major issue is whether any subtractions from the ranks of plaintiffs will be offset by increased numbers of accident victims submitting legal claims. The net impact on defendants, no matter what package of reforms may be passed by a legislature, depends on these opposing pressures.

A recent empirical study of medical malpractice liability trends over the past decade suggests that relief for product liability defendants may prove elusive. Danzon's research shows that both the number of claims and the average size of malpractice awards did, in fact, level off briefly, following a spate of legislation in the 1970s that restricted courts' remedial powers. By the early 1980s, however, both indicators resumed their climb at rates comparable to those preceding legislation.[20] Danzon argues that this net growth comes from the large pool of uncompensated (but negligently caused) medical injuries that have previously failed to reach the judicial forum. According to her estimates, one out of every five such injuries now enters the system, whereas in the early 1970s it was only one out of ten.[21] Even under less accommodating liability rules, in other words, the burdens on defendants continue to grow.

No comparable estimates of uncompensated product injuries are available, partly because any definition of *injury* would need to address the category we have called *environmental accidents*. There is an obvious trap in basing estimates of this pool on formal legal definitions of compensable injuries, whether past, present, or future; in a judicial process such concepts are never self-executing. By any definition, however, the ranks of active plaintiffs will probably keep growing, assuming that current social perceptions of causation and responsibility have been influenced deeply by judicial trends of the past decades, along with recent awareness of environmental sources of personal injury. Danzon's research found that the claimant's "expected net payoff" in suing played a central role in the steady growth of medical malpractice claims filed over the past decade.[22] More important than legislation in shaping the attitudes of potential plaintiffs is the way tort standards (new or old) are interpreted by the courts. Whether tort reform can meet its goals thus depends on the degree of certainty and stability we can expect from the judicial process, even though stability itself is not the final objective.

Tort reformers focus on the problem of legal uncertainty with special persistence, blaming judicial creativity for complicating the insurance industry's rate-making practices that compound the true costs of liability.[23] These critics generally attribute uncertainty to formal changes in doctrine rather than to judicial administration as such. This explains why tort legislation at both state and federal levels displays such spectacular confidence in judicial powers to achieve uniformity of outcomes, despite the courts' case-by-case review of complex factual and legal issues.[24] No doubt there are strong elements of myth and wishful thinking wrapped up in this position; if we sing the praises of the traditional tort system long enough, that tune may shed its harmonic dissonances. We must remember, however, that under formal standards of adjudication uniformity is *procedural* only. The advocates of tort reform are looking for uniformity of *outcomes*, an instrumental measure affected by uncontrolled external factors impinging on litigation.

There are excellent reasons to expect that judicial administration will produce nonuniform results no matter how much doctrinal rigidity is mandated by legislation.[25] Applying complex doctrines to individual facts is merely the beginning of the judicial art; beyond lie vast areas of procedural discretion, along with formidable techniques of doctrinal interpretation. We can only assume that, over time, these standard features of judicial administration will generate highly unpredictable results. Current doctrines of strict liability, for example, were built mainly on such subtle extensions of traditional tort and contract principles, and divergent results were visited on defendants well before the courts gained sufficient courage to pin new doctrinal labels on their creations. To be sure, legislation proscribing specific doctrines, such as liability for failure to warn and for design defects, would alter judicial discourse; but the immediate or long-term impact need not be uniform. The same outcomes reached by doctrinal innovations can often be sustained on alternative grounds, using either older rules or newly created doctrines.[26] A judiciary in the habit of accommodating plaintiffs should have no trouble finding new paths to similar ends.[27]

Guido Calabresi has offered several reasons why courts ought to play a more active role in the construction of statutes, arguing that in some instances they should have the same flexibility they enjoy in applying common-law principles. Moving with obvious caution and disavowing any promiscuous use of judicial powers in defiance of legislative majorities, Calabresi nonetheless believes that, in some areas of the law, a court should decide

when a rule has come to be sufficiently out of phase with the whole legal framework . . . it can only stand if a current majoritarian or representative body reaffirms it. It is to be the allocator of that burden of inertia which our system of separation of powers and checks and balances mandates. . . . It is this task (so like that exercised by courts in updating the common law) which desperately needs doing in a checked and balanced statutory world like ours, and it can be done by courts using traditional judicial methods and modes of reasoning.[28]

Calabresi is not completely clear which statutes he has in mind. Much of his theory is developed in general terms that presume widespread statutory obsolescence, but the mere passage of time does not seem to be the critical factor. He obviously means to include statutes passed during periods of "crises—real or imagined—engendered by rapidly changing technologies and ideologies," among which he lists recent medical malpractice and product liability legislation.[29] These and other statutes "at war with the then prevailing legal fabric" would seem especially ripe for broad judicial interpretation, under Calabresi's approach—and in the shortest of long-runs.[30]

All that is needed to destroy uniformity is *some* judges willing to follow a creative path.[31] Moreover, under fifty state systems (with laws interpreted simultaneously by both state and federal judges), discrepancies across jurisdictions would impede the degree of national uniformity deemed essential to protecting corporations and insurers with nationwide scope.[32] It is clear from recent litigation over environmental accidents that maverick opinions embolden new claimants and their attorneys to test the judicial system at every vulnerable point. Where a potentially large number of cases are circumstantially traced to a common substance—the pattern defining environmental accidents—attorneys, clients, and the general public are suddenly more aware of apparent inconsistencies in judicial treatment of accident cases. And as more plaintiffs enter the system, there arise new opportunities for variations in an expanding cycle.[33] As we saw earlier, the entry of new plaintiffs into the judicial system can eventually defeat the real objective of tort reform: to reduce the net financial burdens on defendants and their insurers.

Finally, we note that states are embarking on this statutory revolution at different times and with different doctrinal configurations, each in response to political bargaining over the many dozens of legal points that hold strategic importance between plaintiffs and defendants.[34] As Calabresi points out, any sudden legislative reversal of a consistent common-law trend is likely, in itself, to shatter uniformity, as was arguably the result of state no-fault automobile liability statutes in the early 1970s.[35] This problem was anticipated in the late 1970s by the federal Interagency Task Force on Product Liability, which raised the idea of a uniform product liability statute to be adopted by each state.[36] Even the task force, however, echoed the doubts voiced by a companion study that uniform statutes could ultimately avoid deviations based on selective drafting, amendments, and subsequent judicial interpretation.[37] And in fact, commentators on another campaign to impose statutory order on common law—the thirty-year drive toward state adoption of a Uniform Commercial Code—have documented that decline from uniformity over time, mostly as a result of judicial interpretation.[38]

Federal Legislation: Stalemate Over Liability Doctrines

Most tort reformers now acknowledge the limitations of state remedies and press for national legislation, hoping to overcome political and constitutional obstacles that earlier defeated national standards for no-fault automobile plans and medical malpractice.[39] In seeking to unify substantive reforms more effectively than uniform statutes, federal action would conserve political energy and limit constitutional challenges.

In the mid 1980s, advocates of tort legislation also hoped to use the special power of federal statutes to launch a new reform strategy—different from the no-fault procedural reforms of the 1970s, and going beyond state laws placing selective limitations on courts' remedial powers. This bolder strategy called for a direct attack on strict liability by reintroducing elements of the traditional fault doctrine, extending once more to defendants the protections offered by standards of reasonable prudence and proximate cause, as well as several affirmative defenses. By adding these reforms to others aimed at court jurisdiction and remedies—such matters as statutes of limitations, punitive damages, joint and several liability, and the collateral-source rule—this new legislative model covered virtually the entire wish list of the most ardent tort reformer. In fact the first bill of this type, introduced in 1982, anticipated the ambitious program later endorsed by former Attorney General Meese's Tort Policy Working Group in its 1986 and 1987 reports.[40]

Even this first bill, however, was a product of compromise between opposing interests, and as the legislative debate unfolded over the next five years its pro-defendant bias was steadily diluted under pressure from powerful plaintiffs' groups. After four major revisions, indeed, there was nothing left of doctrinal reform, and even defendants apparently decided to channel their energies into the elusive search for administrative alternatives.

The campaign for federal liability policy started with a massive study carried out by the federal Interagency Task Force on Product Liability, whose final report appeared in 1978.[41] That study explored the complex relationship between an expanding common law and insurance industry practices in creating the product liability crisis of the mid 1970s. In contrast to the Attorney General's Tort Policy Working Group in the mid 1980s, the task force did *not* blame the crisis on activist judges; at least equal responsibility was assigned to the insurance industry and to the larger fact that, in a technologically advanced society, consumers and workers pay a substantial toll in personal injuries.[42]

This assessment of the compensation problem—recognizing both the number of product injuries and their close connection with socioeconomic trends—led the task force into lengthy consideration of alternative compensation procedures to tort law. Inspired by this analysis, one early draft bill would have established a national mandatory arbitration scheme for product-related accidents, while another would have made the federal government the insurer of last resort.[43] Of course, these plans were not primarily motivated by tender concern for injured plaintiffs, but more by alarm over the documented administrative costs of tort litigation. The product liability problem was thus briefly situated in the same reform environment as no-fault automobile accident schemes.

But the political climate was shifting in the late 1970s, and Congress was clearly reluctant to impose major institutional changes in an area of private law, especially one so rich with potential financial obligations. Notwithstanding the continuing burdens of liability, major public criticisms of tort *procedures* were suddenly muted.[44] Economic theories reconciling an idealized tort law with market institutions helped justify this change in reform strategy, and the growing popularity of analytical moral philosophy did nothing to hurt it.[45] Both bodies of academic lore were available throughout the 1970s, but their skeptical orientations to political action suddenly matched the political mood that greeted the Reagan era.

For whatever reasons, the private-law procedures of the tort system ceased for a time to be direct targets of legislation. The new strategy began by urging states to adopt the Uniform Product Liability statute published by the Commerce Department in 1978,[46] but reformers quickly surmised that state action alone would probably not help (and might even hurt) the campaign to lower defendants' insurance costs. Instead, in a stunning reversal of the Reagan administration's conventional wisdom on "federalism," there began a drive to federalize tort law starting with the pro-defendant model of the uniform statute.[47] During 1982 the first such bill was introduced in the Senate and was reported favorably out of the Commerce Committee.[48] In the previous year, insurance industry regulation had been addressed in modest fashion by a new federal law permitting corporations and other groups to establish their own insurance-risk pools.[49]

Four separate Congresses have wrestled with successive versions of the 1982 national product liability bill, generating volumes of testimony from partisan interests, attorneys and judges, and the academic community.[50] Given the dozens of strategic angles surrounding tort doctrines and their impact, it is scarcely surprising that "political horse trading"[51] accompanied every stage of this process. The most important shift came during the final summer of the Ninety-ninth Congress, when Commerce Committee supporters abandoned the effort to change liability doctrines. They proposed instead an uncertain mixture of reforms aimed at courts' jurisdictional and remedial powers, alongside an administrative scheme designed to divert most product liability claims from the judicial system. That procedure will be discussed along with related models in the next section, but we simply note here that its sudden appearance was at least a faint reminder of the no-fault approaches of the 1970s.

The sequence of bills leading up to 1986 reveals a shifting series of compromises between the presumed strategic interests of plaintiffs and defendants, covering dozens of doctrinal and remedial powers. It can scarcely comfort the advocates of tort reform that plaintiffs' interests gradually gained strength between 1982 and 1986, even though the final bill retained a number of provisions strongly desired by defendants. If the intense bargaining over statutory drafts is any indication of how legislatures and courts would further adjust an eventual statute, we can appreciate the enormous odds against achieving a uniform and stable body of liability rules.

Even the earliest bills avoided a complete repudiation of strict liability principles.[52] They would have confined the return of negligence to two important categories of manufacturer liability: cases involving design defects and the duty to warn. At the same time these bills would have strengthened at least three affirmative defenses, including a version of the "state of the art" defense, plus the arguments that a product was "unavoidably dangerous" and that its dangers were obvious to the ordinary user.[53] Each of these doctrinal standards was really only a lid sitting atop a bin full of legal complexities; we can sort through each bin and find dozens of points on which courts have built further substantive or procedural distinctions. Only a small number of subordinate issues were ever addressed in these bills, the rest being specifically left to state judicial interpretation.

In addition to liability doctrines these bills also addressed judicial procedures—in common with state legislation. These sections remained part of the 1986 bill (S. 2760) in attenuated form, representing both symbolic victories for the tort reformers and real-life changes, the ultimate impact of which would be difficult to predict. The compromise over statutes of limitations is a good illustration of how the bargaining has worked out. The time period for bringing a tort claim would have become more favorable to plaintiffs (in comparison with many state laws) by incorporating the *discovery rule*, which starts the limitations period only after a claimant learns (or should have learned) of an injury, not when the injury was actually caused.[54] But the bill also imposed the presumption that products lose their ability to cause harm ten years after leaving the manufacturer. The factual and strategic burdens thus placed on plaintiffs, especially important in environmental cases, were the apparent price extracted for adopting the discovery rule.

Punitive damages were another disputed topic, which in earlier drafts had been subject to monetary limits although never eliminated completely. In S. 2760 punitive damages were permitted only if a claimant could show willful negligence by the *clear and convincing* standard of evidence. That standard, although appearing less favorable to plaintiffs than mere *preponderance of the evidence*, still leaves enormous room for juries to assess damages, while increasing the powers of appellate courts to revise awards selectively.[55] For both limitations and punitive damages, in other words, the real impact of statutory change would have depended heavily on later judicial implementation. It would seem that the bargaining over S. 2760 produced compromises that carefully avoided any appearance of clear victories or defeats for either side, but only at the cost of ensuring future instability and uncertainty.

In a similar give and take, S. 2760 avoided outright repeal of the joint-and-several liability approach, but also made it more likely that defendants could at least trim their losses.[56] Juries awarding non-economic damages would have been required to apportion those damages across multiple defendants according to their comparative responsibility, even though the main judgment might well have been reached under a strict liability standard.[57] Thus one more contentious issue was compromised under a solution that imposes unique and costly burdens on the judicial process. Earlier drafts would have brought the plaintiff into the same calculation of comparative responsibility: by imposing a *pure* comparative negligence standard on the states, such statutes would have eliminated all remaining traces of the old common-law contributory negligence theory, but only in return for giving fault concepts a permanent foothold in the process of apportioning damages.[58]

Finally, S. 2760 avoided explicit adoption of a collateral source rule, but it gave defendants much the same relief for workplace accidents by barring the victim's employer from seeking reimbursement for workers' compensation benefits.[59] In this case, the cost of compromise was displaced onto a group not directly represented in the statutory bargaining process.

There is little point in wading through the putative merits of these doctrinal controversies. Litigants and their lawyers have been debating them for generations, and their arguments were fully aired in the volumes of printed hearings.[60] This summary is only meant to illustrate the level of grim bargaining that accompanies the scramble for a unified doctrinal statement of tort law—one favorable to defendants but still acceptable to national politicians. None of the compromises reached in S. 2760 should be seen as clear choices between neatly opposing positions; each one merely locates a point (or perhaps a region) along some wide doctrinal continuum. Just as the drafters of successive bills have been swept back and forth along those continua by political winds, so will future legislative draftors be pressured to make other marginal adjustments—a process likely to continue even after some version of federal product liability law should eventually clear the Congress.

In addition, any state or federal court interpreting these provisions in an approved statute could expand along the same wide continua, not only by construing statutory language but also by skillfully matching words to facts. One may assume, for instance, that any national law of torts requiring courts to base liability on proximate cause has not yet found a secure path to certainty and uniformity.[61] Reinstating this doctrine was simply one more way to give back to defendants—at least for the short run—something that they had lost in many jurisdictions; and perhaps that vague advantage was worth the political struggle. Indeed the very exercise of drafting a national body of tort law requires lobbying groups to translate their most minute and ephemeral interests into resonant doctrinal language. For lobbyists who are also lawyers, that task is remarkably similar to and perhaps less demanding than everyday advocacy within the judicial system.

Estimating in advance the net impact of tort reform on defendants is unfortunately no easier for federal legislation than for state law. The struggle over statutory language is probably better understood as symbolic politics rather than a process of rational planning.[62] In reality the long-term liability burden of defendants will be largely determined by factors that are entirely missing from the doctrinal debate. These include the number of product injuries expected in the future and the proportion of those injuries that will enter the judicial system, no matter how delicately we have balanced liability and procedural doctrines.

Any legislative relief to defendants will also depend on further action by the states. Every federal bill drafted during the 1980s would have allowed the states to follow their own reform programs whenever the federal statute remained silent.[63] As the Senate Report on S. 2760 noted,

> A number of state legislatures have considered the question of tort liability, including product liability, and some have adopted measures dealing with this matter. It is not the Committee's intention that this legislation preempt such state legislation—or any other rule of State law—that provides for defenses, places limitations on the amount of damages that may be recovered, or covers other topics that are not addressed by a rule in this bill.[64]

This provision sustains every lobbyist's hope that territory lost through compromise at the federal level might be regained under state law. A state could, for example, proceed to enact those changes in liability doctrines that were scrapped as part of the Commerce Committee's final round of bargaining, although this would presumably frustrate the delicate incentive structure designed to lure parties into settlement negotiations (under a procedure to be described in the next section).

Courts would also face the thorny question of when a topic of state legislation is indeed *addressed* by federal law, given the lush briar patch of implicit compromises hidden within the legislative background. The Commerce Committee report suggests that states might impose lower limits on damages than those required by federal law, but why should the states not just as well *raise* those limits? In the zero-sum game defined by tort litigation, every provision (and every *lack* of a provision) represents an advantage to one interest group at the expense of another. At the very least, the deviations in state law encouraged by this rule, along with costs of litigating its meaning, will surely weaken the uniformity and administrative efficiency that such bills were designed to strengthen.

It seems curious that the subject of environmental accidents was seldom mentioned in these hearings, except by a few lobbyists from highly specialized organizations.[65] But there is little doubt that fear of future liability epidemics resembling the asbestos cases stiffened the resolve of tort reformers to seek whatever legislative relief they could find. In a candid analysis of legal strategies, two experienced attorneys have argued that the most valuable legal doctrines for defendants in toxic-injury cases are statutes of limitations, strict interpretations of causation, and requirements that injuries be traced to specific products and defendants.[66] Despite the pro-plaintiff trend in successive drafts of federal legislation, each of these defenses would likely be strengthened, even in S. 2760. But no one can predict the actual impact, since that same bill would have deferred a number of central legal issues to judicial implementation.

Defendants have received still more pointed advice about environmental accidents from one of the staunchest promoters of federal tort reform. Victor Schwartz, who chaired the Working Task Force for the federal interagency study during the 1970s, has warned that litigation alone cannot handle personal injury claims on the order of the asbestos cases, but will ultimately require the federal government to establish special compensation procedures. In other words, federal tort reform will neither dispose of these claims nor make the underlying problems go away; thus defendants still face costly litigation unless alternative schemes reduce some part of that burden. Schwartz also argues that new federal compensation procedures are the only way to hold the federal government accountable for its role in regulating environmental harms, given its virtual absence from the private-law tort system.[67] Up to now the courts have shielded the federal treasury from indemnity suits by manufacturers in such cases, including asbestos and Agent Orange.[68] But a tort system under the statutory control of Congress would have a harder time preserving that immunity, especially if plaintiffs and defendants both see an opportunity to get their hands into the deepest pockets of all.[69]

The stage is thus set for a further transition in perceptions of the tort crisis, which has been with us now for more than a decade. Rather than defining the conflict solely as a battle between activist judges and overburdened professional or corporate defendants, reformers in future crises may seek to draw the federal government into more central institutional and financial roles. For reasons we have already discussed, it seems inevitable that more substances in our environment—many of them contained in products covered by proposed legislation—will be identified as possible sources of serious personal injuries among easily defined groups of people. If along the way the federal government takes new responsibility for the general outcomes of tort litigation, it can scarcely avoid an active role by blaming creative judges, venal attorneys, and underhanded insurers for all the problems experienced by plaintiffs and defendants.

As Calabresi reminds us, critics of the tort system sometimes forget "that the 'uncertainties' they would abolish to a large extent only reflect the risks inherent in manufacture and use of complex and even of simple products. Uncertainty and risk are allocated and occasionally misallocated by the tort system, but they are not caused by it."[70] Nor are the social costs of risk and uncertainty always best remedied by tort procedures. If those costs remain high, both for injured persons and for future defendants (and their insurers), alternative procedures for compensation and regulation will not be hard to find. And that dance, once begun, knows no end, short of a radically transformed national policy on accidents.

Two-Tiered Compensation Procedures

Any product liability statute passed by Congress will probably include controversial plans for supplementing litigation with additional compensation processes. As we saw above, the most recent bill to reach the Senate floor contained a modest first step in that direction: an expedited settlement procedure that either party could invoke at an early stage of formal litigation.[71] Proponents of that plan hoped it might divert the bulk of liability claims from the judicial system, thereby reducing administrative costs and giving claimants more reliable assurances of at least some compensation. Although not as ambitious as schemes put before Congress in the late 1970s,[72] this plan nonetheless survived intense political bargaining in the Senate Commerce Committee. Without much fanfare, Congress has apparently returned to an earlier view that tort reform should include some kind of compensation alternative, in addition to doctrinal changes.

Sponsors of product liability bills in the early 1980s wanted to defer the whole matter of alternative compensation systems. They tried to confine the issue to harmless proposals for expert studies, ignoring the excellent survey of compensation models published in 1978 by the Interagency Task Force—which has yet to be surpassed.[73] Tort-reform advocates knew perfectly well that litigation spawns its own alternatives: the informal and largely unsupervised bargaining that actually disposes of most tort claims before they ever reach judicial resolution.[74] However, in view of the hostile climate for political intervention, they preferred to leave those practices alone. Meanwhile academic exponents of the invisible hand were ready to show how out-of-court bargaining was just another aspect of the self-regulating system that already encompassed tort doctrines and private market forces.[75]

In addition to heeding these diffuse ideological voices, lobbyists for tort reform weighed the prospects that streamlined compensation might actually increase the payout burdens on defendants, perhaps even enough to equal the high administrative costs of litigation.[76] Their goal, of course, was to cut back on both compensation costs and administrative costs, based on the theory (overly optimistic, as we have already suggested) that doctrinal reform would thin the ranks of plaintiffs. Besides, it must have seemed like good politics to line up solidly behind litigation, since the powerful trial lawyers oppose no-fault schemes even more vehemently than simple tort reform.

As author of the amendment that brought alternative procedures back into the spotlight, Senator Dodd sounded themes that echo the no-fault debate of the 1970s:

> I believe that the original fault system was a harsh and unfair one
> . . . , and while the move back towards strict liability has been

beneficial for many injured persons, the system still fails to compensate many people who deserve compensation and the lawsuit system is a remarkably inefficient and expensive way of delivering those benefits. The result has been a dramatic rise in the costs of the system.[77]

Dodd's appeal finds its strongest support within the legislative arena, where broad humanitarian goals are voiced less hesitantly than in the more formal context of judicial reasoning or academic theorizing. From the noninstrumental perspective internal to the judicial system, doctrines are self-executing: compensable injuries are simply those that are actually compensated. As for out-of-court settlements, it is possible to view them as part of an extended judicial umbrella, under which the equities on both sides of a settled dispute are protected by reference to active judicial principles.[78]

This brand of legal formalism finds a sympathetic defense in the noninstrumental approach of recent moral philosophy, as we saw in Chapter 5. But academic theorizing can also muster instrumental grounds for preserving traditional litigation. The reigning abstractions of welfare economics can very quickly transform the personal and social costs of accidents—negative externalities, unexpected losses, and all the rest—into unconsummated or unwise economic bargains. Given this approach, even the least ideological welfare economist places a heavy burden on policies interfering with this world dominated by calculation and contract; such policies carry a presumption of irrationality and illegitimacy, and at best are analytically condemned as inefficient.

In a political forum, however, it is harder to dismiss the problem of uncompensated accident victims, and even lobbyists for consumers were put in a tough spot by Dodd's appeal. Groups like Ralph Nader's Public Citizen's Congress Watch, led by lawyers who earned their spurs in litigation, distrust alternatives that promise claimants less than the damages available within the tort system; anything smaller is a compromise with legal rights.[79] And yet, when the time came for political horse trading, each group (except the trial lawyers) found it possible to accept a version of Dodd's amendment. Assuming that such a process may eventually become part of a nationally mandated tort system, how might it work, and where will it lead?

Like everything else in S. 2760, the expedited settlement procedure is only one possible model among many, and doubtless not the only plan Congress will have an opportunity to consider.[80] Thus we need to take a general view of procedures that combine litigation with some type of administrative alternative. These two-tiered or dual compensation schemes have long been championed by Professor Jeffrey O'Connell: they may be elective or mandatory, contractual or statutory, restricted to only one kind of accident or more comprehensive.[81] Originating in the 1960s, they bear a family resemblance to state no-fault plans for automobile accidents.[82] And exactly like those plans, their primary challenge is to find a stable balance between two entirely different ways of treating accidents.

In two-tiered plans a streamlined claims process (usually voluntary, sometimes mandatory) is made available to plaintiffs and/or defendants as an alternative to tort litigation, which nonetheless remains as a residual option. By creating an alternative, legislators expect the more streamlined procedure to shoulder the overwhelming number of claims, leaving judicial procedures to handle the exceptional cases: those that are factually or legally complex, those in which grave injuries or large sums are at stake, or any other highly contentious cases.[83]

But if no-fault is good for easy cases, why is it not even better for the harder ones—those that cost the most and tend to destabilize the dual system by keeping the "forensic lottery" alive? Other countries (most notably New Zealand) have severely curtailed their tort systems in favor of administrative schemes.[84] And early in this century most Western democracies, including the United States, followed this more radical approach for industrial accidents.

When no-fault plans were first considered by states in response to the automobile insurance crisis, both constitutional challenges and political opposition quickly dimmed any prospects for a pure administrative alternative.[85] Constitutional rulings on tort reform over the past two decades have been as diverse as everything else connected with tort law.[86] But they send a general message that plaintiffs cannot be asked to sacrifice all their common-law prospects merely for the sake of lowering the administrative costs of the tort system; plaintiffs must retain at least some strategic advantages.[87] Preserving litigation as a procedural option is thus one way to offset, at least in a formal sense, the disadvantages for plaintiffs whose tort damages may exceed the statutory limits found in all no-fault programs. Under this sort of constitutional constraint, dual compensation systems would appear inescapable, at least for state legislation.

Constitutional challenges are now virtually an automatic sequel to tort reform of any sort, given the enormous resistence and litigious appetites of trial lawyers.[88] Such issues are raised against all levels of reform: changes in courts' remedial powers, in liability doctrines, and in compensation procedures. At the state level, constitutional battles have been waged unabated from the days of no-fault automobile-accident insurance plans, continuing through the malpractice episode, and surviving all the way into the current product liability era.[89] While a few state constitutions contain explicit language restricting statutory interference with tort law, most challenges are based on legal theories of unequal treatment or denial of due process.[90] Diverse rulings on such general standards by state appellate courts represent yet another dismal episode in the statutory campaign for uniformity in tort law.

In this instance federal courts could easily restore uniformity under federal constitutional standards of equal protection and due process. Decisions by federal courts upholding federal statutory reforms would override state constitutional doctrines, and could eventually close off the resort to judicial review. (To the extent state reforms are allowed to supplement federal law, of course, such challenges would doubtless continue.) There are relatively few precedents on which to base a prediction of how federal courts would decide constitutional issues raised by a federal tort statute. But most commentators believe that federal courts are more likely than state courts to uphold alternative compensation procedures on constitutional grounds.[91] The major issue for future accident policy is whether federal courts will demand a *dual* system of compensation in which tort litigation plays a necessary part, or whether federal law may, at least for certain kinds of accidents, eliminate tort procedures altogether. Based on rulings for highly specialized federal programs, abolition appears constitutionally defensible, when it may protect the integrity of an alternative compensation process deemed to serve an important public function.[92]

Turning from constitutional issues to political reasons for accepting two-tiered compensation schemes, we know that most efforts to place tort procedures beyond the reach of plaintiffs are hotly contested. Resistance goes well beyond the raucous opposition by attorneys: many consumers' groups are also unwilling to surrender all prospects for substantial recoveries under tort procedures.[93] As part of the political compromise that inevitably accompanies no-fault plans, benefits from an expedited claims process are generally capped at levels that defendants can easily insure. But plaintiffs who believe their injuries justify greater compensation want to preserve the option of taking their claim to the tort system, for whatever satisfaction that system can provide.

Retaining the option of litigation also maintains a critical role for attorneys, even at the settlement stage. Attorneys would be necessary for interpreting whatever leverage the tort alternative may offer, even though most cases would never reach that level.[94] Inevitably some threshold connects the two procedures—the monetary value of the claim, some aspect of the underlying event, or (as in the product liability bill) the decision whether to accept a settlement offer from the other party. Attorneys for both sides can assess the comparative advantages of both systems, and when conditions seem favorable they display consummate skill in maneuvering their client across that threshold into litigation. In sum, potential parties to accident disputes are often reluctant to sacrifice their opportunities for the potential awards (and powerful defenses) they earnestly believe the tort system can provide. And trial lawyers, by using every opportunity to keep the tort system moving down its historical expansionary path, seek continually to augment the comparative advantage of litigation.[95]

Professor O'Connell has tirelessly promoted these two-tiered plans as reasonable political trade-offs, mutually advantageous for all parties (except perhaps the attorneys) because funds already being spent on costly litigation can be converted to compensation. Whether instituted for specific types of accidents (automobile collisions, medical malpractice, product liability) or more comprehensively, dual plans with expedited compensation procedures are meant to offer greater certainty of recovery to injured claimants, plus a less expensive and more insurable risk to defendants. Backing up this process all the while is the tort system, for any cases that should elude the preestablished categories of events triggering no-fault recovery.

The scheme contained in S. 2760, inspired by O'Connell's writings, was a relatively simple example of this strategic compromise between tort litigation and no-fault. Once an alleged product-related injury has occurred, either party would be entitled to propose a settlement: the plaintiff as part of filing a legal complaint, or the defendant in answering that complaint. The incentive for plaintiffs to settle was the prospect of relatively quick compensation—within ninety days after the offer was accepted. For defendants, the incentive to extend a settlement offer was an automatic cap on liability exposure: damages could not exceed the plaintiff's actual economic costs (reduced by contributions from such collateral sources as workers' compensation, sick pay, and social security) plus a limit of $100,000 for "dignitary loss," a concept meant to roll into one sum all the intangibles of tort compensation, including pain and suffering. These were the inducements offered to each side; the penalties for failing to accept an offered settlement were (for the defendant) higher limits on recovery should the plaintiff prevail in litigation, and (for the plaintiff) enforcement of the collateral source rule.[96]

This summary is merely the skeleton of a scheme rich with details, all part of the delicate balance needed to maintain something of value for both sides, since either party had the power to veto the settlement procedure.[97] Because time is a central strategic factor in accident litigation, careful limits had to be placed on how long either side was permitted to prolong the settlement process. Defendants generally feel that time is on their side since their interest in any one case has little urgency; plaintiffs often need immediate financial assistance. On the other hand, plaintiffs' attorneys frequently use up time in whole clusters of cases in order to extract damaging information from the defendant during the discovery process. Because the settlement scheme in S. 2760 set time limits that were too short for either strategy to be employed effectively, the potential uses of time became a larger issue for both sides in deciding whether to veto settlement and assume the enhanced risks of litigation.

The treatment of time limits illustrates the larger challenge of two-tiered systems, particularly those where either side may exit the process. The plan must closely balance incentives to encourage mutual agreement under the expedited procedure, but it must also preserve incentives for parties to stick with settlement rather than litigation—if the cost-saving objectives of settlement are to be realized at all.[98] Designing such a scheme is truly a stab in the dark considering our lack of reliable theories on legal bargaining strategies, plus our lack of proper data to apply those theories to a field like product liability. Faulty design of alternatives to litigation carries the risk that costs of enduring the settlement process, in both time and money, will merely be added to the steeper costs of litigation.[99]

The likelihood that mass settlement procedures will become one more hurdle on the tortuous course of litigation has been dramatically demonstrated in the asbestos cases. As long as a dynamic judicial process holds even imagined advantages for either party, then the litigation battle is merely lengthened by whatever time it takes that party to wrest the case from its preliminary settlement stage. Moreover a claimant would be foolish to enter the first tier of such a system without expert legal advice, since defendants can be expected to view in wholly strategic terms their response to the entire class of incoming claims.[100] As seems evident from the asbestos cases, the presence of attorneys on either side helps to stretch out settlements over longer periods of time, thus reducing the opportunity cost of litigation.[101]

Having identified certain tendencies driving two-tiered systems toward the nightmarish extreme of higher-cost litigation, we should not ignore dynamics leading in the opposite direction. It is always possible to structure the *second* tier (that is, tort law) to be so unfavorable to one side or the other, that the comparative advantage of settlement to that party is restored. Something of this sort was probably intended in S. 1999, the predecessor of S. 2760, which retained many of the pro-defendant doctrinal reforms found in earlier legislative drafts. As we saw in the last section, however, the impact of doctrinal reform on the tort system is by no means predictable. Doubtless some plaintiffs would be discouraged from entering a tougher litigation process, but it is impossible to predict whether new plaintiffs will be attracted at a high enough rate to increase, on balance, the compensation costs of defendants. Advocates of S. 1999 thought they could keep plaintiffs out of litigation by reducing the volatility of judicial interpretation. But it is doubtful whether even the most pro-defendant set of doctrines—given time and the scope of judicial creativity—could ever achieve enough stability to stanch the influx of plaintiffs into the claims process.

We thus conclude this discussion by noting several independent sources of uncertainty in tort legislation using two-tiered compensation procedures. We do not know and cannot know in advance which incentives will be effective in encouraging parties to negotiate a settlement in good faith, which incentives will discourage those parties from maneuvering their claims into formal litigation, and which set of liability rules (if any) will reduce the net burdens on defendants after adjudication has had its say.[102]

Conclusion: New Directions for Legislation

Intense struggles among lobbying groups over the crisis in product liability have achieved far less than tort-reform advocates had expected. To be sure, many states are now debating various reform packages, and some have made initial statutory inroads into judicial autonomy on liability doctrines and remedies. But Congress has not been able to answer the call for a national product liability policy, which is about the only hope for bringing even modest statutory uniformity to this area of the law, along with eventual protection from continual constitutional attack. Whether competing interests can ever find a satisfactory compromise is difficult to predict, although the recurring cycle of premium increases in the insurance industry will undoubtedly maintain the semblance of crisis for years to come.

The analysis in this chapter has sketched one possible set of variations for any future legislative dance based on federal tort reform. The moves rehearsed thus far in congressional committees follow several different patterns: a gradual shift from pro-defendant to more neutral reforms, compromises that defer complex issues to later judicial administration, and an emerging focus on elective alternatives to judicial procedures. These routines follow the classic choreography of modern legislation: incrementalism, compromise, and delegation.[103] It is a formula calculated to test the stamina of all participants—including the courts, whose scope would simultaneously be limited and expanded. Creative judging would still play a central role in this drama, but with unpredictable consequences.

In the next two chapters we will be looking at a different legislative scenario, one based less on micromanaging tort law and more on reconstructing the procedures for handling compensation and accountability. Measured by these more ambitious programs, product liability reform appears rather tame, if not reactionary; and it may be precisely this incrementalism that has hamstrung the political process. By trying to preserve the basic structure of tort law, these reforms have heightened the adversarial interests that divide parties in the traditional lawsuit. The polarized encounter of litigation is brought directly into the legislative arena, where it can be replayed as a ritual battle among professional lobbying groups. Here we see reflected in epic dimensions all the intricate details of liability doctrines, the countless jurisdictional and remedial powers of courts, and the limitless informal dimensions of litigation. Once legislative bodies seek control over any part of this structure, the entire domain is inevitably brought along; in the zero-sum world of lawsuits, what the legislature does *not* say is just as important as what it does say.

By encroaching on judicial territory at all, legislatures intent on tort reform risk disturbing a complex equilibrium of countervailing forces. The problem is to gain control over enough variables that some new and acceptable level of repose can be found. As the economists would be glad to tell us, we should expect long-run effects to differ substantially from those of the short run. Indeed the whole market equilibrium analogy seems especially apt in explaining the anomalies of legislative tort reform. Changing a single aspect of judicial doctrine is like introducing an economic subsidy or penalty and then watching it ramify through the entire system. We might expect advocates of the invisible hand to sound the classic warning that selective intervention eventually leads us down the road to serfdom, in this case toward ever-expanding legislative responsibilities.[104] Ironically it has been the corporate lobbies and conservative legal minds of the Reagan administration who have led the charge for legislative intervention.

We may conclude that tort reform on the model proposed for product liability is a short-lived strategy. Even if comprehensive legislation were eventually approved, it is not likely to achieve the results intended by reform advocates. Instead of returning us to an Eden of liability protection—said to exist before activist judges took the first bite into strict liability—tort reform would more likely take us into a future with greater uncertainties and higher costs of litigation. Perhaps the Commerce Committee caught a glimpse of that future when it began to shift its focus from judicial doctrines to the whole matter of procedures. If the costs of the tort system continue to increase, we may see even bolder experiments than these two-tiered systems resurrected from the days of no-fault automobile-accident insurance plans.

As emphasized throughout this study, the problems raised by environmental accidents present the gravest challenges to traditional judicial procedures. Both the scale of such accidents and the difficulty (including costs) of responding through conventional litigation will only accelerate the search for new legislative approaches, closer in structure to the preemptive model of workers' compensation. Concern over environmental injuries naturally seems to open the way for more radical experiments. For one thing, claims based on environmental accidents can be more efficiently processed in an aggregated scheme, rather than case by case.[105] But more important, by breaking apart the rigid two-party structure of formal litigation, alternative schemes can deal separately with the complex issues of compensation and accountability. This would allow—indeed it would require—a more active role for the federal government in addressing both sets of issues.

Legislation rarely moves in great leaps, however, so that our first perspective on statutory alternatives to litigation—the topic of Chapter 8—is an intriguing compromise between old and new. In certain instances the federal government, rather than dispensing with litigation processes entirely, has offered itself as a substitute for either plaintiffs or defendants. In the swine flu vaccine cases, for example, the government took the place of drug manufacturers as defendants in personal-injury suits. It has also assumed various burdens of plaintiffs, notably in environmental cases under the Superfund law. In these and other instances the federal presence both perpetuates and transforms conventional legal patterns. Rules of liability (whether judge-made or legislatively modified) are allowed to structure *either* compensation or accountability, while leaving the other function open to political oversight.

In the end, however, such hybrid models featuring the federal government as a surrogate plaintiff or defendant will probably yield to more stable structures, where legislation would control policies for both compensation and accountability. Programs of this sort are already found in the field of occupational injury and disease, including workers' compensation and more specialized schemes like the federal Black Lung Program. As we shall see in Chapter 9, administrative models have been proposed to handle virtually the entire scope of environmental accidents.

Chapter 8

Federal Responsibility: Some Common-Law Fictions

> *The modern welfare state [bases] immunities on the conception of a democratic sovereign which must have the freedom to define the public interest, even when the effect is to impose disproportionate costs on some members of the community. Rather than pitting the individual against the state, the government liability question now pits the individual as individual against the individual as a member of the community.*[1]

Why Not Privatize Public Responsibility?

If all our responses to personal injury had to pass through the narrow definitions and institutions of tort law, we would have to abandon a large portion of our contemporary experience. Despite all the creative fictions of common law, it is impossible to confine our notion of accidental events to those occasions when the courts can certify viable plaintiffs and defendants—linked by the requisite causal/factual nexus. Earlier chapters have explored the many ways environmental accidents fail to fit this private-law mold, and thus far we have concluded that adequate reforms cannot be expected from further judicial innovation, or from statutory management of judicial rules. The social response to accidents has to rest on broader shoulders than common law.

This chapter deals with one of tort law's most troubling omissions: its systematic neglect of how the modern state influences the rate and incidence of personal injury. Of the many contextual sources contributing to contemporary accidents, none are more pervasive than policies under the control of the federal government. This is not to downplay the concurrent actions of other institutions in modern society, or of course the important contributions from individual behavior. But along with the rise of the regulatory state, federal power has become an increasingly significant partner in almost every organized private activity. And since the early 1970s, federal authority has played perhaps the dominant role in identifying and regulating potential hazards in our larger environment.

No social response to accidents that is centered on accountability and compensation can afford to ignore the vast reach of the public sphere. It will prove increasingly impractical, if nothing else, to promote optimal deterrence or to expand mass tort compensation while leaving government behavior and financial resources out of the equation. The omission of the U.S. government from the Agent Orange cases, for example, was the proverbial instance of *Hamlet* without the Danish prince. Because it treats human behavior and events as exclusively individual and private, tort law necessarily obscures the impact of public action, along with any trailing notion of public responsibility.

A distinction between public and private modes of accountability has its roots in both political tradition and law.[2] The American political system professes an abiding concern with holding the government responsible to the sovereign people, but until recent decades no one has proposed to use the common law of torts as a means for enforcing public accountability. Up to now the common-law shield of *sovereign immunity* has protected the federal government from tort liability, and the Eleventh Amendment to the Constitution has generally closed the federal courts to civil suits against individual states.[3] Within state courts, similar immunities have been claimed by state governments throughout most of our history. Despite the mysterious origins of immunity doctrines, there is no reason to assume that differential treatment of public and private responsibility is bound up with metaphysical abstractions of sovereignty. It is rather the natural expression of our pluralistic culture that seeks to distinguish between public and private spheres of action, each observing separate procedures for accountability. In American democracy governments are held accountable through the political process of election.[4]

Throughout this study we have defined environmental accidents as testing the limits on what can be reasonably understood as purely private, interpersonal action. Social responses to personal injuries that rely mainly on common law and market systems tend to deny these limits, trying to salvage at least the skeleton of private action even where the flesh has to be abandoned. In documenting the intrinsic weaknesses of those approaches, our general argument has instead pushed the problems of personal injury into a collective context. We now augment that argument by noting the unique nature of government policy as: (1) an irreducible contextual element in environmental injuries, (2) a highly articulated structure for controlling future accidents, and (3) a financial medium for shifting accident losses among discrete groups. Later chapters in this book will describe an approach to accident policy based on these essential public functions, in which common-law adjudication and market systems play a subordinate role.

We might suppose that even the most atomistic theories of action would be forced to concede the collective nature of government behavior, along with the pervasive influence of federal policy on the rate and incidence of environmental accidents. But having already seen throughout this study the remarkable durability of private-action concepts, we must take seriously the possibility that public policy can itself be brought under the Procrustean concepts of private law. Instead of seeing government action as a dominant feature in the social environment of accidents, we may instead try to look through the opposite end of the telescope and see government behavior as the last frontier to be conquered by the institutions of private law.

This chapter explores three areas where the line separating public and private action has grown especially faint, as federal policy flirts with public roles that borrow heavily from common-law procedures. The settings all relate to environmental accidents: injuries from mass immunization programs (the swine flu episode), pollution from toxic wastes (Superfund cleanups), and nuclear accidents (the Price-Anderson Act). In these programs the federal government has taken on the respective roles of private law defendant, private law plaintiff, and insurer of last resort. Together they constitute three steps toward possible privatization of public responsibility: civil liability for individualized harms caused by government policy, a duty to impose individualized accountability on third parties for harms to the common environment, and a guarantee of adequate financing for market-based insurance.

We shall conclude, however, that even these carefully contrived applications of tort-law models to public action have failed to accomplish their intended goals of equity and efficiency, and indeed have worked against those goals. In addition, the inordinate time delays and money costs of tort procedures have diverted resources that could otherwise be spent on the substantive aims of public programs. Far from describing a path toward privatizing government responsibility, in short, these programs reaffirm the vast gulf separating public and private action. That gap will become even clearer in later chapters, as we consider alternative personal injury policies that largely abandon common-law procedures.

This chapter builds on the analysis of Chapter 7, since each program to be discussed below is a creature of statute. Up to the late 1980s, courts have been unsuccessful in undermining sovereign immunity—at least at the federal level.[5] In 1946, however, Congress passed the Federal Tort Claims Act (FTCA), a statutory framework for waiving federal sovereign immunity for government activities that are essentially identical with private sector behavior: negligent operation of government vehicles, negligence by employees of government proprietary enterprises, and a host of other carefully limited circumstances.[6] The Supreme Court in 1984 reaffirmed the central exclusion from FTCA liability of government acts deemed "discretionary," or actions growing out of the regulatory functions of government.[7] While this intriguing boundary line will inevitably undergo further judicial testing, it is unlikely to yield significant expansion of government liability in the absence of congressional approval.

We must note, however, that courts have not completely ignored the issue of government liability; indeed they have developed several creative ways of circumventing both federal and state sovereign immunity. Their main vehicle has been the civil rights tort suit: an action for money damages or injunctive relief primarily aimed at state and local officials.[8] Such cases have grown at a rapid pace since the 1960s, spurred by the civil rights movement and the Warren Court's due-process principles. Similar challenges have also been allowed against individual federal officials for violating personal constitutional rights.

Given the individualist structure of tort law, it is not surprising that judicial activism in the field of government tort liability has focused on actions by individual plaintiffs against individual defendants, with the harm defined as a violation of personal rights. Among other causes, the Warren Court's approach to due process helped to focus judicial scrutiny on the many arbitrary decisions made by relatively low-level public employees—the street-level bureaucrats who have become equally popular targets of sociological study.[9] What might otherwise appear as system-determined behavior has been creatively recast by the judicial system as the failure of individual officials to base their actions on fully specified legal rules. The harms in question are often structural and chronic, but the litigation strategy calls for translating plaintiffs' misfortunes into violations of personal rights, including rights based on a new form of "property": the numerous statutory entitlements recently created by federal welfare programs.[10]

Contrasting these developments with the parallel growth of tort actions against private defendants, we find several important differences. Organizational behavior in the private sphere can be more directly challenged, since corporations (unlike public agencies) are not immune from liability.[11] Moreover, once corporations are placed in the defendant's seat, their monetary resources (backed by liability insurance) are available to fund both the losses experienced by injured parties and the high administrative costs of the judicial system. Extending this process requires only that judges pursue the pro-plaintiff doctrinal trends worked out by progressive commentators. Tort actions in the public sphere, on the other hand, are predominantly confined to suits against named individual employees. Instead of money damages, the frequent aim of litigation is to seek injunctions forcing public officials to revise individual decisions and procedures. However, as public agencies increasingly indemnify employees held liable for civil damages, the civil rights tort suit may eventually find deeper pockets for financing both compensation payments and administrative costs, in a manner closer to private litigation.[12]

Hemmed in by sovereign immunity, civil rights tort litigation has not produced equivalent doctrines to the common-law's vicarious liability and strict liability. Unusually creative judges have sometimes been willing to infer collective intent by a governmental unit to violate constitutional or other civil rights of plaintiffs, but these cases remain the exception and have been heavily disputed.[13] In other instances, courts have been willing to shift the burden of proof to defendants on critical doctrinal issues—one of the central creative devices used by plaintiffs in the private sphere. But these cases remain closely tied to well-traveled constitutional paths; and even so the momentum has recently swung back to more neutral ground, as a more conservative Supreme Court plods through a series of contentious race discrimination suits.[14]

In one respect, however, the civil rights tort cases have evoked even stronger judicial activism than tort cases in the private sphere. With the emphasis on injunctive relief rather than money damages, some judges in the 1970s undertook bold campaigns to restructure public institutions and policies deemed responsible for widespread deprivations of civil rights.[15] Thus a host of decisions imposed judicial administrative authority on public institutions like prisons, hospitals for the mentally ill and disabled, local housing authorities, and school districts found to have discriminated on the basis of race and other factors. Although the outcomes of these experiments have yet to receive dispassionate assessment, it seems evident that judicial capacities and the legitimacy of judicial intrusion are severely taxed in the service of enforcing institutional reform.[16] Lasting accomplishments in areas of social services will require less adversarial and more administrative cooperation between courts and the bureaucracies they seek to improve, and ultimately the legislative process holds the key to both funding and policies for ensuring more enlightened institutions.[17]

Personal injuries from environmental accidents are especially difficult to redefine as deprivations of civil rights. Activist judges and the civil rights bar have so far paid little attention to expanding federal liability in ways directly analogous to private or corporate liability. We may therefore leave behind this approach to government liability through the civil rights tort suit as having little to contribute to accident policies dealt with in this book.

The Swine Flu Vaccine Program: Federal Government as Defendant

What began in early 1976 as a public health initiative of unprecedented scope ended that year as an emblem of both political opportunism and the unforgiving spirit of medical technology. The swine flu program was created to protect Americans from an expected outbreak of disease that many feared would repeat the deadly world pandemic of 1918. But the outbreak never came, and soon the vaccine itself was found to be a source of illness, causing as many as 400 cases of the disabling and often fatal Guillain-Barré Syndrome.[18] Among its unintended social side effects, the swine flu program gave us an opportunity to observe the federal government's response to liability claims like those defended daily by private industry.

The liability issue emerged only as a late-inning crisis in the frenzied effort to produce enough vaccine, within a few short months, to achieve President Ford's announced goal of inoculating "every man, woman, and child in the United States."[19] Congress had already appropriated funds to launch the program, which deftly telescoped the stages of vaccine development, testing, production, and distribution under the guidance of the Public Health Service. In early summer, however, insurance companies notified the four private manufacturers who had contracted to produce the vaccine that their product liability policies would not cover certain claims most likely to arise in a mass vaccination program. And so Congress, under pressure to protect its investment before the fall flu season (and perhaps partly in reaction to the nation's brief panic over Legionnaire's Disease), agreed in August 1976 to a special compensation mechanism, allowing the federal government to take the place of private companies in all suits resulting from the initiative.[20] Public Law No. 94-380 modified the Federal Tort Claims Act to make the United States the sole defendant in all personal-injury suits tied to swine flu vaccine.[21]

Insurers were responding to the same product liability trends that were summarized in Chapter 6. The two most worrisome precedents, both involving mass administration of the Sabin live-polio vaccine, held that a manufacturer was liable for failing to warn vaccinees about the 1 in 4 million chance of catching polio from the vaccine itself.[22] This type of strict liability caused wide dismay in the corporate and insurance worlds. There was no suggestion of traditional negligence or breach of federal regulatory standards by the vaccine manufacturer, nor did the courts spend much time delving into causation—supposedly the plaintiff's burden to establish. Out of all this came the plausible inference that at least some courts intended to make drug companies absolute insurers against side effects from mass-immunization programs. The circumstances of the swine flu campaign bore an eerie resemblance to the earlier polio cases, and they were about to be played out on the grandest possible national scale. In retrospect, these were prescient fears of serious health risks now associated with flu vaccine.

In response to these liability concerns, the swine flu program assumed the added goal of assuring "an orderly procedure for the prompt and equitable handling of any claim for personal injury or death arising out of the administration of [swine flu] vaccine."[23] Congress did not, of course, anticipate the scale of eventual damage claims, determined partly by the unforeseen connection between flu vaccine and Guillain-Barré Syndrome. Out of 40 million persons receiving vaccinations, about 4,000 administrative claims were eventually filed seeking $3.3 billion in damages. More than 1,200 of these cases went to the federal courts, and ten years later the last of them were still fighting their way through the appeals structure.[24] Instead of providing prompt and equitable handling of claims, the swine flu compensation scheme encountered the inevitable delays and inconsistencies of the tort system, and thereby became a costly failure.

This failure is especially notable considering the carefully controlled procedural framework provided by the FTCA, along with some bold and creative judging. In many respects, the swine flu compensation mechanism mirrors the procedural models currently under consideration by Congress for national product liability legislation, and thus its weaknesses should bear special scrutiny. First, under a two-tiered compensation model, swine flu claims were initially diverted into an administrative process, as required by FTCA. Lawsuits could not be filed until an administrative claim was denied, or if no settlement had been reached after six months. Once such claims pass into the tort system, the FTCA mandates an austere, basically pro-defendant procedural regime. All cases must be heard in federal court with no option for jury trials. No punitive damages or injunctions are permitted, and attorneys' fees are strictly controlled at rates well below the standard contingency rate.[25]

The normal state doctrinal standards of liability were preserved, even though the FTCA otherwise precludes recovery based on strict liability. The whole reason for special congressional action was to offer the federal government as a surrogate defendant for private parties, and thus recovery under the swine flu act could be predicated on "any theory of liability . . . that would govern an action . . . under the law of the [state] where the act or omission occurred, including negligence, strict liability in tort, and breach of warranty."[26] This of course encompassed the duty-to-warn theory that had caused the vaccine manufacturers to balk.

With unvarnished state tort-law doctrines as the sole standard of equity, it was essential for both claimants and defendants to employ every affirmative or defensive weapon in their respective arsenals. The pleadings for both sides were model compendia of technical legal arguments. At the pretrial level, parties waged lengthy battles over production and authentication of documents, admissibility of written evidence, and depositions of key figures. As it turned out, however, the pretrial process received an unusually extensive and timely dose of judicial consolidation. Despite continual resistance of both sides, the 1,200 cases were joined in a single federal district and bound by extensive pretrial findings. This phase of litigation was presided over in the strongest possible managerial style by Judge Gerhard A. Gesell, who completed his task in the remarkably brief time of a year and a half.[27] During this time, plaintiffs were represented by a professional panel of experienced attorneys. Communication among plaintiffs was enhanced by the publication of a commercial reporting service, helping to circulate accurate information and uniform pleadings.[28]

As cases were remanded to federal district courts across the country for individual hearings, a vast number of complex factual issues were thus completely standardized. Constitutional challenges against the swine flu act were speedily decided in the government's favor and were uniformly upheld through the federal appeals process.[29] There were no problems in establishing the identify of defendants or of apportioning fault among multiple defendants since the law stipulated that the U.S. government would stand alone in the place of any and all defendants. The volume of cases, while larger than anyone expected, was slight compared to other recent examples of mass tort actions. What remained for determination, however, were the complex medical issues of personal injury and causation—the inevitable boundaries to consolidated treatment of mass accident claims. Delays and inconsistencies were thus able to reenter the litigation process, despite the unique procedural background streamlining the disposition of claims.

Why did this process fail to provide the prompt and equitable relief desired by Congress? Problems emerged from the outset with the administrative settlement provisions of the FTCA, which failed to block the path toward protracted litigation. In reflecting on the paralysis, insensitivity, and legalistic posture of the Public Health Service as it responded to some 4,000 claims, we must remember that the major health risk that soon became associated with swine flu vaccine was both unforeseeable and uninsurable. The sudden rush of claims came as a surprise and quickly aroused fears of a financial donnybrook.

The difficulties posed by these claims could easily be compounded in future environmental accidents, should similar medical surprises produce an even higher rate of demonstrable injury. Our awareness of environmental accidents depends on a number of special factors. If somehow the inoculation of 40 million people had occurred without the high visibility, the organized distribution and surveillance, and the compact timing of the swine flu program, it is difficult to say whether Guillain-Barré side effects would ever have been discovered. However, once the possibility of vaccine-related injury reached the public media, some 40 million people were in a position to question whether recent physical ailments might possibly be due to the vaccine.

Considering the joint uncertainties of liability exposure and causal connections, it seems fair to say that the Public Health Service responded like any prudent potential defendant. The six-month period for administrative settlement, comparable to recent proposals for national product liability procedures, was clearly insufficient to allow the orderly processing of claims, each of which would have required individualized information establishing the claimant's alleged injury, the circumstances of vaccination, and past medical history. The association between flu vaccine and Guillain-Barré was not to be scientifically demonstrated for several years.[30]

Had the Public Health Service made sudden pledges of compensation to claimants, it could well have invited an even greater barrage of claims based on other untested medical theories. This much is clear from the response of swine flu claimants in 1978, after Health, Education and Welfare (HEW) Secretary Califano released a statement apparently announcing that the government would not press the causation issue in cases involving Guillain-Barré Syndrome.[31] Within six months the number of claims alleging Guillain-Barré injuries nearly tripled, with total damages rising beyond $1 billion, forcing Secretary Califano to beat a hasty retreat. These new claims were also accompanied by the sudden organization of a plaintiffs' attorney litigation group, following a pattern seen in later environmental cases. Readers of the *Swine Flu Litigation Reporter* during this period would have detected the influence of career tort lawyers, if no other way, by the number of pleadings seeking damages for loss of consortium and other arcane injuries.

We easily grow skeptical of claims so elastically related to signals of compromise from a deep-pocket defendant. This may be an example of how the threat of trivial claims prevents any prudent defendant from immediately acknowledging the most serious injuries with appropriate settlements. The resulting delays and complexities of litigation weaken the ability of severely disabled claimants and families who have lost a breadwinner to hold out for larger awards. The trouble with this analysis, however, is that no one really knows which claims are trivial and which are serious, pending decisions by the courts, if tort-law standards provide our only measure of equity. Thus no expedited settlement process reasonably could have hoped to reduce those factors pushing plaintiffs and defendants alike toward protracted litigation.

Nor can we take issue with the Justice Department's strategy of using all the arguments and tactics employed by defense counsel for private industry. At nearly every stage, the federal government conducted its legal defense against swine flu claimants in an adversarial but fully professional manner. The high visibility of the program, its political disrepute after control of the White House switched to the Democrats, the awkward fact that swine flu never developed into an epidemic—all combined with the sudden rush of personal-injury claims to place the federal government on the legal defensive.

This defensive posture was prefigured, in fact, before the tragic dimensions of the program were ever realized. Officials at the Centers for Disease Control (CDC) had planned to rely on consent forms signed by all vaccinees to forestall later claims based on strict liability. According to one source, they "seemed to have expected that the duty to warn, once they assumed it, would be discharged too well for penalities."[32] Congress strongly encouraged this strategy by requiring the CDC to consult with the National Commission for the Protection of Human Subjects in developing a consent form.[33]

Career health officials could scarcely be expected to oppose educating the public about the risks of vaccination, and indeed they took some effort to provide standard medical information. This meant, however, that the consent forms were not tightly drafted from a defense lawyer's point of view. Warnings of possible paralysis or cardiovascular effects were not included. The forms did caution against mild side effects like tenderness at the site of the shot, fever, chills, headache, and muscle aches.[34] However, reflecting conclusions drawn by a technical report prepared for the CDC in early 1976, the forms flatly declared that "flu vaccine has rarely been associated with severe or fatal reaction."[35] While plaintiffs were later to challenge this claim, it was probably a fair summary of the available medical evidence.

The ethical goals of informed consent are put to a severe test in any voluntary mass immunization program. In this case the government had an interest in encouraging public participation by stressing the advantages of inoculation, but also an interest in protecting itself from liability by issuing legally effective warnings about possible side effects. Neither of these conflicting goals is easily reconciled with the purpose of making the patient an informed and responsible agent in choosing his or her own medical care. The swine flu program strove for both legal protection, by its use of consent forms, and for mass participation through public advertising.

The invitation to legalistic distortion of the consent process was embedded in previous court decisions involving the legal duty to warn. Judicial creativity may have eased the path to compensation for a single generation of plaintiffs, but it practically assured that all future participants in mass health programs would face an uphill struggle contesting the adequacy of any warnings provided under the question-begging rubric of signed consent forms. In its initial legal defense against swine flu claims, the federal government answered every formal complaint with the formulaic response that vaccinees who signed the forms assumed the risk of side effects.[36] By invoking this defense, the government seized important strategic ground on a factual issue that it knew would be decided case by case by federal judges under FTCA procedures—not by juries, as in ordinary civil trials. Although such tactics are a frequent source of delays and inequities in tort law, they are unavoidable elements in a process where common-law principles are the sole standards of eligibility for compensation.

Along with the legal issues of duty to warn, informed consent, and assumption of risk, the burden of establishing causation is an inescapable element in applying tort-law compensation principles. In Chapter 9 we shall explore the consequences of removing this burden from claimants, as in the federal Black Lung Program; but in the swine flu episode, as Secretary Califano quickly learned, it was too late for the government to renounce its legal defenses. Even after the eventual medical discovery of a causal connection between flu vaccine and Guillain-Barré Syndrome, individual cases had to be decided by federal judges on the basis of specific testimony. Thus we would expect the results of actual swine flu trials to show a number of inconsistencies. Based on reported opinions, it is impossible to find factual differences that could distinguish cases where courts have accepted the causal theory of the Guillain-Barré plaintiff, from those where they have not.[37] Such discrepancies are magnified, of course, by variations in damages awarded by different judges in those cases where plaintiffs have prevailed. In other words, nothing in this record contradicts the pattern of inconsistency that has been documented on a broader scale for the asbestos cases.

While our verdict on the swine flu compensation mechanism is that it failed to provide prompt and equitable handling of claims, we should note one limited sense in which it was successful. Federal assumption of liability did in fact persuade vaccine manufacturers and their insurers to maintain production, thereby keeping the program on a timetable dictated by public health concerns. Although the aftermath of the swine flu program should make Congress wary of following the same route again, it is nevertheless a stop-gap solution whenever liability rules governing private industry appear to frustrate public initiatives. A similar approach could well be taken, for example, in military-related production, as an alternative to extending the government's civil immunity to federal contractors. Energy production in times of national emergencies might also tempt Congress to go down that same legalistic road.[38] Whenever the federal government is the customer of private industry (even under nonemergency conditions), it is entirely reasonable that the costs of the civil liability system should be passed on to the public in one form or another. Federal assumption of liability remains one possible form.[39]

Although the swine flu legislation was designed primarily as a compensation scheme, it is important to consider briefly its implicit approach to the coordinate issue of accountability. As with compensation, we may seriously question any extension of accountability principles from tort law into the public realm. Of course, by comparison with strict adherence to sovereign immunity, opening the federal treasury to personal-injury suits would seem to increase the level of accountability. But the principle of immunity should instead be seen as allowing the government to define responsibility in its own terms, spelled out by other legislation. The FTCA was never intended to preempt other approaches to accountability, but was simply a practical mechanism that allowed the federal government to submit itself to civil suit whenever its activities approximated those of private persons—as with government vehicles involved in traffic accidents. This was an ancillary form of accountability, added to whatever other steps might be taken through the political process.[40]

In the swine flu cases, however, tort law seemed to operate as a shield against more broadly conceived responsibility. As seen solely through the FTCA, the federal government was not responsible to vaccine victims for the consequences of its many policy decisions: to establish the flu program, to distribute vaccine on a mass scale through local health departments, to accept the results of clinical trials. It was responsible only if the patchwork of state liability rules, applied to several-thousand individual circumstances, so determined.

It was, furthermore, the duty of the federal government to play its role of defendant as aggressively as possible, even to the point of urging the courts to consider the following ingenious (and revealing) defense. Ordinarily the FTCA bars suits against the federal government based on strict liability theories like the duty to warn.[41] Thus the swine flu act was necessary to transfer the strict liability of manufacturers to the federal government—an ad hoc exercise in vicarious liability. So far so good. But the Justice Department argued further that, under this approach, the government was accountable only for the actions or omissions of third parties, not for its *own* failure to warn. Since the government itself undertook to provide all warnings, there was no failure by third parties, and thus no vicarious liability under the statute. In sum, the paradoxical logic of this position says that the federal government may escape legal liability to the degree it treats as government policy all phases of the program.

Judge Gesell rejected this line of reasoning—so clearly out of step with congressional intent in amending the FTCA.[42] But it is an instructive example of dilemmas that result from translating public accountability into common-law terms. Creating exemptions under the FTCA may expand federal liability, but it diminishes overall accountability if we also reduce that concept to a mere series of exceptions to sovereign immunity. Instead, some affirmative standard of responsibility beyond common-law doctrines seems essential for building an effective policy of government accountability. We should still be able to hold government accountable for the swine flu vaccine injuries, even if there had been no involvement whatsover of third parties—if the government had gone the last step and manufactured the vaccine in its own laboratories. The search for independent principles of government accountability may not be simple, but it is vain to seek them only in legal fictions and analogies with private action under common law.

The Superfund: Federal Government as Plaintiff

A different kind of public initiative was also launched in 1976 when Congress passed the Resource Conservation and Recovery Act (RCRA).[43] This law founded a comprehensive federal system for discovering and tracking toxic chemicals and other hazardous substances generated by U.S. industry, imposing strict regulations on their safe disposal as waste products. Although this complex monitoring system was designed for future control, the public was more alarmed about immediate health dangers from existing chemical dump sites—locations with memorable names like Times Beach, Love Canal, and the Valley of the Drums. By 1980, Congress agreed to begin the Augean task of identifying and cleaning up the country's most dangerous sites. Just days before the Carter administration left office, Congress approved the Comprehensive Environmental Response, Compensation, and Liability Act (CERCLA), popularly known as the Superfund.[44]

Federal regulation of the environment is governed by statutes dealing separately with air, water, and land pollution.[45] Many states have passed parallel legislation, likewise divided among specific objectives.[46] As with most major regulatory programs in the United States, popular objections to highly centralized administration and financing have led to cumbersome cooperative structures for environmental control, creating a process open to continual marginal adjustments and political bargaining.[47] Cleaning up hazardous-waste sites under CERCLA was assigned to the Environmental Protection Agency (EPA) for administrative enforcement, a task carried out with such scandalous lassitude that Congress intervened in 1983 to force changes in top EPA leadership.[48]

While EPA was dozing, technical reports steadily raised their estimates of potential cleanup sites and the costs of ensuring long-term safety. Instead of the initial target of some 400 sites, by 1985 the EPA was forecasting as many as 2,000.[49] Meanwhile the Office of Technology Assessment (OTA) was reporting to Congress that the number of existing sites was probably closer to 10,000, with another 8,000 soon to join the list.[50] After nearly a decade of surveillance under RCRA, it was also becoming clear that both immediate abatement and long-term control over toxic dump sites would require more expensive measures. For its 10,000 sites, OTA predicted a program extending fifty years and costing $100 billion. Thus in 1986, when Congress reauthorized Superfund for an additional five-year period, it raised the funding level to $8.5 billion—a fivefold increase.[51]

Leaving aside many features of this complex statute, we shall focus here on Superfund's approach to accountability. Unlike other programs considered in this book, Superfund does not attempt to compensate personal-injury victims, although in 1982 an official study group proposed adding personal-injury provisions to CERCLA.[52] Nor does Superfund directly compensate individuals for property damage caused by hazardous waste, although like other environmental statutes it eases the way for individuals to file private lawsuits.[53]

Instead of compensation issues, we shall focus on how the statute determines who should pay these extraordinary sums for cleaning up toxic dump sites. As a recent survey appropriately noted, "The conventional wisdom holds that CERCLA's intent and effect were to make generators, transporters, and disposers of hazardous wastes bear the full social costs of their activities."[54] Although the actual financing formula adopted in 1986 suggests a much broader philosophy,[55] much of the rhetoric behind Superfund centers on CERCLA's tortlike scheme for exacting penalties from parties held responsible in civil proceedings. As we shall see, the gap between collective and individual accountability looms very large in the Superfund debate—both in the rhetoric and implementation of the law.

The original Superfund law and its 1986 amendments have established a special statutory regime, borrowed principally from tort law, which permits the fund to seek reimbursement for cleanup costs at specific sites by suing parties deemed responsible for creating hazardous conditions.[56] This portion of the law casts the federal government in the role of private plaintiff using the judicial process to promote individualized accountability, modeled on common-law principles. In effect Superfund uses litigation to compensate itself out of the pockets of individuals, corporations, and even governmental entities who may be found causally responsible for contributing to hazardous-waste pollution.

Just as the FTCA provides a statutory framework allowing the federal government to structure its own liability as a defendant, CERCLA provides a thick statutory filter for altering the traditional concepts and procedures of common-law liability. No purely private plaintiff has this singular authority to specify applicable liability standards, to set procedural limits on settlement and judicial review, to expand the pool of defendants by codifying theories of vicarious responsibility, and to require courts to apply evidentiary or factual presumptions in its favor. To be sure, congressional ambivalence in exercising these options has allowed the courts to play a major role in shaping Superfund liability; but lobbyists, litigants, and insurers are equally aware that parameters will doubtless be set, from time to time, by legislation.[57]

The Superfund law is. thus a unique regulatory program that employs statutorily modified tort law to accomplish certain of its ends. These ends are as ambiguous as tort law itself: for adherents to various moral theories, the goal is to achieve individualized corrective justice;

for partisans of welfare economics, the goal is an efficient level of future deterrence. Either way, for believers in tort law this ingenious mechanism appears as a socially costless way (perhaps even an optimal way) to funnel revenue into a major environmental endeavor. For critics, however, the prospects look quite different:

> The new hazardous waste cleanup regime [is] a hybrid "administrative-litigation" monster, whose presence in our federal courts is becoming an increasing burden. Meanwhile all the inefficiencies of the litigation system—delays and transaction costs (mostly the legal and consultant fees of all involved)—are accumulating on a grand scale.[58]

As we have seen in other contexts, accountability based on tort law will scarcely be costless. In what is apparently the only systematic forecast of legal costs facing all parties involved in cleanup operations, one researcher has estimated that litigation costs for Superfund enforcement will amount to somewhere between 34 and 55 percent of total direct cleanup expenses.[59] Meanwhile the net addition to Superfund resources from interest, fines, and litigation awards is estimated by Congress at $125 million per year, a mere 7 percent of anticipated Superfund resources.[60] EPA's own legal costs will consume at least twice that amount, while private parties will pay ten times more in litigation expenses.[61] If we accept the Office of Technology Assessment's study, the next five years are only a down payment on a program destined to become a permanent obligation of public policy, with similar costs continuing at least over the next fifty years.

These estimates are even more disturbing when we recall that Superfund litigation is able to avoid some of the most costly features of private tort law. The overall statutory scheme is national in scope and handled primarily by federal courts. Although there are many statutory gaps that require interpretation by individual judges, a uniform, federal common law appears to be emerging; thus parties are spared the wide doctrinal diversity to be found, for instance, in product liability law.[62] Second, since the federal government is the sole plaintiff, litigation strategy and costs can be more efficiently organized than in the standard mass-tort case.[63] The professional plaintiffs' bar is not a major factor, thus the variables of contingent fees, emotional pleas to the jury on questions of medical causation, and the demand for punitive damages are absent. Third, the federal government has the opportunity, at least in principle, to dictate by legislation the doctrinal and procedural framework for litigation. According to advocates of national product liability legislation, such power should reduce litigation costs by promoting both uniformity and certainty in judicial outcomes.

Why, then, does the federal government's resort to tort procedures in this regulatory context threaten to reach cost levels comparable to other types of mass-tort litigation?[64] In the first place, environmental damage disputes are inherently complex; and even though the doctrinal structure may be relatively easy to control, the underlying facts behind hazardous-waste pollution stubbornly resist the conceptual framework of individualized responsibility. As courts have interpreted CERCLA's reach, the range of "potentially responsible parties" (PRPs) includes not only those persons popularly identified as polluters (generators or disposers of waste materials), but also parent and successor corporations, landowners, and state and local authorities—all of whom may have some remote connection to the site, the materials, or the financial assets of the actual polluters.[65] In short, the courts (with the encouragement of both EPA and Congress) have borrowed the deep-pocket concept from private tort law, enriching the common-law principle of responsibility with all the fictional and vicarious shadings taken from product liability. Because of the lengthy history of chemical disposal and the structure of pollution insurance, it is not uncommon in major cases for several hundred potentially responsible parties (including dozens of insurance companies) to find themselves on the receiving end of Superfund litigation.[66]

Factual issues that might determine relative shares of responsibility among such large classes of defendants are rarely open to direct causal proof. As with litigation of environmental accidents in general, identifying the specific causes of present hazardous conditions at a single dump site forces the courts to rely on presumptions, statistical evidence, and long chains of factual inferences. Although CERCLA never explicitly adopts a standard of strict liability, the courts have been quick to read one into the statute, thus sparing EPA the additional burden of demonstrating proximate cause. But even so, findings of specific causal connections remain vital to any tort theory of personal accountability.[67] Even when such findings are augmented with all the creative techniques of progressive judges, or are imputed to remote defendants under theories of vicarious action, important factual issues remain about the long-term polluting effects of substances released into the environment: questions about their interaction with other substances, about background levels of contributing causes, and about the precise timing of long-term environmental effects.[68]

The federal government has found an ingenious way to reduce its *own* litigation costs—notwithstanding the inherent complexities of hazardous-waste litigation—but such methods succeed only by shifting the most expensive legal issues to private parties. The fundamental technique on which EPA enforcement rests is that old friend of progressive tort law—joint and several liability. EPA has openly declared that keeping its own legal budget within terrestrial range depends on being able to target a relatively small number of solvent defendants from among those potentially responsible under the statute. It then becomes a task for well-financed individual defendants to seek out others, through private lawsuits for contribution, to offset their joint and several liability under CERCLA.[69] It is this secondary phase of litigation that may entail hundreds of parties, inherently undecidable questions about individual accountability, and astronomical attorneys' fees.[70] Since the number of dollars at stake in a cleanup can be many hundreds of millions, and occasionally even more than a billion, deep-pocket defendants have no choice but to pursue this costly strategy against their insurers and any other implicated parties.[71]

In sum, the kind of tort system currently being shaped by the architects of Superfund—both in Congress and in the judiciary—is the progressive, activist version that favors vicarious liability, strict liability, joint and several liability, looser statutes of limitations, and various burden-shifting evidentiary devices on issues of causation.[72] The Reagan administration unquestionably experienced some cognitive dissonance in supporting this approach.[73] But once thrust into the role of plaintiff's advocate, environmental attorneys for both EPA and the Justice Department tend to argue the government's position with the same legalistic vigor and professionalism that we noted (albeit for the defense) in the swine flu cases. Ironically, the Reagan administration's Justice Department otherwise was among the most outspoken critics of pro-plaintiff tort trends—espousing the concerns of corporate defendants in product liability suits. In particular, former Attorney General Meese's Tort Policy Working Group extolled traditional negligence law as a kind of return to old-time religion.[74]

Congressional supporters of the Superfund litigation scheme, along with EPA administrators appointed by the Reagan administration, resort to a familiar argument for defending both the high transaction costs and the blatant departure from traditional tort-law standards of moral accountability. These methods are transitional, they maintain, until such time as EPA works out a better process of arranging formal settlements as an alternative to litigation.[75] As we saw in Chapter 6, proponents of the tort system tend to be optimistic about the self-healing powers of judicial control. With the unique leverage provided by CERCLA's statutory framework—its ability to stack the liability odds heavily against defendants—EPA hopes eventually to force parties into negotiation, thereby reducing litigation costs.[76]

As we noted, settlements that reduce EPA's own litigation costs may only sharpen the subsequent legal battle for apportioning liability among potentially reponsible parties.[77] Accordingly, certain provisions in the recent amendments to Superfund were evidently meant to address this secondary problem as well. For example, EPA is now required to provide extensive information to all PRPs, including names and addresses of other PRPs, any specific knowledge EPA may have about the volume and nature of substances connected with each PRP, and a ranking by volume of all substances deemed causally responsible for hazardous conditions. EPA is also encouraged to suggest a "non-binding preliminary allocation of responsibility" as an impetus to settlement negotiations among the parties themselves. Finally, EPA now has explicit authority to contribute its own funds to negotiated settlements, as an alternative to holding deep-pocket defendants jointly and severally liable for the full cost.[78]

On balance, however, both the general framework of Superfund and recent amendments will probably impede the whole process of settlement—contrary to the predictions of tort-law partisans.[79] EPA's help in identifying the full range of PRPs is more likely to promote vigorous litigation than peaceful settlement. And while EPA's non-binding allocations of responsibility are declared to be inadmissable as evidence in later contribution suits,[80] it seems probable that creative attorneys will find ways to get them in anyway—perhaps in third-party claims based on personal injury or property damage, or through government suits for damage to natural resources under §107 (a)(4)(C). EPA has always had the power to contribute its own funds toward "mixed" financing of cleanup costs, but budget pressures imposed by Congress provide little incentive for EPA to exercise restraint when dipping into the deep pockets of private defendants.

Whatever the effect of these statutory nods in the direction of settlement, some further additions to CERCLA are likely to extend formal litigation. Procedurally, settlement agreements can no longer be authorized by EPA administrators, but now require a formal consent decree approved by the federal courts.[81] Parties to settlement negotiations can thus be assured of a day in court to challenge any formula for apportioning damages, a power that "may well result in litigation and accompanying expenses that will make the decree itself unappealing to those who would otherwise be willing to accept it."[82]

New rules also permit formal participation by the general public and/or state governments in developing offical cleanup plans, in negotiating settlements, and in interpretating state environmental regulations.[83] The principle of community involvement is well established in other environmental protection statutes, including the development of long-range planning documents. But the same kind of participation in complex negotiations over remedies at specific sites "is likely to [extend] considerably" both the settlement and litigation process under CERCLA. At nearly every site there are "plenty of issues that can create polarizing and time-consuming argument during the development of a remedy, particularly since more parties with frequently diverse interests must be invited to participate in the choice of remedies."[84]

The adverse interests of state and local authorities are indeed sharpened by recent amendments, which explicitly deny immunity to "any state or local government which has caused or contributed to the release or threatened release of a hazardous substance from the facility."[85] This provision codifies a trend that was already emerging in Superfund case law, under which states may be treated as ordinary defendants by EPA or by potentially responsible parties seeking contribution. In the celebrated case of the Stringfellow Acid Pits, for example, the state of California was held to be a responsible party based on its "active role in site investigation, geological studies, subsequent representations to third parties, supervision and regulation of site construction, operation, and maintenance of the site."[86]

State immunity from civil suits in federal court, protected under the Eleventh Amendment, is now deemed to be waived by state involvement in federal environmental programs.[87] Such a loss of immunity is particularly eventful as this whole area of law moves closer to absolute liability, steered by the combined pressure of vigorous federal enforcement, federal judicial interpretations, and federal statutory language. State conduct in designing environmental policies and implementing regulations will additionally provide a stronger basis for third-party actions against the states, following the lead of CERCLA case law.[88]

There may ultimately be implications for future federal liability behind this erosion of sovereign immunity. Although federal cradle-to-grave regulation of hazardous substances began only in 1976 with the passage of RCRA, the time is approaching when conditions at many dump sites will have been shaped in some fashion by federal regulatory standards, or at least by their implementation. EPA has reason to worry about its own eventual joinder as a defendant in third-party suits[89]; and while courts cannot impose money damages on EPA without specific authority under the FTCA, they could reduce the CERCLA liability of third parties by apportioning responsibility to federal agencies.[90]

Other future areas for increased litigation concern the procedural rights of Superfund defendants, under both the Administrative Procedures Act and the Constitution.[91] EPA has been largely successful in insulating itself from most procedural challenges until relatively late stages of cleanup operations. When EPA begins investigating a particular site, its actions are subject to immediate judicial review, although courts have generally upheld the broad investigatory powers now backed by statutory amendments. However, once EPA has decided to proceed with cleaning up a site, courts have consistently deferred procedural challenges by Superfund defendants until EPA files an action for reimbursement of funds.[92] Thus EPA can effectively postpone meaningful judicial review of its decisions and methods until well after commitments to specific remedies have already been made.

Balanced against the costs and delays of Superfund litigation, we must ask what sort of accountability our society may eventually hope to achieve. The individualized justice of traditional common law—with or without the moral halo bestowed by the Tort Policy Working Group—is scarcely discernible as CERCLA staggers into its second five-year term. Judicial interpretation had already tilted the Superfund tort process sharply in the direction of absolute liability, and recent statutory amendments have only pushed it further. Critics of this trend know to borrow their rhetoric of moral dismay directly from Justice Department attacks on judicial activism in product liability law. "Why in the name of justice," asks one of these critics, "should the courts impose liability on the innocent when the government has a cause of action against the guilty?"[93] At least in product liability cases, judges are arguably responding to the suffering of innocent personal-injury victims, in the absence of any statutory alternatives to common law. Superfund lacks both these conditions that sometimes justify the liberal trend in private law: it has unique statutory means to bring the "guilty" into court, yet it prefers to rely on overbroad liability doctrines for the sake of enhancing its revenues.[94]

An alternative goal for accountability is future deterrence of harmful behavior. The most popular elaboration of this principle, Calabresi's theory of general deterrence, envisions a partnership between the unregulated market and courts as the custodians of tort doctrines. By excluding both legislatures and public administrative agencies—both of which regulate by command rather than by market signal—tort liability doctrines are supposed to enhance the power of markets to produce efficient social decisions about aggregate levels of environmental pollution. This theory has little to say, however, about using tort rules in a regulatory context. As one EPA administrator pointed out, Superfund is "a liability allocating system that is more like a tax than a tort."[95]

The extent to which either taxation or tort liability can micromanage individual behavior in the disposal of hazardous wastes is undoubtedly limited.[96] Any stable connection between sanctions and future behavior depends on the ability of future actors to make reliable judgments of similarity between past liability decisions and future hazardous activities. In environmental areas, where evidence of causation is intrinsically statistical and the measure of long-term damage highly speculative, the most efficient sanctions would necessarily deal with aggregate harms and industrywide behavior.[97] David Rosenberg's description of a deterrence system for environmental torts provides a number of analytical reasons for dealing with mass tort behavior in collective terms. Although Rosenberg's own preference seems to remain with judicial administration of liability systems, he allows the prospect that administrative agencies might play an important role in implementing the procedures he recommends.[98]

For Superfund cleanups, the institutional demands on a liability system are far less complex than the usual mass-tort action. There is no personal compensation process to be coordinated with accountability issues, and the federal government follows a completely separate script (under RCRA) in regulating hazardous substances. It remains an open question at what level of aggregation one might best allocate the costs of cleaning up toxic dump sites: among all active generators or disposers of chemical substances, among companies that make use of chemical substances in production, or among businesses generally. Even if one accepts EPA's rosiest forecast of individualized cost recovery under CERCLA litigation, most of Superfund's cost will be imposed on one or more collective levels. Despite the frequent call by economic critics for more individualized cost accounting, CERCLA's broader approach to cost internalization is probably as individualized as it ought to be.

Federal Preemption of Private Liability: Nuclear Accidents

The lively controversy over nuclear power in the United States has been further enlivened since 1957 by decennial renewals of the Price-Anderson Act,[99] the federal law that structures civil liability for damage from nuclear energy. In 1987 Congress was unable to agree on terms for renewal, leaving a gap of nearly one year before the statute was reauthorized—this time for fifteen years.[100] Meanwhile the congressional debate has raised important options for future approaches to accidents involving nuclear power.

Some proponents of privatization have argued that the statute is unnecessary: that the nuclear industry is sufficiently mature to coexist with a combination of private insurance and the prevailing tort system to see it (and everyone else) through a nuclear accident.[101] Critics of nuclear power oppose statutory caps on private liability, balking at any policy that would make commercial operators less than fully responsible for their deeds. Tort-law conceptions of accountability thus conveniently serve the political goals of those opposing commercial development of nuclear energy.

As the latest Price-Anderson debate dragged on, however, doubts about privatization were heard from numerous quarters. The nuclear power industry, not surprisingly, had no desire to see its potential civil liability uncapped; and critics of tort law argued that the compensation system would break down in any case, once the value of claims surpassed the current threshold level. Both positions warn that federal policy should be more concrete about how it plans to handle compensation claims exceeding any statutory limits.

In addition, public attention has increasingly focused on nuclear energy programs directed by federal agencies. While opponents of commercial nuclear power concentrate mainly on the 109 licensed commercial facilities, the Price-Anderson Act also covers some fifty-seven nuclear reactors currently operated by federal agencies and nonprofit educational institutions, as well as the more than fifty federal contractors responsible for implementing national nuclear policy in the fields of research, transportation, and waste disposal.[102] Recent legislation expanding federal programs, such as the Nuclear Waste Policy Act of 1982,[103] places these public activities closer to center stage in the overall drama of nuclear power. The public nuclear energy sector, as it grows more active and diverse, is certainly of no less concern to public safety than the commercial power sector. And it is here that privatization meets its most serious challenge.

For the past thirty years, after the federal government changed its initial policy of maintaining a monopoly over the peaceful development of atomic energy, private industry has been willing to pursue its research and production roles only after receiving statutory protection from catastrophic liability.[104] This protection has taken two basic forms: statutory limits on total civil liability that may result from a single nuclear accident, and federally guaranteed financial schemes to ensure that compensation funds are available up to that limit. Under the pre-1988 Price-Anderson formula, liability limits diverged slightly for accidents involving commerical power facilities and federal contractors: in 1987 those limits were $705 million and $500 million, respectively.[105] Since only the former figure had changed (slightly) since 1957, most people agreed that increases were long overdue. The 1988 renewal raised coverage tenfold to around $7 billion, which represents a compromise between those wanting to maintain current levels and those favoring removal of all limits.[106]

The insurance aspects of Price-Anderson differ significantly for commerical facilities and federal contractors. The former have reached sufficient numbers and financial stability to pay the full costs of insuring against claims, based on a federally guaranteed system permitting retroactive collection of "deferred premiums"—divided equally among all facilities—should an accident occur at any one of them. Indeed, the profit picture seemed healthy enough in 1988 to finance the ten-fold increase in liability limits approved by Congress. The federal government's major role is in structuring large payouts: dividing compensation costs retrospectively among all commercial facilities, and spreading its collection of deferred premiums over sufficient years to preserve the industry's profitability.[107] Federal contractors, on the other hand, presently require direct indemnity agreements fully underwritten by the Department of Energy; and thus the federal treasury is responsible for reimbursing private parties for all civil penalties incurred, up to the statutory limit. The same procedure for full federal indemnification continues under the new $7 billion threshold level. [108]

The Price-Anderson Act, in its various editions, offers a baroque example of the American impulse to privatize questions of collective responsibility. To its great good fortune, the United States has been spared any serious nuclear accidents that would have put this structure to the test. In the absence of case studies, and faced with conflicting scientific views on the impact of significant nuclear damage, lobbying groups are able to take refuge in convenient assumptions about the behavior of private markets and the common-law liability system as solutions to large-scale social problems.

Experience from the swine flu and Superfund programs, however, ought to alert us to the capacity for confusion, delay, and inequity inherent in tort-law processes—notwithstanding the use of statutes to fine-tune the private legal system. These results, along with the mounting disarray of tort processes in handling asbestos claims, were scarcely mentioned in congressional discussion of Price-Anderson revisions. As in the product liability debate, tort reform in the field of nuclear accidents is surrounded by a haze of legal rhetoric, interest-group bargaining, and naive confidence in the behavioral efficacy of finely balanced economic incentives.

Basic distinctions between public and private responsibilities cannot, however, be made to disappear as easily as advocates of privatization might suppose. The Price-Anderson Act began with the federal government's decision to spin off to the private economic sector the development of atomic energy resources for peaceful, commercial uses. Encouraging nuclear safety, however, was *not* left to private market forces; through the Atomic Energy Commission and its successor agencies, the government has developed a strong regulatory presence in the field of nuclear power. [109] No one today maintains that the tort system is an adequate substitute for continued regulation, although opponents of commercial nuclear power now assert its vital importance in the total system of safety incentives.

The second continuing role for public accountability relates to the statutory limits on civil liability: what lies beyond those limits? To give the private insurance scheme any chance to work, federal law must interdict all liability beyond an amount that can be conveniently financed. In thus setting a numerical boundary line to private responsibility, the law intimates that some form of public accountability is already waiting on the other side. Congress, however, will commit itself to addressing these excess liability claims only after the fact.[110] Like the far side of the moon, the realm of truly large-scale damages remains blocked from view, obscured by the private accountability system. With liability limits now raised to $7 billion, we hope that federal responsibility will never be tested.

The rising importance of noncommercial nuclear activity will, nonetheless, force the issue of public accountability back into the limelight. By increasing liability limits for commercial nuclear facilities, Congress also accepted those same limits in its indemnity program for private contractors.[111] But consider, for instance, the relatively new federal role in supervising the disposal of nuclear waste: the combined lessons of the swine flu and Superfund programs ought to arouse some caution before Congress opens its doors to billions of dollars in liability claims.[112] It is unlikely that any statutory tinkering with litigation procedures could produce a regime more favorable to a government defendant than the swine flu mechanism. But a mere 4,000 administrative claims—based on relatively swift medical reactions to a common exposure—have required more than a decade of litigation to award damages totaling less than $100 million, or about 1.5 percent of the new Price-Anderson liability ceiling. A nuclear accident, even one approaching the relatively limited scale of Chernobyl, would face at least three additional substantive complexities: latent injuries spread out over thirty or more years, human susceptibility to a wide number of life-threatening ailments, and the co-presence of widescale property damage.[113]

Should a nuclear accident occur as part of the federal hazardous-waste disposal program, federal indemnity arrangements would appear to make the government vicariously responsible for acts of its contractors, assuming a liability regime similar to that developed under the Superfund cost-recovery effort. What the federal government has sown as plaintiff in that tortlike program, so would it most likely reap as a surrogate defendant in private litigation. In addition, the level of damages would need to cover not only the costs of cleanup—as in Superfund actions—but also compensation for personal injury and property damage. The volume of compensation claims would be substantially increased by whatever degree the pro-plaintiff presumptions found in Superfund litigation were carried over into private litigation of nuclear damage claims. Could the federal government depend on later contribution suits to recover from private parties? Only if it could argue its way around some one hundred Department of Energy indemnification contracts, presently covering fifty prime contractors and 70,000 subcontractors and suppliers.[114] Even so, it would probably face formidable burdens of proof in shifting responsibility onto other parties, given its extensive involvement in coordinating nuclear waste policy.

These substantive and strategic problems of defining public responsibility for nuclear accidents were largely neglected in the Price-Anderson debate, which centered mostly on adjusting the private responsibility of commercial nuclear facilities. If private models cause confusion in the realm of public accountability, they are scarcely less muddled in the nominally private sphere. For nuclear accidents at commercial facilities, the Price-Anderson Act attempts to combine the compensation procedures of tort law with a financing mechanism designed to insure funding up to the statutory limits of private liability. This mixture suggests the kind of public use of private-law procedures favored by the progressive movement in tort reform. The fact that the federal government's own resources have been necessary for structuring the insurance program creates little tension for progressive analysts. Moreover, the policy of spreading insurance premiums across the entire nuclear power industry anticipated the recent judicial innovation of "market share" apportionment of damages in mass-tort litigation.

Inheritors of this policy tradition are among today's strongest advocates of shifting still more responsibility into the private sphere.[115] Noting the increased financial resources of commercial power facilities, they argued strongly in Congress for removing all limits to civil liability—and held out for a substantial increase as the need for political compromise became clear. As was argued earlier, this emphasis forces public responsibility farther into the background, confining it to supervising the orderly spreading of insurance costs across the entire industry and (if necessary) over time. This recommendation, however, encounters one of the central ambiguities of responsibility under tort law: whether it should aim to individualize accountability, or to leave it at the broader level of aggregate liability. Those who express the greatest confidence in microeconomic efficiency (along with tort-law mechanisms) would envision further litigation to indemnify "innocent" commercial operators, imposing the full costs of compensation on defendants, including equipment designers, manufacturers, subcontractors, vendors, or any other potentially responsible parties.[116]

As with the Superfund effort to pinpoint responsibility, this approach overlooks the tension between a rhetoric of individualism and the creative judicial doctrines that are necessary for handling mass tort claims under common-law procedures. Tort law cannot easily shift accident losses in environmental cases without the benefit of progressive liability doctrines: imposing strict or enterprise liability, disallowing the major common-law defenses to liability, shifting the burden of proof on causation, recognizing some version of joint and several liability, and extending the statute of limitations. Experienced litigators in the toxic-torts field have stressed the central importance of these doctrines,[117] and the federal government's Superfund effort has aptly dramatized their effect. By the time we import these convenient fictions, however, the rhetoric of accountability has lost its intuitive appeal. After all, the progressive approach to tort law created these tools to meet the compensation interests of plaintiffs.[118] As a system of apportioning personal accountability, it has been strongly disputed by both moral philosophy and welfare economics.

We turn, therefore, to the question of victim compensation under the Price-Anderson Act. This statutory concoction of the 1950s, along with its later accretions, anticipated many of the problems that have since unfolded with mass tort cases: the vast scale of damages, likely to exhaust the resources of individual defendants; the unavailability of private insurance in a volatile legal system; the need to spread potentially large risks more broadly than the liability process can manage; and difficulties encountered by plaintiffs alleging latent but statistically predictable injuries. It also anticipated some of the major statutory techniques lately proposed for national product liability reform, vaccine injuries like the swine flu incident, and hazardous-waste cleanup under Superfund.

Compared with other statutory schemes, the Price-Anderson Act does relatively little to increase the effectiveness of ordinary tort procedures for dealing with environmental accidents. The standard rhetoric surrounding all discussions of Price-Anderson emphasizes its commitment to compensate the public "fully" and "promptly."[119] But it relies on tort doctrines and procedures that differ very little from what the courts would routinely apply in the late 1980s, absent statutory guidance.[120]

Price-Anderson's major doctrinal innovation, adopted in the late 1960s, permitted the Nuclear Regulatory Commission (NRC) to transform the governing liability standard into one of strict liability, by classifying a given accident as an "extraordinary nuclear occurrence."[121] In most states, surely, nuclear accidents of almost any sort would be treated as ultrahazardous activities subject to strict rules of liability favoring the plaintiff.[122] But the major burden on plaintiffs in nuclear injury cases would remain: proof of medical causation. As both the swine flu and the asbestos cases demonstrate, courts are badly equipped to render individual decisions on medical causation where the evidence is inherently probabilistic.[123] The factual inquiry into causation consumes extensive pretrial investigation, while it also imposes a heavy strategic burden on the plaintiff.[124] The major statutory means for removing this hurdle from the plaintiff's path is some type of burden-shifting presumption, as we shall see in Chapter 9. So far that approach has not received serious attention in the legislative debate over Price-Anderson, which remains focused more on accountability issues.

By far the most significant nuclear incident yet to occur in the United States—the accident at Pennsylvania's Three Mile Island facility in March 1979—was not, as it turned out, an "extraordinary nuclear occurrence."[125] In making its judgment, the Nuclear Regulatory Commission had to conjure with statutory language limiting such "extraordinary" events to instances where property damage or personal injury was caused by an actual release of radioactive materials. Although some excess radioactivity did escape into the atmosphere around Three Mile Island, the major contamination was contained within the facility itself. It was rather the fear of radioactive danger that motivated Pennsylvanians to abandon their homes and jobs, for which they later sought compensation. While damages of more than $40 million were ultimately awarded for these and other claims, they had to be heard under state tort rules, not the strict liability standard of Price-Anderson.[126] The House bill that became law in 1988 "makes it clear that the Act does cover the cost of precautionary evacuations" in cases where a radiation release "appeared imminent but did not occur."[127] It does so, however, only if state liability rules would allow such claims in particular situations.

The official declaration that an accident counts as "extraordinary" has the additional procedural effect of requiring all cases to be consolidated in the federal district court for the district where the accident occurred. Without that declaration, federal courts would typically lack jurisdiction to hear nuclear accident claims. When the NRC reached its decision about the Three Mile Island accident, claims that had already been consolidated in federal court had to be dismissed.[128] The 1988 revision of Price-Anderson now authorizes exclusive federal jurisdiction for all nuclear incidents.[129] However, as in the swine flu cases, federal courts are still expected to apply unreconstructed state legal doctrines; thus claims from a nuclear accident in Pennsylvania would be heard under a different body of law than an accident in New Jersey. By contrast, some versions of national product liability legislation have tried to standardize liability rules for the country as a whole. Program models examined in Chapter 9 take even more drastic steps to shield compensation rules from the variations across state jurisdictions.

Missing also from the Price-Anderson debate was any consideration of a two-tiered structure to expedite the informal settlement of claims. When we examined this device in Chapter 7 (in the context of national product liability legislation) and again in this chapter (in the context of swine flu), we found reasons to doubt whether the administrative tier would (or could) meet its intended purpose. The chief architect of such plans, Jeffrey O'Connell, has criticized the specific form of some two-tiered statutory models but misses few occasions to restate the general principle.[130] Whatever we finally think of this approach, the failure of Price-Anderson to incorporate any alternative dispute-resolution mechanisms seems a serious omission. Perhaps the statute's 1950s origins and competing issues at each renewal period have conspired against any consideration of expedited settlement procedures. Although nothing we have seen in this book suggests that such procedures are effective in the context of environmental accidents, everything we *have* seen suggests that mass tort litigation encounters monumental congestion—causing innovative minds (both judicial and legislative) to look for procedural alternatives.[131]

From another standpoint, however, the Price-Anderson model follows a unique two-tiered structure that may direct our attention beyond the O'Connell formula. Instead of running compensation claims through the gauntlet of administrative processes followed by tort law, Price-Anderson envisions two entirely different compensation approaches: falling back on some unspecified public liability principle whenever tort law has reached the limits of its capacity. This ordering anticipates the most innovative statutory models for handling environmental-accident claims: those that abrogate the tort-law system altogether. Several of these models will be examined in Chapter 9. They differ from statutes examined in previous chapters by treating tort law—at best—as merely a first stage. Some proposals for compensating occupational disease eliminate the tort system entirely, using the strategy of workers' compensation.

The Price-Anderson Act suspends the tort system when the private sector runs out of money.[132] Given recent estimates on what the commercial nuclear power industry can afford in the way of accident insurance, these tort-law horizons have now been pushed back farther than the eye can currently see. But the problem of underfunded defendants in mass-tort cases has only recently received proper attention, following the well-publicized bankruptcies of Johns-Manville along with several other asbestos producers, and A. H. Robins, Inc., producers of the Dalkon Shield contraceptive device.[133] While some commentators on these cases have suggested that bankruptcy proceedings offer the freedom needed by judges to take proper hold of mass-accident claims,[134] the sad fact is that compensation funds from private defendants often run out before full compensation can be achieved. If future environmental diseases are discovered that replay the asbestos experience, we can expect those claims to end up in bankruptcy court as well. And if legal costs continue to absorb the same high percentage of defendants' resources, a sizable proportion of funds otherwise available to compensate victims will have been squandered on preserving the judicial process.

Price-Anderson, despite its faults, was an early recognition that we need to devise entirely new compensation procedures, at least for those situations where tort-law procedures fail. The spectre of a catastrophic nuclear accident, by keeping before us the prospect of aggregate claims beyond comparison even with past environmental cases, requires us to explore those alternative procedures in some detail.

As the last several chapters have suggested, American policy makers display varying degrees of confidence in tort procedures—but nearly all of them are overly optimistic. Even if the commercial nuclear industry is well-enough financed to pay some very large compensation claims, it may not be sensible to devote such bountiful resources to paying high administrative costs for a system ill designed to adjudicate environmental injuries. But more important, the asbestos

cases have shown that environmental injuries based on other toxic substances may suddenly grow beyond the bounds of defendants' resources. Defendants may not always come as neatly labeled as nuclear
power plants—which are already under agreement to spread compensation costs among themselves. Nor, without the unique level of planning for the insurance aspects of Price-Anderson, will other defendants be as prepared to bear billion-dollar burdens.

This analysis suggests that concrete administrative alternatives to
tort law are a necessary supplement to the policies we have surveyed
in previous chapters. The Price-Anderson Act, even after months of
heated debate, refused to get specific about what lies in store after the
entire tort system has been suspended. Congress has avoided the issue by repeatedly threatening to "study" it—always at some later
date. But we already have useful models of publicly administered compensation systems, ranging from fully implemented programs to blue-
prints for future policies. They are invariably responses to the special
inadequacies of tort-law procedures in the context of environmental
injuries.

Conclusion: The Road to Public
Responsibility

Persistent calls for a *public* tort law suggest one possible future for the
American legal system as it confronts the unprecedented challenges of
environmental accidents. It takes little effort for lawyers and judges
steeped in the creative fictions of tort doctrines to exploit the analogy
between public and private action. After all, if private corporate action
has been assimilated into common-law individualism, the same can
happen with government action. Perhaps the cruel randomness of environmental injuries compels us to cling to traditional concepts of action and responsibility, protecting our native confidence that we can
still control our destiny.

The civil rights lawsuit, mentioned at the beginning of this chapter, is probably the purest expression of the trend toward privatization
of public responsibility. Taken to its Lockean extreme, the private
view of public life makes the state into an instrument for violating
personal liberties—except for its minimal peace-keeping services. As
Richard Epstein has argued, it follows from this premise that federal
regulatory policies are "takings" of property interests, typically with-

out compensation. The concept of a "public" is completely absent from this social universe, just as it is absent from the realm of private law, where action is individual and harms are unjustified violations of personal rights. Epstein's question is very simple: "Would the government action be treated as a taking of private property if it had been performed by some private party?" Using this approach, "every transaction between the State and the individual can thus be understood as a transaction between private individuals."[135] A revival of litigation strategies challenging federal regulation as violating the constitutional protection against uncompensated "takings" is only the latest manifestation of this conceptual individualism.[136]

As any common lawyer knows, however, analogies rarely work in only one direction. Private law concepts have a Protean nature that can point just as easily toward expansion as reduction. Pursuing this thread, we may see government liability as a path out of this Lockean universe, leading instead toward a recognition of social interdependence. In this alternative world, harmful events on any major scale cannot be reduced to interpersonal transaction without leaving an important remainder, which calls forth a qualitatively different type of responsibility. As a small and ambiguous step in that direction, the private law concept of liability applied to government policy may preserve the notion of public responsibility from utter fragmentation. As our society becomes increasingly aware of serious risks endemic to the modern environment—generalized in source but specific in their random effects—we can expect this powerful metaphor to ramify widely. What we cannot plausibly attribute to individuals may instead require some collective response.

The metaphor suggests that responsibility generates liability, and that the state might ensure compensation for the random injuries associated with environmental accidents. But responsibility on the public level can be further identified with accident prevention and the regulation of future behavior. The two functions of compensation and accountability are closely linked under common law, where they are traditionally applied exclusively to individual persons and events. Public responsibility breaks the mutual dependence of these two functions whenever our environment denies us the warm comfort of specificity. Individual victims may find compensation, even when their injuries cannot be traced to specific defendants. Individual and corporate producers may face standards of accountability, even when their actions cannot be tied to specific harmful occurrences. Purely private responsibility would require both functions to be mutually defining; public responsiblity recognizes that we live in a more complex world. We shall explore in Chapter 10 how these two functions, precisely because of their separation, can become more effectively coordinated.

The various studies in this chapter have shown how the concept of liability in federal programs inspires new approaches to emerging problems of social interdependence. Unfortunately, the metaphor brings with it strong institutional commitments to judicial *procedures*, to which technocratic hubris adds a thin veneer of statutory fine tuning. In recent decades, as the federal government has often reluctantly played a growing role in public health, environmental protection, and energy development, it has assumed the guise of both surrogate defendant and surrogate plaintiff. Policy experts on both the right and left wings of the political spectrum have encouraged this trend toward discharging public responsibilities through private decision-making systems (conceived as some kind of mixture of economic markets and civil liability procedures). Private-law procedures, however, invariably obscure the public goals of government action. Their high administrative costs are only symptomatic of this misplaced emphasis.

Marx comments on the irony of historical change, by which revolutionary forces, "in creating something entirely new . . . conjure up the spirits of the past to their service and borrow from them names, battle slogans and costumes." The creative fictions of tort law have found new life in cloaking the forms of government policies aimed at complex environmental issues. But beneath those threadbare metaphors, a more fundamental change is taking place in our national policies. Shifting to another overworked Marxian image, the challenge is to find the "rational kernel within the mystical shell." The tort system is that shell, heavily reinforced by our common-law legal tradition, the American softness for incrementalism, and recent fashions in welfare economics and moral philosophy. What about the kernel?

We have caught glimpses of it in our discussions of the swine flu vaccination program, the Superfund cleanup campaign, and recent policy debate over nuclear safety. In each case, we have found a distinction (summed up neatly by Robert Radin) between "two models of liability, a traditional model based on a two-party accident situation and a present-day context in which risks are collectively generated and imposed on an unwary aggregation of victims."[137]

In the Superfund program Congress has tried to combine both models, using a costly and time-consuming process borrowed from traditional tort law to help gain control over the collective generation of toxic hazards. Despite the formidable techniques available under modern tort law for confronting the social dimensions of the hazardous-waste problem, EPA's litigation program diverts economic resources from the ultimate goal of increasing public health and safety. As Radin notes, "the problems raised by the numerical aggregation of potentially responsible parties—multiple generators, transporters, and operators in the hazardous waste disposal chain—create complexities that are not easily accommodated by the traditional torts process."[138]

It is worth recapitulating the many auxiliary devices Congress has mobilized in order to give this anachronistic battle every possible chance for victory. First, Congress had to create a statutory structure giving itself (as well as private parties) the power to sue potential defendants—thus bypassing the private-law barriers of standing, jurisdiction, limitations, and burden of proof. Next it had to insinuate (loudly enough for interpreting courts to hear) a standard of strict liability, to overcome the intrinsic limits of traditional liability standards based on individualized fault. And in a host of other provisions, Congress had to ensure that the deck was stacked against defendants on such matters as causation, vicarious action, and joint and several liability. But even with these statutory crutches, Congress has not been able to create a litigation device for converting environmental damages into individualized torts. We thus reach Radin's conclusion: "Once an effort is made to cabin a mass tort episode within the structure of the traditional tort process, the litigation takes on a life of its own. Consolidation engenders lawyers' committees, hybrid pre-settlement procedures, trade-offs on claims, pooled responsibility for risk."[139]

The Superfund experiment treats the federal government as a consolidated plaintiff—the surrogate for all those aggrieved by hazardous-waste pollution. The swine flu program made the federal government into the sole defendant, and the source of all compensation for those injured by the ill-fated vaccine. With the Price-Anderson Act, the federal government added the role of mobilizing enormous financial resources, without which the private liability system could not function. We sincerely hope that this last program will never be tested, but the lessons of the other two can only increase our trepidation. Each program offers the illusion of individualized justice to mask the growing costs of collective living.

Chapter 9

Administrative Compensation Systems

> *Institutionally, it is difficult for courts and legislatures to go fast or far within a compensation system, since the traditional limits of the system help define its legitimacy, and its legitimacy in turn suggests definite limits.*[1]

Workers' Compensation: The Pioneer Administrative System

The most extensive statutory incursion into tort-law procedures was also one of the first. By 1920, following trends in Europe during the late nineteenth century, most states had passed workers' compensation laws in response to heightened concern about workplace injuries.[2] Despite continuing variations among state programs, for seventy years these statutes have provided the major administrative alternative to common-law compensation procedures.[3] In contrast to recent tort-reform proposals, workers' compensation abandoned the strategy of managing judicial rules by statutory edict. Instead it created an entirely new claims procedure, in which workplace victims could receive limited benefits without meeting the most onerous doctrinal tests of common law: negligence, assumption of risk, and contributory negligence.[4]

Current workers' compensation programs require the claimant's employer to pay compensation no matter who might have caused an injury (even including the victim). But benefits have remained substantially below what is potentially available to plaintiffs under tort law: in addition to medical expenses, successful claimants receive only partial replacement of lost income.[5] They are not directly compensated for intangible losses (including pain and suffering) nor may they seek punitive damages. Employers must either purchase insurance or otherwise guarantee adequate funding.[6]

Workers' compensation introduced a nettlesome and much-litigated eligibility standard by covering only those injuries "arising out of or in the course of employment." As we shall see, such attempts to remove specific categories of injury from the judicial process are only partly successful, owing to the intrinsic vagueness of statutory boundaries. Within the workers' compensation structure, as a result, employers and victims have guided the administrative appeals process toward increasingly adversarial forms. In addition, creative judges are steadily reinventing ways for injured workers to initiate claims within the tort system.[7]

Under such pressures the administrative costs of state workers' compensation systems have risen steeply, especially for environmental work-accident claims.[8] Although some analysts appear confident that administrative systems can respond effectively to occupational diseases,[9] the record so far suggests a more ambiguous future. One possibility, assuming further development of adversarial trends, is eventual merger with tort law. Alternatively, administrative systems may adopt broader, more inclusive statutory presumptions affecting eligibility, evidence, and benefits. As they move in this direction, however, such programs inevitably cross an invisible border into the larger social-welfare structure. Both futures are prefigured in the American experience with workers' compensation and selected occupational disease programs.

Absent any definitive study of how workers' compensation developed in the United States, the topic has provided "a battleground for historians of differing ideological persuasions."[10] Some commentators dwell on the plight of injured workers under early common-law doctrines favorable to employers, while others contend that judicial reform was already changing those doctrines, thereby threatening employers with higher costs.[11] Most analysts agree, however, that abandoning tort law for an insurance scheme was a practical compromise meeting the minimal expectations of both employers and labor.

Insurance, with its periodic payment of fixed premiums, made the cost of industrial injuries more predictable for employers than the quixotic system of liability suits. It substituted small regular payments by all employers for infrequent but enormous damage payments by a few. For employers, then, insurance removed a great deal of the risk of doing business that had been created by the liability system. For workers, it substituted a greater likelihood (if not certainty) of small payments to all injured workers for the small chance of successful litigation and a large award to a very few injured workers.[12]

The term *insurance* is initially confusing as a description of workers' compensation. It is employers who purchase insurance (or who self-insure) to guarantee direct payments to injured employees. This is different from a system of social insurance, under which workers would apply to the government for benefits, paid from a fund derived from either general revenues or special levies.[13] In both the original British scheme and American legislation, the costs of benefits were placed on employers on the theory that "losses should be allocated to the enterprise that creates the hazards that cause the losses, and ultimately distributed among those who consume its products."[14] Thus workers' compensation was also meant to promote industrial safety by imposing economic incentives on employers to prevent at least some accidents from occurring. Although permitting (and indeed requiring) employers to purchase insurance would seem to dilute these incentives, some preventive effect might be rescued if insurance premiums reflected the individual accident records of particular employers.[15]

The political compromises that create a program are not always able to sustain it over the long run. Although workers' compensation is now entrenched in fifty state-administrative structures (in addition to special programs for federal employees), it faces a completely different policy environment at the close of the twentieth century from that at the beginning. Perhaps the major difference—along with the change in scale and diversity of American industry—is the massive growth of federal authority in both industrial regulation and social welfare. Regulation under the Occupational Safety and Health Act of 1970 has tried to reduce the number of accident victims, not just compensate them; and public welfare programs based on need or entitlement now provide an essential safety net for injured workers. These trends simultaneously protect and challenge the workers' compensation system, but recent signs suggest that the challenges are becoming more serious. Above all, the unmet problems of occupational disease suggest the time has come to reexamine the entire system.

Why Workers' Compensation Is No Longer Enough

Under late twentieth-century conditions, political compromises on compensation must reckon with a whole new set of issues. From our earlier survey of recent tort-reform proposals, we can identify two major departures from the original workers' compensation model.[16] First, the federal government is now the focal point of reform, even though its role is viewed with great ambivalence. Second, nearly all recent proposals provide some continuing function for tort law, although it too is regarded with ambivalence. These two changes are central to current debate over occupational disease, and through that topic they invariably raise questions for the entire administrative framework of workers' compensation. Although its formal design excludes federal oversight and civil liability procedures, the operating reality of workers' compensation suggests that state administrative control is not absolute. In this section we will take a closer look at encroachments from both federal policy and judicial procedures.

Chapters 7 and 8 traced the growing federal orientation of tort-reform proposals in the fields of product liability and mass accidents involving vaccines, hazardous waste, and nuclear power. This trend echoes more fundamental socio-economic developments in the United States, made possible by changing constitutional theories of federal legislative power. By the time Congress passed the Occupational Safety and Health Act (OSHA) in 1970,[17] the commerce clause had emerged victorious over pre–New Deal doctrines of federalism. When workers' compensation first came along, however, the scope of national regulation was much more limited. Congress could not have organized workers' compensation on a national basis, even though it was able to start its own program for federal employees.[18] (The federalism of this period had its anomalies: in 1917 the Supreme Court upheld a national compensation statute for railroad workers.[19]) By the 1950s, with constitutional barriers falling away, the Department of Labor cautiously began planning a model workers' compensation statute—an idea that surfaced several times during the 1960s. On these occasions states rejected any suggestion of a possible federal takeover, and they were supported by business interests who feared higher benefit costs from any increased federal role.[20]

The closest approach to a uniform statute was the 1972 report by the National Commission on Workmen's Compensation Laws. That document outlined potential mandatory federal standards and urged congressional action unless states complied voluntarily with some nineteen basic reforms, including substantial increases in benefit levels.[21] Despite a flurry of state activity the commission's recommendations were only partly implemented, but Congress balked at any further federal initiatives.[22] As one essay on this episode has suggested, worries over the growing burden of federal disability programs probably weakened congressional resolve to improve compensation standards.[23]

Notwithstanding the endurance of state control, federal regulation or preemption in the future will probably depend on how states react to three major challenges facing workers' compensation: rising administrative costs, growing litigiousness, and a recent surge of occupational-disease claims. All three problems have plagued the system since its beginning, but they have grown notably more acute over the past two decades. The occupational-disease challenge has received the most attention, since it overlaps with other compensation crises facing the judicial system. In particular, the search for legislative solutions to the asbestos problem has reopened the case for federal reform of workers' compensation.

Most business lobbyists have objected strenuously to federal initiatives for occupational disease.[24] But as the debate over national product liability reform shows, escalating awards and administrative costs in diverse state programs may eventually promote federal action—if only to ensure more uniform, predictable costs within state programs. As occupational-disease claims enter the workers' compensation system in greater number, their cost in administrative terms could turn out to be quite high—especially if litigation is allowed to penetrate further into the appeals process.

We must also remember that companies with the greatest interest in these issues are not merely employers; many of them are also producers vulnerable to product liability suits. Since a high percentage of product liability claims are based on workplace accidents, some of these defendants might welcome federal reorganization of workers' compensation if it diminished the threat of injury suits against third parties. This explains why asbestos manufacturers—several of whom faced bankruptcy in defending mass tort claims—became the strongest supporters of federal programs for occupational disease. Just as state compensation systems currently protect employers from liability, a federal policy could immunize all who contribute to a central occupational-disease compensation fund.

The asbestos industry also hoped that some of the compensation burden could be shifted to the federal treasury, based on the theory that federal policies over several decades were at least partly responsible for the wide deployment of asbestos.[25] For reasons explored in Chapter 8, state administrative systems and tort law are both unlikely to reach questions of federal responsibility. By contrast, a number of federal statutory strategies have already been tested, including sovereign-immunity waivers (the swine flu model) and private and public insurance for catastrophic levels of injury (the Price-Anderson model). Considering the substantial growth of federal regulation over the past two decades, national policies on workplace safety and exposure to toxic materials will have a commanding impact on future rates of workplace accidents, including occupational disease. A federal compensation statute is perhaps the only way to confront federal and industry accountability on comparable terms.[26]

In addition to federalization, the major difference between workers' compensation and recent tort-reform models is the current fashion for preserving at least some tort features in statutory compensation schemes. No doubt this institutional nostalgia betrays the central role of trial lawyers in legislative horse trading. But we have also seen that all the major players—and their lobbyists—find compelling reasons to support two-tiered procedures. Plaintiffs are reluctant to surrender all recourse to tort law, since their current political bargaining strength owes nearly everything to judicial activism. Manufacturers, employers, and other defendants still hope to find justice by restoring common law to its earlier doctrinal condition; under the spell of tort reform they imagine that a few good statutory slaps will bring judges to their senses. Along with these converging interests of erstwhile adversaries, the whole climate in government over the past decade has encouraged greater use of private solutions to public problems—solutions generated by economic markets and civil litigation. Until these various perceptions change, legislators will continue to look for ways to weave tort law into public policy on accidents.

In the original compromise that yielded workers' compensation, tort procedures were abandoned only "when both sides became convinced that the game was mutually unprofitable."[27] Today, however, that conviction has eroded, with the result that litigation has already made serious inroads into what was meant to be a purely administrative system. In its daily operation, workers' compensation has assumed many features of the tort system, including costly and time-consuming appeals, along with heavy evidentiary burdens falling on claimants. With many of the statutory boundaries of workers' compensation now facing judicial challenges—especially the line between injury and disease—it is probably too late for state administration to regain full autonomy. The varied responses of more than fifty systems to the complex challenge of occupational disease show the difficulty of maintaining separate administrative schemes in a society where tort law is the final arbiter of personal injury issues.[28] If workers' compensation is not eventually broadened under some federal statutory model, the alternative may be gradual annexation by state judicial systems.[29]

Although the administrative model was a major departure from the legal status quo when workers' compensation was created, its reform image has since been eclipsed by judicial activism. Looking back to the early years of the century, it may have been important in the days of unbridled capitalism to interpose a neutral authority between worker and employer in the aftermath of workplace accidents. But when the central issue became automobile accidents, the economic class conflicts of industrialism were replaced by discrete disputes between ordinary drivers. There seemed little need to supplement the private system of litigation with anything more bureaucratic than first-party insurance bought on the open market. Damages under tort law gradually became greater and more flexible than workers' compensation benefits, while the doctrinal burdens on plaintiffs were substantially relaxed. On the whole, conventional political wisdom grew to prefer the incrementalism of litigation to building up state bureaucracies.

As judicial activism transformed fields like professional malpractice and product liability, employers came to see the workers' compensation system as a relatively safe haven compared to the heavy seas of civil litigation. State legislatures could be counted on to resist the increases in damages and social-welfare entitlements introduced by the courts and by Congress during the 1960s and 1970s. Thus workers' compensation today is often criticized as a reactionary holdout against the trend toward complete judicialization of accident policy. In contrast to the compromising spirit that attended its birth, the administrative model has settled into a confrontation with judicial activism. And although employers as a group enjoy stronger fortifications than do product liability defendants, the workers' compensation system is already under heavy siege from litigation. Defenders of the system tend to blame its problems on too much litigation, while the attackers insist there is too little.[30]

It may be impossible to sort out cause and effect, but there is at least a strong correlation between the central problems of workers' compensation and the trend toward litigation. Rising administrative costs, system delays, and award inequities all have been accompanied by increased litigation over the major legal boundaries of workers' compensation. These include the distinctions between injury and disease, work-related and non–work-related disability, employers' vicarious responsibility and third-party liability under tort law, and injury compensation and social-welfare entitlements.[31] Also in contention are the benefit levels offered by each system. After states enacted some recommendations of the 1972 National Commission on Workers' Compensation Law, benefits began to move slowly in the direction of award levels and categories recognized by tort law. This has sharpened controversy over the adequacy of workers' compensation payments: cost increases from even small changes have alarmed employers,[32] while labor groups still measure these programs by common-law standards. Employers thus feel greater urgency in challenging claims, while employees are encouraged to try for larger awards.

This adversarial climate is not confined to occupational-disease litigation, but extends throughout the workers' compensation system. In a review essay, James R. Chelius recently found it "ironic that most commentaries on workers' compensation emphasize the inefficiency of its extensive use of lawyers, while many other legal areas point to the 'streamlined' workers' compensation system as a model to be emulated."[33] Despite its original resolve to abandon common law, workers' compensation has steadily become more litigious and formalized. Edward Berkowitz summarizes the record as follows:

> An increasingly contentious system bred formality by encouraging the participation of lawyers. The presence of lawyers, despite the efforts of early administrators to exclude them, defeated efforts to hold hearings with relaxed rules of evidence and cross-questioning. Nor did the harm end there. Because of the demands on the lawyers' time, their participation increased the delays in the compensation process and raised old questions about the financial status of the worker and his potential dependence on public programs. The participation of attorneys also invited concern about

the competence of one lawyer compared with that of another and about the persistence of the mismatch between the comparatively rich insurance companies and the relatively poor workers.[34]

Workers' compensation was conceived as a purely administrative system for handling injury claims, but in practice it now shares many features of two-tiered compensation statutes. It removed doctrinal defenses for employers, but it introduced eligibility criteria that have become the focus of equally adversarial disputation. It provided alternative procedures to tort law, but those procedures have grown more formalized, and appeals to the judicial process allow claims to be replayed under standard rules of litigation. Finally, it was designed to operate without participation by lawyers, but the choice of how to present a claim or whether to contest a decision routinely requires professional judgment. "In most states," Berkowitz concludes, "it remains advisable for those seeking workers' compensation to employ the services of a lawyer."[35]

For reasons explored in Chapters 6 and 7, it seems unlikely that extra layers of litigation can successfully adapt the workers' compensation system to the hazardous workplace environments of the late twentieth century. As we shall see in the next section, most occupational-disease claims fail to clear the hurdles of either system. For more ordinary injuries, workers' compensation benefits for long-term injury are often supplemented by social entitlement programs, particularly Social Security Disability Insurance. And for some employees, private pensions and disability insurance raise benefit levels still further.[36] These supplementary disability schemes are obviously even more critical for injury victims who never file workers' compensation claims, or whose claims are denied; such is the probable fate of many disease victims whose illness cannot be easily classified as work related.[37]

If social-welfare programs plug holes in workplace compensation coverage, federal safety regulation does the same for workplace accountability. According to one recent study, half of private industry's investment in safety and health during the period 1972 to 1978 was the result of inspection and enforcement measures taken by OSHA.[38] By contrast, both workers' compensation and the tort system have been estimated to promote inconsequential levels of deterrence, given the low proportion of total accident costs registered by either system.

Perhaps the most remarkable observation which can be made is that despite approximately three-quarters of a century of public concern and controversy, one cannot conclude, on the basis of data generally cited to demonstrate the superiority of workers' compensation over negligence, that workers' compensation has effected any improvement in terms of the wage loss compensation and deterrence objectives over the evolving negligence system it replaced.[39]

A great deal of care has been expended on modeling the deterrence effects of various insurance options under workers' compensation.[40] But the relevance of formal models is considerably lessened by actual insurance practices; premium rates for many employers, for example, are not adjusted for each firm's particular accident record. And for those larger employers who are experience rated, premium costs are too small in relation to total payroll expenses to have significant impact on safety investments.[41] Most studies of deterrence under workers' compensation consider only the effects of insurance premiums, which represent a small portion of workplace accidents costs. If significant numbers of occupational disease claims never enter the compensation system, they can scarcely be registered even by the most sensitive insurance mechanism.

Additional pressures on both workers' compensation and tort law could result from federal and state programs requiring employers to publicize toxic hazards in the workplace.[42] While such right-to-know laws (along with federal medical-surveillance regulations) may ultimately bring more disease claims into one or both compensation systems, they do not address the vital issues of proof and causation. More complete social accountability for workplace injuries depends on bringing new cases into a compensation system, but only if they can be dealt with equitably and consistently. These were the goals of recently proposed administrative alternatives to state workers' compensation, which attracted increasing congressional interest as asbestos claims began to clog the judicial system.

Federal Occupational Disease Initiatives: Asbestos Statutes

Delays and inequities in claims processing under workers' compensation programs are difficult to substantiate beyond an anecdotal level, but evidence is beginning to emerge about the fate of occupational disease claims. Unlike traumatic accidents in the workplace, diseases may remain latent for many years before disabling their victims. Moreover the causal relationship between almost all serious diseases and toxic substances present in the workplace is statistical, corresponding to the concept of *environmental* injury used throughout this book. For a few diseases like mesothelioma, an accurate medical diagnosis almost certainly names the material source of illness; but for most other cancers, cardiovascular diseases, and respiratory ailments the possible sources are many—and most likely interactive. These claims are no easier to resolve under administrative procedures, where eligibility for benefits requires evidence of some causal link to the workplace, than in other compensation systems.[43]

Disease claims are currently a small share of the workers' compensation caseload, although the potential number of valid claims is undoubtedly quite large. And while the data are fragmentary, as Peter Barth reminds us in his survey of the literature, it seems plain that only a tiny portion of occupational-disease victims now file workers' compensation claims. According to one study, for example, only 3 percent of occupationally caused radiation illness was reflected in formal claims.

The volume of claims for delayed consequences of radiation exposure is surprisingly small. There appear to be fewer claims filed than would be expected, considering (a) present medical knowledge of biological effects and (b) the number of serious accidental exposures known to have taken place. . . . Although the examined claims cover a wide variety of alleged diseases there is a noticeable absence of claims for some diseases which have been demonstrated through medical research to be among the consequences.[44]

Similar conclusions have been reached in several studies of asbestos claims.[45]

Barth has analyzed the course of occupational-disease claims that were actually filed, using data from a 1975 closed-claim study by the federal Interdepartmental Workmen's Compensation Task Force. He found that disease claims were far more frequently contested by employers, less likely to be settled after being contested, subject to disproportionate delays, and ultimately less likely to be compensated.[46] Certain disease claims deviated from this pattern to the extent they looked like ordinary injuries: skin diseases, poisoning, and hearing loss were all found to have processing rates nearer those for all other workers' compensation claims. For dust diseases and respiratory conditions, however, the differences were striking; employers contested some 90 percent of such claims, in contrast to the normal 10 percent rate. In addition, these contested disease claims were about five times less likely to receive compensation than contested claims for other accidents. And among all contested claims, the average disease case took three times longer to be resolved, whatever the outcome.

Considering these patterns, it is scarcely surprising that many disease claims never enter the workers' compensation process. Barth's conclusion, based on data from a variety of sources, suggests that workers' compensation is no more successful than the tort system in handling personal injuries that take the form of diseases:

> As the frontiers of compensation of occupational diseases are pushed back by medical advances and administrative decisions, these cases will grow in importance. For this group of occupational disease cases, given the level of controversion and incidence of compromise settlements, it would be fair to question whether the workers' compensation system is "handling" these cases at all. It is difficult to justify the use of the term "no-fault" to apply to a group of cases that have, in the overwhelming majority, been controverted on the question of compensability. These claimants' typical experience with the workers' compensation system bears little resemblance to the theoretical or textbook description of the operation of the system.[47]

As long as recovery is something of a lottery, we might as well play for the higher rewards potentially available under tort law, including the money for paying legal fees.

For administrative compensation systems to become more effective than tort law in handling environmental accident claims, they have to find better ways to attract more claims into the system, to process them more quickly, and to compensate more equitably a higher proportion of claimants. Such schemes will invariably pay out larger benefits than those available under workers' compensation programs, thereby inviting opposition from employers eager to minimize insurance premiums. But employer premiums are rising anyway under the current system, driven partly by processing costs for an increasingly litigious claims system. Political compromise—at least on claims for particular diseases—should become more attractive as litigation absorbs a larger percentage of the potential compensation pool.[48]

Although an early federal asbestos compensation plan reached Congress in 1973, the concept seemed to ripen quickly during the period of 1981 to 1985 as asbestos litigation suddenly reached its current unmanageable state.[49] The major proposals would have replaced tort law (used heavily by workers to sue asbestos manufacturers) with various administrative alternatives: federally modified state workers' compensation programs, exclusive federal compensation schemes, and hybrid plans combining both state and federal proceedings. Although some of these bills would have brought significant changes to workers' compensation, they echoed that system's original spirit of practical compromise: nearly all proposals before 1985 assumed that asbestos victims would have to forgo access to the tort system in return for more expeditious, less adversarial, but also less lucrative benefits.

By the mid 1980s plaintiffs' lobbyists hardened their terms by endorsing an asbestos compensation plan that retained tort law as its second tier, following the pattern of national product liability bills.[50] Plaintiffs' stake in pending litigation had presumably reached a level where they could no longer afford to bargain away all recourse to the tort system. Perhaps this explains why Congress shifted its attention during the years 1986 to 1988 to the twin regulatory tasks of monitoring occupational health hazards and notifying workers at risk of excess exposures to disease.[51] These initiatives, without significant structural changes in compensation procedures, can only augment litigation in administrative and tort-law arenas—even though both systems have shown their inability to handle the complex factual issues raised by occupational disease. If this latest congressional strategy ultimately draws more disease claims into adversarial combat, perhaps litigation weariness will then force both sides to recalculate their long-term interests. By referring intractable statutory conflicts to the judicial system, Congress may be reacting to the same impasse it faces for federal product liability.

Among asbestos claims procedures that would have abolished tort-law remedies, we find a bewildering number of compensation and accountability options. Most plans were designed to supplement state workers' compensation, which became in effect the first stage of a two-level process.[52] These plans varied more in the funding of compensation awards, by spreading the burden in different ways among present employers, asbestos manufacturers and distributors, other industries, and the federal government itself.[53] Most plans were ominously silent on how claims authorities (whether federal or state) were to handle complex questions of medical diagnosis and causation. A few included statutory presumptions for directing case outcomes; but by 1981 this technique was already viewed with skepticism, having been blamed for widespread chaos in the federal Black Lung Program.[54]

Two-level systems preserving some features of workers' compensation share a common objective with hybrid compensation models that salvage elements of tort law: the goal is to combine the most desirable parts of two distinct systems. From workers' compensation, the first procedural level would preserve state autonomy, the employer's exemption from civil liability, and lower, more predictable benefits than tort damages. Meanwhile the second procedural level—federal and administrative—would offer important new possibilities: ensuring national minimum benefit standards, extending the liability exemption beyond employers to other asbestos defendants (thus ending product liability suits against asbestos manufacturers), and distributing costs beyond the employer to other "responsible" parties, including the U. S. government. This second level contains something of value for claimants, whose benefits would likely be raised (or even rescued entirely) by a nationally administered program. But the major advantages would accrue to defendants in asbestos litigation, who could replace their full exposure to tort liability with contributions to a federally administered compensation fund.

Just how much they would gain depends, of course, on who else contributes. The asbestos victim's present employer was generally the first contributor under two-level plans, up to the maximum benefits mandated by each state's workers' compensation system. Even if most such awards were later topped up by the federally administered fund, asbestos manufacturers could at least share those costs with a wider circle than fellow defendants in tort actions. Some bills, in addition to including importers and minor distributors of asbestos products in their financing formulae, would have required substantial contributions from the federal government based on its unique role as importer, buyer, seller, contract specifier, stockpiler, and regulator of asbestos since the 1930s.[55] As mentioned earlier, a federal scheme that excludes tort law in some fashion is probably the only way to hold the United States financially accountable for its own past actions—so long as the courts and Justice Department support a strict sovereign-immunity defense in asbestos cases.

All this careful positioning of compensation burdens could mean very little, however, unless some fact-finding process can successfully resolve the complex issues of medical causation present in most asbestos cases.[56] Barth's analysis shows that about 90 percent of such cases making it into the workers' compensation system are contested by employers, thus provoking a secondary litigation crisis surrounding appeals. His conclusion (quoted earlier) questions the capacity of workers' compensation to handle these cases in any meaningful sense, and certainly not according to the "theoretical or textbook" (or nonadversarial) premises of workers' compensation. We suspect that industry supporters of these bills, while exuding confidence in the workers' compensation process, would actually prefer litigation on these terms, in exchange for their present burden under tort law. But lobbyists and lawyers for asbestos plaintiffs just as surely hope to shift litigation entirely into the civil liability arena.

Black Lung and the Problem of Statutory Presumptions

Whether or not they can retain access to tort law, plaintiffs favor statutory presumptions requiring state or federal compensation authorities to resolve doubtful medical and causation issues in their favor. Among the asbestos bills taken up in congressional hearings, only the 1982 proposal sponsored by Representative George Miller (D-Cal.) included such presumptions. Even that bill left much ground for future litigation, stipulating simply that workers who were exposed to asbestos and later developed either asbestosis or mesothelioma would enjoy an "irrebuttable" presumption that the disease was occupationally caused, while those with lung cancer would have a "rebuttable" presumption.[57]

Both presumptions were coolly received by parties scheduled to pay into the federal compensation fund.[58] The irrebuttable presumption raised two separate issues. First, although asbestosis and mesothelioma are highly correlated with asbestos exposure, they do not (indeed cannot) correlate perfectly. But more important, claimants hoping to win automatic benefits could arguably find doctors willing to stretch medical diagnoses (about which there can always be some doubt) into these two categories. Critics were even more opposed to the rebuttable presumption for lung cancer, which has been linked epidemiologically with many substances besides asbestos. "Such a presumption," said one group, "is tantamount to legislating a diagnosis which medical and epidemiological data does not support."[59]

These arguments notwithstanding, the failure of most compensation proposals to address medical causation raises a further set of issues. Without some use of presumptions, the workers' compensation system may, for all practical purposes, prevent many disease claims from ever reaching the second procedural level. As Barth's analysis shows, that system imposes a substantial burden by requiring each claimant to establish both a medical diagnosis and occupational causation. This is an especially costly procedure in both financial and strategic terms, given the propensity of employers to contest respiratory-disease claims. It also seems highly impractical from a general policy standpoint to impose this burden separately on many thousands of individuals seeking compensation in fifty separate jurisdictions.[60] These are some of the reasons why the Miller bill, through statutory presumptions, chose to shift at least part of that burden onto the federally administered fund.

Apart from standard objections based on the welfare-economic theory of optimal deterrence,[61] opposition to statutory presumptions is often based on the notorious experience of the Black Lung Program, the only existing federal compensation scheme devoted to a single occupational disease. A brief look at Black Lung is thus essential for any evaluation of other federal compensation models. It leaves us, however, facing an important dilemma. On the one hand, occupational-disease proposals lacking statutory presumptions would probably founder on the litigious shoals of current workers' compensation and tort procedures. On the other hand, including such presumptions could place any compensation scheme on a collision course with a whole armada of social-welfare programs. The black lung experience shows the need to coordinate discrete programs with other social policies, not the wisdom of excluding statutory presumptions from specialized occupational disease programs.

The Black Lung Program burst on the scene in 1969 after some shrewd political maneuvering by Congress members from coal-producing states.[62] It was designed to compensate victims (and their survivors) of several respiratory disabilities popularly lumped together under the name "black lung." In epidemiological terms, mining and exposure to coal dust have been associated with these diseases, including "coal workers' pneumoconiosis," a specific disease defined partly in terms of occupational etiology. Congress declared its intent to compensate victims of "pneumoconiosis," but it was unclear whether it meant one specific disease or the whole family of black lung maladies. The statute defined "pneumoconiosis" as "a chronic dust disease of the lung arising out of employment in an underground coal mine." But the Department of Labor regulations seemed to go further, saying that,

> For the purpose of the Act, "pneumoconiosis" means a chronic dust disease of the lung and its sequaelae, including respiratory and pulmonary impairment, arising out of coal mine employment. . . . For purposes of this definition, a disease "arising out of coal mine employment" includes any chronic pulmonary disease resulting in respiratory or pulmonary impairment significantly related to, or substantially aggravated by, dust exposure in coal mine employment.[63]

We may briefly recall that the late 1960s was a period of severe depression for the mining industry and a time of particular bitterness for miners. In order to compete with the growing popularity of oil and gas, coal-mine operators in the 1950s had undertaken an extensive mechanization campaign. This process significantly increased the levels of coal dust to which miners were exposed, even as it hastened the reduction of employment opportunities; between 1950 and 1969 the work force in America's coal mines shrank by some 70 percent.[64] Amid economic decline and a rise in disease and disability, many miners found themselves without adequate recourse in either workers' compensation (because of problems in proving the work connection for dust diseases),[65] federal Social Security Disability Insurance, or even their own pension funds.[66] Grass-roots organizations in mining states captured the political attention of several members of Congress, who introduced the eventual formula for compensation during a House-Senate Conference Committee called to reconcile two more modest proposals.[67]

One commentator has noted the improbable patchwork of goals resulting from these volatile conditions:

> My own view is that Congress, in enacting the Black Lung Law, created a hybrid mechanism of some parts medical, some parts compensation and large parts combat pay. The difficulty, aside from the administrative problems of handling that law, is that it was

unfortunately characterized as a workers' compensation program, although it had many of the elements of a pension program or a social security compensation system and an insufficient number of the elements of a true disability compensation program. The worthiness of it should not be in dispute, merely the nomenclature under which it was presented through Congress to the public.[68]

While it is natural for legislation to reflect a variety of political and social goals, the multiple objectives of the Black Lung Act gave birth to a host of unusual and conflicting statutory presumptions. Through these presumptions broader social objectives were forced into the framework of a workers' compensation plan. During the 1970s Congress twice amended the law by adding presumptions openly designed to expand the number of successful claims, producing a Byzantine structure of interlocking inferences concerning occupational causation[69] and at least four other issues:

- the degree of disability (anyone with "complicated pneumoconiosis" was irrebuttably presumed to be totally disabled, or to have died from that cause)[70]
- the medical diagnosis of specific symptoms ("pneumoconiosis" was rebuttably presumed in cases lacking X-ray evidence, whenever there was "other evidence" of "respiratory or pulmonary impairment")[71]
- methods of establishing medical facts (including the use of autopsy reports by local physicians, and affidavits by survivors describing a deceased miner's medical condition)[72]
- the very definition of who was actually exposed to coal dust (anyone employed "in or around a coal mine or coal preparation facility")[73]

It is futile to deny the single-minded thrust of these and a long list of further presumptions and administrative practices: to increase the number of successful claims and the average size of awards. Barth's conclusion seems to sum it up neatly: "If the goal of the program was to get federal money to the coal miner community, primarily to the older workers or the survivors of miners, the program was very largely successful."[74] By 1981, faced with rapidly increasing costs and a new political climate, Congress scaled back some of these statutory provisions.[75] But compensation costs have remained higher than anticipated, and there is little doubt that the Black Lung Program will continue to be vastly more expensive than its sponsors ever predicted.[76]

Such a collection of ad hoc provisions tells us very little about how more limited presumptions would work in asbestos compensation proposals. The black lung law should not, therefore, be ritually invoked as a test case for other occupational-disease programs. A great many state workers' compensation laws contain presumptions that connect particular jobs with certain toxic substances or resulting diseases; indeed, as Leslie I. Boden points out, some states include negative presumptions in their workers' compensation guidelines. While all such provisions "have the potential to increase efficiency and fairness of compensation systems," Boden concludes that they "have not appeared to dramatically reduce litigation and substantially increase compensation of occupational disease claimants. . . . If any conclusion is supportable from these sparse observations, it is that the drafting and administration of presumptions is very important, and that their mere existence means little." Moreover, where claims procedures encourage adversarial strategies, presumptions are likely to clog up the system, since they "serve to educate workers and attorneys about the possibility of successful claims."[77]

The Black Lung Program is a timely reminder that categorical and administrative limits for any one program face expansionary pressure from broader social goals concerning disability, income maintenance, and pension support.[78] This implicit but powerful relationship may explain sharp differences of perspective on the Black Lung Program. Those who perceived it as a form of workers' compensation saw nothing wrong in the meticulous and time-consuming scrutiny of claims, based on normal uncertainties about the occupational relation of diverse medical conditions. Those more concerned about the economic impact of disability were quick to consider black lung benefits to be like Social Security Disability Insurance. Finally, those interested in the economic welfare of a depressed and disillusioned geographic community saw a chance to patch up gaping holes in the social safety net.[79]

As Barth emphasizes, neither sponsors nor critics of the program understood the need to coordinate a specialized compensation program with social-welfare policy.[80] In Chapter 10 we will consider some possible coordination strategies, but here we may simply note the inevitable crises that await incrementally designed compensation plans. The Black Lung approach tried to straddle conflicting perspectives within Congress, leaving some parts of the program to be administered by the Social Security Administration, and other parts by the Department of Labor. In neither case, unfortunately, was the program administered well. The costs of the entire scheme—every step of the way—were consistently underestimated; unanticipated delays and inconsistencies in processing claims were the source of universal dismay; and formal appeals and litigation were allowed to magnify those delays and inconsistencies.[81]

Similarly, the funding structure pointed the program in opposing directions. Part of the burden was placed on the mining industry under the Superfund principle, while residual responsibility for funding stayed with the federal treasury. Some partisans understood the federal portion to represent a kind of combat pay for a socially exploited work force, while others saw it as simply an insurance fund of last resort. Needless to say, when costs began to outstrip available resources, parties with adversarial interests in the funding process increased their level of acrimony.

Hazardous-Waste Injuries: Extending the Superfund Financing Strategy

In 1986 Congress expanded its regulatory campaign against environmental dangers from chemical and industrial wastes, increasing fivefold the amount of money available through the Superfund mechanism for cleaning up hazardous-waste sites around the country. But it also maintained an exclusive focus on cleanup costs, turning back a Senate committee proposal for a small demonstration project aimed at compensating personal injuries.[82] This was the modest offshoot of a broader proposal developed in 1982 by a congressional study group, to which the original Superfund law had referred the problem of personal injury compensation.[83]

Congress has thus failed to approve any of the accumulating proposals for federal compensation programs in the areas of product liability, occupational disease, and hazardous-waste injuries. Alongside their common lack of success, these proposals have gradually come to resemble each other in basic outline and may profitably be compared for analysis. Each grows out of distinct failures of existing compensation processes: the hyperextension of the tort system for product injuries, the underperformance of administrative procedures in handling occupational disease, and the inability of multiple common-law forms to respond to environmental hazards. These problems are alike in their resistance to individualized evidence, and they pose parallel challenges to traditional policies linking entitlements and accountability.

Another mark of their common fate is the lure of creative judging as a possible remedy, evident in the power of product liability doctrine to draw all three categories of personal injury into its orbit. Unless federal legislation manages to restructure the entire field, present inertia could deliver many of these issues into the judicial process. Victims alleging occupational or environmental injury are now accustomed to naming product manufacturers as defendants—following examples set in the asbestos and Agent Orange cases. As we saw in Chapter 6, these cases also illustrate the judicial system's inability to supply compensation in a fair and efficient manner, or to carry out a comprehensive or realistic policy of accountability. Nevertheless, the unresolved problems of hazardous-waste injuries, occupational disease, and product liability are all converging on the judicial process.

In drafting its legislative compensation model for hazardous-waste injuries, the Superfund study group retraced the same path followed by product liability and occupational-disease reformers. After lengthy assessment of existing state judicial remedies, the group concluded (with seemingly genuine regret) that tort law and creative judging were insufficient responses to environmental injuries, absent major statutory intervention. Their solution followed the predictable pattern: an elaborate two-tiered compensation process, retaining tort law (in slightly friendlier form for plaintiffs) while professing to channel the vast majority of claims toward a more streamlined administrative procedure.[84] Although the study group expected state administrative and judicial systems to process individual cases, it wanted to establish uniform national standards under federal authority. It did not, however, suggest any mechanism for handling federal responsibility in terms comparable to private liability.

It seems striking that federal compensation proposals have achieved this degree of uniformity in three distinct areas, while Congress remains unable to follow through on any one of them. In earlier discussions of both product liability and occupational disease, we suggested that political compromises between organized plaintiffs and defendants should be considered unstable so long as each side defines its self-interest within the strategic terms of litigation. This is true even in the occupational-disease debate, where reform proposals are no longer confined to the purely administrative realm of workers' compensation. Apart from interest groups with special reasons for shedding tort law (like the asbestos companies), the major parties seem to view the judicial process as a kind of insurance policy—assuming it can be insulated from "abuse" by other groups. The two-tiered model is destined to surface in this political context, since it allows each side to take refuge in its idealized vision of litigation.[85]

The Superfund study group's proposal was a notably fragile and unworkable example of political compromise. Its two-tiered plan offered victims a no-fault administrative claims procedure in return for a cap on benefits modeled on workers' compensation. But unlike workers' compensation, this was not an exclusive remedy for victims, and no potential defendants were protected from liability. In addition, at least some claimants were promised evidentiary presumptions on the critical issue of medical causation—although all the specifics were to be supplied later by scientific panels and implemented though state judicial proceedings. Finally, unsuccessful claimants were allowed to appeal adverse administrative decisions, or to initiate entirely new claims through the tort system.[86]

As one of the group's members noted in a separate statement, the result was an unsteady compromise between two widely opposing views:

> To compromise differences arising between a few panel members who strongly preferred that no statutory intervention at all occur to hasten the evolution of existing remedies at common law, and other panelists who favored one statutory scheme or another because they believed that existing common law remedies were inadequate, we designed a plan that tried to please both. In so doing we did what attorneys do very well—we created new legal remedies to be coupled to those already in existence. Designing new procedures is the policy-minded lawyer's stock-in-trade. But at some point managing conflict by generating procedures becomes the jurisprudential equivalent of the treasury's printing new money, with analogous results.[87]

While this compensation mechanism fits into a familiar pattern, the more distinctive aspect of Superfund is its approach to accountability. As we saw in Chapter 8, the Superfund law places the primary costs of hazardous-waste cleanup on all tax-paying businesses, with special surcharges imposed on the production of crude oil and chemical feedstocks. About one-quarter of the Superfund comes from general revenues, and only one-eighth is projected from interest, fines, and litigation awards.[88] It was the rhetoric and reality of the last source that captured our attention in Chapter 8, where we examined the government's campaign to marshall the forces of tort law against a vast field of "potentially responsible parties." Despite much talk about tracking down polluters, the tools provided by litigation are much better designed to impose costs on a relatively small number of corporate deep pockets.[89] For all practical purposes, the Superfund formula breaks the connection between financing of environmental remedies and individualized accountability, leaving the latter goal to other regulatory programs.

Broad-based compensation funds approach the whole issue of accountability in much the same way that administrative systems deal with compensation. Both processes take a perspective on events which stays with generalities, rejecting the individualized premises of tort law. Just as an injured worker has no need to prove the specific employer's fault, the contributors to administrative compensation funds do not have to be linked to particular injuries. In both cases, however, generalization is subject to certain limits: workers' compensation confines responsibility to the class of employers, while Superfund singles out specific industries for special taxation. Such groups are often in a good position to redistribute the burden in the form of higher prices, and thus society as a whole ends up sharing much of the cost. But policy makers seem reluctant to abandon entirely the principle of internalizing accident costs, no matter how broadly construed. A similar reluctance places categorical limits on administrative compensation programs—even though the line drawn between deserving and nondeserving victims is often highly arbitrary.

Despite its anomolous frontiers, the Superfund strategy has the potential to structure accountability across a wide class of compensation programs. Considering the convergence of federal compensation models for product liability, occupational disease, and hazardous-waste accidents, we might also expect to find a unified principle for distributing the costs of such programs. The underlying injuries, after all, are often difficult to separate. A significant proportion of all product liability actions stem from workplace injuries.[90] Hazardous wastes and other toxic materials are a major source of occupational disease.[91]

All three areas are major targets of federal regulatory action, just as all are decisively affected by federal spending and resource development policies.

The Congressional study group that proposed the personal injuries scheme assumed that compensation would be financed under the same formula as other Superfund expenses. A similar model was proposed in most of the asbestos compensation statutes, which variously included asbestos manufacturers, distributors, miners, and importers; current and past employers of asbestos victims; the cigarette industry; and the federal government.[92] The formula is thus broad enough to encompass multiple, if not conflicting, theories of accountability borrowed from product liability doctrine, workers' compensation, and government liability; all differences of kind are neatly covered over by precise quantitative proportions.

Moreover, the inclusion of any one funding source can be rationalized by a variety of interest groups. Federal contributions, in particular, may be understood as a response to liability (whether of federal policy makers, agencies, or the public as a whole), as social-welfare payments, or merely as a financial guarantee of private sector solvency. Any particular formula still needs political agreement, but it does not require adversaries to resolve all differences of perspective. Asbestos victims, for example, may feel vindicated by the inclusion of asbestos manufacturers in a funding plan, but the manufacturers themselves might simply feel relief at substituting excise taxes for civil liability.

The general compensation fund contains yet another kind of flexibility. It provides a reliable source of money for compensation awards, whether or not a specific, solvent responsible party is ever identified; but it does not preclude transferring those costs later on if a particular culprit is ultimately identified. The retrospective pursuit of individual wrongdoers can take place through the judicial process, as with the EPA's cost-recovery campaign under Superfund; but it is by no means restricted to judicial action. Indeed, considering the enormous costs and time delays of a regulatory strategy based on litigation, we suspect that its primary purpose is rhetorical. It seems to satisfy (at least in theory) the partisans of strict microeconomic efficiency and individualist moral philosophy.

It is usual to find noble generalities about cost internalization in the preamble to administrative financing plans. One model bill for asbestos compensation, for example, declared its intention "to assess contributions in an equitable manner reflecting each responsible party's role in the use of asbestos." But the fine print reveals that each manufacturer's specific contribution was to be based on objective measures of market sales, averaged out over arbitrary time periods. Likewise, employers' contributions to the fund would have been allocated under varying insurance-based systems used by fifty state workers' compensation systems.[93]

Even though compensation funds seem to abandon the classic individualist ideals of microeconomics and deontology, they generally retain some reference to the goal of internalizing accident costs. At least part of the reason must be the economic climate over the past decade; high interest rates, growing federal deficits, and resistance to higher taxes—all pervasive trends throughout the 1980s—make it fiscally imprudent and politically impossible to fund remedial compensation programs out of general revenues. When society already feels responsible for too many things, it is predisposed to believe that environmental accidents are someone else's fault. Society's duty can thus be rhetorically hedged by declaring that the true culprits shall be identified and forced to pay.

The Superfund concept of financing presupposes political compromise along much the same lines as two-tiered schemes for compensation. New compensation burdens continually push the funding formula toward broader, more generalized classes of contributors, while individual companies and entire industries concentrate on showing that they did nothing wrong, and should thus be excused from payment. While they produce very little money, cost-recovery efforts like those under Superfund generate enormous political conflict spilling over into the program's regulatory goals. As federal lawsuits target deep-pocket corporations—who in turn seek to implicate endless ranks of insurers, landowners, transporters, governmental units, and other potentially responsible parties—the political support for Superfund goals can expect to undergo similar fragmentation.[94]

These opposing tendencies were apparent in the 1986 Superfund amendments, which reauthorized the overall program for its second five-year period. The amendments' sponsors took a significant new step toward broader accountability by imposing a tax surcharge on all businesses, whatever their relationship to hazardous wastes. Characterized by supporters as a temporary measure, it will, we suspect, become an enduring feature. But the amendments also declared a new resolve to step up cost recovery efforts by strengthening the government's litigation powers and expanding the scope for third-party litigation.[95] These same strategies were strongly recommended in 1982 by the Superfund study group, whose plan for personal injury compensation was carefully balanced by its vigorous commitment to individualized cost allocation through litigation.[96]

In sum, compensation funds illustrate once again the dilemmas of placing clear boundaries around the problems of accidental injury—especially environmental accidents. By shedding the assumption that accountability must be tied to individual actions and specific injuries, compensation funds provide a practical way to finance the higher compensation costs that accompany broader definitions of personal injury. They also supply a mechanism—unavailable to litigation—for taking account of government's unique role in shaping the economic and natural environment. At the same time, political conflicts surround the negotiation of precise formulae for distributing costs among industries and other potential contributors. Such conflicts could be disabling if funding levels are perpetually revised upward. Just as administrative compensation schemes tend to overreach their original mandates, as happened in the Black Lung Program, the same can probably be said about funding formulae. And just as compensation programs in operation merge imperceptibly into general welfare schemes, compensation funds could easily move beyond limited excise taxes toward broader levies on production, consumption, or employment.

Vaccines and Biomedical Research: Arguments for Public Responsibility

Administrative compensation schemes are generally designed to solve some crisis in another system—most often the judicial system. The crisis itself can variously be described as a failure to compensate deserving victims (or at least to compensate them fully), a failure to treat defendants equitably, or simply the high administrative costs of the judicial process. Recently, as we saw, administrative systems have been proposed for combating a similar condition in the workers' compensation system itself.

In every case, the decision to curtail an existing compensation procedure requires intense political negotiations. Competing interest groups, formed according to the strategic contours of litigation, must somehow agree that they have nothing substantial left to win from judicial procedures; and for a variety of reasons such compromises are increasingly difficult to bring off. Under complex two-tiered proposals—the emerging standard in federal tort reform—administrative schemes have become further weapons in the adversarial struggle. It would be a mistake, however, to leave the discussion of administrative systems on these purely strategic terms. Quite apart from private interests, there are times when broad public goals seem to demand more effective compensation procedures. The most compelling examples can be found in federal public health programs.

Compensating blameless victims is in many ways a natural extension of federal policy in areas like vaccine development and biomedical research, where the government already plays a dominant role in planning, funding, and regulation.[97] Both programs carry a strong sense of collective purpose, even though they coordinate a vast range of private and organizational behavior. Without this unusual degree of federal supervision, we would probably treat such complex activities as an aggregate of private decisions held together by a network of market transactions, voluntary choices, and regulatory sanctions. But at least for vaccination programs and biomedical research, federal coordination has become essential for mobilizing private efforts on behalf of widely accepted public health goals.

Both programs, while accomplishing much that is beneficial, are also responsible for an unknown number of unavoidable, random injuries. Even a small number of accidents can compromise federal program goals, especially when they ramify through the existing judicial process. The swine flu episode is perhaps the clearest example, where sudden doctrinal shifts in a handful of court decisions provoked a sharp rise in insurance costs for high-risk, low-profit vaccine production. Well-publicized injuries can also inhibit public participation in voluntary vaccination programs or clinical research procedures, thereby limiting the scope and pace of federal initiatives. Under these circumstances, the public as a whole cannot escape the consequences of personal injury, even if it ultimately chooses to do nothing. A public response in some form is unavoidable, whether it is based on pragmatic, economic, legal, or ethical grounds.

Over the past fifteen years, federal health officials have investigated several models for highly specialized administrative compensation procedures. Most recently, Congress approved (and President Reagan reluctantly signed) the National Childhood Vaccine Injury Act of 1986, the first new federal compensation system since the Black

Lung Program of 1969.[98] Among the many compensation proposals before Congress, the childhood-vaccine law tackles the smallest number of past and future injuries. But its symbolic meaning was clear to supporters and opponents alike, who considered it an important precedent for more ambitious federal compensation legislation.

Compared with other federal compensation proposals, the new vaccine statute contains some fresh inducements for claimants to abandon the judicial system. It provides an administrative alternative to state tort law for a restricted set of injuries, substituting a claims procedure administered by federal courts.[99] For these proceedings, the law creates a series of presumptions about causation, based on medical data linking vaccines with known side effects;[100] and it imposes a new excise tax on vaccines to fund compensation awards.[101] In addition to covering medical costs and lost (mostly future) earnings, the law authorizes lump-sum damages up to $250,000 for pain and suffering or death.[102] Finally, the statute follows the two-tiered structure now common to federal compensation proposals, under which claimants have the right to initiate a tort suit after completing the claims procedure. In these cases, however, courts cannot base liability on the controversial duty-to-warn theory, which has become the primary doctrinal tool for extending strict liability to cases of vaccine injury.[103]

The statute is primarily concerned with injuries from the combined vaccine for diphtheria, pertussis, and tetanus (DPT).[104] This vaccine has achieved good results in reducing illness and death from pertussis in the United States and other countries, but it has also been linked to a number of acute and permanent neurological disorders. Projections of serious side effects of DPT vaccine vary widely, ranging from 1 case in 10,000 vaccinations to 1 in 300,000. A recent cost-benefit study estimates that, for every sixteen lives now being saved, one new case of serious neurological damage will be caused by the vaccine itself.[105]

While the net benefits of vaccination are universally acknowledged, the Childhood Vaccine Act came in response to a crisis involving vaccine manufacturers and parents of past and future vaccinees. Faced with rising insurance costs after several DPT liability suits, manufacturers gradually withdrew from the market, leaving only one U.S. producer of DPT vaccine by 1985. Even with reliable supplies, however, public participation in state-administered vaccination programs began to decline as parents became more aware of potential side effects. Public health specialists knew that interrupting vaccination programs in other countries was associated with increased mortality, and they urged Congress to take swift action to stabilize production and respond to public apprehension.[106] As in the swine flu episode, an imminent threat to public health was enough to force Congress to reach agreement on curtailing litigation. The goal of vaccinating school-aged children was firmly established in the *public* domain, unlike the more diffuse (and ostensibly private) interests at stake in fields like product liability, occupational disease, and hazardous-waste injuries—problems with vastly greater human and economic cost than vaccine injuries.

The Childhood Vaccine Act generated its share of controversy, despite its modest scope as a compensation program. The legislative debate featured the usual battle of interest groups, including a well-organized association of parents seeking expanded tort remedies for their allegedly injured children. The two-tiered compensation procedure, the use of federal courts for processing claims, and provisions for pain and suffering in the expedited recovery scheme are all evidence of the parents' bargaining power, assisted by skillful lawyer-lobbyists.[107] Opposing interests were presented by pharmaceutical companies and insurers, whose position followed the same basic script found in other congressional debates: stop the runaway tort system with statutory controls on pro-plaintiff doctrines.[108] In many respects it was the same tired story, only this time Congress understood that children's lives would be spared if only some compromise could be found.

The childhood-vaccine program emerged after more than a decade of sporadic discussion about special compensation schemes to accompany the expanding federal role in vaccine development. The topic was raised officially in 1976 as part of the swine flu debate, when Congress asked federal health officials to study "the scope and extent of liability for personal injuries or death arising out of immunization programs and of alternative approaches to providing protection against such liability (including a compensation system) for such injuries."[109] Unfortunately, when HEW submitted its report in May 1978, the compensation issue was already buried in political fallout from swine flu, leaving the department with little to say beyond underscoring the dilemmas of each alternative.[110] Some of these plans would have shifted liability from one defendant to another, ending up with someone legally inaccessible to plaintiffs. One proposal, for instance, wanted to shift the duty to warn from manufacturers to federal agencies, where it could be harmlessly discharged in the normal course of drug inspection and approval. A later variation had the federal government transferring this burden to state health departments, which are often protected under state-immunity doctrines.[111]

The report also outlined a "public compensation system" for all vaccine injuries, which merits a closer look here as part of our survey of administrative models.[112] It is the prototype of the childhood-vaccine compensation program approved by Congress in 1986, although it would have gone further in restricting litigation and was designed to cover injuries from any vaccine. This proposal barred personal injury litigation against drug manufacturers and other defendants, and substituted a claims procedure to be administered by the Public Health Service. Limited benefits similar to workers' compensation were to be available on a no-fault basis to vaccinees who suffered "designated compensable injuries" (DCIs)—injuries known to be associated with particular vaccines. The list of DCIs was to be composed and periodically revised by a panel of scientific experts. Adverse decisions on the initial claim could be appealed only by bringing a new claim under the Federal Tort Claims Act, which (as we saw with swine flu) initially channels claims into a separate administrative process.

The most obvious bottleneck in this system was the burden on claimants to establish the causal connection between vaccines and DCIs. Unlike the schedule later enacted for childhood-vaccine injuries, the DCIs carried no presumption of causation; they simply removed the claimant's traditional burden of establishing negligence. We sense enormous frustration over this issue within the work group that designed the proposal. Completing its work just months after the swine flu program self-destructed, it acknowledged the overriding importance of the causation issue but found no practical way to meet it. "We are referring to persons who have had the shot, have become disabled, and now believe that the shot was the cause. By order of magnitude, victims in this class may be ten times as numerous as those who became disabled because of the shot."[113]

Even if medical criteria were able to distinguish between these two types of claimant, the report ruefully concluded, "it is doubtful that any 'system' constructed in today's societal climate would permit the distinction to be made."[114] Faced with the option of compensating all vaccinees who suffer designated injuries, the proposal chose instead to leave the burden of causation on claimants. But in 1986 the decision went the other way: the Childhood Vaccine Act includes causal presumptions, despite their odious repute in Congress. The swine flu cases left little doubt that causation issues can paralyze an administrative claims system just as thoroughly as the tort system. In retrospect, it is clear that the liability work group's proposal would have failed to ensure "prompt and equitable relief" for the most serious injuries from swine flu vaccine—the very problem that prompted the whole study of compensation alternatives. Even worse, Guillain-Barré Syndrome would never have appeared on the original list of DCIs, prior to the start of the swine flu program.

Federal vaccine policies illustrate perfectly the social dimensions of environmental accidents. They combine the most benign accomplishments of modern medicine with some of its deepest frustrations. Vaccines now protect us from many diseases that have long plagued mankind, but they do so invariably at some price. We desperately want the chance to pay that price as long as vaccines rid our world of its most feared diseases. We may try to avoid such morbid calculations, but there is no doubt about the public interest in continuing to use the safest possible vaccines. We also understand, however, that this social decision imposes a heavy cost on a few randomly selected persons.

Those participating in vaccination programs obviously serve their own self-interest, but mass vaccination carries additional medical and economic benefits for society as a whole: increased medical security derived from "herd immunity," and economic and social protection from the varied costs of disease. These benefits are sufficient, in extreme cases, to justify mandatory participation; but in recent years federal health officials have concentrated on voluntary campaigns like the swine flu program. Even so, the government plays a central role in perpetuating the small but statistically inevitable risk of vaccine-related injury.[115]

Throughout the 1970s health officials experimented with both practical and ethical reasons for including compensation as an integral part of public health policy.[116] And for independent legal and economic reasons, their surveys of compensation models tended to favor administrative alternatives to tort law. Apart from vaccine policy, federal programs for biomedical research became an active field for generating new compensation procedures; issues in human experimentation were gaining new attention, and for a while ethical speculation mixed freely with legal and practical concerns. In 1975 the National Institutes of Health established the Task Force on the Compensation of Injured Research Subjects to explore, among other topics, "possible compensation mechanisms." The task force understood its mission in broad terms, seeking testimony from "ethicists, economists, compensation experts, and clinical investigators."[117]

As with vaccine injuries, a small but unknown number of accidents were thought to be associated with research conducted by, sponsored by, or regulated by federal agencies. The task force produced its own survey and found little evidence of injuries that could be directly tied to routine biomedical research, although the question of causation became rather murky for "therapeutic" research involving experimental treatments for extremely ill patients.[118] Given the small number of potential cases, we may wonder why the task force persisted in spinning out compensation procedures, embroidering its analyses with broad ethical declarations. The most plausible reason appeared briefly in the final report: a concern that lawsuits filed by research subjects would increase time delays and costs of federal programs.[119]

Without the drama of colorful and exotic injuries, the report comes across as a somewhat abstract ethical discussion. After consulting widely with experts in the emerging field of biomedical ethics, the task force concluded that,

> Because society is both the beneficiary and the sponsor of research, compensatory justice may come into play for the redress of injuries. . . . Compensatory justice goes beyond humanitarian beneficence, which, however laudatory, remains morally optional. . . . Compensatory justice recognizes an obligation on the part of society to make an effort to redress injuries.

The task force's leading ethical expert, H. Tristram Engelhardt, Jr., expanded on this theme in his section of the report:

> Society is in debt to those who agree to contribute to its good in programs it authorizes, and for which it directly or indirectly solicits volunteers who could properly and reasonably require such a debt.
> Society should not use its members for the common good without at the same time protecting those members' rights to their continued security.[120]

Despite these bold speculations, the report broke little new ground in its survey of compensation alternatives, restricting itself to a review of current federal models: the Federal Employees' Compensation Act (FECA, the equivalent of state workers' compensation for federal employees), the Black Lung Program, Veterans' Service-Connected Disability, and National Flood Insurance.[121] Among these models, it gravitated toward the workers' compensation approach as requiring the smallest increment of change. By treating some research subjects as federal employees, it turns out, the federal health agencies could stop the litigation threat in exchange for relatively modest benefits. The task force failed to pursue the logic of compensatory justice to the point of requiring benefits closer to common-law damages. Nor did it make any special allowance for the causation problem—which remains a burden for claimants in FECA proceedings as in state workers' compensation.

Even this minimal answer to the call for public responsibility was never adopted. Almost immediately after the task force report was submitted, the matter of personal safety in biomedical research got caught up in the privatization movement. The first sign of change was new HEW regulations consigning the problem of personal injury to private insurance—a move anticipated by the task force. Under these arrangements federal contractors were required to insure themselves against civil damages, but claimants' were given no additional tools for establishing liability, beyond standard tort procedures.[122] Meanwhile the federal government managed to avoid direct liability in medically related injury cases, as federal courts consistently upheld the Justice Department's vigorous sovereign-immunity defense. It is possible, of course, that the problem of injured research subjects vanished from public attention because there never were very many cases—a conclusion supported by the task force's own survey. However, as with other accidents for which causation issues are central, it is hard to measure the true number of uncompensated accidents using definitions based on judicial liability standards.

The problem of injured research subjects was further privatized in the dramatic expansion of federal regulations governing *informed consent*. This development is a peculiar variation on the ethical stance adopted by the task force, which stressed the collective obligations of society in its complex relation to blameless victims of biomedical experimentation. As an alternative to compensation, however, the victims themselves may be said to ratify their own injuries by granting prior consent to risk-bearing procedures. In recent years this position has been elegantly developed by Engelhardt, the ethical expert relied on extensively in 1978 by the Task Force on Injured Research Subjects. Using a moral philosophy reminiscent of Richard Posner's approach to tort law, Engelhardt (along with other ethical specialists) believes, in effect, that accidents *cannot* happen when individuals have voluntarily chosen to assume a relevant package of risks.[123]

This argument was explicitly rejected by the task force in 1978, which dissented from this portion of its professional ethicist's advice:

> The Task Force concluded that informed consent does not negate or waive the obligation to provide compensation. The case is similar to that of persons who have been injured in the course of voluntary military service. . . . Informed consent in the research setting functions as a recognition of and a protection for a person's integrity and autonomy, but does not imply a waiver of the right of the person to compensation in the event of injury.[124]

Other commentators on informed consent concur with the task force in separating liability issues from the ethical principle of respecting personal autonomy.[125] But Engelhardt's position is obviously convenient for federal health authorities and private health researchers who, only a decade ago, were desperately searching for ways to avoid liability. We need not cast doubt on the integrity of Professor Engelhardt or the architects of federal regulations covering consent procedures in medical settings; their arguments all have secure roots in individualist approaches to moral philosophy. But the recent surge of federal regulation around patient consent, combined with the utter disappearance of concern about compensation, is probably not coincidental. The most extreme option for privatizing problems of personal injury, in short, is to "ethicize" them. We saw a similar strategy at work in legal commentary on the tort system,[126] but in the field of biomedical research it has taken the further ironic turn of creating its own quasilegal bureaucracy.[127]

Part Four

Comprehensive Accident

Policies

W e have now surveyed the intense activity that pervades the American legal system in its increasingly futile effort to manage the problems of environmental accidents. Where is all this activity leading us, and what can be done to channel it into more productive paths?

To find answers, we need to stand back from the situational elements in specific tort-reform battles. Even more, we must retreat momentarily from the technocratic goals of most tort surveys, which confidently seek out optimal institutional structures, based on analytical models examined in Part II. American discussion of accident policy has managed to construct impressive interpretive schemes, but it has lacked any clear vision of how the underlying problems may be changing. None of the popular reform strategies mentioned in Part III offers any prospect for stabilizing a volatile set of issues. An eclectic mix of those strategies provides analysts a chance to hedge their bets, but only underscores the ephemeral or strategic nature of their solutions. Safest of all is the recent call for massive collections of data about the tort system. Certainly more data could provide a refreshing change from the abstractions of legal, economic, and moral theory. But unless we are clear about how to interpret new data—and what data we need to consider in the first place—chances are such evidence may be used mainly to fortify old policy positions.

Chapter 10 attempts to speculate on where the legal system is actually moving, especially as it responds to a new set of claims based on more complex premises about the natural and social environment. In contrast to the individualist spirit of current legal institutions and commentary, this chapter explores an entirely different framework of conceptual and normative assumptions about events, causation, and responsibility. This environmental or social orientation is not in itself a policy model, but rather an occasion for clarifying the central presumptions behind existing policies for personal injuries. More important, it defines the major assumptions which appear to govern the mysterious evolution of American legal policy: interdependence of events, statistical causation, and collective responsibility. No one has yet organized these perspectives into a conscious policy, but they can explain the circuitous path through instrumentalist reforms of legal doctrine covered in Chapter 1, plus the increasingly radical departures from case-by-case adjudication surveyed in Part III.

As the United States moves slowly toward open acceptance of these new assumptions, we should discover deeper connections between the ambitions of the tort system and larger policies currently in place for dealing with personal disability and environmental regulation. A new approach to personal injury, based on an environmental orientation, would pursue the twin social goals of compensation and accountability through separate policies tied to the social-welfare system and administrative regulation, respectively. Changes in both these areas of public policy over the past two decades help confirm the hypothesis that tort crises are merely symptoms of greater challenges, whose solution lies well beyond piecemeal strategies for reforming the judicial process. From this point of view, the main issue in incremental tort reform is not to solve all the political battles, but rather to understand the slow yet inevitable process of turning private law functions over to political institutions governed by public values. The principle of public responsibility captures the structural and normative implications of this important transition.

The full task awaiting the United States becomes much clearer in the context of policies developed by other industrialized nations, which are briefly discussed in Chapter 11. In countries with less robust tort systems but more extensive programs for social welfare, the main outlines of public responsibility have been clearly anticipated.

The most intriguing experiment occurred in New Zealand, which in 1972 replaced the judicial process with an administrative scheme for compensating all personal injuries. Even more important than this stunning institutional change was the philosophy behind the New Zealand program, which foreshadows the major lesson in social interdependence that awaits us all in an era of environmental accidents. For the remainder of this century—in a time when social-welfare policies in most countries seem to have lost their sense of commitment and direction—it may yet be possible to concentrate on compensation and accountability as goals for restoring a sense of common purpose to public life.

Chapter 10

The Public Responsibility Model

I think underlying all our problems with the civil justice system is the inability of this country to decide whether it wants to have a pure compensatory system or whether it wants to have a fault-based liability system. . . . My personal assessment is that we are experiencing the disadvantages of trying to operate both systems in tandem, the worst of both worlds. We are attempting to compensate everyone within a fault-based system and we are incurring huge social overhead costs by attempting to do so. I believe it is time to focus on that overall choice and to be rational in doing so.[1]

Two Ways of Structuring Environmental Uncertainty

The battleground of accident policy is littered with military metaphors. Alas, more will rise to take their place, as long as American policy tries to impose archaic order on a dynamic world. As with many campaigns that endure for generations, it is no longer entirely clear what the larger battle is about—beyond the endless tactical struggles that consume our political energy and social resources.

The system originally administered by the courts under the banner of tort law has been irreversibly altered by instrumentalist reforms of the past century. There remains only symbolic strength in the traditional model of interpersonal duties, discrete events, and formal adjudication, although loyal remnants continue to mount "desperate scholarly rearguard action[s]"[2] on its behalf from their academic redoubts. Even with a pragmatically reformed judicial process, however, some decisive encounters with environmental accidents during the past two decades have exposed what may prove to be fatal weaknesses. The survey in Part III was meant to show that American policy has been sampling a wide range of alternatives to the case-by-case procedures of the judicial system—at least for this new class of accidents. The battle now is over *which* procedures to use in place of standard litigation.

Having lost so much ground over the past century, and with nothing but further losses in sight, the traditional approach to personal injury requires fundamental reassessment. Behind the institutional system of courts, doctrines, and piecemeal alternatives stands a particular world view which needs to be challenged. We may describe it as a distinctive approach to risk and uncertainty, built on a series of tacit presumptions that disguise the collective environment of personal injuries. Reinforced by past American policy, current institutional structures, interest-group conflicts, and academic theorizing, this atomistic or individualist orientation remains surprisingly strong. It is generally subtle enough to avoid direct assertions that the world is a rational place, that we understand the basic causes of events, and that we know the limits of everyone's social duties.[3] Nonetheless, it craftily imposes a weighty burden on anyone who suggests otherwise—on anyone who believes, in short, that this rationalistic order is *not* the world in which most personal injuries occur.

The individualist orientation presumes, for example, that serious illness is an isolated event, until somebody (usually the claimant) can persuade the courts that someone else caused it.[4] Only when the presumption of isolation is overcome does the event turn into a potentially compensable "accident." The same test was also applied over the years to traumatic injuries, although by now most proof barriers have been substantially lowered. Indeed, this whole orientation has maintained itself in the modern world of highly complex events by radically changing the operational meaning of agency and causation.

Another important component of the individualist framework concerns accountability. Two normative presumptions supplement the atomistic view of public events: the idea that responsibility attaches to past actions only when there is some breach of preexisting social rules or standards, and the notion that liability depends on finding a specific person who violated those standards. Only when these additional requirements are met does the individualist approach permit a remedy, usually in the form of compensation. Thus for years consumers were unable to sue manufacturers of defective products unless they had established a direct trade relationship, preferably one in which the quality of goods was explicitly warranted.[5] Here too the legal system has responded to modern pressures by broadening its terms, as we saw in Chapter 1. Against product manufacturers, it is now fairly easy for some injured consumers to overcome traditional legal barriers to compensation. But with other defendants (such as the remote disposers of toxic wastes) these presumptions still provide significant protection.

Imagine now a completely different orientation to events and personal relations. Let us presume that personal disabilities in modern society are intrinsically linked to unspecified environmental forces. Of course, careful research may be able to isolate specific (often probabilistic) sources of injuries—perhaps a combination of substances, persons, and organizations. But while this kind of knowledge becomes useful in planning future prevention, it is not required for the initial labeling of specific injuries as "accidents." Indeed we expect that our inquiry will always leave some residue of unexplained causation.[6] This approach to uncertainty thus assumes an infinitely expanding environmental context, to be filled in only as specific evidence warrants. A familiar example would be current epidemiological research on the occupational, environmental, and genetic sources of respiratory disease.[7]

Let us extend the environmental approach to accountability as well. Who is responsible for life's many misfortunes, and how can we promote a safer future? Here the system of presumptions places residual responsibility on society as a whole, but it also allows partial assignments to individualized sources (organizations, groups, individuals), to whatever degree they can plausibly be identified. Accountability is presumed to follow from causal associations of the type explored by epidemiology, which focuses on opportunities for future prevention more than reconstructing past events. Taking the example of vaccine injuries, responsibility resides first with the community that collectively endorses a vaccination program. Additional responsibilities can also be assigned, based on specific policies or actions of federal agencies, health care organizations, doctors, and even patients. At any level of attribution, accountability under this model does not exclude some kind of remedial response (fines or punishment) for past accidents, but it concentrates more heavily on preventive action for future accidents.

This social or environmental orientation is not introduced here as a self-standing philosophy, nor does it provide a ready-made blueprint for American accident policy. Its main purpose is to draw attention to the unchallenged role of its polar opposite in shaping current American theories and policies. Both frameworks—environmental and individualist—are alternative ways of structuring society's reactions in the face of uncertainty over accidents. In lawyers' terms, they control the burden of proof; they tell us what to do whenever our knowledge or judgment is unable to fit actual events into preexisting categories. Considering how little we really know about environmental accidents, these two orientations will yield completely different policy structures, based on identical starting information. Just how different they turn out in practice depends partly on how firmly each approach stands by its presumptive standards.

Defining these two orientations serves a useful analytic purpose. The social or environmental framework is a heuristic device for drawing out implications for policy and values in the remaining sections of this chapter. But it is not a model policy or a concrete value scheme.[8] Nor will we be able to stage a confrontation of alternative frameworks like a clash of rival hypotheses, facing their conclusive test. Unlike Gustave Shubert, whose remarks quoted at the beginning of this chapter anticipate some process of rational choice, we do not envision any final battle of the titans.

For one thing, any criteria we might use (legal, economic, moral, or even pragmatic) to select one scheme over the other would probably be drawn from *within* either system, and would thus reflect the particular orientation of either scheme. In Part II we saw how individualist premises from a variety of disciplines have been used to prop up the sagging structure of traditional tort law. One could readily find comparable support for the social or environmental framework in the same disciplines: in the civic republican tradition in political theory, in institutional economics, and in communitarian and cultural perspectives on moral philosophy.[9] These are important theories that may someday enrich the debate over accidents, but they cannot settle the issue of basic frameworks as a matter of rational choice. In themselves they are no more conclusive than interest-group liberalism, free-market economics, and libertarian moral philosophy.

We can, nonetheless, use the social or environmental orientation to clarify the direction of major trends in American accident policy. Recall first the evidence from Chapter 1, showing the way instrumental reforms have gradually eroded the traditional underpinnings of common-law doctrines. Add next the policy survey in Part III, which suggests an incipient trend away from traditional litigation in current public responses to environmental accidents. In the late twentieth century, case-by-case adjudication has lost its privileged institutional status as an ideal, even among those who still favor the courts for their own strategic purposes. An environmental orientation reinterprets these trends in an *affirmative* way, as something more than a rejection of antiquated policy assumptions about a complex world. The environmental model, in short, reveals what American policy has been implicitly reaching *toward*.

Rather than spending all our time and resources debating further surgery for a moribund system, we should begin to explore these problems from an entirely new direction. Events themselves are urging us to do so—as we grapple with the extraordinary challenge of environmental injuries. With a new orientation to accidents, it is possible that more supportive economic theories, moral philosophies, and political models can eventually be roused as well.

Separating Compensation and Accountability

An environmental approach allows us to divide compensation and accountability into separate policy branches. It suggests an entirely different set of programs and institutions to replace judicial processes as the primary form of public response to personal injuries. What might such programs look like when they are not just selective deviations from the judicial system? Does the comprehensive model tell us anything useful about the "mixed" institutional structures that are likely to characterize American policy in the years ahead?[10]

In responding to environmental accidents, courts and administrative schemes have already tried to put some distance between issues of compensation and accountability. The judicial process tends to hide this separation behind a doctrinal curtain, but despite the rhetoric it seems clear that a diffuse instrumental policy favoring plaintiffs has fostered an expansion of traditional accountability rules. The individualist orientation to events and obligations requires courts to maintain a queasy equilibrium between compensation and accountability concepts, but their initiatives have obviously been inspired by a transparent emphasis on compensation.[11]

Despite this centrality of compensation for judicial activism, most commentators agree that legislation can potentially meet compensation goals more efficiently.[12] Legislative programs can award benefits while avoiding the expense and duplicity of correlating victims and agents in particular cases. Claimants can be compensated without having to pinpoint the individual source of injury, while agents can be held accountable even without evidence of actual damages already caused.[13] As we saw in Chapter 9, political bargaining sometimes turns to administrative schemes as an opportunistic response to judicial crises, when the costs of individualized decisions become intolerable. Some recent proposals in the areas of product liability and occupational disease were explored in Part III.

The politics behind most legislative spinoffs from the tort system still call for maintaining a correlation between aggregate compensation costs and accountability.[14] Thus the costs of compensating asbestos victims were expected to come from special funds supported by assessments on industries related to the asbestos trade. The case for preserving some kind of correlation can derive from judicial rhetoric as well as from economic theories of future cost internalization. But usually interest-group bargaining is enough to keep accountability from straying too far from its traditional correlation with compensation. Those funding the scheme have a partisan interest in avoiding payment for accidents that they never "caused," as we saw in connection with federal Superfund concept, as well as the Black Lung Program. And groups supporting future compensation and deterrence have an interest in imposing accountability on specific organizations they want to regulate—like nuclear power plants and producers of other toxic hazards.

An environmental orientation has little room for these rhetorical or strategic attempts to maintain the traditional correlation between compensation and accountability. From this standpont the concept of a compensable accident is independent of any particular causal source—whether statistical or mechanical. In a pure compensation policy, social decisions about priorities and amounts for individual compensation are completely separate from the task of identifying potential funding sources. Funding and accountability are treated in a separate policy system, in which penalties for past actions and incentives for future behavior are developed without regard for benefits awarded to injured persons. Of course, some loose form of coordination between these two branches of public policy may still be warranted by political and fiscal practicalities. But decisions within each system do not require individual correlation for the sake of legitimacy or efficiency in the overall approach.

American policies already show some impatience to explore these broader options for organizing compensation and accountability. In the National Childhood Vaccine Injury Act of 1986, for example, Congress established a special compensation mechanism for the statistically in-evitable victims of a widely used but sometimes dangerous product.[15] One objective was to prevent the courts from financing the compensa-tion of these victims by imposing liability on vaccine manufacturers, using fashionable duty-to-warn doctrines. The new law suggests that injured children should be compensated, even though no one in par-ticular can be held accountable for injuries caused by proper admin-istration of childhood-disease vaccines. This reverses a major pre-sumption of the individualist framework, whose associated legal, economic, and moral theories can all be mobilized against shifting such losses away from victims.[16] An environmental orientation makes compensation the natural presumption.[17]

Other American policies illustrate how this new orientation would apply to problems of accountability. The environmental approach en-courages regulation of activities with probable connections to future harm, notwithstanding the paucity of specific evidence linking past injuries to particular causes. For new technologies like genetic engi-neering, federal regulatory standards have already been planned for reducing the potential threat from unanticipated accidents.[18] Sim-ilarly, for recent scientific discoveries like the depletion of ozone in the earth's atmosphere, no one can be sure just how many personal inju-ries have already occurred; but the United States (along with other nations) has nevertheless launched a policy aimed at reducing future harms.[19] As we shall see later in this chapter, accountability policies can recognize broad categorical distinctions based on probabilistic evi-dence. They can fill in the causal landscape without affecting compen-sation policies, since their exclusive purpose is to guide social strat-egies for prevention and retribution.

These and similar examples of an independent accountability pol-icy reveal the importance of underlying presumptions in social re-sponses to environmental uncertainty. Even when policy makers rely on formal techniques for regulatory decision making, there is always a residual presumption at work: either we *reject* regulation unless our model shows it *is* socially necessary, or we *support* regulation unless our model shows it is *not*. Sometimes these presumptions may be en-tirely hidden behind analytical techniques like environmental model-ing or cost-benefit analysis, but their presence is manifest in a society's overall approach to regulation.

With its ability to separate compensation and accountability, the environmental orientation permits each branch to develop in an appropriate policy context. Compensation thus becomes an aspect of social entitlement and occupies a place within the larger social-welfare system. Accountability connects with several distinct policy areas, reflecting the multiple levels of attribution on which accidents can be explained. At all levels, however, accountability becomes part of a broader policy of public regulation designed to influence future behavior of organizations, groups, and individuals. The emphasis on accident prevention through multiple forms of regulation does not rule out retribution, especially where accountability can be readily personalized. Thus taxes, fines, and even imprisonment have a potential role to play in a comprehensive accountability policy, which may overlap with the criminal-justice system.[20] The environmental orientation is thus compatible with a variety of institutional structures and programs.

Compensation: The Presumption of Comprehensive Entitlement

An environmental approach to compensation policy would eliminate all distinctions in social entitlement based on causal categories.[21] This is the logical endpoint of legal trends explored throughout this book, and provides a useful sense of where future reforms may actually be leading. For some time the eclipse of causal conditions was scarcely noticeable, as courts shielded their instrumental doctrinal changes by retaining the old vocabulary of proximate cause. For defendants to be found liable, their causal connection to the specific injury had to be fully demonstrated; but progressive judges gradually psychologized that connection, on the way toward discarding it entirely through the doctrine of strict liability.[22] Judges who are inclined to compensate plaintiffs have never been entirely patient with causal criteria; the needs of the badly injured victim are completely indifferent to whether the source of injury was a careless rifle shot, a lightning bolt, or a socially beneficial drug. The cause of injury was important only for knowing whom to blame, and thus from whom to collect.

The institutional reforms discussed in Part III treat the whole concept of causation with even greater abandon, generally searching for some equilibrium between the compensation interests of victim groups and the protection of others (including the federal treasury) from boundless accountability. Courts and legislatures know how to manipulate causal presumptions and burdens of proof, and the tendency is to move causal categories toward the periphery of group eligibility for compensation. Causality provides a *jurisdictional* limit to compensation procedures, as is seen most clearly in purely administrative programs. Workers' compensation—the most notable example—covers only those accidents that "arise out of or in the course of employment."

Other administrative procedures with broad causal presumptions still have to wrestle with borderline issues, as we saw in Chapter 9 with the Black Lung Program. Indeed, even the most comprehensive administrative scheme in existence—the New Zealand Accident Compensation Act—has to distinguish "personal injury by accident" from other forms of disability, notably organic disease.[23] As Terence Ison and Jane Stapleton have noted, these causal classifications are vestiges of the tort system from which alternative compensation programs were originally derived.[24] Their survival has nothing to do with the quality of need among those who receive benefits, but instead relates to the politics and financing of particular programs. Causal criteria disappear from compensation policies only when we reach the most fundamental level of presumptions: the issue of residual responsibility, and whether it rests with the injured victim or with society as a whole.[25]

From an environmental orientation, likewise, there is no reason to treat compensation as a series of monetary replacements for distinct categories of loss. Nonetheless, most administrative schemes (including New Zealand's) have preserved tort classifications in their schedule of benefits, even to the point of including special payments similar to pain and suffering.[26] A broader compensation system would replace this catalogue of more or less constructive losses—based on the fiction that accidents can be pinpointed like historic events—with at least three major categories of benefits: medical services, income maintenance, and rehabilitation assistance.

Accident compensation thus merges into general entitlement programs for disability, which have risen to sudden prominence in all industrialized societies over the past three decades.[27] By absorbing residual responsibility for many victims of environmental injuries, national disability policy has tacitly assumed a vital public function that is pointedly excluded from judicial procedures limited to providing compensation. From the environmental perspective, disability programs exist precisely to meet the basic social obligation to *compensate* the disabled, and not just to administer social insurance or to serve the meliorative ends of ordinary "welfare."[28]

In their current form, disability policies present their own weighty practical and conceptual problems. For example, the very definition of disability straddles the dichotomy between individual and social orientations: between a clinical assessment of individual physiology, on the one hand, and the broader capacity to participate in socioeconomic life, on the other.[29] An environmental definition of disability contains the critical notion of the capacity to *work*—a relational concept that presupposes as much about the labor market and social structure as it does about individual performance. From this viewpoint, general economic conditions are partly responsible for the recent surge in disability claims experienced by industrialized Western societies.[30]

To be sure, disability programs raise enough complexities to rival those of the traditional tort system.[31] This is especially true in the United States, with its diverse combination of employment-related private insurance, pension plans, and public programs for medical assistance, income transfers, and direct services.[32] We have completely different ways of handling disabilities, for example, depending on whether they are total or partial, and whether they are short or long term. In addition, we know little about potential conflicts between the goals of compensation and rehabilitation, despite considerable speculation on the disincentives of public-welfare programs.[33] Controversies over eligibility and fiscal integrity in disability programs also have a way of spilling over into the judicial process, with predictable results for both equity and efficiency.[34]

Since these coordination problems already haunt American disability policy, we might balk at compounding them by adding compensation cases rescued from the faltering civil liability process. But such caution ignores a far more important possibility: that the systematic failures of judicial compensation are *already* contributing to the extraordinary pressures on public (as well as private) disability programs.[35] Paradoxically, a more deliberate blending of both systems might stimulate greater coherence in disability policy—especially if, along with uncompensated injuries, the normative weight of public responsibility could somehow be shifted to the social-welfare domain. As economist George Rohrlich has pointed out, a public commitment to a single entitlement process for personal disability would ensure wider attention to the values of equity and consistency. Although improving program integration is a difficult challenge, Rohrlich asks whether this is not "the solution that is ultimately inevitable to cope with the ubiquitous and literally uncontainable disability hazard, which in this nuclear age beset with environmental hazards resembles nothing so much as the 'genie out of the bottle.' "[36]

Looking at tort reform in the context of public disability policy is nothing new. Twenty years ago, advocates of fundamental reform in accident compensation clearly identified the need for changes in both systems.[37] Their aim was to combine the abolition of tort law with the creation of more extensive public programs for disability; indeed the latter was viewed as the political quid pro quo for doing away with tort law. In Great Britain, New Zealand, and Australia, where these proposals had their greatest impact, conditions for comprehensive reforms in both areas were more favorable than in the United States, with its hyperactive tort system and underdeveloped social-welfare structure. New Zealand took the first step down this road, and for a while it seemed that Australia and Great Britain might follow. But comprehensive plans lost their appeal by the late 1970s, and along with them the prospects for fundamental changes in tort law quickly vanished.

If this coherent, politically balanced strategy now seems out of place, social and economic changes over the past two decades may provide the reasons. In the United States, for example, we have witnessed the selective expansion of tort-law doctrines, major increases in Social Security disability claims, rising costs of medical care, growing militancy for rehabilitative services on the part of the disabled, a lively private market in employee benefits, academic disaffection with the politics of regulation, and daunting fiscal constraints on social-welfare expenditures. Under these conditions, substituting a national disability scheme for the entire tort system seems hopelessly utopian. After all, Congress spent the 1980s deadlocked over relatively trivial statutory changes in product liability doctrine.

Opportunities for single-stroke legislative reform have further diminished along with the fading distinction, based on underlying causation, between traditional accidents and other forms of disability. As Jane Stapleton has convincingly shown, little justification remains for dividing comprehensive plans into separate components for accidents, disease, and congenital disability.[38] From an environmental perspective these distinctions have never been defensible, whether for the tort system or some administrative substitute. Similar reservations were voiced even by the architects of the New Zealand policy, who for practical reasons found it necessary to confine their plan to "personal injuries."[39] Thus the New Zealand program tackled only a small portion of the disability problem, in effect allowing a favored minority to receive preferential benefits, based on the fugitive distinction between accidents and disease. Today we understand even better that the New Zealand compromise perpetuates inequities among groups of people, based on outmoded causal descriptions of their disabilities.[40]

The New Zealand experience provides an interesting contrast with the reform challenges now facing countries like the United States and Great Britain, which chose not to follow that same path. With clearer insight into the environmental sources of disease, it is tempting to dismiss the New Zealand policy as just a lot of trouble in exchange for relatively minor progress. In a sense this is true, and some advocates of comprehensive programs now seem disillusioned with what was originally greeted as a revolutionary approach.[41]

From a practical point of view, however, the New Zealand model has one major advantage: by attacking a problem that could be neatly defined (at least in 1972) as personal injury, New Zealand was able to abolish the major part of its common-law tort system. If that country now faces the further task of reconciling categorical differences among benefits for all disabled persons, it is no worse off than any other modern industrial nation. Indeed it is much *better* off with its institutional options now confined to the social-welfare sphere. Over time, other countries will want to see if New Zealand has an easier time consolidating its policies for the disabled. At the other extreme is the United States, where future progress on disability must contend with the anachronistic appeal of a lively tort system.

It is doubtless too late for other countries to follow the New Zealand pattern. Any decision to eliminate tort law altogether must now come with alternate procedures for handling not just accidents (under the old definition) but also a much wider range of personal disabilities.[42] Despite their endemic crises, the more self-confident tort systems of the 1980s have raised the stakes in interest-group haggling over no-fault options, at least in the United States. We see this, for example, in the evolution of no-fault legislative proposals into two-tiered plans, as described in Chapter 7. Under the influence of academic trends discussed earlier in Part II, political assessment of compensation issues has been virtually blinded by the refulgence of individualist theories in support of tort law, reducing the chance for fundamental change in American compensation policy. For the foreseeable future, then, litigation is likely to move from crisis to crisis, following the patterns described in Part III.

The notion of comprehensive entitlement is nonetheless vital for predicting the long-term future for both tort compensation and disability programs. Although it is not an option for immediate reform, it is the implicit standard by which incremental changes in both systems will continually be judged—and found wanting. An era of environmental accidents thus presents us with the fundamental irony that our ultimate destination is clear, but we are fated to choose the most circuitous route for getting there. The more dynamic our tort reforms and the more creative our solutions to specific environmental problems, the more we eventually undermine the distinctions separating compensation from other forms of entitlement. This happens not only because causal boundaries to eligibility are inherently weak, but also because the responsibility for intervention is slowly passing from the judicial process to the political system. The more open instrumentalism of politics reduces the likelihood that legal formalism, economic abstractions, or moral philosophy will ultimately preserve the individualist framework of discrete events and limited social duties.[43]

Unless causal boundaries are treated with almost absolute reverence, the long-term dynamic that favors universal entitlement is easy to summarize. Consider the current American workers' compensation model, which purports to compensate all workplace injuries, whether caused by a careless foreman or a lightning bolt. But what happens to the worker who is injured by a careless driver on the way home? If we expand the worker's compensation program to cover transport accidents to and from work, there remains the problem of the worker who slips and falls on her own doorstep. Extend coverage to all mishaps of the worker, and we are still left with the worker's child who slips in the bathtub.

For each step along the way, causation may seem to provide a logical, natural boundary; and those who currently fund any limited scheme have an equally natural interest in holding to the status quo in eligibility. But if causation counts for nothing *within* a compensation program, why should it exclude the next class of victims closest in description to those who already qualify? For political purposes, interest groups can form among those who are potentially eligible, just as surely as among those who would actually be liable. Environmental approaches to causation vastly complicate this struggle by blurring all existing causal criteria of eligibility. Thus more intense battles may occur around the boundaries of existing programs, as we saw earlier in the case of both workers' compensation and product liability. Unless we cling stubbornly to the individualist framework and its associated legal, economic, and moralistic theories, there is no way to divert the ultimate logic of comprehensive entitlement. Sometimes a court or a legislature manages to strengthen a causal barrier that was earlier breached, but elsewhere five more fortresses are about to be overrun.

In an era of environmental accidents, compensation as a *public* function challenges our usual tolerance of inequity and inefficiency in the social-welfare system. Why should children with vaccine injuries have more generous benefits than other children with equivalent disabilities? Why should coal miners have an easier time collecting benefits for occupational respiratory disease than asbestos workers? And if we help the asbestos workers, then why not those who suffer from other work-related diseases?

The expanding political supervision of tort procedures suggests that the public agenda may soon become crowded with issues of equity in compensation. The whole cafeteria of tort-reform options laid out in Part III can affect this process in several ways. To the extent specific reforms are actually adopted, they may delay the long-term trend toward comprehensive entitlement by momentarily reducing political tension, by preserving an institutional role for litigation, or by expanding the stakes of special-interest groups in preserving selective programs. In the short term, special classes of victims defined in relation to toxic agents like asbestos or dioxin have strategic reasons to embrace the categories of individualism (skillfully extended to *their* group circumstances by legal metaphors). The presence of an active tort system is thus likely to multiply inequities in compensation, at least in the immediate future.

Meanwhile *all* the strategies surveyed in Part III tend to erode the institutional base of traditional litigation, thereby undermining the structural support for individualism. We can briefly illustrate this self-defeating effect of incremental reform using the examples of asbestos, Agent Orange, and nuclear power. In the United States, asbestos litigation has benefited little from structural reforms in adjudication designed to streamline the processing of cases, as we saw in Chapter 6. But it has been the occasion for unprecedented research on how diverse courts cope with large numbers of claims, based on similar exposures and diverse but comparable injuries. After summarizing the many factors that frustrate the courts' ability to process asbestos claims promptly and equitably, the Rand study draws the following conclusion:

> A basic problem with asbestos litigation is that through group disposition processes it has sacrificed attention to individualized injuries and needs that supposedly characterizes our litigation process without achieving the reduction in transaction costs that usually accompanies less individualized administrative processes. This transformation of the historical case-by-case posture of litigation into a partially administered group approach is significant not only because it focuses attention on the trade-offs in any system between consistency and individualization, but also because it has come about in such a remarkable fashion—without plan, without debate, and without much public awareness. The rather sudden and unpublicized nature of this important alteration in the character of litigation seems to fly in the face of the slow, careful, incremental, and public way of change that has been characteristic of Anglo-American common law for centuries. [44]

This quotation—perhaps unwittingly—captures the essential irony of incremental tort reform, in its demand for *public* debate over changes in common-law adjudication. Far from "flying in the face" of traditional legal change, the absence of systematic planning and public awareness (fully documented by this research study) is the *essence* of that incremental process. But today we expect more structure, consistency, and public discussion for routine adjudication—now that we have learned to scrutinize these claims as a group, instead of 50,000 unique injuries. What the Rand research team finds shocking about asbestos claims is what earlier critics of the tort system have been pointing out for years, only now it is much easier to document.

Our concerns about equity and efficiency are no doubt made more urgent by the possibility (documented by another Rand study) that this litigation could cost as much as $65 billion, of which only $24 billion may get beyond the attorneys into the hands of plaintiffs. [45] We should take a long, hard look at that $65 billion figure, and try to imagine what could be accomplished if somehow it were invested in health, income, and rehabilitation services for victims of respiratory disease. Remarkably, there seems to be no practical way for Americans to make *this* economic choice at a political level, unless we pursue

more drastic reform measures like the administrative proposals for occupational disease analyzed in Chapter 9. So far such public action has
been blocked by litigants on both sides, who wish to protect their
individual losses while hiding behind the neutral language of tort
rights and economic efficiency.

Another intriguing round of litigation involved more than 200,000
claims from Vietnam veterans alleging long-term health and reproductive effects of their exposure to the herbicide Agent Orange. As we
saw in Chapter 6, this complex litigation ended in 1984 with a settlement, under which several product manufacturers agreed to establish
a $180 million fund for distribution by the court.[46] Compared to other
judicial ordeals, the Agent Orange litigation set an unbeatable standard for the speed and thoroughness with which the knotty legal issues of toxic torts were resolved. As a demonstration of how the volatile forces of litigation can be contained by a superb trial judge, we
cannot imagine a more inspired performance. From just about every
other standpoint, however, the outcome raises troubling concerns.

Although the amount of the agreed settlement was (at the time) the
largest ever negotiated in a toxic-tort case, the enormous number of
claimants (potentially an estimated 600,000 veterans exposed to Agent
Orange) means that the award will have to be spread very thin. Because of the likely expense of trying to prove individual exposure levels and their inscrutable connections to injuries occurring years later,
Judge Weinstein wisely chose to distribute the fund according to the
standards of "compensation" rather than "tort."[47] In other words, he
rejected the standards that courts ordinarily use to determine liability
and damages for typical common-law cases (including asbestos litigation). He treated the fund more like a social-welfare program, developing criteria of entitlement based on severity of need among all
600,000 members of the potential class of recipients. After setting
aside $45 million for research, surveillance, and other projects bene-
fiting the class as a whole, he established a fixed schedule of awards for
death and disability, available to any Vietnam veteran with any degree
of exposure to Agent Orange.[48]

Schuck concludes that Judge Weinstein "established precisely
what Congress had rejected just prior to the 1984 elections—a large
new federal benefit program for Vietnam veterans."[49] This correctly
suggests the relevance of political and administrative criteria for evaluating the outcome of the Agent Orange case, at least from the standpoint of compensation. On that basis, however, the benefit program

scarcely seems "large." The United States spent $23.6 billion in 1986 on medical and disability programs for all veterans. Figures available for 1983 show some $2.5 billion annual expenditures for death and disability payments for around 600,000 Vietnam-era veterans (excluding any claims specifically tied to Agent Orange).[50] Even if we add the approximately $120 million in legal costs used in this litigation up through 1984,[51] the amount in question seems relatively modest. As for the size of individual awards, the Weinstein plan falls well short of benefits provided by most state workers' compensation programs and Social Security Disability Insurance. The disparities are even greater in comparison with benefits in the federal Black Lung Program, not to mention the more lurid compensation levels sometimes provided by the tort system itself.

The difficulties encountered by plaintiffs in these cases, even with the planful assistance of an enlightened judge, suggest that future mass dispositions of environmental injury claims will receive low marks for consistency, adequacy, and cost effectiveness. As comparable events come to light, pressure for more consistent political oversight seems a likely result. This does not guarantee, of course, that more drastic interventions will be forthcoming, let alone that merger with social-welfare programs will suggest itself as a solution. No one can predict the actual route for reform, although it is safe to expect that current tort reform strategies will fail to satisfy even their own political partisans.

Although it is painful to contemplate, a truly stunning mass accident could test our society's tolerance for ineffective piecemeal reforms. We can gain some sense of potential political sentiment by looking at the Three Mile Island litigation, and its effect on federal legislation defining future liability. The United States's only major encounter with nuclear accident claims followed a curious episode in which the release of radioactivity was too insignificant to trigger the strict liability provisions of the Price-Anderson Act, the federal statute regulating nuclear liability litigation.[52] But personal claims were filed anyway in the aftermath of the Three Mile Island incident by people who were afraid of possible radioactive leaks, and who had allegedly incurred expenses and psychic trauma from evacuating the immediate area.[53]

A sober legal reading of the statute restricted special claims procedures to incidents where losses are *caused* by radioactivity; to a defendant this means something entirely different from the plaintiff's *fear* of radioactivity. From a political perspective, however, the difference created a highly unpopular gap in liability coverage. When the Price-Anderson Act was renewed in 1988, despite a number of paralyzing questions, the law was changed to permit easier recovery after any future nuclear scare like the one at Three Mile Island.[54] In a case where Congress has dominant legislative oversight over the entire structure of liability procedures, changing the boundaries of causation is much like creating a new entitlement program. Indeed it is much simpler, since in this case Congress does not have to appropriate the actual funds.

If at some point a greater number of accident claims fall under this same degree of congressional stewardship, it seems reasonable that the bounds of eligibility will expand rather than contract—and will expand very quickly in the aftermath of any major panic or catastrophe. It is sad to think that it may take the pressure of dramatic environmental accidents to break the appeal of incremental strategies for tort reform. But whatever it takes for Americans to focus on inconsistencies in their wide-ranging programs for compensation, we can expect the number of anomalies to multiply over the years, as environmental accidents (large and small) bring all compensation procedures under closer political scrutiny.

Returning to the broader environmental framework, it may seem that a system of comprehensive entitlement loses sight of compensation in the general stream of social welfare. While it is true that a social policy for compensation assumes a different quality the farther it strays from the traditional judicial context, the distinctive meaning of compensation is by no means lost. Indeed, social-welfare theorists have sometimes reached for precisely this broad concept of compensation as a central justification for the whole social-welfare system. The British theorist Richard Titmuss, for example, described one of the main goals of modern welfare programs as providing "compensation for the 'diswelfares' of change experienced by the individual and the community at large because we cannot identify and legally charge the causal agents of change."[55] If we can now refer all causation matters to a separate policy for accountability, Titmuss's notion of compensatory social welfare captures the essential meaning of public responsibility toward accident victims, according to the environmental perspective.[56]

But compensation is only one branch of the public-responsibility model. Although its separate design makes it independent from accountability issues in matters of detail, compensation must find its place in a larger policy framework. Left entirely to itself, a comprehensive approach to compensation is open to attack from both ends of the political spectrum. Traditionalists like to identify compensation with invitations to idleness. In accident policy they depend on welfare economics or moral theory to raise accountability goals to the dominant position within some massive trade-off, where compensation is presumed to diminish wealth or fairness.[57] From a very different point of view, other critics have attacked welfare programs as efforts by elites to buffer their exploitation of the powerless.[58] An independent compensation system could thus be accused of buying off the disabled (no doubt at favorable rates), and thereby distracting attention from more fundamental questions of social and economic equality.[59]

Quite obviously, no separate policy on compensation can satisfy both camps at the same time. But we shall see how the natural flexibility of an independent accountability strategy, in conjunction with compensation, can cover almost any position between these two extremes. Whatever its shape, an accountability policy does not have to compromise the independent goal of comprehensive entitlement.

Accountability: The Presumption of Public Responsibility

An environmental framework encourages the separate development of policies for compensation and accountability, but it preserves their ultimate unity in the principle of public responsibility. Nowhere is the contrast with individualist presumptions more evident than with this concept, the practical effect of which is to convert both compensation and accountability into imperative tasks for public action. To be sure, it is individual people who actually receive compensation; just as it is specific agencies, organizations, groups, and individuals who cooperate under any working scheme for accountability. What remains indissolubly collective is the *responsibility* to ensure that such policies are actually formulated and implemented.

As a practical matter, public responsibility can be expressed through a wide number of programs and institutional structures. As we have just seen, a policy devoted to compensation would probably build on designs already being used by industrial nations in responding to social problems of disability. In the area of accountability, a greater variety of options are available for assigning responsibility to organizations and persons.

Accountability itself can be divided into two branches: retribution for past actions, and modification of future behavior. The former is identified with the criminal-justice system and its formal procedures, but it also includes the fines and other penalties administered by public regulatory bodies. To whatever extent findings of civil liability are thought to be useful expressions for public retribution (apart from other functions of compensating victims and deterring future behavior), they too can be included in this inventory. While it has become uncommon in the twentieth century to think of retributive systems as fully independent of public goals for future prevention, the structures for retributive policies are still firmly in place.[60] They remain as options for public policy, even when compensation may be administered by entirely separate institutions.

We shall concentrate here on the preventive goals of accountability, which have gained increasing importance over the past century as part of the legal turn toward instrumentalism. In most commentaries, strategies for accident prevention have been heavily restricted by the analytical goal of coordinating prevention with existing compensation systems. A common approach is to attribute primary inducements for preventive behavior to judicial distributions of compensation or liability. Liability (according to the progressive critics of tort law) creates incentives for potential defendants to promote future safety, but compensation (according to economist critics) counters that tendency by reducing similar incentives for potential plaintiffs.

Based on this approach, most academic treatments of accountability have become obsessed with the technique of guiding future safety efforts by adjusting civil liability mechanisms. Even for critics who allow a legitimate role for other forms of public regulation, the concern for optimal deterrence remains an important analytical exercise, and a kind of ritual homage to the virtues of efficiency.[61] At times it seems that analytical elegance alone is responsible for keeping judicial compensation procedures alive, as purely ancillary to the goal of optimal accident prevention.[62]

Separating compensation and accountability into distinct policies frees both systems from the institutional constraints of the judicial process. It also brings both policies squarely into the political arena, beyond the full reach of the invisible hand of procedural justice or market equilibrium. Under these conditions, injury prevention becomes part of a general policy of public regulation. In that context, however, the influence of tort law's individualized framework of duties remains quite powerful. Just as the burden of accidents falls on inevitable victims in the form of injuries, the burden of regulation falls on specific groups and persons in the form of fines, fees, or taxes. Unlike injuries, however, which are allocated randomly, costs must be distributed through some social process—political, legal, or economic.

The necessity for publicly financing regulation thus perpetuates the perennial lure of individual responsibility; if *I* didn't cause any harm, then *I* shouldn't be made to pay for it. Hence the appeal of would-be "neutral" funding mechanisms: administrative schemes that pay for themselves, legal liability, and general deterrence. The central irony of public regulation is that collective control over a common environment, which is indispensable to modern industrial societies, is captivated by retreating metaphors of individual responsibility. Over the past two decades, intellectual fashions have reinforced the resistence to regulatory policy, chiefly by trying to undermine its institutional base in the political system.[63]

From an environmental orientation, accident prevention policy is presumed to be the result of public deliberation, and not merely the spontaneous product of an institutional structure—whether political, judicial, or economic. The political process is thus expected to formulate substantive policy (at least in broad outlines), leaving judicial findings and economic calculations confined to the lesser role of aiding implementation. This different orientation vastly expands the available strategies for preventing future accidents. It need not ignore those strategies favored by courts and markets, which restrict prevention to a process of manipulating economic incentives. But other strategies can be used as well, including broader incentives for altering individual or group behavior, direct changes to the environment itself, and controls placed on destructive agents within that environment. In other words, an environmental perspective builds its preventive strategies directly on the complex model of events used by epidemiology, rather than working exclusively through the psychology of economic self-interest.

Using epidemiological concepts, William Haddon, Jr. has elaborated a convenient inventory of regulatory strategies for responding to accidents. His scheme begins with the basic model of victim, agent, and environment, which is augmented by temporal distinctions among actions taken before, during, and after the injurious event.

Over a period of twenty-five years, Haddon has refined this matrix into a series of ten strategies for injury control, listed here with his own illustrations.

1. To prevent the creation of the hazard in the first place. Examples: prevent production of plutonium, thalidomide, LSD.
2. To reduce the amount of hazard brought into being. Examples: reduce speeds of vehicles, lead content of paint, mining of asbestos.
3. To prevent the release of the hazard that already exists. Examples: pasteurizing milk, bolting or timbering mine roofs, impounding nuclear wastes.
4. To modify the rate or spatial distribution of release of the hazard from its source. Examples: brakes, shutoff valves, reactor control rods.
5. To separate, in time or space, the hazard and that which is to be protected. Examples: isolation of persons with communicable diseases, walkways over or around hazards, evacuation.
6. To separate the hazard and that which is to be protected by interposition of a material barrier. Examples: surgeon's gloves, containment structures, childproof poison-container closures.
7. To modify relevant basic qualities of the hazard. Examples: altering pharmacological agents to reduce side effects, using breakaway roadside poles, making crib slat spacings too narrow to strangle a child.
8. To make what is to be protected more resistant to damage from the hazard. Examples: immunization, making structures more fire- and earthquake-resistant, giving salt to workers under thermal stress.
9. To begin to counter the damage already done by the environmental hazard. Examples: rescuing the shipwrecked, reattaching severed limbs, extricating trapped miners.
10. To stabilize, repair, and rehabilitate the object of the damage. Examples: posttraumatic cosmetic surgery, physical rehabilitation, rebuilding after fires and earthquakes.[64]

An environmental approach to prevention starts from this range of options and works backwards to the question of accountability. Who should be held accountable for seeing that these strategies are defined, compared, and carried out for various types of accidents? For

Haddon the answer is the purely functional consequence of who has control and authority to undertake each kind of intervention. This broadens the possibilities for assigning responsibility beyond the limited roster of defendants in the judicial process, which starts with the traditional classes of persons having private legal duties, and ranges only as far as instrumentalism can safely go—perhaps no farther than corporate defendants with deep enough pockets to finance a more ambitious compensation system. Even the most creative judges still have to impute some causal link between defendants and an injury that has already occurred. Haddon's analysis, by contrast,

> does not center on causation per se—despite the frequent usefulness of relevant knowledge of causes—but rather on the means available for reducing the specific kinds of undesirable morbidity and mortality that are of concern. . . . In fact, with this orientation and focus, reductions in undesirable end results can often be achieved without exhaustive knowledge of their exact causes. In illustration: pasteurization and water purification can control milk and waterborne diseases even in the absence of specific knowledge as to which pathogens would otherwise reach the publics to be protected.[65]

A series of complementary responsibilities thus fall on the general public, regulatory bodies, public and private organizations, persons within those organizations, and, finally, individual actors. A general policy on accountability would adopt a preventive strategy mobilizing all of these levels in appropriate roles. It is not realistic, for instance, for the general public or its legislative representatives to vote on specific designs for baby cribs. Nor is it likely that legislative bodies could readily agree on particular strategies for broad types of accidents—such as highway accidents or occupational diseases. The responsibility of the electorate is primarily to ensure that a regulatory structure is in place to supervise those decisions. Legislative bodies would also be expected to monitor agency performance and to intervene in exceptional circumstances.

Although a comprehensive preventive structure of this type looks quite formidable in the abstract, the general outline may suggest useful ways to build more coherence into U.S. policy for environmental and safety regulation. Regulatory agencies have a responsibility to specify more precise duties for the organizations they regulate; and those organizations in turn must define responsibilities for specific personnel. In the past two decades, a vast scholarly literature has explored the options for communicating regulatory goals at various levels of the enforcement hierarchy, centering on the distinction between regulation by explicit command and by economic incentives. A coordinated national regulatory policy would undoubtedly have to make use of both techniques, with comparatively greater use of economic information at the most specific levels of enforcement, where the number of actors being controlled becomes largest.[66]

From the late 1960s through about 1980, the federal government began to build a regulatory structure for promoting health and safety in the environment.[67] Although it developed in the piecemeal style that has characterized most public initiatives in this country, each step toward this emerging policy of comprehensive environmental regulation was an implied rejection of accident prevention measures based solely on civil liability systems. At a time when no-fault alternatives to judicial compensation were getting serious attention in state legislatures, civil liability was viewed with equal skepticism as a monitor for social interests in environmental protection. In many cases involving accidents from hazardous substances, the courts had scarcely begun the process of matching individual injuries with viable, well-funded defendants. Given the number of economic actors (agencies, organizations, and individuals) potentially involved in implementing the above list of strategies, it was unrealistic ever to expect that courts, by making individual liability decisions, could establish an exhaustive system of economic incentives.

The litigation process made perhaps its strongest conceivable bid to construct a prevention system in the field of product accidents during the 1970s, using doctrinal tools like strict liability and a variety of creative procedural devices.[68] (Similar changes occurred in adjudication of medical malpractice claims, where the introduction of standard negligence doctrines brought a flood of claims into the judicial process.) The product liability initiatives launched by a number of creative courts fueled a lively controversy over possible *public* functions of tort law, a lofty vision that reflected the American preference for decentralized, incremental approaches to social policy.[69]

Advocates of strict liability were completely unsentimental in their dismissal of the moralistic language of fault, and emphasized instead the instrumental value of liability doctrines that imposed more of the costs of product accidents on manufacturers.[70] To be sure, their dominant goal was to win more compensation for personal injury victims; but progressive critics also understood the future-oriented sense of causation. According to this view, our ability to prevent future injuries was the practical payoff for delving into the source of past injuries. Future accident prevention thus became an independent reason for stretching traditional legal rules and procedures. By legally attributing past accidents to those who were in the best position to prevent them in the future, we could advance the public interest in regulation—as well as compensation. Best of all, the public interest would be articulated by the neutral voice of impartial justice, insulated from the need to gain consensus in the rougher world of politics.

From an environmental perspective, this approach is a somewhat tentative expression of the public responsibility principle. But asking the *courts* to administer the public's response to accidents placed severe limits on preventive strategies, and it unwittingly provoked a feisty individualist counterreaction. Ironically, it was the economic premise hidden within the public law tort model that was used most successfully to blunt the reformist edge.

The civil-law strategy for preventing accidents put its major emphasis on economic incentives, rather than moral exhortation, criminal sanctions, or administrative commands. This left it vulnerable, however, to the searching questions of economic-welfare theorists: how much regulation do we really need? And how does the distribution of costs affect the overall level of safety? Implicit in the first question is the idea that some regulation may cost more than it is worth. The second question turns the tables on progressives by pointing out that compensating plaintiffs has an opposing effect on overall safety incentives, directly offsetting the purpose of imposing liability on defendants.

Both arguments were inevitable applications of broader theories attacking public regulation in its political manifestations, which gained attention soon after the federal government launched its new environmental initiatives in the late 1960s. The field of economics has a complex history of commentary on public regulation, much of it supportive.[71] But the particular brand of economic criticism leveled against environmental regulation and public tort law embodies almost perfectly the set of presumptions that we identified earlier with an individualist orientation to events, persons, and social responsibilities. It adopts an especially narrow perspective on economic questions, ignoring, for the most part, issues like income distribution and the limits of market information—precisely those problems that are emphasized by the opposing environmental framework.

The current brand of economic criticism is less notable for its economics than for its institutional biases. Consider the following synopsis:

Administrative regulation is, from the economic viewpoint, a presumptively disfavored instrument because it tends to centralise determination of prices, outputs, and production processes in the government, displacing decentralized decisions by producers and consumers. This leads to inefficiencies because government agencies cannot generate and process all of the information employed by the market price system.

Other economic policy instruments—instruments such as taxes or subsidies . . . make greater use of market incentives and allow for greater decentralised flexibility. They are accordingly presumptively preferred.

Economic incentives are superior because they promote a least-cost allocation of abatement efforts (firms that can control pollution cheaply will do more abatement and pay less in fees or for permits, while firms with high abatement costs will control less and pay more). They reward firms that develop environmentally superior processes and products.[72]

Stewart's summary of this standard antiregulation argument brings out the crucial role of presumptions derived from an individualist orientation. Information found in existing markets is the preferred means of recognizing the normative presumption in favor of individual consumer sovereignty. This is certainly one way to organize the social response to environmental uncertainty: if a present risk is not already reflected in market prices, then it bears the enormous burden of earning public notice through the irrational institutions of politics.

In addition, spontaneous market judgments, based on comparisons among market-priced alternatives, are presumed to be superior to judgments rendered by political institutions. In the field of accident policy, the economic theory of tort law amends this second point to allow civil liability awards (when properly generated) to influence the pricing of choices among possible preventive strategies, as well as the more fundamental economic choice between prevention and compensation.[73]

By now the opposing presumptions of the environmental orientation should be familiar. Prevention information expressed by unregulated markets is presumed to be less comprehensive than what is potentially available through epidemiological research. The judicial process is unable to remedy this systematic weakness in market data, given its traditional orientation to individual cases, private parties, and causal connections. The only way to make market data reliable instruments for microdecisions about accident prevention is to supplement them with information and value choices drawn from the political process. Thus the economic signals sent out to corporations and private persons—to all those in a position to affect the future accident rate by marginal adjustments in behavior—must pass through regulatory bodies, which in turn are answerable to the voters.[74]

Nothing prevents regulatory policy from relying heavily on decentralized forms of decision making by corporate and individual actors; indeed that is the point of recognizing multiple levels of accountability within a national policy of accident prevention. Instead of allowing unregulated markets to dictate terms for those decisions, however, the environmental model assigns that role to regulatory agencies, and ultimately to the electorate. Under persistent political oversight, environmental accidents may well yield more fully to organized control through either command regulation or a system of economic incentives. Under the market-judicial approach, these accidents will continue to escape our attention.[75]

An awareness of environmental accidents helps reestablish the unity of political and economic issues, contrary to the presumptions of recent welfare-economic theory. Reversing the analytical abstractions described in Chapter 4, we may formulate three conclusions about the economic aspects of regulation, using an environmental perspective. *Optimal deterrence* becomes the responsibility of politically regulated market systems. *Cost reduction* encompasses a range of social and distributional concerns expressed by the political process—not just the analytical goal preferred by current welfare economic theories. Finally, economic concerns as a whole reach a central point of contact with *normative* issues. The model of public responsibility treats economics as an instrument of social policy—the very opposite of treating public policy as the residue of self-regulating economic systems.[76]

While it seems clear that politics rather than markets will determine how far the United States can go in regulating environmental health and safety, it is also true that politics is shaped by economics through the process of public funding. How much accident prevention we can support—politically—depends in part on who is paying; and the same is true for compensating the victims of personal injury. Concepts from traditional tort law inhibit cost spreading across the widest possible range of taxpayers—both corporate and individual. While perhaps only a few market enthusiasts want to delegate national health and safety policy entirely to the free market and civil liability, the constituencies opposing public regulation are enhanced as more costs are redistributed from injury victims onto the rest of society.

Just as the long-term trend in compensation appears to be toward universal entitlement, over time the personal costs of accidental injury have been redistributed with increasing breadth. In practical terms, the most limited regime for redistributing accident costs was the traditional tort system operating under negligence standards.[77] Although the past century has seen steady erosion of the doctrinal constraints on negligence, the problems of assigning costs have complicated the process of moving beyond mere doctrinal reform. When legislatures become active in drawing the boundaries of liability for future accidents, potential defendants (and their insurers, who often become the defendants' defendants) can resist under cover of moral intuition, economic analysis, or sheer political clout. The principle of equity pays an ironic visit to these discussions, wanting to know why taxpayers who "did nothing wrong" are being forced to pay as much as those who are caught red-handed.

Today the most significant investments in accident prevention occur entirely outside the tort system—even beyond the politically managed doctrinal boundaries of product-liability law. As we saw in Chapters 8 and 9, financing more systematic prevention in the natural environment requires mobilizing federal revenue powers. These two chapters covered alternative methods of financing large-scale regulatory action. One method tries to mimic the tort system's method of allocating costs, based on individualized findings of wrongdoing. The Superfund cost-recovery program—small in terms of dollars but immensely powerful in its symbolism—illustrates the federal government's determination to apply individualist rhetoric to the financing problem. The other framework uses the language of insurance, and seems especially popular in administrative programs that have to coordinate regulation and compensation, like workers' compensation and special funds for childhood-vaccine injuries. For nuclear accidents, both insurance and tort concepts are combined in the Price-Anderson approach to allocating accident costs.

Perhaps the most likely solution to financing the future costs of regulation has already been found in the recent eclectic formula adopted after the 1986 reauthorization of the Superfund law. Cost recovery through litigation is only a small source of projected revenue for Superfund activities, with the bulk of financing coming from other sources: general revenues, a surcharge on all corporate taxpayers, and a special excise tax on industries whose production methods most contribute to the nation's hazardous-waste burdens.[78] The political flexibility of such an approach was explored in detail in Chapter 9, where we noted the potential advantages of a unified funding scheme for controlling environmental accidents in the workplace, the natural environment, and the product market. As we concluded, the Superfund model—an artifact of political bargaining—nonetheless reflects the eclectic nature of our knowledge about environmental injuries.

Critics who evaluate the model by its own opportunistic rhetoric about internalizing accident costs are justified in condemning it as a tool for future prevention. But the real issue here is not prevention—which is the task of regulatory policy as a whole—but rather *financing*, and the political wiles of distributing prevention costs across the entire population. Everyone except the most rabid market economist concedes that prevention and financing are distinct issues, especially when political institutions have seized the initiative for long-term environmental regulation. The problem is to find politically palatable ways to fund those efforts, along with the inevitable future costs of compensating greater numbers of accident victims.

The Superfund financing formula is broad enough to reach the vast resources that will be required over the next several decades, although its categorical distinctions weakly reflect the rhetorical appeal of individualized accountability. The formula takes some notice of where existing environmental hazards come from, but it is broad enough to impose the major costs on industries that will play an even stronger role in creating the environment of the future. It permits us to quantify accountability for diverse categories of agents, including the federal government. Although it defines cost burdens on a generalized level, it does not rule out more discriminating adjustments of tax burdens should we learn enough to make taxation a major tool for future prevention.

The central presumption behind this funding method, however, is that the economic burdens of regulation must be broadly distributed, unless we find plausible reasons to focus them in more specific ways. The amount of regulation our society is able to afford is thus not determined by how well we are able to justify our methods of cost internalization. To implement a regulatory strategy based on the full range of epidemiological insights, our public-finance needs will inevitably outstrip our institutional ability to internalize costs. Given the tendency of all revenue schemes to awaken individualist protests from the contributors, any choice among funding mechanisms must be politically astute.[79] The eclectic Superfund formula may well be sufficiently vague and diverse to allow it to play an expanded role in future regulatory initiatives.

Apart from the inevitable public choices among prevention strategies and funding mechanisms, the central question for public responsibility is the overall choice between prevention and compensation. Faced with this daunting challenge, the two policy areas of compensation and accountability must eventually overlap. The compensation needs of a society are, in some sense, a measure of failure in prevention policies; and marginal adjustments in the amount of prevention will determine changes in the burden of compensation. More research on vaccine safety, for example, may result in fewer children being seriously disabled by rare side effects. More safety devices in consumer or industrial products can reduce the rate of disabling accidents. A more ambitious nuclear waste disposal program can lower the chances of future injuries, with their attendant compensation costs.

The economic aspect of this trade-off has made it the centerpiece of market-dominated theories. If somehow we could invent a market system (perhaps with the help of courts) with prices reflecting all our collective values, all potential strategies for accident prevention, and all future environmental contingencies—then perhaps we could sit back and let the market decide how to allocate resources between compensation and regulation.[80] We obviously do not have—and never will have—such a market, and continued tinkering with liability rules will not move us any closer to that elusive goal.

Even a perfect market system would bypass important normative questions. Personal injuries, by their very nature, represent major shifts in the distribution of social welfare. The judicial process translates injuries into monetary losses, but it necessarily ignores the difference in kind between the enjoyment of good health and money in the bank. The market system (unless subject to public regulation) is even less concerned with this distributional change; under some welfare-economic theories, an accidental loss to one person can be paid for by a large enough gain in someone else's income. Under either approach, we cannot rule out the possibility that personal injuries in modern society are, in part, the product of prevailing economic, social, and political inequalities.

To be sure, it is technologically futile to expect to eliminate accidents entirely from our world, even if the environment were more cooperative.[81] At least some personal injuries are inevitable and unavoidable, but in the end societies must make a political choice about how many injuries they are willing to accept—quite apart from how many they may be willing to pay for. This is the major obligation of any political approach to accident policy. If the concept of public responsibility means anything, it stands for the inescapably political nature of this decision.

Practical Reform: The Irony of Incrementalism

Most surveys of alternatives to tort law end somewhat wistfully, with the admission that dramatic changes are unlikely to take place in U.S. accident policy. The role of litigation in personal injury claims seems firmly entrenched, despite the fact that the traditional forms have been irreversibly changed by instrumental judging, by political oversight, and by selective public forays into the structure or administration of compensation. Our survey in Part III analyzed these various strategies, noting how bitterly the battles over tort reform are being fought—often to no avail. Most of the compromise plans being viewed as reforms may do little more than raise the costs of litigation without adding much to the compensation of victims or the prevention of future accidents. More complexity and disorder in accident policy seem the probable outcomes of these volatile conditions, and not comprehensive reform.

Although tort law has become mired in perpetual crises, the future of accident policy may well be settled in an entirely different arena. Over the past three decades, the United States has made modest but significant efforts to develop national policies for both personal disability and environmental regulation. More than all the turmoil in our judicial system, these changes appear to be carrying us into an entirely new era of public responsibility for personal injuries. Like everything else in the American political process, the design of future social welfare and regulatory policies is being worked out in piecemeal fashion, in response to urgent but vaguely articulated pressures; and neither field has lacked for critics. But these policies are now firmly established, and the projected scale of public investment suggests that we will be devoting the next few decades to finding greater coherence in both areas.

An environmental orientation provides an argument for shaping future disability and regulatory policies around the problem of personal injury—understood not in the language of tort law and its derivatives, but as an inescapable feature of human interaction in all industrialized societies. Ultimately, policies based on *this* framework offer the only practical, realistic alternative to the present chaos of tort law—not the incremental reforms analyzed in Part III. Even now, disability programs are meeting more of the compensation needs of injury victims than the tort system, and regulatory policy is a far more potent force for accident deterrence. More resources are already being spent under their auspices than through the channels of accident litigation, notwithstanding the high administrative costs of the judicial system.

So far debate in this country has resisted the long-term implications of these new programs. Indeed, since the mid 1970s it has been popular to challenge the legitimacy of public initiatives for disability and environmental control. The theoretical outlook of neoconservatism, combined with the market ideology of Reaganism, has sought to perpetuate a world view in which private action still calls the shots. At most, however, this historic confluence of anachronistic intellectual and political forces has managed only to slow the expansion of disability and regulatory programs. Having survived such challenges, those programs now show every prospect for renewed expansion in what remains of this century.

Despite our strong historical and intellectual attachment to individualized procedures for responding to accidents, our practice as a nation has already moved far ahead of our ideology. When it finally comes, we suspect that the shift to an environmental orientation will be greeted as an obvious and welcome rationale for public responsibilities that are already embedded in our social structure. We may never know what to do about the tort system, but it will suddenly be recognized as an expensive and largely irrelevant adjunct to other ways of handling the problem of accidents. Instead of just building reforms onto that system, a more realistic accident policy will find ways to limit the costs and intrusions of litigation while other programs try to address more pressing public needs.[82]

Among the possible futures for accident policy, certainly the *least* practical would be a disorganized public agenda superimposed on an active litigation system. Gustave Shubert warns against this same dismal prospect.[83] The internal tensions he finds within the current judicial system reflect the opposing forces of what we are calling the individualist and environmental orientations. By grafting social concerns onto the traditional apparatus of litigation, he notes, we mainly gain higher administrative costs and little resolution of underlying conflicts. But perhaps we do not need to wait for theorists to discover some "rational" way to compare the costs and benefits of alternative systems. The United States has, in effect, already set its course toward public responsibility by committing itself to long-term policies for personal disability and environmental regulation.

Today's heated controversies over the future of tort law seem oblivious to larger social dynamics. It is not surprising that this particularly antiquated corner of our legal heritage, with its extraordinary staying power, is able to constrain our view of potential alternatives. For some time yet, we may continue to design optimal arrangements within a structure that is daily being repudiated by our social environment. Our confidence in incremental reform compels us to spin elaborate theories around the problem of tort reform, all the while blocking our view of overarching issues of personal disability and environmental regulation.

Fine-tuning the tort system, ironically, is the inevitable route to making it obsolete. The reason has little to do with incremental reform as such, but with being incremental in too small an arena. As the tort system moves under increased political scrutiny, its inequities and inefficiencies will eventually be recognized and absorbed by incremental trends within the broader contexts of social welfare and environmental regulation. By labeling the problem of personal injury as primarily a tort crisis, the United States seems intent on delaying that moment of discovery as long as possible.

We are not questioning the fundamental value of prudence in social life. Especially in a social environment that we barely comprehend, we would be ill advised to trust our fate to abstract theories about ideal (or even optimal) arrangements. But our prudence will do us some good only if we apply it to our everyday environment, with all its complexities, rather than saving it for an imaginary world of cerebral design.

There has never been a time in politically organized societies when prudence was other than indispensable. But the cognitive requirements of prudence in our world are savagely more demanding and the scale of risk, to the species as a whole and to particular human collectivities within it, is breathtakingly more extreme. In its modern form, therefore, the challenge to understand what it is to be prudent—as individuals, as members of communities or classes, as citizens or political leaders—is necessarily an unnerving one.

But it is not a challenge from which we can, with honour, simply turn away.[84]

Chapter 11

Comparative Policy Perspectives

> *We fool Americans will go on for fifty or seventy-five years before we . . . undertake . . . what they have already achieved in New Zealand.*[1]

The New Zealand Experiment

Other industrialized democracies have struggled with the problems of personal injuries, and they all face the relatively new challenge of environmental accidents. Their responses have taken significantly different paths from the American experience, however, based on differences in their legal systems, social welfare structures, and underlying values.

The international exchange of ideas on accident policy has remained a purely academic exercise. For earlier social reform movements, by contrast, foreign models were a vital force in American debate. Workers' compensation, our major exception to the judicial monopoly over accident compensation, was influenced by programs in Bismarckian Germany and Edwardian England—not to mention New Zealand.[2] But other deviations from judicial models have found no echo in American policy, and for the past three decades the accident problem in the United States has been discussed with parochial assurance that our problems are uniquely complex. Perhaps that belief has fulfilled itself, since our unique failure to exploit meaningful alternatives to tort law has now greatly complicated our search for practical responses to environmental accidents.

The American pattern retains a more prominent role for courts, lawyers, and legal commentary on accident policy than we find in any other industrial country. But the difference in legal culture is probably less the cause than the effect of underlying views on social relations and social welfare. Western European countries along with the Commonwealth nations of Australia and New Zealand have embraced more fully the values of the modern welfare state. They have adopted more comprehensive programs for public medical services (in most cases a national health system), and they offer a more extensive series of income supports and social services.

These programs not only provide more adequate assistance for victims of personal injury and disease, but they quite naturally limit the role of the judicial process. Since World War II, countries other than the United States have viewed accident compensation as a matter of coordinating benefits and setting priorities, based on their assumption of political responsibility for the essential fabric of public life. While they all retain some residual role for civil liability, they have witnessed nothing like the sudden expansion of personal injury litigation in the United States. Their orientation to public responsibility principles has kept the judicial process under firmer political control, relegated to subordinate status in national policy.

The most spectacular institutional reform in the area of personal injury occurred in New Zealand in 1972 with the adoption of the Accident Compensation Act (ACA).[3] The New Zealand approach had a brief but powerful influence on policy discussions in Australia and Great Britain, providing a focus for political, legal, and philosophical debate over future directions of public welfare.[4] In New Zealand itself the ACA arrived with bipartisan support from the majority conservative party and the liberal opposition, and with only muted criticisms from legal practitioners, insurance companies, organized labor, and other interest groups. Among the complex reasons why such reform succeeded in New Zealand, we must credit that country's pride in its history of social innovation.[5] Its self-image as "the political laboratory of the world" has been reflected in the judgment of foreign observers for most of the past century: "The new light that has been growing for years in the Southern sky, till now it illumines the world, is . . . but the rising glory of a new civilization . . . the Aurora Socialis of New Zealand."[6]

Against this background of social-welfare values and traditions, the ACA is perhaps the most radical alternative to tort litigation as a means for compensating personal injury victims. Going beyond more selective programs for specific injuries (such as workplace or automobile injuries), New Zealand abolished the tort action for "personal injury by accident," replacing it and the workers' compensation system with a single entitlement program. Persons injured in the workplace, on the highways, in the home, or anywhere else in New Zealand are equally eligible for benefits administered by the newly created Accident Compensation Corporation. Medical care and rehabilitation services are provided through parallel state systems. Compensation levels are defined by published schedules, and they are virtually independent of the source of injury, the claimant's own behavior, or the identity of putative defendants.[7]

The ACA set a new pattern for social benefits, different from entitlements under social security or the superseded workers' compensation system. In response to perceived inadequacies in both programs, the ACA borrowed categories of loss from common law, including earnings-related benefits (without a means test), separate compensation for permanent partial or total incapacity, and a further payment for "intangible" loss, reminiscent of pain and suffering. While these parallels with common-law damages helped to consolidate political support for the ACA, they were generally consistent with independent efforts to reform the social security benefit structure.[8] As the ACA moved through successive drafting stages, however, important conflicts between these two frameworks rose to the surface. Political opposition was never passionate enough to defeat the new law, but it did manage to shift benefits closer to the traditional legal model.[9]

Establishing the ACA was a remarkable political feat by any standard. Perhaps most striking was the underlying philosophical case, laid out in a series of reports inspired by the distinguished jurist, Sir Owen Woodhouse.[10] The Woodhouse Report associated fundamental change in tort law with a renewal of public commitment to social welfare. Both projects were united by a common set of objectives:

1. More substantial benefits than those provided under either social security or workers' compensation, based on the common law standard of "compensation for loss."
2. Along with compensation, parallel commitments to rehabilitation and more vigorous accident prevention.
3. Acceptance of a philosophical principle which held the "community" responsible for the overall incidence of personal inju-

ries, with clear implications for expanding the national commitment to social welfare. [11]

The last point shares a distinct kinship with the principle of public responsibility used throughout this book. The Woodhouse notion of *community responsibility* deliberately equivocated between common-law and social-welfare traditions. It was in part a creative extension of the liability concept, intimating that society as a whole bore residual accountability for accidents. The Woodhouse Commission typically applied this argument to workplace and highway accidents, whose aggregate occurrence they associated with industrial and consumption patterns of modern societies, especially the demand for high technology. The report did not overlook more personalized accountability, but recommended criminal penalties and regulation as the appropriate responses. [12] Later in this chapter we will return to the community responsibility principle to examine its connections with social-welfare themes.

Despite the breathtaking sweep of this legislation, it was nearly eclipsed by a more ambitious proposal for Australia in 1974. That plan started with an approach to personal injury similar to New Zealand's, but would have allowed the same benefits for illness and congenital disability. Sir Owen Woodhouse was again the major architect of the plan, which saw its prospects fade with the Labour government of Gough Whitlam. [13] By the time the bill died in 1975, formidable practical and constitutional objections had been raised. [14] Although the particular scheme was abandoned, individual Australian states have continued to investigate more limited no-fault accident programs, and by the late 1980s the national government was reexamining its social-welfare structure in terms reminiscent of the mid 1970s. [15]

Its political fortunes aside, the proposed Australian scheme was the most fully articulated national policy combining illness and injury in a single compensation program. It would have removed personal injury actions from the judicial process, while reorganizing and raising social security benefits for the disabled. The new benefit structure reflected common-law categories of loss: medical services, lost income, and additional payments for permanent incapacity—but not the pain-and-suffering provisions of the New Zealand act. [16]

The declared purpose of this bold proposal was to put accidents on the same footing as other personal misfortunes, providing for comparable entitlements. Since personal injuries were to be removed from the judicial process, awards would no longer be based on fault, but tort concepts were nonetheless influential in raising benefits to a new standard, opaquely named *real compensation*. The final product was to become part of the state-administered social security system, where it would have taken the place of means-tested, flat-rate benefits.

The New Zealand principle of community responsibility was somewhat overshadowed in this ambitious program. To be sure, the phrase was retained, but the concept lost its powerful reference to legal liability and moved closer to the language of enlightened altruism.[17] Paradoxically, this shift betrayed an underlying assumption that illness and injury were differently related to collective action in modern society. Only personal injuries, apparently, were considered the inevitable, statistical results of consumer tastes and industrial practices in high-technology societies.[18] If accident victims were now to be treated identically with other disabled persons, the reasons had less to do with social causation than with the ethical appeal of horizontal equity—the equal treatment of similar groups.

The New Zealand ACA acknowledged the presence of occupational diseases and included them under the statutory definition of personal injury, accepting the prevailing classification of diseases found in many workers' compensation programs.[19] The Australian proposal seemed even less worried about the etiological boundaries of disease, since it was prepared to offer comparable benefits for victims on either side of the frontier.[20] By an ingenious bootstrap method, it used the social causation premise from the New Zealand report to establish the justice of higher benefits for personal injury victims, and then shifted to the ethical principle of equal treatment. "Once the principle of community responsibility is applied to alleviate the plight of the injured, then the same community assistance cannot as a matter of social conscience be withheld from the sick."[21]

Both the New Zealand scheme and the Australian blueprint represent significant milestones on the road to reforming common-law systems of accident compensation. Both countries heard mounting internal criticism of judicial procedures, especially in their handling of automobile accident claims.[22] Experiments with no-fault compensation from Canadian provinces planted ideas for reform, as did the Ontario workers' compensation program. Still more encouragement for the Woodhouse Commission's comprehensive approach came from Terence Ison's influential study.[23] Ison catalogued the common ailments of tort law—delays, doctrinal complexity, strategic asymmetries, and violations of the universal entitlement principle. Noting the basic similarity in complaints concerning workplace and automobile injuries, Ison postulated that further areas of judicial expansion would follow the same pattern. Ison's book summarized more than a decade of arguments for no-fault alternatives to tort law, and its conclusions matched closely those of the Woodhouse Commission, whose members read the book while it was in manuscript form.[24]

Another source for the New Zealand strategy came from the indigenous welfare-state perspective, skillfully invoked and extended by the Woodhouse Commission. The tort system appears especially weak when measured against these normative criteria, rather than the internal norms of common law. Perhaps this explains why the Woodhouse plan differed fundamentally from contemporary reforms suggested by progressive critics in the United States.[25] The failure of judicial procedures to deliver roughly equivalent benefits to persons injured in comparable ways violates the welfare commitment to social equity.[26] In the end it does not really matter whether the gap in equal treatment occurs because of the fault doctrine, because the judicial system costs too much or takes too long, or because there is no apparent source of injury—the violation of horizontal equity remains the same. All the practical objections to tort law catalogued by legal critics come together in this central flaw: the judicial system cannot satisfy the ethical demands of universal entitlement for comparably situated people.

From this perspective, we cannot expect the tort system to mend itself, or even to play a significant part in granting compensation; administrative procedures in the social-welfare system were clearly better equipped to meet these expectations for consistency. The underlying cause of injury is usually irrelevant to other forms of social entitlement: for emergency medical services under the national health scheme, income support, or rehabilitation programs. In the days before economic efficiency adhered to the technical jargon of welfare economics, the Woodhouse Commission also noted that a state-administered scheme could provide compensation at considerably lower cost than the judicial process.[27]

The Frustration of Welfare Objectives: Britain's Pearson Commission

As these comprehensive schemes took form in the antipodes, the American tort debate had already come under the influence of economic welfare models. This was not yet the case in Britain, however, when in 1973 hopes for comprehensive change were raised by the appointment of a Royal Commission on Civil Liability and Compensation for Personal Injury, known as the Pearson Commission.[28] The Commission took a careful look at the New Zealand and Australian reform models, whose value premises were sympathetically viewed by proponents of Britain's social-welfare policies. A significant treatise was prepared by one of the designers of the Australian plan, which admirably summarized the failures of tort law as a compensation system and noted its inability to satisfy the demands of horizontal equity.[29]

Public sentiment in Britain had also been stirred by the badly disfigured children whose mothers had taken the notorious drug thalidomide. The grotesque encounters of these families with the judicial process brought an unprecedented public outcry against the personal injury system, and became one of the main reasons for creating the Pearson Commission. Other concerns on the nation's agenda included health and safety in the workplace, which had been subjects of an earlier government inquiry.[30] The Pearson Commission approached its task on a grand scale, collecting an enormous amount of evidence about the tort system and other compensation schemes. By the time the final report was issued in 1978, however, prospects had dimmed for comprehensive change in either the legal or social security system, let alone in both. A year later the Thatcher government came into power, and from that time forward the underlying values of Britain's social-welfare structure were themselves called into question.

The Pearson Report anticipated this change of heart in its tepid recommendations, despite its prodigious efforts to document weaknesses in the civil liability system. One commentator—an advocate of comprehensive reform—described the results as "timid and vulnerable to the suspicion that it indeed preferred a less comprehensive no-fault solution for reasons it would rather keep to itself."[31] In retrospect this seems an uncharitable judgment, considering not only the weighty interests opposed to dramatic institutional change, but also the subtle shifts in welfare-state commitments brought on by inflation and other economic concerns.

But the Report undeniably served up a massive collection of compromises, and it failed to project a coherent or commanding set of principles like those contained in the New Zealand Woodhouse Report. The most important recommendations adopted the familiar strategy of selective administrative alternatives to litigation. Thus a proposed no-fault program for automobile injuries simply followed the pattern of Australian states like Victoria and Tasmania, and were thus scarcely sufficient to ensure Britain's position as the "social-democratic model for the latter twentieth century."[32] In most other areas, proposals bogged down in tedious levels of incremental detail—"a plethora of mini-issues."[33] In the end the Commission presented some 188 separate recommendations, nearly all of which were quickly forgotten in the change of government. In retrospect their caution looks like an early indication of the malaise that overtook the British commitment to welfare principles.

The Pearson Commission's primary recommendations included: (1) a no-fault plan for automobile accidents, to be funded out of increased gasoline taxes; (2) improved benefits in the Industrial Injuries program, funded by increased contributions from employers to the existing national insurance program; and (3) a new social security benefit for all children severely disabled by accident, illness, or congenital disease. On paper these results might appear as only a minor retreat from the New Zealand plan. The two largest classes of accident claims—workplace and automobile injuries—were moved farther from the judicial process, and social-welfare benefits available to many accident victims were to be strengthened. On a philosophical level, the Commission endorsed the principle that tort compensation and social security should be linked together, with tort eventually becoming the "junior partner" in that association. "Social security should be recognized as the principal means of compensation," the Report insisted.

> Although we have been concerned with many issues, at the heart of our enquiry has been the relationship between tort and social security. They are derived from different philosophies. In the past they have been allowed to develop side by side as though they had little to do with each other, so that they even use different words to describe what are basically the same things. The Monckton Committee surveyed some aspects of their interrelationship thirty years ago. But, since then, social security provision for the injured and bereaved has greatly expanded and has become much more complicated, and the common law of tort has further evolved and been supplemented by a number of statutory provisions. It was high time for a further review.

In the event, we have not recommended that tort should be abolished. But the changes which we have proposed represent a considerable shift of emphasis from the tort to the social security system of compensation.[34]

These are verbal winks and nods suggesting that tort law should be allowed to fade away gracefully, instead of being precipitously uprooted.

At the same time, the Commission preserved a clear function for the doctrines and institutions of tort law, unlike the New Zealand and Australian models. An unspecified portion of the Commission subscribed to "a factor which goes deeply into the structure of society": the fault principle. As enshrined in tort law, that principle promotes "a sense of responsibility for the effect of one's actions on others," and it prevents "general irresponsibility."[35] On a more practical level, this fraction of the Commission emphasized that tort law provided a more satisfactory level of compensation than state-administered welfare benefits—using the "objective loss" concept rather than more variable standards of need.

The Pearson Commission's chief critics included some who were instrumental in the New Zealand experiment.[36] For them it was a particular disappointment to hear yet again the traditional defense of tort law, based on an individualist orientation to public morality; their various studies (starting with Ison's work) had documented the failure of actual tort systems to serve that very principle. It is not surprising, therefore, that Fleming suspects hidden reasons for maintaining separate judicial procedures for most cases. Indeed we would expect powerful interests like the Law Society to try to persuade the Commission to resolve its ambivalence in favor of a dual system.

More fundamentally, however, the Pearson Report marked a retreat from the ideal of horizontal equity—the notion that persons with comparable needs should be given comparable benefits. As we have seen, the New Zealand ACA seemed to create a disturbing anomaly with its preferential treatment of personal injury over disease and other disablements. This tension was only precariously resolved—more in practice than in principle—in the Australian proposal, and since that time horizontal equity has become the dominant value behind repeated calls for the abolition of the tort system.[37] The Pearson Commission was not insensitive to this principle; indeed it made an emphatic point of expanding its proposed scheme for disabled children to eliminate causation as a criterion of entitlement. But it invoked horizontal equity for just such special cases, on behalf of victims deemed eminently deserving. Besides, for such a limited program the additional benefits would not have raised costs by any significant amount.

With hindsight, the transition to more conservative policies under the Thatcher government helps clarify the Pearson Report's ambivalence. There is little doubt that welfare-state ideals central to the New Zealand and Australian plans had lost some of their earlier appeal. It may also be true that the Commission lacked the sagacity of Sir Owen Woodhouse or the political courage to propose major structural changes; but the Commission was also concerned about costs, about state interference with personal autonomy, about individual self-reliance, and about diversity in the institutional life of the modern state. In the past decade, all these themes have moved to the center of debate about the future of the welfare state in all its forms.[38]

Welfare Principles and Tort Reform: Community Responsibility

Before political trends took a turn in the late 1970s, the movement for comprehensive tort reform produced a highly concrete set of proposals, based on a common body of principles. The failures of the tort system were sharply magnified under scrutiny by social-welfare criteria. Unlike American instrumentalism, which concealed its values behind judicial formalisms, tort-law criticism in the Commonwealth nations managed to find a critical stance outside the judicial framework. In the debate that moved from New Zealand through Australia to Great Britain, the prime concerns were equity and adequacy in the social response to personal disability. The tort system, always steeped in one crisis or another, was the occasion for this controversy, but never the controlling theme.

The principles underlying this movement were all closely tied to the values of British social democracy. They also presented a challenge, within the welfare-state framework, to social policies identified with what Richard Titmuss labeled "residual welfare" and "industrial, achievement-performance" models. The former describes the Reagan and Thatcher safety-net approach to welfare, under which the only distinctive public role is to address temporary failures in the dominant social institutions of market and families. The second model accepts need-based welfare programs as permanent adjuncts to industrialized economies, and thus as components of politically managed capitalism. Under both approaches to social welfare, state-administered benefits are limited to selected groups near the bottom of the economic scale. Their purpose is to sustain the lower strata in order to keep them functioning in a social system defined primarily by market processes.[39]

By contrast, Titmuss's "institutional-redistributive" model of welfare contains the values assumed by advocates of new compensation systems. This model rests on "theories about the multiplier diswelfare and disrupting effects of change, industrial, technological, social, and economic, and in part on a conception of social justice which sees man not only as an individual but as a member of groups and associations." The purposes of welfare, according to this view, are "to promote integrative values, to prevent future diswelfares, to penetrate economic policies with social welfare objectives, and in all these ways to bring about a redistribution in command over resources over time." In promoting these ends, Titmuss said, the redistributive welfare model

> challenges different societies at different stages of development . . . to determine a particular infrastructure of universalist services. . . . The fundamental problem which this model sets for government is to find the "right" balance between the integrative role of universalist services and the social equality role of selective (or priority) developments. They are inter-dependent roles, subject to continuing adaptation and change, but often in conflict because of limited resources.[40]

The desire to expand universal entitlements in the economic climate of the late 1960s explains the attraction of horizontal equity. In addition, a concern for the disabled person's integration in society explains the push for income-related benefits and rehabilitation services, in contrast to the minimal supports provided under other welfare models. Of course, limited social resources may require the state to concentrate benefits on people whose needs are greatest (the long-term disabled, and those completely incapacitated), but everyone in modern society is at some risk of joining these categories. Thus the moment had finally arrived, according to the Woodhouse Commission, to unify the system of accident compensation—tort, workers' compensation, and social security—and to eliminate differential treatment based on the cause of injury. In addition, the level of benefits provided as compensation must be enough to maintain injured persons and their families as fully functioning members of their society.

> Clearly, if compensation is to meet real losses it must provide adequate recompense, unrestricted by earlier philosophies which put forward tests related merely to need. Such an approach may have been appropriate when poverty was a widespread evil demanding considerable mobilisation of the country's financial resources. But average modern households, geared to the regular injection of incomes undreamed of at the turn of the century, have corresponding commitments which do not disappear conveniently if one of the hazards of modern life suddenly produces physical misfortune. Increasing affluence has brought with it additional social hazards for every citizen; but fortunately, at the same time, it has left society better able to afford their real cost.[41]

In the course of applying these emerging welfare principles to the problems of personal injury, the Woodhouse Commission made a unique contribution to both welfare theory and tort reform with its principle of community responsibility.

> This . . . principle is fundamental. It rests on a double argument. Just as a modern society benefits from the productive work of its citizens, so should society accept responsibility for those willing to work but prevented from doing so by physical incapacity. And, since we all persist in following community activities, which year by year exact a predictable and inevitable price in bodily injury, so should we all share in sustaining those who become the random but statistically necessary victims. The inherent cost of these community purposes should be borne on a basis of equity by the community.[42]

Community responsibility speaks to the fundamental relation between the individual and modern society in finding a new balance among public costs, private gain, and individual loss. While not denying a level of individual accountability for accidents, the Woodhouse Report fastens on the environmental context, shaped by the growth of modern technology, in which most accidents occur. The community as a whole benefits from these productive advances, but certain individuals pay a disproportionate price as the "statistically necessary" victims.

This idea became the central value behind the New Zealand ACA, although some proponents of universal compensation have reacted to it with skepticism. Atiyah, for example, questioned the apparent tautological sense of responsibility that unites all accidents in one collective context: the worker injured by dangerous machinery along with the child who slips in the bathtub—not to mention the proverbial lightning bolt. This common perspective on injuries becomes even more artificial, according to Atiyah, when contrasted with organic illness, which he associated with natural causes and thus assumed to be outside the scope of community responsibility altogether.[43] For purposes of merging tort into the social security system, the Woodhouse principle of collective causation seemed to conflict with the principle of horizontal equity, which demanded that personal injury and disease be treated in comparable ways.

The community-responsibility principle now requires another look, however, in light of epidemiological methods of connecting environmental forces with many kinds of disease. Indeed, it is much easier to apply the central argument in the Woodhouse Report to the new problems of environmental disease, where scientific evidence and ordinary custom prevent us from reducing events to a purely individualized level of causation. For the kinds of accidents dealt with in the Woodhouse Report—automobile, workplace, and household accidents—the community's responsibility seems to deny more individualized explanations that have become almost intuitive under common law. We routinely attribute road accidents to the carelessness of one or both drivers in a collision, just as earlier generations assigned workplace injuries to the carelessness of injured workers, co-workers, or supervisors.

The Woodhouse Commission resisted these tendencies, putting such an overriding emphasis on the social context of accidents that it appeared to ignore possible overlapping levels of causality and responsibility. Twenty years later, based on the initial U.S. encounter with environmental accidents, we are in a better position to understand what the Commission was really trying to say. The community's responsibility for personal injury is not forced to supplant other levels of accountability; it defines a distinct public role with implications for compensation procedures as well as environmental regulation. With his lawyer's appreciation of strategically placed analogies, Sir Owen Woodhouse found a critical link between the common-law concept of compensation for loss and the evolving obligations of the modern welfare state.

In the economic climate at the close of the twentieth century, the Woodhouse concept of community responsibility may prove vital to further changes in the personal injury system, as well as the entire disability portion of social security. (It could also strengthen national policies for health and safety regulation, as we shall see in a moment.) More than timidity, the modest yield from the Pearson Commission reflected the widespread failure of modern welfare systems to preserve a fundamental sense of common purpose in public intervention. As long as economic resources were increasing during the late 1960s, the transition from "residual welfare" models to more universal services seemed like the only natural course for public policy. As a principle, horizontal equity is intrinsically optimistic; it assumes the electorate wants to move the relatively disadvantaged person up to the level of the most highly compensated. But horizontal equity could just as easily be used to scale benefits down to the lowest common denominator; it is simply one part of a larger value scheme, the rest of which must provide cogent reasons for public intervention in the first place.

During the 1960s horizontal equity was doubtless an appropriate theme in reform movements for both personal injury and the larger field of disability. It was easy to demonstrate the comparable social claims of injured persons, whether or not a viable tort plaintiff could be found, or indeed whether the injury met the prevailing legal definition of accident. The logic of horizontal equity encouraged society to "top up" the benefits of all disadvantaged people, using as a benchmark the notion of most-favored victim—who, following the Woodhouse Report, was properly identified as the fully compensated plaintiff under tort law. But the direction of that logic, as it turned out, was contrary to the movement of public resources, or at least to the willingness of voters to put resources into public welfare. The Pearson Commission obviously sensed this retrograde motion in 1978, and its caution now looks like prescient anticipation of public moods in the following decade.

Community responsibility, as it was elaborated by the Woodhouse Report, captures the elusive *public* aspect of personal security, given the hazardous conditions of modern technological society. Our ability to identify this common interest is greatly improved by recent epidemiological evidence showing how the web of environmental causation spreads beyond the workplace and the highway. It necessarily includes more subtle injuries and complex illnesses that we still only partly understand.

As Claus Offe has written, the disillusionment with welfare principles in social-democratic systems can be traced to a decline in the sense of social solidarity. To restore that sense, "the critical sociological variable is some notion of commonality of interest and fate, of 'sameness,' or a sufficiently binding conception of a durable collective identity, which is the ultimate resource that keeps cooperation intact beyond its initial phase."[44] Personal vulnerability in a world of environmental accidents starts from the most narcissistic impulse for physical integrity. It incorporates the self-regarding desire for continued participation in the public economic and cultural order. As recent toxic encounters have shown, we are all part of a larger social system in which anyone—regardless of wealth, social status, or individual talent—may encounter harmful agents like asbestos and other hazardous substances, true dangers of which are appreciated too late to prevent serious harm to a "statistically inevitable"[45] number of people.

What unites individuals, from an environmental perspective, is their common vulnerability to contemporary hazards, a condition that reaches back to the past as well as into the future. The implications of community responsibility are perhaps even greater for future regulation than for retrospective compensation. For both time dimensions, the central requirement is an adequate structure for responding to disparate needs, coordinating where possible the actions of specific groups and individuals.[46] Although the Woodhouse Report was read primarily as a statement on compensation, it has equally powerful implications for a social policy on prevention: "Injury arising from accident demands an attack on three fronts. The most important is obviously prevention. Next in importance is the obligation to rehabilitate the injured. Thirdly, there is the duty to compensate them for their losses."[47]

If we extend the concept of community responsibility beyond the limited field of workplace and highway accidents, the potential scope for prevention becomes much greater than anything the Woodhouse Commission imagined. In any case, the administrative agency created by ACA was designed to transform collective resources into individualized benefits; it would have required entirely different powers to

perform a similar transformation of collective accountability. Beyond
the exhortative value of public education programs, the Accident
Compensation Corporation itself has been able to contribute very little to the cause of "accident" prevention.[48]

In its plan for financing the scheme, the Woodhouse Commission
became entangled in some revealing controversies, which likewise
haunt more limited administrative alternatives to tort law. The civil
liability analogy, lurking in the community-responsibility principle,
gave rise to an awkward question: whether the financial burdens of the
program would fall on "innocent" people—people who had done nothing wrong, or who did not cause any tangible harm. The *community*
might be responsible in theory, but in practice the money for the
scheme was to come directly from employers and from drivers of
automobiles.

This method of financing the ACA was mainly a political artifact,
since it tapped the two major revenue sources already in existence
under private insurance programs for workers' compensation and personal automobile coverage. It was probably vital to the political success of the ACA that it could offer more comprehensive benefits without altering the kinds or amounts of premiums.[49] No-fault plans are
generally sold with this guarantee, and it is important to note that an
administrative scheme for "all accidents" was unable to prevent revenue payers from reindividualizing the causal relation. Perhaps the
only way to obviate such quarrels is by general revenue funding.

A second objection, although politically less explosive, concerned
the conflict between the ACA's method of funding and the economists'
approach to accident prevention through market-based deterrence.[50]
It was only a matter of time until this latter gospel reached the Southern Hemisphere, and defenders of the faith have been quick to dismiss
the New Zealand scheme for failing to implement general deterrence
principles. As we saw in Chapter 4, this theory finds unexpected virtues in tort law, despite its failures as a fair or adequate system for
meeting the needs of accident victims. Rather its purpose is to send
helpful signals to the market about future accident costs, based on
individualized judgments about past events.

Nothing could be more opposed to the logic and spirit of community responsibility. Even though the New Zealand law chose not to
engage in vigorous enforcement measures, its underlying principle
requires the political system to exercise final judgment over the selec-

tion of strategies for accident prevention—not the market system. It also protects the community voice in determining the balance between public investment in prevention versus compensation—a voice that the theory of general deterrence tries its utmost to silence. Nothing prevents public authority from using market pricing as a regulatory tool, to whatever extent highly individualized calculations may promote better decisions at the margins of prevention. As things turn out in New Zealand, however, the Accident Compensation Corporation has been largely unable to adjust premiums for employers or drivers according to any reliable predictions of future accident-causing behavior. It has therefore used highly aggregated categories for assessments—much like the system of private insurance before it.[51]

In criticizing the New Zealand scheme, the economic theory of general deterrence reveals its hidden conceptual and normative assumptions, as well as its idealized vision of how tort law actually operates. The rigorous internalization of costs converts social causation back into individualist terms. If accident-producing activities are not fully attributed to discrete events and specific human decisions, whether for lack of data or for political or administrative lack of resolve, a prevention policy cannot be "efficient," under the general deterrence definition. From there it is a small step to questioning the basic justice of the ACA: if it is not efficient in the narrow welfare-economic sense, then it must be redistributing resources, shifting the burden of accidents to those who have not caused them (and cannot even prevent them). The Woodhouse Commission's cavalier attitude toward cost internalization in designing its funding structure was what we might expect from cumbersome, "irrational" bureaucracies. Behind this critique stands the tacit presumption that the free market and tort system were already doing an exemplary job of internalizing accident costs—or could be made to do so with minor adjustments in liability rules.

The Woodhouse Commission was not ignorant of these perspectives, but it was skeptical of their relevance to an operational scheme. Community responsibility does not refer to particular causal influences associated with specific accidents; it is a collective responsibility shared by everyone who participates in modern society and cannot be precisely apportioned. On this view, no adequate criteria exist even in theory, but certainly not in practice, for internalizing the costs of accidents. Given the Commission's views on the vast number of accidents that escape the tort system, there is every reason to doubt that the market is institutionally equipped to register accident costs in any systematic way.

Ironically, this suggests that the community-responsibility principle corrects a serious operational flaw in the macroeconomic use of general deterrence, which begs the definition of an *optimal* rate of accidents for society as a whole. General deterrence does not seek to eliminate all accidents, but only those that are more expensive than their prevention, according to market criteria. But how can prevailing market signals be trusted to price these alternatives properly, under a legal system that recognizes only those accidents involving *specific* agents, victims, and events? The community-responsibility perspective suggests that, up to now, the price of technological progress has not been paid by the majority of those who benefit from it. Instead those costs are falling primarily on the "statistically inevitable" victims of social progress, and thus are excluded from the market calculus that decides between compensation and prevention.

Other West-European Models:
Two-Tiered Social Security

Nothing as revolutionary as the New Zealand and Australian plans has come out of European countries, where negligence law has long been subordinated to social security policy. Yet issues of compensation and accountability still arise, and the way they are now being handled provides some insight into future problems for welfare states in responding to environmental accidents. Just as the American tort system has been forced to consider selective alternatives, social security has been pressured to make selective additions for specific groups of accident victims. The likely result is a proliferation of secondary entitlement programs, funded more or less like independent insurance schemes, on top of public benefits available to victims of short- or long-term disability. These new programs are supposed to fill the gaps in the social-welfare network, displacing private liability actions into a tertiary role.

At least three major surveys of personal injury policies in Western Europe have been presented over the past twenty years, each emphasizing different elements in the convergence of social security and tort systems, covering three distinct phases of development. The survey completed by André Tunc in 1970 was devoted to special compensation plans for automobile accidents, seen generally as no-fault alternatives to civil liability. Tunc's influential article virtually *defined* the challenge of contemporary tort reform around this single problem.[52] Three years earlier the Woodhouse Commission in New Zealand had questioned the entire concept of civil liability for personal injury, as well as the prevailing structure of social security. The Commission's theory of community responsibility was meant to infect the social-welfare system with a new sense of collective obligation, building analogically on evolving liability principles. By comparison, Tunc's approach kept the two structures apart: social welfare was primarily meliorative, while compensation belonged to private law. The only complication was the automobile.

> If cancer, or even, in some respects, the common cold, is a social problem, it is of a nature which cannot be imputed to anyone or anything. Only social legislation or personal insurance, therefore, can alleviate its evil. . . . On the other hand . . . traffic accidents are caused by a special category of things: motor vehicles. . . . It is the existence of motor-cars which first makes such accidents possible. No cars, no accidents![53]

The pioneer no-fault scheme for automobile accidents belonged to the Canadian province of Saskatchewan, but by 1970 other proposals were circulating in North America and Europe.[54]

Eight years later, when the Pearson Commission surveyed Britain's European neighbors, the issues had broadened beyond the special problem of highway accidents. Social security and tort were viewed in many countries as alternative approaches to similar ends.[55] Some no-fault automobile accident schemes had been enacted in North America, Australia, and Sweden, and the idea of extending no-fault to other accidents had come under wider discussion—not only in New Zealand.[56] More significant, however, was the growing awareness that compensation systems interact with each other, and that social security was emerging as the dominant framework for coordination. Closer integration of compensation benefits and horizontal equity were thus major themes during the 1970s, occasionally leading to important policy changes. In 1976, for example, the Netherlands combined its workers' compensation program with basic disability coverage under social security.[57] Although the Pearson Commission did not visit Israel, it noted an early government study that would have substituted a unified social insurance scheme for both workers' compensation and civil liability for automobile injuries.[58]

In 1986, after another eight years, representatives from primarily West European countries met in Uppsala, Sweden for an international conference on current compensation issues.[59] Papers from that conference compared the status of major legislation, but more specifically they responded to recent Swedish alternatives to civil liability for workplace accidents, pharmaceutical injuries, and medical malpractice. In these areas, Sweden has established "voluntary" insurance programs to supplement social security benefits.[60] A similar program for automobile accidents became mandatory in 1976.[61]

These insurance schemes are meant to fill gaps between the level of benefits provided under social security and the theoretical standard of "full compensation for loss" defined by civil liability, including the intangible loss known as pain and suffering. As we have seen, the New Zealand and Australian Woodhouse Commissions undertook a similar task, but drew on philosophical assumptions that would have extended comparable benefits to all accident victims, and eventually to all disease victims as well. The basic structure of social security disability programs was to be altered, moving welfare benefits uniformly upward, while inevitably lowering the final target somewhat from the highest reaches of tort-law damages. By abolishing the institutional base of tort law, New Zealand also curtailed the power of common law to define a compensation standard beyond the social security system.

The Swedish approach, on the other hand, begins with a more generous baseline level of social security benefits, adds further public support for favored victims (especially those injured in the workplace), and lastly fosters a quasiprivate insurance plan for raising benefits to ideal tort levels—but only for specific kinds of accidents. (Civil liability remains in existence for accidents left outside the insurance scheme, not really as a practical alternative, but more as a reference point for invidious comparisons with welfare benefits.) The result is a multitiered series of programs, providing benefits for certain injuries that approach the private law ideal through alternative structures.

The expression "the Swedish alternative" refers mainly to the system on the top level, and quite particularly to the types of voluntary insurance that are based on group agreements. . . . The Swedish type of no-fault insurance differs entirely from the American variety by covering not basic losses but those parts of the loss that are compensated neither by social insurance nor by . . . supplementary means. . . . This no-fault insurance applies to injuries arising in what would otherwise be major fields of tort liability: motor traffic accidents, industrial injuries, medical malpractice and an important section of products liability [drug injuries]. . . . For better or for worse, the system singles out some types of injury and leaves others to be dealt with by traditional tort law.[62]

It is not entirely clear what prompted Sweden to offer these additional forms of personal injury compensation. There is probably no social-welfare system in existence that owes more to ideals of horizontal equity, even though actual programs display a wide diversity.[63] Introducing new distinctions into the existing categories of entitlement, based on the cause of personal injury, must therefore reflect equally strong pressures from some other value source. Unlike the United States, the Swedish civil liability system had not been inundated with malpractice claims from which it sought legislative relief. In fact, prior to the patient insurance scheme introduced in 1975, only about ten injured patients each year were able to gain recovery through private litigation, and "it was generally thought that so-called treatment injuries should be indemnified to a much greater extent than was possible under applicable tort law." The insurance program now grants compensation in some 4,000 cases each year, or around 65 percent of all reported injuries. "About 60 percent of the compensation paid out relates to pain and suffering or other kinds of non-economic losses."[64]

Civil liability was unable to provide relief for most malpractice injuries, but social security was unable to compensate to the fullest extent. It would seem that Sweden was responding, in a more limited way, to the same goals already cited by the New Zealand Woodhouse Commission: maintaining personal-injury victims near the same socioeconomic level as before their accidents, and doing so through a program that collectivizes risk.[65] Although these plans are labeled "voluntary," participation is not left up to the individual citizen to purchase insurance on the open market (as neoconservatives have proposed[66]), nor is it subject to individual bargaining in exchange for the right to sue (as Jeffrey O'Connell has advocated for the United States[67]). The terms of coverage are negotiated through collective bargaining in industry, by public councils with oversight responsibilities for medical services, and by the producers of pharmaceuticals (with public oversight).[68] The "Swedish alternative" should not be mistaken for a return to judicial institutions or market solutions, although it does reflect a recent trend away from centralized bureaucracy, and toward privatization of public services in the modern welfare state.[69]

The Swedish approach is not directly applicable to the American scene, but is rather an alternative to the strategy used in West Germany and other countries to expand private litigation by selective adoption of strict liability rules. West Germany currently recognizes

> about ten provisions, almost all of them included in special statutes, that grant compensation for personal injury suffered as a result of specific hazardous activities. These statutes cover practically all land and air traffic, pipelines and other means of conveying energy, all nuclear activities, all activities resulting in water pollution and, most recently, production and distribution of pharmaceutical products.[70]

These statutes govern procedural matters including evidentiary presumptions, defenses to liability, and limits on damages. "Usually, though, these limits are exceeded by the courts, in appropriate cases by simultaneously basing the judgement on fault."[71] The German approach is slowly extending the dominant European strategy for automobile accidents to additional categories of personal injury. The ad hoc nature of the extensions are evident to all commentators—Swedish, German, and the rest—and the threat to welfare principles of equity is at least mildly disturbing to most.

The general spirit of the Uppsala presentations reflects none of the *Sturm und Drang* of the American debate over tort reform; yet it was in some ways an equivalent discussion. Against the backdrop of two completely different attitudes toward social obligation and public welfare, a group of anomalous compensation claims has arisen to test both ideologies. First there was just the automobile (although before that there was the hazardous workplace, and still earlier the railroad). By the 1970s, rising economic expectations of middle-class citizens placed increasing demands on public authorities for protection against the kind of precipitous loss of socioeconomic status that commonly follows from accidental injury. Although public benefits under social-welfare programs had been increasing, so were claims; and the pressure to move benefits upward eventually became impossible to satisfy.

Maintaining personal security requires more than a residual welfare or safety net approach, but now only relatively favored groups can successfully gain that additional support. The conditions in Israel are perhaps the most extreme example of fiscal pressures facing most industrialized countries:

> The trend in inflation-plagued Israel is, unfortunately, to reduce social welfare services, even in most vital areas, such as health and education. There is a concomitant retreat from plans to extend social insurance coverage to new categories of people. In addition, there is a marked tendency to reduce government involvement in activities which can be managed by private agencies. The purpose is to restrict the public service sector.[72]

Just as in the United States, the gradual discovery of environmental accidents promises to increase the tension in European responses to personal injury. Although U.S. courts seem to have a special knack for dramatizing the collective effects of certain toxic epidemics, the pressure on European governments to raise social entitlements in selective cases has been strong despite prevailing calm in the civil justice system.[73] There is still a tendency to see these situations as exceptions in a social order where entitlements can be neatly separated from compensation. But the list cannot keep growing forever. As more categories join the roster of injuries receiving special treatment, the causal boundary lines become increasingly suspect. As long as possible, European countries may seek to avoid the full implications of an environmental perspective on personal injury. More ad hoc programs can perhaps postpone that recognition, but they will also complicate the technical problems of reshaping the overall system.

Even the New Zealand model will have to rethink its jurisdictional boundary between personal injuries and the more common misfortunes of disease and disability. Having discarded its tort system at the right historical moment, however, New Zealand finds its task vastly simplified. It still may not be easy to unite the personal injury and social security branches of the New Zealand welfare system, but at least the future of both programs rests with the same institutional authority. After pondering the complex options that await the German system, Eike von Hippel was keenly aware of the political obstacles faced by European (and American) accident-compensation policies.

Existing systems of accident compensation suffer from a whole series of deficiencies. To be sure . . . these problems might be resolved or at least reduced, even without the introduction of comprehensive social insurance, by a host of strategic measures.
Nevertheless I see in comprehensive social insurance the model of
the future, since it allows an optimal, combined solution to all the
relevant problems. Thus other states need to establish expert commissions, following the example of New Zealand and Australia, to
probe the question of comprehensive reform.[74]

Public Responsibility in the Welfare State

In projecting future directions for accident policy, we must begin with
the evident decline in political support for the collective values that
inspired the brief attraction of "institutional-redistributive" approaches. The erosion of that support was evident in the timid recommendations of the Pearson Commission (for all their modesty, too liberal for the Thatcher era), and the willingness of other European
countries to create horizontal inequalities through selective benefits
for accident victims. These trends are also inseparable from resurgent
individualist perspectives in academic theory, notably in welfare economics and moral philosophy.

Claus Offe's sociological approach to political change suggests that
these are not mere passing fashions.

> Encompassing alliances of a pro-welfare-state orientation thrive in
> the "good times" of economic growth and full employment (i.e.,
> positive-sum games) and tend to decompose under zero-sum con-
> ditions. The potential for "public-regarding" and solidaristic politi-
> cal commitments appears to be exhausted in many countries. . . .
> In that sense, the economic crisis of the welfare state generates
> individualistic political attitudes and orientations and thus trans-
> lates, without much liberal-conservative mass mobilization and po-
> litical organization needed, into a political crisis of the welfare
> state.[75]

According to Offe, declining economic resources are the occasion but
not the major cause of changing political attitudes. What matters even

more is the change in philosophical orientation of individuals and groups, a movement away from collective values and toward "an interpretive pattern that is deeply distrustful of social policies as 'public goods,' and that tends to unravel such policies in terms of gains and losses, exploitation, free-riding, redistribution, and so on—that is, in individualist 'economic man' categories." This sudden change in orientation rests, finally, on social structures that fail to reinforce our social sense of common fate, or sameness.

In all such cases, the decisive change is not on the level of objective events and facts, but on the level of interpretive frameworks and the strategic adoption of beliefs and expectations. The calculative attitude toward individual and short-term costs and benefits is therefore nothing that is inherent in human nature or an eternal standard of rational action; to the contrary, it is the product of disintegration and decomposition of cultural and structural conditions that constrain and inhibit such utilitarian orientations.[76]

On this interpretation, we cannot expect any sudden return to the period when democratic majorities responded favorably to the call for broader social security entitlements, universal eligibility, and horizontal equity. Individuals and groups may still find limited strategic or ideological value in these goals, but they are at least momentarily displaced in most industrial societies—even those with much more advanced welfare systems than the United States. If Offe's diagnosis is correct, even a sustained economic upturn would not automatically change the interpretive framework through which most people form their impressions of public responsibility.

The prospects for comprehensive legislation on personal injury, therefore, may never again appear as favorable as they did in the mid 1970s, when Australia and Great Britain briefly considered extending the New Zealand model to all forms of personal disability. This does not mean that the problems of personal injury will disappear from the public agenda. As we saw in Chapter 10, the problem of "accidents" has been largely supplanted by the more diffuse issues of disability policy and environmental regulation. In the United States, recurring crises of the tort system ensure continuing attention to cases on the boundary line of legal categories—what we have been calling *environmental accidents*. For the foreseeable future, however, public attention and academic commentary remain focused on a growing repertoire of ad hoc solutions, technocratic nostrums, and institutional compromises. Our incrementalist faith tells us reassuringly that the crises of tort law can be ameliorated by prudent choice among the limited alternatives discussed in Part III.

But this confident assessment assumes that we are using suitable categories to describe the problems that lie ahead. If instead we are imposing anachronistic legal, moral, and economic concepts on a complex environment, pragmatic solutions may only compound our problems. Personal injuries in modern societies illustrate the paradox of collective goods and individual welfare. Even the most clever policies are unable to reduce factional conflict, which can yield only to deep-seated perceptions of common interest.

> In order for a "good" to be a "public good," there must be a collectivity, the members of which refer to themselves as "we." It is only the self-conception of a collectivity . . . that puts an end to . . . reasoning in terms of individual and group payoffs and replaces it by a discourse of collective benefits. . . . Without notions of "sameness" and collective identity, public goods cannot be produced (or, if produced, commonly perceived as "public" and as "goods").[77]

Notes and Index

Notes

Prologue

1. Emile Durkheim, *Montesquieu and Rousseau* (Ann Arbor: University of Michigan Press, 1960), p. 59.
2. Irving J. Selikoff, *Disability Compensation for Asbestos-Associated Disease in the United States* (New York: Mt. Sinai School of Medicine of the City University of New York, 1982), p. 4.
3. Nigel Hawkes et al., *Chernobyl: The End of the Nuclear Dream* (New York: Random House, 1987), p. 209. Some more recent estimates have been scaled down; see "Chernobyl and the Europeans: Radiation and Doubts Linger," *New York Times*, June 12, 1988, p. 1.
4. See Charles Perrow, *Normal Accidents: Living with High-Risk Technologies* (New York: Basic Books, 1984). Perrow's theory is discussed in Chapter 2.
5. The terms *injury* and *personal injury* raise other definitional issues that will not be resolved here. This study deals with injuries to people rather than property interests, although the dividing line is sometimes difficult to draw. A fully operational accident policy would need to define this division, as well as the further boundary with contract law. The personal injuries considered here are not restricted to physical as opposed to intangible harms.
6. In contrast to this approach, David Rosenberg has deliberately preserved all contextual associations in the following definition: "An 'accident' is an event in which personal injury occurs as a result of tortious conduct.

353

'Tortious conduct' is defined by currently prevailing substantive standards of liability" ("The Causal Connection in Mass Exposure Cases: A
'Public Law' Vision of the Tort System," *Harvard Law Review* 97 [1984]:
851). Rosenberg's article is discussed in Chapter 6.

7. Quoted from *Encyclopédie des chemins de fer et des machines à vapeur*
(1844) in Wolfgang Schivelbusch, *The Railway Journey: The Industrialization of Time and Space in the Nineteenth Century* (Berkeley and Los
Angeles: University of California Press, 1986), pp. 131–32.

8. For centuries prior to industrialization—in the Age of Exploration—European exports of flora, fauna, and micro-organisms were responsible for
periodic environmental shocks in many parts of the world. See Alfred W.
Crosby, *Ecological Imperialism: The Biological Expansion of Europe,
900–1900* (Cambridge: Cambridge University Press, 1986).

9. The word *paradigm* is *not* meant to invoke any of the many senses used
by Thomas Kuhn in his historical speculations on scientific theory. It is
borrowed instead from the less ambitious sphere of recent linguistic philosophy, in which paradigm cases—simple, concrete applications—are
used to define the essential differences among multiple theoretical positions. For an amusing deflation of any claims to profundity surrounding
"the argument from paradigm cases," see Ernest Gellner, *Words and
Things* (London: Penguin Books, 1968), pp. 33–40.

10. See Peter W. J. Bartrip and S. B. Burman, *The Wounded Soldiers of
Industry: Industrial Compensation Policy, 1833–1897* (Oxford: Clarendon Press, 1983) and Deborah A. Stone, *The Disabled State* (Philadelphia: Temple University Press, 1984), chap. 2.

11. For general background see Herman M. Somers and Anne R. Somers,
Workmen's Compensation (New York: John Wiley & Sons, 1954), chap. 2.

12. The debate is summarized in Lawrence M. Friedman and Jack Ladinsky,
"Social Change and the Law of Industrial Accidents," *Columbia Law Review* 67 (1967): 50–82.

13. The term *progressive* has no standard use in this context, but G. Edward
White, in chap. 3 of *Tort Law in America: An Intellectual History* (New
York: Oxford University Press, 1985), discusses a representative group of
writers including Leon Green, Charles Gregory, Francis Bohlen, Fowler
Harper, and William Prosser. One could also mention other legal realists
like William O. Douglas. For a systematic presentation of accident law
closest to the point of view here called *progressive*, see Fowler V.
Harper, Fleming James, Jr., and Oscar S. Gray, *The Law of Torts*, 2nd
ed. (Boston: Little, Brown, 1986). The first edition of 1956 was an even
purer example.

14. For a historical treatment see Joseph A. Page and Mary-Win O'Brien,
Bitter Wages (New York: Grossman, 1973).

15. See, for example, Francis H. Bohlen, "The Basis of Affirmative Obligations in the Law of Torts," *American Law Register* 53 (1905): 209–39, 273–310, 337–77.
16. White traces this theme in the early works of Leon Green, specifically his confidence in the judicial process as an instrument of reform (*Tort Law in America*, pp. 75–83). See Green's later essay, "Tort Law Public Law in Disguise," *Texas Law Review* 38 (1959 and 1960): 1–13, 257–69.
17. For an argument linking the early approach to industrial accidents to more recent theories of "enterprise liability" in the context of product accidents, see George L. Priest, "The Invention of Enterprise Liability: A Critical History of the Intellectual Foundations of Modern Tort Law," *Journal of Legal Studies* 14 (1985): 461–527 (especially p. 520).
18. See the discussion in Harper, James, and Gray, *The Law of Torts*, vol. 3, pp. 127–30 (§13.1). For an analytical discussion see William O. Douglas's early essay, "Vicarious Liability and Administration of Risk," *Yale Law Journal* 38 (1929): 584–604, 720–45. See also Priest ("The Invention of Enterprise Liability," pp. 480–83), who deals with the tension between goals of internalizing costs and using insurance as a means of cost distribution.
19. Priest is not alone in crediting William Prosser's work as catalyzing this change through his influence on the American Law Institute's *Restatement (Second) of Torts*. See Harper, James, and Gray, *The Law of Torts*, vol. 5, pp. 537–48 (§28.27).
20. White, *Tort Law in America*, p. 178.
21. Influential texts from this period include Alfred F. Conard, *Automobile Accident Costs and Payments: Studies in the Economics of Injury Reparation* (Ann Arbor: University of Michigan Press, 1964); Walter J. Blum and Harry Kalven, Jr., *Public Law Perspectives on a Private Law Problem: Auto Compensation Plans* (Boston: Little, Brown, 1965); Robert E. Keeton and Jeffrey O'Connell, *Basic Protection for the Traffic Victim* (Boston: Little, Brown, 1965); and Guido Calabresi, *The Costs of Accidents: A Legal and Economic Analysis* (New Haven, Conn.: Yale University Press, 1970). Calabresi's book provided the analytical framework for subsequent applications of economic theory to tort law problems. For early consideration of automobile accidents as a distinctive class, see former President Nixon's prescient essay, "Changing Rules of Liability in Automobile Accident Litigation," *Law and Contemporary Problems* 3 (1936): 476–90; and the symposium, "Compensation for Automobile Accidents," *Columbia Law Review* 32 (1932): 785–824.
22. An early treatment of automobile accidents shows closer ties to progressive values, emphasizing the effects on low-income drivers. See (in addition to the *Columbia Law Review* symposium just cited) Committee to

Study Compensation for Automobile Accidents, *Report to the Columbia University Council for Research in the Social Sciences* (Philadelphia: International Printing, 1932).

23. See the study published by Temple University's Insurance Department, *Total Research Approach to the Study of Automobile Accidents* (Philadelphia: Temple University, 1968). Other evidence is cited in Harper, James, and Gray, *The Law of Torts*, vol. 3, pp. 90–97 (§11.4). For an intriguing cultural analysis of "accident consciousness" in the context of driving and alcohol policy, see Joseph R. Gusfield, *The Culture of Public Problems: Drinking-Driving and the Symbolic Order* (Chicago: University of Chicago Press, 1981).

24. See Conard, *Automobile Accident Costs*, p. 127.

25. Priest argues that the response to automobile accidents in the work of Fleming James was a major repository of earlier progressive attitudes, and he elevates James to central importance in the emergence of enterprise liability in the 1960s ("The Invention of Enterprise Liability," pp. 470–83). In my view, James was a transitional figure who allowed the progressive concern with retribution to wither, while emphasizing the more neutral goal of cost internalization. Calabresi's economic theory inherited this emphasis, transposing it into the idiomatic logic of welfare economics. James's parallel concern with cost distribution through insurance occupies an important spot in Calabresi's overall scheme, although it stands outside his influential theory of market-based general deterrence. Calabresi's work is discussed in Chapter 4.

26. See references in note 21.

27. See Harper, James, and Gray, *The Law of Torts*, vol. 3, pp. 90–97 (§11.4) and references cited therein.

28. In addition to Calabresi, a number of other academic lawyers have contributed to developing the economic approach, with a range in political positions from liberal to conservative. See, for example, Richard A. Posner, *Economic Analysis of Law*, 3rd ed. (Boston: Little, Brown, 1986), especially chap. 6; and William M. Landes and Richard A. Posner, *The Economic Structure of Tort Law* (Cambridge, Mass.: Harvard University Press, 1987). For additional references see Chapter 4. Despite some analytical similarities, these writers differ substantially on policy recommendations, based on underlying value assumptions. A sampling of recent policy recommendations based on economic analysis can be found in Robert E. Litan and Clifford Winston, eds., *Liability: Perspectives and Policy* (Washington, D.C.: Brookings Institution, 1988).

29. See Guido Calabresi, "Concerning Cause and the Law of Torts," *University of Chicago Law Review* 43 (1975): 69–108.

30. By contrast, essentially all cases of mesothelioma (a rare cancer of the

lining of the lung) are associated with asbestos exposure. See Selikoff, *Disability Compensation*, p. 4.

31. Deborah R. Hensler, William L. F. Felstiner, Molly Selvin, and Patricia A. Ebener, *Asbestos in the Courts: The Challenge of Mass Toxic Torts* (Santa Monica, Cal.: Rand Corporation, 1985).

Chapter 1

1. G. Edward White, *Tort Law in America: An Intellectual History* (New York: Oxford University Press, 1985), p. 243.

2. Donald Harris et al., *Compensation and Support for Illness and Injury* (Oxford: Clarendon Press, 1984), chap. 12. Similar studies are being conducted in the United States by the Rand Corporation's Institute for Civil Justice.

3. This perspective on law and the judicial process is discussed both historically and systematically by Robert S. Summers, *Instrumentalism and American Legal Theory* (Ithaca, N.Y.: Cornell University Press, 1982). Summers is a somewhat ambivalent exponent of instrumentalism, having been influenced also by Oxford analytical legal theory, which in many respects opposes instrumentalism. See the review by Roger Brownsword, *Modern Law Review* 48 (1985): 116–20.

4. Oliver Wendell Holmes, Jr., *The Common Law* (Boston: Little, Brown, 1881), pp. 77–129. On the role of this essay in defining the American law of negligence, see White, *Tort Law in America*, pp. 12–19.

5. One prominent instrumentalist defender of negligence is Richard Posner, especially in his essay "A Theory of Negligence," *Journal of Legal Studies* 1 (1972): 29–96. The dissenting voices to instrumentalism will be considered more systematically in Chapter 5; their approach to questions of policy is based on a sharp distinction between purposes and rights. See, for example, Richard A. Epstein, "A Theory of Strict Liability," *Journal of Legal Studies* 2 (1973): 151–204. A more general argument for a rights-centered approach to legal issues can be found in Charles Fried, *Right and Wrong* (Cambridge, Mass.: Harvard University Press, 1978).

6. See, for example, Benjamin Cardozo, *The Nature of the Judicial Process* (New Haven, Conn.: Yale University Press, 1921).

7. For general background see Wilfred E. Rumble, *American Legal Realism* (Ithaca, N.Y.: Cornell University Press, 1968).

8. Richard A. Posner, *The Economics of Justice* (Cambridge, Mass.: Harvard University Press, 1981), pp. 60–87.

9. In addition to these formal expectations, it bears repeating that courts are

expected to execute their tasks effectively in a high percentage of potential cases.

10. A standard treatment combining pragmatic and traditional theories of legal reasoning is Edward A. Levi, *An Introduction to Legal Reasoning* (Chicago: University of Chicago Press, 1949). For the influence of legal realism see (in addition to Summers and White) Karl Llewellyn, *The Common Law Tradition* (Boston: Little, Brown, 1960), and William L. Twining, *Karl Llewellyn and the Realist Movement* (Norman: University of Oklahoma Press, 1985). An alternative approach to adjudication appears in Ronald Dworkin, *Taking Rights Seriously* (Cambridge, Mass.: Harvard University Press, 1977), anticipating more recent deviations from instrumentalism.

11. In addition to the works just cited, a more pessimistic treatment of this tension can be found in current views of the critical legal studies movement. For a general summary see Mark Kelman, *A Guide to Critical Legal Studies* (Cambridge, Mass.: Harvard University Press, 1987).

12. Both White (*Tort Law in America,* especially chap. 5) and Priest have attempted to document this influence (George L. Priest, "The Invention of Enterprise Liability: A Critical History of the Intellectual Foundations of Modern Tort Law," *Journal of Legal Studies* 14 [1985]: 461–527).

13. Throughout this chapter, general references on tort law doctrines will be confined to two leading treatises: Fowler V. Harper, Fleming James, Jr., and Oscar S. Gray, *The Law of Torts,* 2nd ed. (Boston: Little, Brown, 1986); and W. Page Keeton, *Prosser and Keeton on the Law of Torts,* 5th ed. (St. Paul, Minn.: West Publishing, 1984). For a brief summary of legal doctrines in their institutional context, see John G. Fleming, *The American Tort Process* (Oxford: Clarendon Press, 1988). An overview of recent empirical research on the tort system is available in Deborah R. Hensler, Mary E. Vaiana, James S. Kakalik, and Mark A. Peterson, *Trends in Tort Litigation: The Story Behind the Statistics* (Santa Monica, Cal.: Rand Corporation, 1987).

14. Prosser's two essays—"The Assault upon the Citadel (Strict Liability to the Consumer)," *Yale Law Journal* 69 (1960): 1099–1148, and "The Fall of the Citadel (Strict Liability to the Consumer)," *Minnesota Law Review* 50 (1966): 791–848—bring the story up to its modern period. An earlier segment is most charmingly told in Levi, *Legal Reasoning,* pp. 8–27. For a discussion of related developments in the contract doctrine of implied warranty, see Harper, James, and Gray, *The Law of Torts,* vol. 5, pp. 444–532 (§§28.15–28.25A).

15. Donoghue v. Stevenson [1932] A.C. 562 (H.L.).

16. P. S. Atiyah and Peter Cane, *Accidents, Compensation and the Law,* 4th ed. (London: Weidenfeld & Nicolson, 1987), pp. 62, 60.

17. For a standard treatment, see Charles O. Gregory, "Trespass to Negligence to Absolute Liability," *Virginia Law Review* 37 (1951): 359–97. Alternative studies, such as Posner's influential essay "A Theory of Negligence," are more tergiversations from progressive values than strict historical revisions.

18. Academic critics investigating the historical antecedents to Holmes's statement of negligence doctrine have argued that negligence was a fairly recent invention whose historical mission was to protect industrial development. An especially full treatment of this position is found in Harper, James, and Gray, *The Law of Torts*, vol. 3, pp. 107–14 (§§12.2–12.3). According to them, prior to the negligence system propounded by Holmes, defendants could be found liable for any activity that carried an "unreasonable probability of harm," whether or not they met expectations of reasonable prudence (p. 112).

This theory of preindustrial liability, built essentially on causation alone, is generally referred to as *strict liability*, or *liability without fault*. In the language of instrumentalism, "Such conduct is . . . 'tortious'—not in the sense that it is unethical, unlawful, or culpable, but because it is a type of conduct indulged under conditions that, as a matter of social engineering, may become the basis of liability in the event that it is the legal cause of harm to persons not disqualified to recover therefor" (vol. 3, p. 184 [§14.1]). This hypothesized early era of strict liability served as an implicit norm for the reconstruction of tort law under progressive values. Another influential scholar has argued that the development of negligence helped to subsidize new technologies at the expense of the "weakest and least active elements in the population. . . . Indeed, the law of negligence became a leading means by which the dynamic and growing forces in American society were able to challenge and eventually overwhelm the weak and relatively powerless segments of the American economy" (Morton J. Horwitz, *The Transformation of American Law, 1780–1860* [Cambridge, Mass.: Harvard University Press, 1977], p. 99); see also pp. 85–101.

Whether we accept these arguments or not, it seems a fair conclusion that the doctrines associated by Holmes with negligence, particularly the prudent person standard, were a response by nineteenth-century society to a growing number of cases involving persons who had "no preexisting relationship with one another" (White, *Tort Law in America*, p. 16; also see Horwitz, *Transformation*, p. 95). For contrasting historical views, see Gary T. Schwartz, "Tort Law and the Economy in Nineteenth Century America: A Reinterpretation," *Yale Law Journal* 90 (1981): 1717–75.

19. According to White, "A concept of tort law as a 'compensation system' is a distinctly twentieth-century phenomenon, brought about by an altered

view of the social consequences of injuries. . . . The attitudes of educated Americans toward injuries have changed dramatically over the past hundred years. A widespread attitude which associated injury with bad luck or deficiencies in character has been gradually replaced by one which presumes that most injured persons are entitled to compensation, through the legal system or some other mechanism. This transformation in what I have called the prevailing ethos of injury in America has been an important determinant of the state of tort law" (*Tort Law in America*, pp. 62, xix).

20. Such is Terence G. Ison's conclusion in *The Forensic Lottery* (London: Staples Press, 1967).

21. See Harper, James, and Gray, *The Law of Torts*, vol. 3, chap. 18; and Keeton, *Prosser and Keeton*, chaps. 5 and 7.

22. See Harper, James, and Gray, *The Law of Torts*, Vol. 3, pp. 183–84 (§14.1); Atiyah and Cane, *Accidents*, pp. 42–43. Guido Calabresi and Alvin K. Klevorick address this issue in "Four Tests for Liability in Torts," *Journal of Legal Studies* 14 (1985): 585–627.

23. Holmes's statement of the objective test is widely quoted: "The standards of the law are standards of general application. The law takes no account of the infinite varieties of temperament, intellect, and education which make the internal character of a given act so different in different men. . . . When men live in society, a certain average of conduct . . . is necessary to the general welfare. If, for instance, a man is born hasty and awkward . . . no doubt his congenital defects will be allowed for in the courts of Heaven, but his slips are no less troublesome to his neighbors than if they sprang from guilty neglect" (*The Common Law*, p. 108).

24. "A man need not, it is true, do this or that act—the term *act* implies a choice—but he must act somehow. Furthermore, the public generally profits by individual activity. As action cannot be avoided, and tends to the public good, there is obviously no policy in throwing the hazard of what is at once desirable and inevitable upon the actor" (ibid., p. 95).

25. Harper, James, and Gray have catalogued and analyzed these situations: "Many activities there are that create situations fraught with danger to others, but because of the general social utility of the activities, the risk is not regarded as unreasonable. . . . But in many of these activities the dangers from socially desirable conduct are especially great and, when they do result in harm, the innocent victims are especially numerous. In others the person carrying on the activity is greatly benefited therefrom in comparison to the loss to the injured persons. . . . The problem, basically, may be regarded as one of allocating a probable or inevitable loss in such a manner as to entail the least hardship on any individual and thus to reserve the social and economic resources of the community" (*The Law of Torts*, vol. 3, p. 183 [§14.1]). They go on to treat these situations as

appropriate for the rule of strict liability (or liability without fault), drawn from the English case of Rylands v. Fletcher (3 Hurl. & C. 774, 159 Eng. Rep. 737 [1865]; L.R. 1 Ex. 265 [1866], L.R. 3 H.L. 330 [1868]), which persisted as a rule during the same historical period that negligence doctrine was on the rise (ibid., pp. 186–233 [§§14.2–14.5]).

26. Harper, James, and Gray argue that strict liability is only an incremental change from standard judicial interpretations of the prudent-person test in cases involving "unreasonably dangerous products" (ibid., vol. 5, p. 578 [§28.32A]). Other commentators claim the difference is more substantial, and they point to the adoption in 1964 of §402A in the *Restatement (Second) of Torts* as opening the floodgates to producer liability for product injuries. See Priest's history ("The Invention of Enterprise Liability"), and Richard A. Epstein, *Modern Products Liability Law* (Westport, Conn.: Quorum Books, 1980).

27. See White's lengthy discussion of the judicial style of California judge Roger Traynor, one of the leading innovators in tort law doctrinal change (*Tort Law in America*, chap. 6).

28. Richard Epstein, while apparently disowning instrumentalism, made an ingenious attempt to transsubstantiate the progressive doctrine of strict liability into a liability principle even more restrictive than traditional negligence. Epstein thinks we are well rid of the prudent-person test because it opens too many doors to liability, not too few. Instead he wants to confine tort liability within a series of "causal paradigms" as exiguous as his libertarian assessment of social obligation. Epstein is not always clear whether this approach is required by moral intuition, whether it represents the hidden meaning of current case law, or whether it simply recommends itself as good social policy; see "A Theory of Strict Liability."

29. See Calabresi's article "Concerning Cause and the Law of Torts," *University of Chicago Law Review* 43 (1975): 69–108. Epstein, of course, is the major exception.

30. While *proximate cause* introduces a limitation on complexity for functional purposes of restricting liability, the law retains a separate concept of *cause in fact*: to maintain the sense of causation represented by pure physical laws. See Harper, James, and Gray, *The Law of Torts*, vol. 4, chap. 20; Keeton, *Prosser and Keeton*, pp. 263–72 (§41); and Atiyah and Cane, *Accidents*, chap. 4.

31. For an early version of this position, see Henry W. Edgerton, "Legal Cause," *University of Pennsylvania Law Review* 72 (1924): 211–44, 343–75. See also Atiyah and Cane, *Accidents*, pp. 103–14.

32. For an early statement see Leon Green, *Rationale of Proximate Cause* (Kansas City: Vernon Law Book Co., 1927).

33. In re Polemis & Furness, Withy Co., [1921] 3 K.B. 560 (C.A.).

34. Atiyah and Cane, *Accidents*, p. 113.

35. See, for example, Guido Calabresi, *The Costs of Accidents: A Legal and Economic Analysis* (New Haven, Conn.: Yale University Press, 1970), pp. 7, 198.
36. See Calabresi and Klevorick, "Four Tests," p. 600.
37. See William O. Douglas's classic essay, "Vicarious Liability and Administration of Risk," *Yale Law Journal* 38 (1929): 584–604, 720–45.
38. Harper, James, and Gray, *The Law of Torts*, vol. 5, pp. 8–10 (§26.2); Keeton, *Prosser and Keeton*, pp. 499–501 (§69).
39. Harper, James, and Gray, *The Law of Torts*, vol. 5, p. 21 (§26.5).
40. Priest, "The Invention of Enterprise Liability."
41. Albert Ehrenzweig, *Negligence Without Fault* (Berkeley and Los Angeles: University of California Press, 1951).
42. Priest, "The Invention of Enterprise Liability," pp. 463–64.
43. This important qualification appears in his conclusion (ibid., p. 527).
44. Ibid., p. 525. The asbestos case is Beshada v. Johns-Manville Prods. Corp., 90 N.J. 191, 447 A.2d 539 (1982). The critical literature on Beshada has noted that its daring resort to absolute liability was soon modified by the New Jersey Supreme Court in Feldman v. Lederle Laboratories, 97 N.J. 429, 479 A.2d 374 (1984)—in conflict with Priest's overall thesis.
45. For the current status of these rules see Harper, James, and Gray, *The Law of Torts*, vol. 4, chap. 21; Keeton, *Prosser and Keeton*, pp. 480–98 (§68).
46. Harper, James, and Gray, *The Law of Torts*, vol. 4, pp. 352–84 (§§22.12–22.14); Keeton, *Prosser and Keeton*, pp. 462–68 (§66).
47. Third parties may also be assigned a proportion of responsibility; see the discussion in Atiyah and Cane, *Accidents*, pp. 116–26.
48. For a review of current problems see Michael K. Steenson, "The Fault with Comparative Fault: The Problem of Individual Comparisons in a Modified Comparative Fault Jurisdiction," *William Mitchell Law Review* 12 (1986): 1–44.
49. Summers v. Tice, 33 Cal. 2d 80, 199 P.2d 1 (1948).
50. See Harper, James, and Gray, *The Law of Torts*, vol. 3, pp. 1–39 (§10.1).
51. The symbolic potential of these cases is evident to many critics. See, for example, the "allegorical trip down strict liability strip," in a critique of joint and several liability by Paul C. Nelson, "Punishment for Profit: An Examination of the Punitive Damage Award in Strict Liability," *Forum* 18 (1983): 377–79.
52. Sindell v. Abbott Laboratories, 26 Cal.3d 588, 163 Cal. Rptr. 132, 607 P.2d 924, *cert. denied*, 449 U.S. 912 (1980). Other courts have not followed California's approach: for example, Payton v. Abbott Laboratories, 512 F.Supp. 1031 (D.Mass. 1981), Ryan v. Eli Lilly & Co., 514 F.Supp. 1004 (D.S.C. 1981), Zafft v. Eli Lilly & Co., 676 S.W.2d 241 (Mo. 1984).

In 1988 the California Supreme Court issued two DES decisions that place qualifications on the Sindell doctrine; Brown v. Superior Court, 245 Cal. Rptr. 412, 751 P.2d 470 (1988), and Jolly v. Eli Lilly & Co., 245 Cal. Rptr. 658, 751 P.2d 923 (1988).

53. Mike Steenson reports that "in 1986 and 1987, half of the states enacted legislation directed toward joint and several liability" ("Recent Legislative Responses to the Rule of Joint and Several Liability," *Tort and Insurance Law Journal* 23 [1988]: 482).

54. See, for example, Judith Jarvis Thomson's essay "Remarks on Causation and Liability," in *Rights, Restitution, and Risk* (Cambridge, Mass.: Harvard University Press, 1986), pp. 192–224.

55. For a recent summary see Jeffrey O'Connell and C. Brian Kelly, *The Blame Game* (Lexington, Mass.: D. C. Heath, 1987).

56. A recent publication collects information about damages awards nationwide, arranged by portions of the human anatomy; Robert Harley and Maryann Magee, *What's It Worth? A Guide to Current Personal Injury Awards and Settlements* (New York: Kluwer Law Book Publishers, 1987 and supplements).

57. Readers can scarcely fail to be impressed by the banner headline announcing that "$988,000 Is Awarded in Suit over Lost Psychic Power," reporting on a jury award to a woman who claimed that a routine CAT scan had made her unable to continue her practice as a psychic (*Philadelphia Inquirer*, March 28, 1986, p. 1).

58. See Ison's *Forensic Lottery*, and Jeffrey O'Connell, *The Lawsuit Lottery* (New York: Free Press, 1979).

59. These points are discussed in Harper, James, and Gray, *The Law of Torts*, vol. 4, pp. 563–73 (§25.10).

60. Ibid., vol. 4, pp. 526–34 (§25.5A); Keeton, *Prosser and Keeton*, pp. 9–15 (§2).

61. "Robins Reorganization Is Approved by Judge," *New York Times*, July 27, 1988, p. D4. For a summary of the bankruptcy court's efforts in creating a special compensation fund, see Paul Marcotte, "$2.48 Billion Trust Fund," *American Bar Association Journal* 74 (March 1988): 24. For background on the pre-bankruptcy litigation see Nelson, "Punishment for Profit," p. 388. See also In re Dalkon Products Liability Litigation, 521 F.Supp. 1188 (N.D.Cal. 1981).

62. The U.S. Supreme Court passed up a chance in 1988 to rule on the constitutionality of punitive damages; see Bankers Life & Casualty Co. v. Crenshaw, 108 S.Ct. 1645 (1988) ("High Court Taking No Stand Now on Big 'Punitive' Damage Awards," *New York Times*, June 1, 1988, p. 1).

63. Priest notes the many internal differences among this group and the idiosyncratic theorizing of certain key figures, making all the more puzzling his blanket statement that "the theory of enterprise liability [com-

manded] almost complete support within the academic community" as early as the mid 1950s ("The Invention of Enterprise Liability," p. 463).
64. Harris et al., *Compensation and Support*, chap. 12.

Chapter 2

1. Paul Starr, *The Social Transformation of American Medicine* (New York: Basic Books, 1982), p. 189.
2. Ibid., p. 181.
3. Mervyn Susser, *Causal Thinking in the Health Sciences: Concepts and Strategies of Epidemiology* (New York: Oxford University Press, 1973), pp. 25, 3. For other introductions to epidemiology see Brian MacMahon and Thomas F. Pugh, *Epidemiology: Principles and Methods* (Boston: Little, Brown, 1970), Abraham M. Lilienfeld and David E. Lilienfeld, *Foundations of Epidemiology* (New York: Oxford University Press, 1980); and Harold A. Kahn, *Introduction to Epidemiological Methods* (New York: Oxford University Press, 1983). I have chosen in this book to emphasize the research strategies of *epidemiology* over the broader but problematic rubric of *human ecology*. That controversial term continues to receive varying interpretations from the disciplines of biology, sociology, anthropology, and geography, as well as from policy-oriented environmental advocates. See, for example, Frederick Sargent II, ed., *Human Ecology* (Amsterdam: North Holland, 1974), biological emphasis; Michael Micklin and Harvey M. Choldin, eds., *Sociological Human Ecology: Contemporary Issues and Applications* (Boulder, Colo.: Westview Press, 1984), sociological emphasis; Kenneth Hewitt, ed., *Interpretations of Calamity from the Viewpoint of Human Ecology* (Boston: Allen & Unwin, 1983), geographical emphasis. An attempt at overall synthesis can be found in Amos H. Hawley, *Human Ecology: A Theoretical Essay* (Chicago: University of Chicago Press, 1986). Much of the human ecology literature is taken up with programmatic summaries and jurisdictional issues, with surprisingly little attention to problems of personal injury or public control of environmental conditions. See, however, Hewitt's essay, "The Idea of Calamity in a Technocratic Age," in *Interpretations of Calamity*, pp. 3–32.
4. Stephen H. Linder, "Injury as Metaphor: Towards an Integration of Perspectives," *Accident Analysis and Prevention* 19 (1987): 4.
5. See, for example, Committee on Trauma Research, *Injury in America: A Continuing Public Health Problem* (Washington, D.C.: National Academy Press, 1985), and Leon S. Robertson, *Injuries: Causes, Control Strategies, and Public Policy* (Lexington, Mass.: D. C. Heath, 1983).

6. This argument has been worked out at length by David Rosenberg, "The Causal Connection in Mass Exposure Cases: A 'Public Law' Vision of the Tort System," *Harvard Law Review* 97 (1984): 849–929. Rosenberg's article is analyzed in Chapter 6.

7. For an important empirical study of asbestos litigation, see Deborah R. Hensler, William L. F. Felstiner, Molly Selvin, and Patricia A. Ebener, *Asbestos in the Courts: The Challenge of Mass Toxic Torts* (Santa Monica, Cal.: Rand Corporation, 1985).

8. For a careful consideration of how the disease relationship may alter the landscape of compensation, see Jane Stapleton, *Disease and the Compensation Debate* (Oxford: Clarendon Press, 1986).

9. In addition to the study cited in note 7, two additional Rand reports address the issue of costs: James S. Kakalik, Patricia A. Ebener, William L. F. Felstiner, and Michael G. Shanley, *Costs of Asbestos Litigation* (Santa Monica, Cal.: Rand Corporation, 1983); and James S. Kakalik and Nicholas M. Pace, *Costs and Compensation Paid in Tort Litigation* (Santa Monica, Cal.: Rand Corporation, 1986).

10. A lively recent restatement of past criticisms is Stephen D. Sugarman, "Doing Away with Tort Law," *California Law Review* 73 (1985): 555–664.

11. Hensler et al., *Asbestos in the Courts*, p. 2.

12. For an argument that the causal doctrines of common law are in close conformity with intuitions gleaned from analysis of ordinary language, see H. L. A. Hart and Tony Honoré, *Causation in the Law*, 2nd ed. (Oxford: Clarendon Press, 1985). This argument will be criticized in Chapter 5.

13. N. F. Stanley and R. A. Joske, eds. *Changing Disease Patterns and Human Behaviour* (New York: Academic Press, 1980). See also Stapleton, *Disease*, chap. 1. Rosenberg has criticized the judicial system's dependence on "particularistic evidence" of causation in cases of toxic exposure; see "The Causal Connection."

14. See Hart and Honoré, *Causation*, pp. liv, 228–29. For historical background on the burden of proof and a discussion of distinctions within this concept, see John Henry Wigmore, *Treatise on the Anglo-American System of Evidence*, 3rd ed. (Boston: Little, Brown, 1983), §2485.

15. "With few exceptions, the civil justice system has adoped the more conservative position and as yet has been unwilling to change" (Hensler et al., *Asbestos in the Courts*, p. 35).

16. Both examples are cited in ibid., p. 42. Damages awarded to the four plaintiffs were approximately $1 million each, plus an additional $1 million each in punitive damages. This case was later studied at length by Molly Selvin and Larry Picus, *The Debate over Jury Performance: Observations from a Recent Asbestos Case* (Santa Monica, Cal.: Rand Corporation, 1987). For another study of variations, see Irving J. Selikoff,

Disability Compensation for Asbestos-Associated Disease in the United States (New York: Mt. Sinai School of Medicine of the City University of New York, 1982).

17. Hensler et al., *Asbestos in the Courts*, p. 44.
18. See Peter H. Schuck, *Agent Orange on Trial* (Cambridge, Mass.: Belknap Press, 1986); Jack B. Weinstein, "Preliminary Reflections on Law's Reactions to Disasters," *Columbia Journal of Environmental Law* 11 (1986): 1–50. The Agent Orange litigation is discussed in Chapter 6.
19. P. S. Atiyah and Peter Cane, *Accidents, Compensation and the Law*, 4th ed. (London: Weidenfeld & Nicolson, 1987), p. 433 [citing *Research on Road Safety* (London: HMSO, 1963), pp. 3–4]. See also Fowler V. Harper, Fleming James, Jr., and Oscar S. Gray, *The Law of Torts*, 2nd ed. (Boston: Little, Brown, 1986), vol. 3, pp. 90–97 (§11.4).
20. Atiyah and Cane, *Accidents*, p. 414.
21. Cited by Sally Lloyd-Bostock, "The Ordinary Man, and the Psychology of Attributing Causes and Responsibility," *Modern Law Review* 42 (1979): 167.
22. Ibid., pp. 154–55.
23. See Hart and Honoré, *Causation*, p. lxxviii.
24. For the link between epidemiological methods and policy approaches see W. Haddon, Jr., "Advances in the Epidemiology of Injuries as a Basis for Public Policy," *Public Health Reports* 95 (1980): 411–21. Haddon's ideas are clearly summarized in Robertson, *Injuries*, chap. 4. A useful survey of policy implications is Sol Levine and Abraham M. Lilienfeld, eds., *Epidemiology and Health Policy* (London: Tavistock, 1987).
25. See Pete Shields, *Guns Don't Die, People Do* (New York: Arbor House, 1981). For empirical analysis see Gary Kleck, "Policy Lessons from Recent Gun Control Research," *Law and Contemporary Problems* 49 (Winter 1986): 40–41.
26. Charles Perrow, *Normal Accidents: Living with High-Risk Technologies* (New York: Basic Books, 1984). The Three Mile Island study, part of the larger investigation supported by a presidential commission, is cited in this book, where it is extensively summarized in Perrow's chap. 1.
27. Ibid., pp. 3–4.
28. Ibid., p. 16. In Perrow's view, "The performance of all concerned—utility, manufacturer, regulatory agency, and industry—was about average."
29. Both quotes ibid., pp. 4–5.
30. "Risk will never be eliminated from high-risk systems, and we will never eliminate more than a few systems at best. At the very least, however, we might stop blaming the wrong people and the wrong factors, and stop trying to fix the systems in ways that only make them riskier" (ibid., p. 4).
31. These points are culled from ibid., pp. 3–12, and chap. 3.
32. Ibid., p. 85.
33. Ibid., p. 105.

34. Ibid., p. 115.
35. Ibid., p. 76.
36. Ibid., p. 21.
37. Ibid., p. 9.
38. Perrow cites Larry Hirshhorn's analysis of "the limits of 'cybernetic' (self-correcting) systems" (ibid., p. 79).
39. Ibid., p. 8.
40. See, for example, Robert Dingwall, "The Jasmine Beckford Affair," *Modern Law Review* 49 (1986): 489–507, and two articles by Barry A. Turner, "The Organizational and Interorganizational Development of Disasters," *Administrative Science Quarterly* 21 (1976): 378–97, and "The Development of Disasters—A Sequence Model for the Analysis of the Origins of Disaster," in *Man-Made Disasters* (London: Wykeham Publications, 1978), pp. 753–74.
41. Trends in damages awards are the subject of some controversy. The impression we gain from media coverage of large awards is not an accurate indication of how the typical tort victim is compensated. Nonetheless the trend is both toward higher average awards and greater numbers of tort claims, particularly in the areas of product liability and what we are calling *environmental* cases. For general data on current compensation awards, see Kakalik, *Costs and Compensation*. Jury Verdict Research, Inc. collects data on tort awards and publishes periodic summaries; see, for example, *Personal Injury Valuation Handbook* (Solon, Ohio: Jury Verdict Research, 1986). On punitive damages see Mark A. Peterson, Syam Sarma, and Michael Shanley, *Punitive Damages: Empirical Findings* (Santa Monica, Cal.: Rand Corporation, 1987).
42. Richard A. Schmalz, "On the Financing of Compensation Systems," *Journal of Legal Studies* 14 (1985): 812, 816.
43. Hensler et al., *Asbestos in the Courts*, p. 1. Another source states that between 1940 and 1970 some 27 million people were exposed to asbestos in the workplace (Eugene R. Anderson, Irene C. Warshauer, and Adrienne M. Coffin, "The Asbestos Health Hazards Compensation Act: A Legislative Solution to a Litigation Crisis," *Journal of Legislation* 10 [1983]: 30).
44. *New York Times*, July 4, 1987, p. 17. In 1988 federal District Court Judge Robert R. Merhige, Jr. ruled that the remaining claims would be valued at $2.48 billion, as part of a larger reorganization plan under which Robins eventually agreed to be purchased by another company. See "Robins Reorganization Is Approved by Judge," *New York Times*, July 27, 1988, p. D4; Paul Marcotte, "$2.48 Billion Trust Fund," *American Bar Assocation Journal* 74 (March 1988): 24.
45. Arthur S. Olick, "Chapter 11—A Dubious Solution to Massive Toxic Tort Liability," *Forum* 18 (1983): 361–76.

46. See "Developments in the Law—Toxic Waste Litigation," *Harvard Law Review* 99 (1986): 1458–1661.
47. Office of Technology Assessment, *Superfund Strategy* (Washington, D.C.: Government Printing Office, 1985), pp. 18–21.
48. Mark E. Solomons, "Hazardous Wastes and Workers' Compensation: Some Evolving Concerns," *Tort and Insurance Law Journal* 21 (1985): 92.
49. Kakalik et al., *Costs of Asbestos Litigation*, pp. 26–27. For costs of the tort system generally see Kakalik and Pace, *Costs and Compensation*.
50. Anderson et al., "Asbestos Health Hazards," p. 33.
51. Hensler et al., *Asbestos in the Courts*, p. xxvii; see also Selikoff, *Disability Compensation*, pp. 349–518. Recent strategies for expediting the disposition of asbestos claims are unlikely to resolve these problems, as we shall see in Chapter 6.
52. E. J. Mishan, *Economic Efficiency and Social Welfare* (London: Allen & Unwin, 1981), pp. 232–33.
53. Ibid., p. 228.
54. Fred Hirsch, *Social Limits to Growth* (Cambridge, Mass.: Harvard University Press, 1976), p. 3. I am indebted to Jane Kronick for suggesting this application of Hirsch's work. For commentary see Adrian Ellis and Krishan Kumar, eds., *Dilemmas of Liberal Democracies: Studies in Fred Hirsch's Social Limits to Growth* (London: Tavistock, 1983).
55. National Swine Flu Immunization Program of 1976, Pub.L. No. 94-380, 90 Stat. 1113. This statute was briefly codified at 42 U.S.C. §§247b (j)-(l) (1976). See the report by the Controller General of the United States, *The Swine Flu Program: An Unprecedented Venture in Preventive Medicine* (Washington, D.C.: General Accounting Office, 1977). For a factual summary and negative critique of the program, see Richard E. Neustadt and Harvey V. Fineberg, *The Swine Flu Affair: Decision-Making on a Slippery Disease* (Washington, D.C.: Government Printing Office, 1978). On some related public health issues, see Diana B. Dutton, *Worse Than the Disease: Pitfalls of Medical Progress* (New York: Cambridge University Press, 1988).
56. This liability mechanism is described in detail in Chapter 8.
57. U.S. Department of Justice, Civil Division, Torts Branch, "Swine Flu Statistics as of December 1, 1986." The number of Guillain-Barré claims filed was 1,045, but in 1979 a Department of Justice official estimated that as few as 500 were genuine instances of the disease, based on projections of the statistical correlation with taking the vaccine (personal communication, November 7, 1979). By early 1987, 39 claims out of the original 4,172 were still under consideration by the Justice Department. As of December 1, 1986, a total of 704 claims had been administratively settled for $43,639,744; 387 lawsuits had been settled for $36,924,225; and 103

judgments for plaintiffs had resulted in damages awards of $32,755,206. Remaining claims were denied.

58. Hirsch, *Social Limits*, p. 106.
59. Donald Harris et al., *Compensation and Support for Illness and Injury* (Oxford: Clarendon Press, 1984), p. 46. For a description of the survey sample, see p. 35.
60. Ibid., pp. 317–18.
61. Ibid., pp. 76, 319, 328.
62. Deborah A. Stone, *The Disabled State* (Philadelphia: Temple University Press, 1984). See also Richard Abel's review of the Harris study, *California Law Review* 73 (1985): 1003–23.
63. See Peter S. Barth and H. Allan Hunt, *Workers' Compensation and Work-Related Illnesses and Diseases* (Cambridge, Mass.: MIT Press, 1980), chap. 5; and other sources cited in Chapter 9.
64. U.S. Department of Labor, *An Interim Report to Congress on Occupational Disease* (Washington, D.C.: Government Printing Office, 1980).
65. Selikoff, *Disability Compensation*, p. 459.

Chapter 3

1. Opening remarks by Senator Pressler in "Product Liability Voluntary Claims and Uniform Standards Act," Hearings on S. 1999 before the Subcommittee on the Consumer of the Senate Committee on Commerce, Science and Transportation, 99th Congress, 2nd Session, p. 6.
2. For an overview of the Accident Compensation Act, see Terence G. Ison, *Accident Compensation* (London: Croom Helm, 1980).
3. See *Report of the Royal Commission on Civil Liability and Compensation for Personal Injury* (London: HMSO, 1978) (known as the Pearson Report). A decade later, most of the Commission's recommendations have been ignored, and there is little sign of weakening in the tort system.
4. For a general description see *Congressional Quarterly Almanac* 44 (1986): 287–89.
5. Robert A. Dahl, *Dilemmas of Pluralist Democracy* (New Haven, Conn.: Yale University Press, 1982). See also the more withering analysis in Theodore J. Lowi, *The End of Liberalism*, 2nd ed. (New York: Norton, 1979), pt. 2.
6. Among other sources cited in Chapter 5, see Richard A. Epstein, "A Theory of Strict Liability," *Journal of Legal Studies* 2 (1973): 151–204; and Ernest J. Weinrib, "Toward a Moral Theory of Negligence Law," *Law and Philosophy* 2 (1983): 37–62.

7. Dahl, *Dilemmas*, pp. 159–65.

8. See Guido Calabresi, "Some Thoughts on Risk Distribution and the Law of Torts," *Yale Law Journal* 70 (1961): 499–553, and, more generally, Fowler V. Harper, Fleming James, Jr., and Oscar S. Gray, *The Law of Torts*, 2nd ed. (Boston: Little, Brown, 1986), vol. 5, pp. 17–23 (§26.5).

9. See Jerome Frank, *Courts on Trial* (Princeton, N.J.: Princeton University Press, 1949), pp. 80–102.

10. See Charles E. Lindblom, *Politics and Markets* (New York: Basic Books, 1977), p. 5, for reflections on the corporate dominance of legislative lobbying.

11. For hearings in the 99th Congress (in addition to the hearings on S. 1999), see "Product Liability Act," Hearing on S. 100 before the Subcommittee on the Consumer of the Senate Committee on Commerce, Science, and Transportation, 99th Congress, 1st Session (1985), and, from the same subcommittee and session, "Product Liability Act Amendments."

12. "Product Liability Act Amendments," Hearings on S. 100, p. 187.

13. "Two-Pronged Attack on Liability Insurance Crunch," *Congressional Quarterly Weekly Report* 44 (1986): 3059–63.

14. See the testimony of Marshall Shapo and Keith Davidson, Hearings on S. 1999, pp. 71–76. In early 1987, the ABA House of Delegates endorsed proposals for limited changes in state tort rules ("ABA House of Delegates Approves McKay Commission Recommendations," *The Brief* 16 [Spring 1987]: 2–8).

15. See Marshall Shapo, *Towards a Jurisprudence of Injury* (Chicago: American Bar Association, 1984).

16. For a discussion of the economic incentives on lawyers to represent toxic tort claims, see David Rosenberg, "The Causal Connection in Mass Exposure Cases: A 'Public Law' Vision of the Tort System," *Harvard Law Review* 97 (1984): 893–98.

17. Harper, James, and Gray, *The Law of Torts*, vol. 3, pp. 137–48 (§13.4).

18. See Kenneth S. Abraham, *Distributing Risk: Insurance, Legal Theory, and Public Policy* (New Haven, Conn.: Yale University Press, 1986), chap. 2.

19. Ibid., pp. 58–59.

20. The 100th Congress revived some old threats for regulating the insurance industry. For example, H.R. 2727 would have repealed the industry's exemption from antitrust laws. See "Panel Limits Insurers' Antitrust Exemption," *Congressional Quarterly Weekly Report* 46 (1988): 1673, reporting on a vote by the Monopolies Subcommittee of the House Judiciary Committee.

21. For a general discussion of lobbying see Jeffrey M. Berry, *The Interest Group Society* (Boston: Little, Brown, 1984); and Jack L. Walker, "The

Origins and Maintenance of Interest Groups in America," *American Political Science Review* 77 (June 1983) 390–406.

22. See Michael W. McCann, *Taking Reform Seriously: Perspectives on Public Interest Liberalism* (Ithaca, N.Y.: Cornell University Press, 1986), and references therein.

23. In addition to McCann, see the essays in Burton A. Weisbrod, *Public Interest Law: An Economic and Institutional Analysis* (Berkeley and Los Angeles: University of California Press, 1978).

24. McCann, *Taking Reform Seriously*, pp. 113–21. On conservative public interest groups, see Lee Epstein, *Conservatives in Court* (Knoxville: University of Tennessee Press, 1985).

25. The literature is summarized in Jethro K. Lieberman, *The Litigious Society* (New York: Basic Books, 1981), chap. 2 of which is devoted to the product liability debate.

26. For a general introduction to arguments for and against regulation, see Stephen Breyer, *Regulation and Its Reform* (Cambridge, Mass.: Harvard University Press: 1982), chap. 1.

27. See Lindblom, *Politics and Markets*, pp. 190–93.

28. See Michael S. Baram, *Alternatives to Regulation: Managing Risks to Health, Safety and the Environment* (Lexington, Mass.: D. C. Heath, 1982), chap. 9.

29. The history of research on asbestos health effects is available in Irving J. Selikoff's study *Disability Compensation for Asbestos-Associated Disease in the United States* (New York: Mt. Sinai School of Medicine of the City University of New York, 1982), chap. 1. For a highly critical account of the asbestos industry, see Paul Brodeur, *Outrageous Misconduct: The Asbestos Industry on Trial* (New York: Pantheon Books, 1985). A more neutral account is Deborah R. Hensler, William L. F. Felstiner, Molly Selvin, and Patricia A. Ebener, *Asbestos in the Courts* (Santa Monica, Cal.: Rand Corporation, 1985).

30. See, for example, Robert E. Keeton and Jeffrey O'Connell, *Basic Protection for the Traffic Victim* (Boston: Little, Brown, 1965).

31. The reference is to an important article by William Prosser signaling the demise of the "privity of contract" doctrine, thus clearing the way for expansion of product liability suits (*Minnesota Law Review* 50 [1966]: 791–848).

32. See David Held, *Models of Democracy* (Stanford, Cal.: Stanford University Press, 1987), p. 244.

33. This is the paradoxical message of Calabresi's book, which nonetheless articulates the economic model in unsurpassed detail (*The Costs of Accidents* [New Haven, Conn.: Yale University Press, 1970]).

34. See Richard A. Posner, *The Economics of Justice* (Cambridge, Mass.: Harvard University Press, 1981), pp. 48–115.

35. These proposals were culled from chap. 7 of the Interagency Task Force on Product Liability, *Final Report* (Washington, D.C.: Government Printing Office, 1978).
36. Ibid.
37. See Malcolm E. Wheeler, "The Use of Criminal Statutes to Regulate Product Safety," *Journal of Legal Studies* 13 (1984): 593–618.
38. Product Liability Reform Act, S. 2760, 99th Congress, 2nd Session (1986). This and other bills relating to federal product liability reform are discussed at length in Chapter 7.
39. Committee members' remarks at the beginning of the hearings on S. 1999 leave little doubt that the draft of this bill was intended to offer both sides something of value. Although the accommodation reached in S. 2760 was somewhat different, the same spirit of compromise prevailed.
40. Remarks of Senator Danforth, Hearings on S. 1999, pp. 3–4.
41. Ibid., p. 146.
42. Ibid.
43. Ibid., p. 105.
44. Ibid., p. 166.
45. The bill provided only for "reasonable" attorneys' fees in connection with the administrative portion of the scheme.
46. In 1988 the House Committee on Energy and Commerce became the new forum for product liability debate. Yet another compromise bill, H.R. 1115, was approved by the Subcommittee on Commerce, and eventually by the full committee. An interesting new twist to the debate was provided by groups attempting to exempt certain "evil" products from coverage under the statute, presumably so that the tort system could continue to punish them. Anti-abortion groups sought to exempt contraceptives, while women's groups singled out products associated with birth defects (*Congressional Quarterly Weekly Report* 46 [1988]: 1406; for a summary of H.R. 1115 as reported, see House Report No. 100-748).
47. See Lowi, *The End of Liberalism*, p. xvi.
48. Dahl, *Dilemmas*, pp. 162–63.

Chapter 4

1. E. J. Mishan, "Do Economic Evaluations of Allocative Changes Have Any Validity in the West Today?" in Mishan, *Economic Efficiency and Social Welfare* (London: Allen & Unwin, 1981), pp. 259–60.
2. For a brief history of law-and-economics literature, see Cento G. Veljanovski, *The New Law-and-Economics* (Oxford: Centre for Socio-Legal Studies, 1982).

3. See Edward Levi, *An Introduction to Legal Reasoning* (Chicago: University of Chicago Press, 1949), pp. 5–7.
4. Alexander M. Bickel, Jr. offered the most sensitive treatment of this cautious endorsement in *The Least Dangerous Branch* (Indianapolis: Bobbs-Merrill, 1962). More confident though increasingly dogmatic endorsements of the judicial process appeared during the 1970s, with the decline in progressive confidence in legislative government. The most elaborate argument for judicial self-sufficiency is Ronald M. Dworkin, *Taking Rights Seriously* (Cambridge, Mass.: Harvard University Press, 1977).
5. The initial contributions were made by Guido Calabresi, *The Costs of Accidents* (New Haven, Conn.: Yale University Press, 1970) and by Richard A. Posner, "A Theory of Negligence," *Journal of Legal Studies* 1 (1972): 29–96. See also his recent summary analysis, coauthored with William M. Landes, *The Economic Structure of Tort Law* (Cambridge, Mass.: Harvard University Press, 1987).
6. For examples, in addition to Calabresi, Posner, and works cited in Veljanovski, readers should consult the *Journal of Legal Studies*, which has published much of the law-and-economics literature.
7. For an assessment of the respective contributions of lawyers and economists, see Veljanovski, *The New Law-and-Economics*, pp. 126–41.
8. This follows trends in other policy areas, described admirably in Robert H. Nelson, "The Economics Profession and the Making of Public Policy," *Journal of Economic Literature* 25 (1987): 49–91.
9. This condition is the famous notion of a Pareto optimum or, more technically, a potential Pareto improvement. The literature on the Pareto principles is vast. For a relatively nontechnical introduction, see Allen Buchanan, *Ethics, Efficiency and the Market* (Totowa, N.J.: Rowman & Allanheld, 1985), pp. 4–13. Also useful is E. J. Mishan, "Pareto Optimality and the Law," *Oxford Economic Papers* 19 (1967): 255–87.
10. We are leaving aside the influential Hicks-Kaldor modification of the Pareto principle. That theory allows some persons to suffer losses of utility, provided a sufficient surplus is generated elsewhere in the system that could compensate them. In other words, the theory postulates an *economic* measure of losses (defined as the amount the loser would hypothetically accept as ex ante compensation in an imagined exchange). Since this exchange (and indeed the whole welfare economic theory itself) is imaginary, nothing in the Hicks-Kaldor theory requires that such compensation be institutionally enforced. For an economist's discussion see E. J. Mishan, "A Reappraisal of the Principles of Resource Allocation," *Economica* 24 (1957): 324–42. For applications to the law-and-economics debate, see Jules L. Coleman, "Economics and the Law: A Critical Review of the Foundations of the Economic Approach to Law," *Ethics* 94 (1984): 649–79.

11. Francis M. Bator, "The Simple Analytics of Welfare Maximization," *American Economic Review* 47 (1957): 57.

12. Important conceptual problems with the market's ability to coordinate individual preferences in both a complete and consistent way were raised by Kenneth Arrow in the 1950s. Economists are still absorbing the impact of these issues; see for example the discussion in Lawrence A. Boland, *Methodology for a New Economics* (Boston: Allen & Unwin, 1986), pp. 2–8. On Arrow's many contributions see Amartya Sen's review article, "Social Choice and Justice," *Journal of Economic Literature* 23 (1985): 1764–76.

13. See W. J. Baumol, *Welfare Economics and the Theory of the State*, 2nd ed. (Cambridge, Mass.: Harvard University Press, 1965).

14. "A Reappraisal of the Principles of Resource Allocation," in Mishan, *Economic Efficiency*, p. 4.

15. Calabresi, *The Costs of Accidents*, p. 26.

16. See for example the exchange between Posner ("Some Uses and Abuses of Economics in Law") and Frank Michelman ("A Comment on Some Uses and Abuses of Economics in Law") in *University of Chicago Law Review* 46 (1979): 281–315. Posner's position is elaborated in *The Economics of Justice* (Cambridge, Mass.: Harvard University Press, 1981), pp. 88–115.

17. See the classic article by Paul Samuelson, "Evaluation of Real National Income," *Oxford Economic Papers* 2 (1950): 1–29.

18. Bator, "Simple Analytics," p. 28.

19. His subsequent book, *Tragic Choices* (New York: Norton, 1978), is even further removed from policy prescriptions. It compares the formal properties of the market to political and administrative systems, such that even a society's "selection" of a decision-making process becomes an analytic issue. At times, Calabresi incautiously suggests that this kind of choice is itself essentially economic (see pp. 32, 56), and not simply a cultural artifact. For similar reservations, see Brian Barry's review essay, "Tragic Choices," *Ethics* 94 (1984): 303–18.

20. Calabresi, *The Costs of Accidents*, pp. 24–26.

21. Ibid., pp. 26–31.

22. Ibid., pp. 68–69.

23. Ibid., p. 24. When Calabresi finally does return to the subject of justice, he carefully distinguishes the substantive inquiry into justice (into "what a community deems to be just") from a second-order, "critical," or "rational" description of the community's actions in pursuit of justice. In this second sense, justice is a "political fact, a datum to be dealt with like the climate" (pp. 291–92), and that quite neatly sums up Calabresi's own tack.

24. See for example Ronald M. Dworkin, "Is Wealth a Value?" *Journal of Legal Studies* 9 (1980): 191–226, reprinted in Dworkin, *A Matter of Principle* (Cambridge, Mass.: Harvard University Press, 1985), pp. 237–66.
25. See generally Johannes de v. Graaff, *Theoretical Welfare Economics* (Cambridge: Cambridge University Press, 1967).
26. See the history in I. M. D. Little, *A Critique of Welfare Economics*, 2nd ed. (Oxford: Oxford University Press, 1957), pp. 67–83.
27. Ibid., pp. 86–109. For a recent discussion see Robert Cooter and Peter Rappoport, "Were the Ordinalists Wrong About Welfare Economics?" *Journal of Economic Literature* 22 (1984): 507–30. As with many trends, the separation of welfare economics and ethics may be running its course. Recent work by Amartya Sen and others appears to inject certain ethical perspectives into the analytical framework of economics; see, for example, Sen's *On Ethics and Economics* (Oxford: Basil Blackwell, 1987).
28. Calabresi, *The Costs of Accidents*, p. 24, n. 1.
29. Ibid., p. 31.
30. See, for example, Richard Musgrave, *The Theory of Public Finance* (New York: McGraw-Hill, 1959).
31. Calabresi, *The Costs of Accidents*, p. 40.
32. Ibid.
33. Ibid., p. 24, n. 1.
34. Ibid., p. 70.
35. See, for example, the extended treatment by P. S. Atiyah and Peter Cane, *Accidents, Compensation and the Law*, 4th ed. (London: Weidenfeld & Nicolson, 1987), pp. 506–42.
36. Calabresi, *The Costs of Accidents*, p. 69.
37. See, for example, Dennis C. Mueller, *Public Choice* (Cambridge: Cambridge University Press, 1979), and Jon Elster and Aanund Hylland, eds., *Foundations of Social Choice Theory* (Cambridge: Cambridge University Press, 1986).
38. Calabresi's negative characterizations of nonformalistic arguments and institutions are scattered throughout his book (*The Costs of Accidents*, pp. 96–103, 186, 190, 294). This view of regulation is, of course, standard fare in much of the policy literature inspired by economic models; see Nelson, "The Economics Profession."
39. Calabresi himself has extended this market model of social choice into political processes (conceived as analogous to markets), in accordance with emerging theories of "public choice"; see especially *Tragic Choices*.
40. In Schumpeter's phrase, these conclusions are not about "living and fighting" human beings, but are "mere clotheslines on which to hang propositions" (*History of Economic Analysis* [New York: Oxford University Press, 1954], p. 886).

41. See Mark Kelman, *A Guide to Critical Legal Studies* (Cambridge, Mass.: Harvard University Press, 1987).

42. Over the past two decades the circle around Posner has been especially active in extending these basic concepts to other "choices" affecting the design of tort law: definitions of causation, assumption of risk, contributory negligence, punitive damages, and the like. These dispersed treatments have generally appeared in the *Journal of Legal Studies*, and they have recently been pulled together by Posner and his colleague, William M. Landes, into a unified economic theory of tort law in *Economic Structure*. See also the independent work of Steven Shavell, *Economic Analysis of Accident Law* (Cambridge, Mass.: Harvard University Press, 1987). Economic concepts have also been applied to other areas of the law, to the judicial process, and indeed to all of human behavior; for a brief summary, see Veljanovski, *The New Law-and-Economics*. Such economic imperialism has long been identified with academics at the University of Chicago; for a brief historical account see Melvin W. Reder, "Chicago Economics: Permanence and Change," *Journal of Economic Literature* 20 (1982): 1–38.

43. Calabresi, *The Costs of Accidents*, pp. 135–73.

44. Ibid., pp. 293–300.

45. Posner, "A Theory of Negligence."

46. Landes and Posner, *Economic Structure*, pp. 273–74.

47. See Guido Calabresi, "Optimal Deterrence and Accidents," *Yale Law Journal* 84 (1975): 656–71.

48. One finds brief discussions of this problem in Shavell, *Economic Analysis*, chap. 12, and in an earlier article, "A Model of the Optimal Use of Liability and Safety Regulation," *Rand Journal of Economics* 15 (1984): pp. 271–80.

49. Calabresi, *The Costs of Accidents*, pp. 78–94. For a theoretical overview of market failure, see Francis M. Bator, "The Anatomy of Market Failure," *Quarterly Journal of Economics* 72 (1958): 351–79.

50. "The Problem of Social Cost," *Journal of Law and Economics* 3 (1960): 1–44. Coase's theorem is nonetheless much admired by some welfare economics writers because it suggests an *implicit* economic foundation for a nonmarket relationship. It is surprising that some enterprising theorist has not come forward with a corollary postulate: that persons in society do *in fact* strike all the bargains that make economic sense. High transaction costs are thus folded into the economics of bargaining, and the status quo suddenly becomes the optimal level of bargaining across society. (For a similar line of thought, see Boland, *Methodology*, pp. 32–34.) This refinement would, however, make superfluous any judicial role in supporting the market. One might irreverently observe—invoking an economic theory of argumentation—that most law professors would find such a corollary "more than they bargained for."

51. A possible solution, by way of circular logic, is to postulate that whatever the courts *actually* decide is in turn based on valid economic calculations. This appears to be the remarkable route favored by Posner, as we shall see in a moment.

52. This conclusion is supported by David Rosenberg, "The Causal Connection in Mass Exposure Cases: A 'Public Law' Vision of the Tort System," *Harvard Law Review* 97 (1984): 849–929. Rosenberg indicates the major changes in judicial structure that would allow courts to send more appropriate market signals in environmental accident cases, but the scale of those changes argues against their practicality. (Rosenberg's proposal is discussed in Chapter 6). For a more general critique of the signaling capacity of courts, see E. P. Belobaba, *Products Liability and Personal Injury Compensation in Canada: Towards Integration and Rationalization* (Ottawa: Policy Research, Analysis and Liaison Directorate, Policy Coordination Bureau, Consumer and Corporate Affairs, 1983), chap. 6. An empirical study of product manufacturers has shown little evidence that companies are ready to accept economic signals from tort law (George Eads and Peter Reuter, *Designing Safer Products: Corporate Responses to Product Liability Law and Regulation* [Santa Monica, Cal.: Rand Corporation, 1983]).

53. For an extended discussion of insurance issues, see Shavell, *Economic Analysis*, chaps. 8–10.

54. Calabresi, *The Costs of Accidents*, pp. 244–65.

55. In numerous instances Posner concedes at least apparent weaknesses in tort law, especially in cases involving "catastrophic personal injuries"; see Landes and Posner, *Economic Structure*, chap. 9. But he invariably qualifies these admissions by offering more penetrating criticisms of political regulation. And even the demonstrated weaknesses of tort law in mass accident cases are said to be easily redeemable by judges acting on their hidden economic instincts. For some criticisms of Posner, see Walter Y. Oi, "Tort Law as a Regulatory Regime: A Comment on Landes and Posner," *Journal of Legal Studies* 13 (1984): 435–40.

56. On the conceptual ambiguities of "transaction costs," see note 50. Much of the law-and-economics literature has found odd comfort in the economic theory of transaction costs, as though the market might somehow provide its own remedy. In the economic literature on organizations, however, the theory has been used to explain the growth of bureaucratic structures in a market society. See the work of Oliver Williamson: *Markets and Hierarchy: Analysis and Antitrust Implications* (New York: Free Press, 1975); *Economic Institutions of Capitalism* (New York: Free Press,

1985); and *Economic Organization: Firms, Markets, and Policy Control* (New York: New York University Press, 1986).

57. For criticisms by an economist sympathetic to the law-and-economics movement generally, see Veljanovski, *The New Law-and-Economics*, pp. 126–41.

58. Given the low estimation of political processes by most of these theorists, their challenges to policy designers seem especially perverse. For an astute discussion of the "policy scientist's" systematic inability to incorporate implementation into formal policy prescriptions, see Paul Diesing, *Science and Ideology in the Policy Sciences* (New York: Aldine Publishing, 1982), chap. 5.

59. The only theorist in serious danger of accepting this limitation is Posner, whose unique contribution has been to clasp firmly together the two invisible hands found in purely conceived market and judicial structures. But other theorists have been slow to generalize about accidents or other harms defined by institutions other than the judiciary. That can be expected to change with the growth of epidemiological research and a consequent broadening of the meaning of *accident*. See, however, the basically conservative recommendations contained in Robert E. Litan and Clifford Winston, eds., *Liability: Perspectives and Policy* (Washington, D.C.: Brookings Institution, 1988).

60. The data and approach taken in this discussion are based on an essay by S. Leonard Syme and Jack M. Guralnik, "Epidemiology and Health Policy: Coronary Heart Disease," in Sol Levine and Abraham Lilienfeld, eds., *Epidemiology and Health Policy* (London: Tavistock, 1987), pp. 85–116.

61. See Susan P. Baker, Stephen P. Teret, and Erich M. Daub, "Injuries," in Levine and Lilienfeld, *Epidemiology*, pp. 177–206.

62. For general references see Leon S. Robertson, *Injuries: Causes, Control Strategies, and Public Policy* (Lexington, Mass.: D. C. Heath, 1983), and Julian A. Waller, *Injury Control: A Guide to the Causes and Prevention of Trauma* (Lexington, Mass.: D. C. Heath, 1985).

63. Baker et al., "Injuries," pp. 190, 189.

64. Ibid., p. 179.

65. "Do Economic Evaluations of Allocative Changes Have Any Validity in the West Today?" in Mishan, *Economic Efficiency*, p. 257.

Chapter 5

1. Sigmund Freud, *The Interpretation of Dreams*, trans. James Strachey, in *Standard Edition of the Complete Psychological Works of Sigmund Freud* (London: Hogarth Press, 1953), vol. 5, p. 621.

2. Edward Levi, *An Introduction to Legal Reasoning* (Chicago: University of Chicago Press, 1949), p. 1.

3. These assumptions can be traced back to neo-Kantian movements at the end of the nineteenth century, which provided most of the modern academic disciplines with their conception of science. On the sources and development of this philosophical school see Herbert Schnädelbach, *Philosophy in Germany: 1831–1933* (Cambridge: Cambridge University Press, 1984).

4. A central influence in this respect was A. J. Ayer, *Language, Truth and Logic* (1936; reprint, New York: Dover Publications, 1952). For a general critique of emotivism in ethics, see Alasdair MacIntyre, *After Virtue* (South Bend, Ind.: Notre Dame University Press, 1981), pp. 22–34. In economics, the decisive publication was Lionel Robbins, *An Essay on the Nature and Significance of Economic Science* (London: Macmillan, 1932).

5. For a representative selection see Richard Rorty, ed., *The Linguistic Turn* (Chicago: University of Chicago Press, 1967).

6. Herbert Simon, "A Behavioral Model of Rational Choice," *Quarterly Journal of Economics* 69 (1955): 99–118; and *Models of Man: Social and Rational* (New York: John Wiley & Sons, 1957), pp. 196–206.

7. Charles E. Lindblom and David K. Cohen, *Usable Knowledge: Social Science and Social Problem Solving* (New Haven, Conn.: Yale University Press, 1979).

8. For the general philosophical argument see Wilfred Sellars, "Empiricism and the Philosophy of Mind," in *Science, Perception, and Reality* (London: Routledge & Kegan Paul, 1964), pp. 127–96, and Richard Rorty, *Philosophy and the Mirror of Nature* (Princeton, N.J.: Princeton University Press, 1979). For more specific applications see Bernard Williams, *Ethics and the Limits of Philosophy* (Cambridge, Mass.: Harvard University Press, 1985), and Don Herzog, *Without Foundations: Justification in Political Theory* (Ithaca, N.Y.: Cornell University Press, 1985).

9. Ronald M. Dworkin, *Taking Rights Seriously* (Cambridge, Mass.: Harvard University Press, 1977).

10. Lindblom and Cohen, *Usable Knowledge*.

11. The strongest market advocates include those influenced by the Chicago school, including Richard Posner in the field of law-and-economics.

12. While the literature on social and professional ethics is now vast, much of the best work appears in the *Hastings Center Report* and other publications sponsored by the Hastings Center.

13. This phrase, identifying moral reasoning with the behavioral qualities of solemnity, apparently comes from the British philosopher Gilbert Ryle; see Robert E. Goodin, *Political Theory and Public Policy* (Chicago: University of Chicago Press, 1982), p. 100. Today the term generally signals

an elevation of the deontological style of moral philosophy over the instrumental style.

14. See the collection of essays in Daniel Kahneman, Paul Slovic, and Amos Tversky, *Judgment under Uncertainty: Heuristics and Biases* (Cambridge: Cambridge University Press, 1982).

15. The results of the survey are presented by Sally Lloyd-Bostock in Donald Harris et al., *Compensation and Support for Illness and Injury* (Oxford: Clarendon Press, 1984), pp. 139–63.

16. Sally Lloyd-Bostock, "The Ordinary Man, and the Pyschology of Attributing Causes and Responsibility," *Modern Law Review* 42 (1979): 167.

17. Ibid., pp. 154–55.

18. Charles Perrow, *Normal Accidents: Living with High-Risk Technologies* (New York: Basic Books, 1984), p. 7.

19. Robert Dingwall, "The Jasmine Beckford Affair," *Modern Law Review* 49 (1986); 492–93 (emphasis in original). Dingwall cites the disaster studies of British sociologist Barry A. Turner; see, for example, "The Organizational and Interorganizational Development of Disasters," *Administrative Science Quarterly* 21 (1976): 378–97.

20. Judith Jarvis Thomson, "Remarks on Causation and Liability," *Philosophy and Public Affairs* 13 (1984): 101–33, reprinted in *Rights, Restitution, and Risk: Essays in Moral Theory* (Cambridge, Mass.: Harvard University Press, 1986), pp. 192–224 (quotations are from the latter edition).

21. 26 Cal.3d 588, 163 Cal. Rptr. 132, 607 P.2d 924, *cert. denied*, 449 U.S. 912 (1980). DES is a fertility drug used widely in the United States between about 1940 and 1970.

22. Thomson, "Remarks on Causation," p. 223.

23. Michael Sandel, *Liberalism and the Limits of Justice* (Cambridge: Cambridge University Press, 1982), pp. 15–65. Robert Goodin, in a more polemical vein, criticizes the "narcissistic fixation on 'moral character'" along with the preference for "bizarre hypotheticals" found in recent moral philosophy, particularly that published by *Philosophy and Public Affairs* (*Political Theory*, pp. 3–18).

24. In addition to Sandel, see Brian Barry, *The Liberal Theory of Justice* (Oxford: Clarendon Press, 1973), and William Leon McBride, "Social Theory *Sub Specie Aeternitatis*: A New Perspective," *Yale Law Journal* 81 (1972): 980–1003.

25. A somewhat different approach is found in Jules Coleman and Charles Silver, "Justice in Settlements," *Social Philosophy and Policy* 4 (1986): 102–44. Taking the existing civil litigation process as a paradigm of justice, these authors examine arguments for fostering settlements by modifying procedural standards. While they assign the "burden of justification" to advocates of settlement, all they purport to do is "raise doubts"

that settlement is *always* preferable to litigation. The modesty of the goals and results, as well as the assignment of vague burdens of proof to advocates of institutional change, illustrates a common pattern in this literature.

26. H. L. A. Hart and Tony Honoré, *Causation in the Law*, 2nd ed. (1959; Oxford: Oxford University Press, 1985).

27. The phrase is from Ludwig Wittgenstein's *Philosophical Investigations*, 2nd ed. (Oxford: Basil Blackwell, 1958), §38; this book supported the use of ordinary language for dissolving philosophical puzzles.

28. This is Richard A. Epstein's understanding in "A Theory of Strict Liability," *Journal of Legal Studies* 2 (1973): 151.

29. The model is J. L. Austin's essay, "A Plea for Excuses," reprinted in *Philosophical Papers* (Oxford: Clarendon Press, 1961), pp. 123–52. Austin's technique has been irreverently referred to as the "57 Varieties" way of doing philosophy. For a stinging critique of the wider language analysis program, see Ernest Gellner, *Words and Things* (London: Penguin Books, 1968).

30. Michael Martin, *The Legal Philosophy of H. L. A. Hart: A Critical Appraisal* (Philadelphia: Temple University Press, 1987), p. 276. See also the gentle but telling assessment by William Twining, "Academic Law and Legal Philosophy: The Significance of Herbart Hart," *Law Quarterly Review* 95 (1979): 557–80. Before noting the baleful effect of Oxford analytic philosophy on the compensation issue, Twining points out that "if law is to be viewed as a social phenomenon, it would seem to be worthwhile at least to explore the relationship between legal theory and social theory"(pp. 566–67).

31. Martin, *The Legal Philosophy of H. L. A. Hart*, p. 277.

32. "Do Lawyers' References to Common Sense Have Anything to Do with What Ordinary People Think?" *British Journal of Social Psychology* 20 (1981): 162.

33. Hart and Honoré, *Causation*, pp. lxxx–lxxxi (emphasis in original).

34. This statement applies at least to English theory beginning with Jevons. See Mark Blaug, *Economic Theory in Retrospect*, 4th ed. (Cambridge: Cambridge University Press, 1985), p. 301. For speculations on the value theories of Menger and Walras, see Wolfgang Grassl, "Markets and Morality: Austrian Perspectives on the Economic Approach to Human Behaviour," in Wolfgang Grassl and Barry Smith, eds., *Austrian Economics: Historical and Philosophical Background* (New York: New York University Press, 1986), pp. 139–81.

35. For a general discussion see Morton G. White, *Social Thought in America: The Revolt Against Formalism* (Boston: Beacon Press, 1957).

36. A similar interpretation of this theoretical shift can be found in Sidney S.

Alexander, "Human Values and Economists' Values," in Sidney Hook, ed., *Human Values and Economic Policy* (New York: New York University Press, 1967), pp. 101–16.

37. Mill prefaces this remark with the supposition that "a person possesses any tolerable amount of common sense and experience" (*On Liberty* [New York: Norton, 1975], p. 64).

38. See Sen's conclusion: "If interpersonal comparisons of utility are dropped, but nevertheless utility is regarded as the only thing of intrinsic value, then Pareto optimality would be the natural surviving criterion, since it carries the utilitarian logic as far forward as possible without actually making any interpersonal comparisons of utility" (*On Ethics and Economics* [Oxford: Basil Blackwell, 1987], p. 38).

39. A critical account of emotivism appears in MacIntyre, *After Virtue*, pp. 22–34.

40. Sen remarks, "I guess it is a reflection of the way ethics tends to be viewed by economists that statements suspected of being 'meaningless' or 'nonsensical' are promptly taken to be 'ethical.' The peculiarly narrow view of 'meaning' championed by logical positivists . . . caused total chaos in welfare economics" (*On Ethics and Economics*, p. 31). The current distinction between positive and normative economics can be traced back to this same epistemology.

41. The term *consumer sovereignty* appears to date from this period, although it was originally used in a less global fashion. See G. Peter Penz, *Consumer Sovereignty and Human Interests* (Cambridge: Cambridge University Press, 1986), p. 12.

42. Sandel has accurately identified this self as the modern descendant of Kant's transcendental ego (*Liberalism*, pp. 7–11).

43. These points and others have been raised by numerous economists and philosophers; for a summary and citations, see Sen, *On Ethics and Economics*, pp. 40–55, 80–88.

44. The issues in this paragraph are dealt with comprehensively in Penz, *Consumer Sovereignty*.

45. For a critique see E. J. Mishan, "The Folklore of the Market: An Inquiry into the Economic Doctrines of the Chicago School," reprinted in Mishan, *Economic Efficiency and Social Welfare* (London: Allen & Unwin, 1981), pp. 219–55. For an historical overview see Melvin W. Reder, "Chicago Economics: Permanence and Change," *Journal of Economic Literature* 20 (1982): 1–38.

46. Richard A. Posner, *The Economics of Justice* (Cambridge, Mass.: Harvard University Press, 1981), p. 75.

47. Richard A. Posner, *Economic Analysis of Law*, 2nd ed. (Boston: Little, Brown, 1977), p. 10 (emphasis in original). Curiously, this forthright de-

finition has disappeared from the third edition (1986), although one can gather the pieces of it from pp. 9, 11–15.

48. George P. Fletcher, "Fairness and Utility in Tort Theory," *Harvard Law Review* 85 (1972): 537–73.

49. Milton Friedman, "The Methodology of Positive Economics," in Friedman, *Essays in Positive Economics* (Chicago: University of Chicago Press, 1953), pp. 3–43. See William M. Landes and Richard A. Posner, *The Economic Structure of Tort Law* (Cambridge, Mass.: Harvard University Press, 1987), pp. 19–24. Posner's verificationist theory was discussed in Chapter 4.

50. Landes and Posner have systematized these arguments. For another summary see Steven Shavell, *Economic Analysis of Accident Law* (Cambridge, Mass.: Harvard University Press, 1987).

51. On the differences between revealed preferences and reflective attitudes on insurance, see Howard Kunreuther, *Disaster Insurance Protection: Public Policy Lessons* (New York: John Wiley & Sons, 1978).

52. A general argument along these lines is found in Nicholas Abercrombie, Stephen Hill, and Bryan S. Turner, *Sovereign Individuals of Capitalism* (London: Allen & Unwin, 1986).

53. An exception is Jules Coleman's work, discussed in this chapter.

54. Goodin remarks that the "the philosophical world is in the midst of a transition, away 'from a once widely accepted old faith that some form of utilitarianism . . . *must* capture the essence of political morality,' and toward a new deontological faith trading heavily on notions of absolute right and wrong" (*Political Theory*, p. 15). A leading example of this trend is Charles Fried's work, often cited by moral philosophers writing on legal topics; see, for example, *Right and Wrong* (Cambridge, Mass.: Harvard University Press, 1978).

55. Epstein, "A Theory of Strict Liability," discussed in this chapter with additional references.

56. See Fletcher, "Fairness and Utility," and Ernest J. Weinrib, "Toward a Moral Theory of Negligence Law," *Law and Philosophy* 2 (1983): 37–62. On the general theory of liberalism see Ian Shapiro, *The Evolution of Rights in Liberal Theory* (Cambridge: Cambridge University Press, 1986).

57. Rawls's *A Theory of Justice* (Cambridge, Mass.: Belknap Press, 1971) has been the subject of enormous commentary and application; see, for example, Norman Daniels, ed., *Reading Rawls* (New York: Basic Books, 1976).

58. P. S. Atiyah and Peter Cane, *Accidents, Compensation and the Law*, 4th ed. (London: Weidenfeld & Nicolson, 1987), p. 413. Jules Coleman has also raised this point; "The Morality of Strict Tort Liability," *William and Mary Law Review* 18 (1976): 259–86.

59. Atiyah and Cane, *Accidents*, p. 413.
60. Fowler V. Harper, Fleming James, Jr., and Oscar S. Gray, *The Law of Torts*, 2nd ed. (Boston: Little, Brown, 1986), vol. 3, p. 132 (§13.2).
61. See the study by the U.S. Attorney General's Tort Policy Working Group, "Report on the Causes, Extent and Policy Implications of the Current Crisis in Insurance Availability and Affordability" (Washington, D.C.: Government Printing Office, February 1986). This report is discussed in detail in Chapter 7.
62. "Report on the Current Crisis," p. 2. The reader who made this the only source of information about a tort crisis would find no mention of uncompensated personal injury victims. As far as the Tort Policy Working Group is concerned, the "crisis" is the escalating costs to business of insurance premiums. The same limitation affects the analyses in Robert E. Litan and Clifford Winston, eds., *Liability: Perspectives and Policy* (Washington, D.C.: Brookings Institution, 1988).
63. George L. Priest, "The Invention of Enterprise Liability: A Critical History of the Intellectual Foundations of Modern Tort Law," *Journal of Legal Studies* 14 (1985): 525. The reference is to Beshada v. Johns-Manville Prods. Corp., 90 N.J. 191, 447 A.2d 539 (1982).
64. It comes as no surprise that Richard Posner has applied the universal solvent of economic logic to the phenomena of moral intuition; "The Concept of Corrective Justice in Recent Theories of Tort Law," *Journal of Legal Studies* 10 (1981): 187–206.
65. Corresponding to these two extremes are Robert Nozick, *Anarchy, State, and Utopia* (New York: Basic Books, 1974), and Sandel, *Liberalism*. Rawls's work tends toward more progressive forms of liberalism. Another trend grows out of environmental movements, positing "natural" rights that belong to humans as well as to animals and inanimate objects. See, for example, Robin Attfield, *The Ethics of Environmental Concern* (New York: Columbia University Press, 1983); Tom Regan, ed., *Earthbound: New Introductory Essays in Environmental Ethics* (New York: Random House, 1984); and Christopher D. Stone, *Earth and Other Ethics: The Case for Moral Pluralism* (New York: Harper & Row, 1987).
66. Williams, *Ethics and the Limits of Philosophy*.
67. For references see notes 28, 48, and 56. Izhak England has written a highly critical assessment from an instrumentalist point of view: "The System Builders: A Critical Appraisal of Modern American Tort Theory," *Journal of Legal Studies* 9 (1980): 27–69. Jules Coleman provides a philosophical critique in "Moral Theories of Torts: Their Scope and Limits," *Law and Philosophy* 1 (1982): 371–90, and 2 (1983): 5–36.
68. "Nuisance Law: Corrective Justice and Its Utilitarian Constraints," *Journal of Legal Studies* 8 (1979): 49–102.
69. Fletcher, "Fairness and Utility," p. 540, n. 14.

70. Coleman, "Moral Theories of Torts," vol. 2, p. 35.
71. Ibid., pp. 6–8.
72. See 1129a1–1137a31.
73. *Politics*, 1253a1–1254.
74. England, "The System Builders," p. 68.
75. Goodin, *Political Theory*, p. 103.
76. Ibid., pp. 103–4, 106–7. See also Goodin's later book, *Protecting the Vulnerable: A Reanalysis of Our Social Responsibilties* (Chicago: University of Chicago Press, 1985).
77. Perrow, *Normal Accidents*, pp. 62–100.
78. An ambitious effort to relate these cultural factors to the growing pluralism of "secularized" society is found in Mary Douglas and Aaron Wildavsky, *Risk and Culture: An Essay on the Selection of Technological and Environmental Dangers* (Berkeley and Los Angeles: University of California Press, 1982).
79. See Jane Stapleton, *Disease and the Compensation Debate* (Oxford: Clarendon Press, 1986).
80. Sandel, *Liberalism*, p. 183.

Chapter 6

1. Aaron D. Twerski, "From Risk-Utility to Consumer Expectations: Enhancing the Role of Judicial Screening in Product Liability Litigation," *Hofstra Law Review* 11 (1983): 935.
2. An eloquent statement of this position can be found in Alexander M. Bickel, *The Least Dangerous Branch* (Indianapolis: Bobbs-Merrill, 1962). As the 1960s turned more confrontational, progressive commentators became more polarized in choosing between judicial and political leadership. For the former position, see Owen M. Fiss, "The Forms of Justice," *Harvard Law Review* 93 (1979): 1–58; for the latter, Stuart A. Scheingold, *The Politics of Rights* (New Haven, Conn.: Yale University Press, 1974).
3. This problem is explored in the American Law Institute's *Preliminary Study of Complex Litigation* (Philadelphia: American Law Institute, 1987). See also the conclusions of the Judicial Administration Working Group on Asbestos Litigation, *Final Report* (Williamsburg, Va.: National Center for State Courts, 1984).
4. A particularly strong statement of this fear appears in David Rosenberg's review of Paul Brodeur's *Outrageous Misconduct*, *Harvard Law Review* 99 (1986): 1693–706.
5. For a historical review see George L. Priest, "The Invention of Enterprise Liability: A Critical History of the Intellectual Foundations of

Modern Tort Law," *Journal of Legal Studies* 14 (1985): 461–527. For reservations on Priest's overall argument, see the discussion in Chapter 1. As stated earlier, there are reasons to expect a reverse trend in the next several years; those reasons are discussed in Chapter 7.

6. For a general summary, see Fowler V. Harper, Fleming James, Jr., and Oscar S. Gray, *The Law of Torts*, 2nd ed. (Boston: Little, Brown, 1986), chap. 28.

7. For a discussion of the duty to warn as an example of this trend, see Desmond T. Barry, Jr., and Edward Charles DeVivo, "The Evolution of Warnings: The Liberal Trend toward Absolute Product Liability," *Forum* 20 (1984): 38–58.

8. In addition to Priest, "The Invention of Enterprise Liability," see G. Edward White, *Tort Law in America: An Intellectual History* (New York: Oxford University Press, 1985).

9. The emergence of a crisis is outlined in Interagency Task Force on Product Liability, *Final Report* (Washington, D.C.: Government Printing Office, 1977), chap. 1.

10. See the history in Allison B. David and Ali Jalilian-Marian, "DTP: Drug Manufacturers' Liability in Vaccine-Related Injuries, *Journal of Legal Medicine* 7 (1986): 203–16. See also V. Kenneth Rohrer, "Liability of Drug Manufacturers under Failure to Warn Notions," *Missouri Law Review* 36 (1976): 570–76; Mary Elizabeth Mann, "Mass Immunization Cases: Drug Manufacturers' Liability for Failure to Warn," *Vanderbilt Law Review* 29 (1976): 235–66.

11. Howard A. Latin, "Problem-Solving Behavior and Theories of Tort Liability," *California Law Review* 73 (1985): 677–746.

12. Even Richard Epstein, a critic of recent product liability trends, sees some basis for a collective social response to vaccine injuries; *Modern Products Liability Law* (Westport, Conn.: Quorum Books, 1980), pp. 110–11.

13. See Marc A. Franklin and Joseph E. Mais, Jr., "Tort Law and Mass Immunization Programs: Lessons from the Polio and Flu Episodes," *California Law Review* 65 (1977): 754–75.

14. See the report of the Subcommittee on Health and the Environment of the House Committee on Energy and Commerce, "Childhood Immunizations," 99th Congress, 2nd Session (Committee Print: 1986).

15. This point is argued very forcefully in two reports from the U.S. Attorney General's Tort Policy Working Group, "Report on the Causes, Extent and Policy Implications of the Current Crisis in Insurance Availability and Affordability" (Washington, D.C.: Government Printing Office, February 1986) and "An Update on the Liability Crisis" (Washington, D.C.: Government Printing Office, March 1987). The latter report supplies a dozen examples of products taken off the market be-

cause of liability fears and costs (pp. 18–20), although unlike vaccines these products are neither essential to public health nor necessarily "worth" the accidents they might occasion.

16. See Arnold W. Reitze, Jr., "Federal Compensation for Vaccination Induced Injury," *Boston College Environmental Affairs Law Review* 13 (1986): 169–214. See also John G. Fleming, "Drug Injury Compensation Plans," *American Journal of Comparative Law* 30 (1982): 297–323.

17. Richard L. Greenstreet, "Estimation of the Probability That Guillain-Barré Syndrome Was Caused by the Swine Flu Vaccine: U.S. Experience (1976–77)," *Medicine, Science and the Law* 24 (1984): 61–67.

18. U.S. Justice Department, Civil Division, Torts Branch, "Swine Flu Statistics as of December 1, 1986."

19. Frederick H. Fern and Wayne Sichel, "Evolving Tort Liability Theories: Are They Taking the Pharmaceutical Industry into an Era of Absolute Liability?" *St. Louis University Law Journal* 29 (1985): 763–85.

20. Barry and DeVivo, "The Evolution of Warnings," pp. 47, 57. The New Jersey case is Beshada v. Johns-Manville Prods. Corp., 90 N.J. 191, 447 A.2d 539 (1982), but its force is now limited by Feldman v. Lederle Laboratories, 97 N.J. 429, 479 A.2d 374 (1984). On the matter of manufacturers' knowledge, however, see Paul Brodeur, *Outrageous Misconduct: The Asbestos Industry on Trial* (New York: Pantheon Books, 1985).

21. In addition to David and Jalilian-Marian, "DTP," see Alan R. Hinman, "The Pertussis Vaccine Controversy," *Public Health Reports* 99 (1984): 255–59.

22. Centers for Disease Control, "Reinstatement of Regular D-T-P Vaccine Schedule," *Morbidity and Mortality Weekly Report* 34 (1985): 231–32.

23. National Childhood Vaccine Injury Act of 1986, Pub. L. No. 99-660, Title III; 100 Stat. 3755; 42 U.S.C. §300aa. Also covered are measles, mumps, rubella, and polio.

24. §2122 (c).

25. The early case was Reyes v. Wyeth Laboratories, 498 F.2d 1264 (5th Cir. 1974). A different outcome was reached, for example, in Cunningham v. Pfizer & Co., 532 P.2d 1377 (Okla. 1974).

26. See for example Conafay v. Wyeth Laboratories, [1984–85 Transfer Binder] Prod. Liab. Rep. (CCH) ¶10,487 (D.D.C. 1985), remanded on other grounds, 841 F.2d 417 (D.C.Cir. 1988).

27. David and Jalilian-Marian, "DTP," pp. 216–24.

28. Reitze, "Federal Compensation," pp. 210–11.

29. June Osborn, "Relentless Questions on a Vaccine for AIDS," *New York Times*, March 31, 1987, p. 17. See also her remarks in "The AIDS Epidemic: Discovery of a New Disease," in Harlon L. Dalton et al., eds., *AIDS and the Law* (New Haven, Conn.: Yale University Press, 1987), pp. 25–27.

30. David Rosenberg, "The Causal Connection in Mass Exposure Cases: A 'Public Law' Vision of the Tort System," *Harvard Law Review* 97 (1984): 905–6.
31. Ibid., p. 866. Arguments for a "proportional risk" standard of liability appear to have originated with Samuel D. Estep, "Radiation Injuries and Statistics: The Need for a New Approach to Injury Litigation," *Michigan Law Review* 59 (1960): 259–304.
32. Rosenberg, "The Causal Connection," pp. 908–16.
33. Ibid., pp. 861–62.
34. See Stephen D. Sugarman, "Doing Away with Tort Law," *California Law Review* 73 (1985): 555–664.
35. Rosenberg, "The Causal Connection," p. 862, n. 51.
36. Ibid. See Peter Huber, "Safety and the Second Best: The Hazards of Public Risk Management in the Courts," *Columbia Law Review* 85 (1985): 277–337.
37. Rosenberg, "The Causal Connection," p. 852.
38. Ibid., p. 906.
39. See the seminal article by Abram Chayes, "The Role of the Judge in Public Law Litigation," *Harvard Law Review* 89 (1976): 1281–316.
40. "Tort Law Public Law in Disguise," *Texas Law Review* 38 (1959): 1.
41. Ibid., pp. 3, 269.
42. Rosenberg, "The Causal Connection," p. 861.
43. Ibid., pp. 885–87.
44. James A. Henderson, Jr., "Why Creative Judging Won't Save the Products Liability System," *Hofstra Law Review* 11 (1983): 845–60.
45. Rosenberg, "The Causal Connection," p. 927.
46. Ibid., p. 926.
47. Ibid., p. 928.
48. For an overview of asbestos litigation, see Deborah R. Hensler, William L. F. Felstiner, Molly Selvin, and Patricia A. Ebener, *Asbestos in the Courts: The Challenge of Mass Toxic Torts* (Santa Monica, Cal.: Rand Corporation, 1985).
49. This is Irving Selikoff's projection, in *Disability Compensation for Asbestos-Associated Disease in the United States* (New York: Mt. Sinai School of Medicine of the City University of New York, 1982), p. 4. See also Barry I. Castleman, *Asbestos: Medical and Legal Aspects* (New York: Harcourt Brace Jovanovich, 1984).
50. See Nicholas Ashford, "The Magnitude of the Occupational Health Problem," in Subcommittee on Labor of the Senate Committee on Labor and Public Welfare, House Committee on Education and Labor, "Proceedings of the Interdepartmental Workers' Compensation Task Force Conference on Occupational Diseases and Workers' Compensa-

tion," 94th Congress, 2nd Session (Joint Committee Print, 1976), p. 295. See also sources cited in "Note—Compensating Victims of Occupational Disease," *Harvard Law Review* 93 (1980): 916–37.

51. Hensler et al., *Asbestos in the Courts*, p. xxvii.

52. "Year End Report on the 1986 Asbestos Litigation in Philadelphia County," reprinted in *Asbestos Litigation Reporter*, March 6, 1987, pp. 14, 299–302.

53. The figure 50,000 comes from *Asbestos Litigation Reporter*, June 5, 1987, p. 15,029. The average number of defendants is based on claims sampled by Hensler et al., *Asbestos in the Courts*, p. 15.

54. James S. Kakalik, Patricia A. Ebener, William L. F. Felstiner, and Michael G. Shanley, *Costs of Asbestos Litigation* (Santa Monica, Cal.: Rand Corporation, 1983), p. 40. Harry Wellington has observed that "if this trend were to continue it is virtually certain there will *not* be enough defense money to compensate for the victims of asbestos diseases, nor enough insurance to maintain the survival of many asbestos defendants" ("Asbestos: The Private Management of a Public Problem," *Cleveland State Law Review* 33 [1984–85]: 378).

55. Hensler et al., *Asbestos in the Courts*, pp. 36–37.

56. Ibid., p. 67.

57. Kakalik found that asbestos claims reaching the point of trial yielded 3.76 times the average settlement prior to trial (*Costs of Asbestos Litigation*, p. 20).

58. Hensler et al., *Asbestos in the Courts*, pp. 55–57.

59. This dynamic is fully documented for the Agent Orange litigation by Peter H. Schuck, *Agent Orange on Trial: Mass Toxic Disasters in the Courts* (Cambridge, Mass.: Belknap Press, 1986).

60. Hensler et al., *Asbestos in the Courts*, pp. 16–17.

61. Ibid., p. 54.

62. Ibid., p. 65. The jury had awarded damages totaling $7.9 million for the first four plaintiffs. See the follow-up study on this case by Molly Selvin and Larry Picus, *The Debate over Jury Performance: Observations from a Recent Asbestos Case* (Santa Monica, Cal.: Rand Corporation, 1987).

63. Hensler et al., *Asbestos in the Courts*, p. 66. For a discussion of the Ohio Asbestos Litigation Case Management Plan, see Francis E. McGovern, "Toward a Functional Approach for Managing Complex Litigation," *University of Chicago Law Review* 53 (1986): 478–91. For additional data on asbestos awards see James S. Kakalik, Patricia A. Ebener, William L. F. Felstiner, G. W. Haggstrom, and Michael G. Shanley, *Variations in Asbestos Litigation Compensation and Expenses* (Santa Monica, Cal.: Rand Corporation, 1984).

64. See "Developments in the Law—Class Actions," *Harvard Law Review*

89 (1976): 1321–644; and Stephen C. Yeazell, "Group Litigation and Social Context: Toward a History of the Class Action," *Columbia Law Review* 77 (1977): 866–96.

65. 39 F.R.D. 69, 103 (1966); for commentary see Charles Alan Wright, Arthur R. Miller, and Mary Kay Kane, *Federal Practice and Procedure*, vol. 7B (St. Paul, Minn.: West Publishing, 1986), §1783; and James Wm. Moore and John E. Kennedy, *Moore's Federal Practice*, 2d ed. (New York: Matthew Bender, 1987), vol. 3B, ¶23.02 [2.-18]. For analysis and cases see Note, "Class Certification in Mass Accident Cases Under Rule 23(b)(1)," *Harvard Law Review* 96 (1983): 1143–61; Larry S. Bush, "My Brother's Keeper—Some Observations on Federal Rule 23 and Mass Tort Class Actions in the United States," *Civil Justice Quarterly* 5 (1986): 109–22, 201–17; and Irving R. M. Panzer and Thomas Earl Patton, "Utilizing the Class Action Device in Mass Tort Litigation," *Tort and Insurance Law Journal* 21 (1986): 560–72.

66. See In re Temple, 851 F.2d 1269 (11th Cir. 1988), which denied class-action status for asbestos plaintiffs opposing Raymark Industries. For other cases see In re School Asbestos Product Liability Litigation, 606 F.Supp. 713 (J.P.M.D.L. 1985) [property damage claims brought by school districts]; In re Rely Tampon Products Liability Litigation, 533 F.Supp. 1346 (J.P.M.D.L. 1982) [toxic shock cases]; McElhaney v. Eli Lilly & Co., 93 F.R.D. 875 (D.S.D. 1982) [DES cases]; In re No. Dist. of Cal. Dalkon Shield IUD Products Liability Litigation, 693 F.2d 847 (9th Cir. 1982), *cert. denied sub nom.* A. H. Robins Co. v. Abed, 459 U.S. 1171 (1983); In re Bendectin Products Liability Litigation, 749 F.2d 300 (6th Cir. 1984).

67. For a comprehensive survey see the American Law Institute's *Preliminary Study of Complex Litigation*. Discussions of specific points can be found in Roger H. Transgrud, "Joinder Alternatives in Mass Tort Litigation," *Cornell Law Review* 70 (1985): 779–849; Robert E. Vagley and Mary R. Blanton, "Aggregation of Claims: Liability for Certain Illness with Long Latency Periods Before Manifestation," *Forum* 16 (1982): 636–57; Douglas J. Gunn, "The Offensive Use of Collateral Estoppel in Mass Tort Cases," *Mississippi Law Journal* 52 (1982): 765–99; and F. Scott Baldwin, "Asbestos Litigation and Collateral Estoppel," *Forum* 17 (1982): 772–83. For cases refusing judicial notice of asbestos hazards, see Hardy v. Johns-Manville, 681 F.2d 334 (5th Cir. 1982); In re Related Asbestos Cases, 543 F.Supp. 1152 (N.D. Cal. 1982).

68. Francis McGovern, "Management of Multiparty Toxic Tort Litigation: Case Law and Trends Affecting Case Management," *Forum* 19 (1983): 5.

69. See David G. Owen, "Rethinking the Policies of Strict Products Liability," *Vanderbilt Law Review* 33 (1980): 681–715.

70. Federal pressure is also being brought to bear on this doctrine. See the March 1986 report by the Attorney General's Tort Policy Working Group, pp. 64–65.

71. 26 Cal. 3d 588, 163 Cal. Rptr. 132, 607 P.2d 924, *cert. denied*, 449 U.S. 912 (1980). See Note, "Market Share Liability: An Answer to the DES Causation Problem," *Harvard Law Review* 94 (1981): 668–80, and Glen O. Robinson, "Multiple Causation in Tort Law: Reflections on the DES Cases," *Virginia Law Review* 68 (1982): 713–69. In 1988 the California Supreme Court appeared to back away from the Sindell doctrine in two cases involving DES. Brown v. Superior Court, 245 Cal. Rptr. 412, 751 P.2d 470 (1988) and Jolly v. Eli Lilly & Co., 245 Cal. Rptr. 658, 751 P.2d 923 (1988).

72. See, for example, Payton v. Abbott Laboratories, 512 F. Supp. 1031 (D.Mass. 1981); Ryan v. Eli Lilly & Co., 514 F. Supp. 1004 (D.S.C. 1981); and Zafft v. Eli Lilly & Co., 676 S.W.2d 241 (Mo. 1984). Victor E. Schwartz and Liberty Mahshigian, "Failure to Identify the Defendant in Tort Law: Towards a Legislative Solution," *California Law Review* 73 (1985): 941–75.

73. Wellington, "Asbestos," p. 388. See also Leland G. Smith, "Asbestos Claims Facility—An Alternative to Litigation," *Duquesne Law Review* 24 (1986): 833–66. For a discussion of private alternatives to litigation, see Robert A. Baruch Bush, "Dispute Resolution Alternatives and the Goals of Civil Justice," *Wisconsin Law Review* (1984): 893–1034. In opposition see Owen M. Fiss, "Against Settlement," *Yale Law Journal* 93 (1980): 1073–90. An extended discussion appears in Richard L. Abel, "The Contradictions of Informal Justice," in Abel, ed., *The Politics of Informal Justice* (New York: Academic Press, 1982), pp. 267–320. A recent study from Great Britain is, remarkably, the first comprehensive empirical investigation of dispute settlements in personal injury cases: Hazel Genn, *Hard Bargaining: Out of Court Settlement in Personal Injury Actions* (Oxford: Clarendon Press, 1987).

74. The figure of 7,000 settlements was reported in *Asbestos Litigation Reporter*, April 3, 1987, p. 14,579, which also noted that new claims were accumulating at the rate of 2,000 per month. The cost figures are from *Asbestos Litigation Reporter*, January 16, 1987, p. 13,960. For settlement guidelines see Asbestos Claims Facility, "Alternative Dispute Resolution Procedures," reprinted in *Asbestos Litigation Reporter*, March 12, 1987, pp. 14,331–36. The termination announcement, released by ACF on May 24, 1988, was reprinted in a special bulletin by *Asbestos Litigation Reporter*, May 26, 1988.

75. For a general discussion see Note, "Adjudicating Asbestos Insurance Liability: Alternatives to Contract Analysis," *Harvard Law Review* 97

(1984): 739–58. Although many carriers have reached settlements with asbestos defendants, the legal battle continues. The largest such case—still in progress during 1988—has gone against the insurers on most major points of contention. In re Asbestos Insurance Coverage Cases, San Francisco Super. Ct., Dept. 9, Judicial Council Coordination Proceedings No. 1072. The central decision was reprinted in *Asbestos Litigation Reporter*, June 1, 1987, p. 14,960. For informal comments on the course of the litigation, see Judge Ira Brown, "Judging the Mega-Case," *The Brief* 17 (Spring 1988): 12–17, 32–39. For broader insurance implications, see the reprinted papers from a 1988 conference of international reinsurers: John Butler et al., *International Reinsurance: Asbestos Claims* (Brentford, Eng.: Kluwer Publishing, 1988).

76. Hensler et al., *Asbestos in the Courts*, p. 119.
77. Letter to Dean Wellington from Paul W. Whelen on behalf of plaintiffs, December 12, 1986, reprinted in *Asbestos Litigation Reporter*, January 2, 1987, p. 13,927.
78. The antitrust suit was Grimes v. Asbestos Claims Facility, No. 87-813 (W.D. Pa., filed April 15, 1987). Later developments in that case and in lawsuits against ACF are documented in 1988 issues of *Asbestos Litigation Reporter*.
79. Hensler et al., *Asbestos in the Courts*, p. 119.
80. The reorganization plan was approved in In re Johns-Manville Corp. 68 B.R. 618 (Bankr.S.D.N.Y. 1986) and was later affirmed by the District Court, 78 B.R. 407 (S.D.N.Y. 1987). The entire litigation is summarized in the Court of Appeals decision, Kane v. Johns-Manville Corp., 843 F.2d 636 (2nd Cir. 1988). Later in 1988 the U.S. Supreme Court decided not to hear an appeal from a related case, 109 S.Ct. 176. For early background see Note, "The Manville Bankruptcy: Treating Mass Tort Claims in Chapter 11 Proceedings," *Harvard Law Review* 96 (1983): 1121–42. Although the court-approved plan did permit future litigation, it specifically ruled out all payments for punitive damages.
81. 843 F.2d at 640, 650.
82. 843 F.2d at 645.
83. Hensler et al., *Asbestos in the Courts*, p. 22.
84. Ibid., p. 23.
85. Rosenberg, review of *Outrageous Misconduct*, p. 1706.
86. See for example Robert F. Peckham, "A Judicial Response to the Cost of Litigation: Case Management, Two-Stage Discovery Planning and Alternative Dispute Resolution," *Rutgers Law Review* 37 (1985): 253–77. For a skeptical approach see Judith Resnick, "Managerial Judges," *Harvard Law Review* 96 (1982): 374–448. For a general overview see the symposium introduced by E. Donald Elliott, "Managerial Judging and

the Evolution of Procedure," *University of Chicago Law Review* 53 (1986): 306–36.

87. For an engrossing chronicle of the Agent Orange litigation through 1985, see Schuck, *Agent Orange on Trial.*

88. The court order approving the settlement appears in In re Agent Orange Product Liability Litigation, 597 F.Supp. 740 (E.D.N.Y. 1984). Decisions on several ancillary matters, including the distribution plan, begin at 611 F.Supp. 1221 (E.D.N.Y. 1985).

89. 818 F.2d 145 (2d Cir. 1987), *cert. denied,* 108 S.Ct. 695, 2898 (1988).

90. See Schuck, *Agent Orange on Trial,* especially chap. 8.

91. In addition to Schuck, see an account openly sympathetic to the veterans' position, Carol Van Strum, *A Bitter Fog: Herbicides and Human Rights* (San Francisco: Sierra Club Books, 1983). In 1988 a revised Air Force study seemed less certain that dioxin could be exonerated; "New Doubts Raised on Agent Orange," *New York Times,* March 23, 1988, p. 11.

92. For the Court of Appeals' treatment of these issues see 818 F.2d 145, 201, 204, and 210.

93. Schuck, *Agent Orange on Trial,* chap. 2. Judge Weinstein also spoke to these concerns, 597 F.Supp. 740, 747.

94. The procedural history of the entire case is summarized by the Court of Appeals, 818 F.2d 145, 152–61.

95. For a theoretical statement of the position that factual uncertainty in a case fuels litigation as opposed to settlement, see George L. Priest and Benjamin Klein, "The Selection of Disputes for Litigation," *Journal of Legal Studies* 13 (1984): 1–55.

96. Schuck, *Agent Orange on Trial,* chap. 8.

97. Ibid., p. 142.

98. Ibid., p. 160.

99. This is the order appearing at 611 F.Supp. 1396 (E.D.N.Y. 1985).

100. 818 F.2d 145, 171 [citing City of Detroit v. Grinnell Corp, 495 F.2d 448, 455 (2d Cir. 1974)].

101. Schuck, *Agent Orange on Trial,* p. 166 (quoting from *Newsweek*).

102. The critical literature has yet to focus on this general question. A preliminary attempt is Peter H. Schuck, "The Role of Judges in Settling Cases: The Agent Orange Example," *University of Chicago Law Review* 53 (1986): 337–65. Judge Weinstein's observations are clearly set forth in "Preliminary Reflections on the Law's Reactions to Disasters," *Columbia Journal of Environmental Law* 11 (1986): 1–50. See also the symposium, "Mass Tort After Agent Orange," *Brooklyn Law Review* 52 (1986): 329–569.

103. Schuck, *Agent Orange on Trial,* p. 142.

104. Paraphrase of Weinstein quoted in ibid., p. 190.
105. Ibid., chap. 11. For general arguments against the managerial trend in judging see Judith Resnick, "Failing Faith: Adjudicatory Procedure in Decline," *University of Chicago Law Review* 53 (1986): 494–560.
106. 818 F.2d 145, 190.
107. Resnick, "Managerial Judges," p. 426, n. 195.
108. Rosenberg, review of *Outrageous Misconduct*, pp. 1695, 1704–5.
109. See Castleman, *Asbestos*, p. 128.
110. Rosenberg, review of *Outrageous Misconduct*, p. 1695.

Chapter 7

1. Woodrow Wilson, *Congressional Government* (1885), in Arthur S. Link, ed., *The Papers of Woodrow Wilson* (Princeton, N.J.: Princeton University Press, 1968), vol. 4, p. 161.
2. For a comparatively mild statement of the trial lawyers' position, see Larry S. Stewart, "The 'Tort Reform' Hoax," *Trial* 22 (July 1986): 89–96. A former president of the American Trial Lawyers Association, Robert L. Habush, was less restrained: "I am mad at the insurance industry for so deceitfully feeding on public prejudices and misperceptions and inciting the 'mob' to sponsor legislative 'butchery' on the rights of those injured by 'mal-doers'" ("Diary of a Mad President," *Trial* 23 [July 1987]: 5).
3. See the bibliographies published by the American Bar Foundation: Bruce A. Levin and Robert Coyne, eds., *Tort Reform and Related Proposals* (Chicago: American Bar Association, 1979).
4. For an analysis of insurance rate-making procedures as a cause of the 1970s crisis, see Interagency Task Force on Product Liability, *Final Report* (Washington, D.C.: Government Printing Office, 1978), chap. 6. An even more critical analysis is found in Eli P. Bernzweig, *By Accident Not Design: The Case for Comprehensive Injury Reparations* (New York: Praeger, 1980), pp. 102–45. See also Joseph A. Page and Marcy M. Stephens, "The Product Liability Insurance 'Crisis': Causes, Nostrums and Cures," *Capital University Law Review* 13 (1984): 387–404. The insurance industry rebuttal appears in various publications issued by the National Association of American Insurers, the Alliance of American Insurers, the Insurance Information Institute, and similar groups. See also the journal *Business Insurance*. For a recent survey see Scott E. Harrington, "Prices and Profits in the Insurance Market," in Robert E. Litan and Clifford Winston, eds., *Liability: Perspectives and Policy* (Washington, D.C.: Brookings Institution, 1988), pp. 42–100.

5. This campaign has been endorsed by former Attorney General Meese's Tort Policy Working Group in two documents: "Report on the Causes, Extent, and Policy Implications of the Current Crisis in Insurance Availability and Affordability" (Washington, D.C: Government Printing Office, February 1986), and "An Update on the Liability Crisis" (Washington, D.C.: Government Printing Office, March 1987). The Working Group chairman, Richard K. Willard, has discussed the group's philosophy in "Wheel of Fortune: Stopping Outrageous and Arbitrary Liability Verdicts," *Policy Review* 36 (Spring 1986): 40–43.

6. For overstatements see Desmond T. Barry, Jr. and Edward Charles De-Vivo, "The Evolution of Warnings: The Liberal Trend toward Absolute Product Liability," *Forum* 20 (1984): 38–58; and George L. Priest, "The Invention of Enterprise Liability: A Critical History of the Intellectual Foundations of Modern Tort Law," *Journal of Legal Studies* 14 (1985): 461–527. An appropriate corrective to these interpretations may be found in various discussions of current case law; see, for example, "Manufacturer Not Insurer or Obligated to Produce Perfect Products," in *American Law of Products Liability 3d*, ed. Russell J. Davis et al. (Rochester, N.Y.: Lawyers Cooperative Publishing Co., 1987), §10:19.

7. Guido Calabresi argues that "the reasons for the statutorification of American law are powerful, deeply grounded, and for the foreseeable future unlikely to change" (*A Common Law for the Age of Statutes* [Cambridge, Mass.: Harvard University Press, 1982], p. 79). See also Grant Gilmore, *The Ages of American Law* (New Haven, Conn.: Yale University Press, 1977), pp. 95–97.

8. Product Liability Reform Act, Senate Bill 2760, 99th Congress, 2nd Session (1986).

9. For a general overview see Sylvia Law and Steven Polan, *Pain and Profit: The Politics of Malpractice* (New York: Harper & Row, 1978), and Eli P. Bernzweig, "Some Comparisons Between the Medical Malpractice and Products Liability Problems," in Interagency Task Force on Product Liability, *Selected Papers* (Washington, D.C.: Government Printing Office, 1977), pp. 418–45. For specific state legislation see Michael D. McCafferty and Steven M. Meyer, *Medical Malpractice: Bases of Liability* (Colorado Springs: Shepard's/McGraw-Hill, 1985), chap. 5.

10. See Herman M. Somers and Anne Somers, *Workmen's Compensation: Prevention, Insurance and Rehabilitation of Occupational Disability* (New York: John Wiley & Sons, 1954), and Edward D. Berkowitz, *Disabled Policy: America's Programs for the Handicapped* (Cambridge: Cambridge University Press, 1987), pp. 15–40.

11. See Robert E. Keeton, Jr., Jeffrey O'Connell, and John H. McCord, eds., *Crisis in Car Insurance* (Urbana: University of Illinois Press, 1968). For a recent survey see Josephine Y. King, *No Fault Automobile*

Accident Law (New York: Wiley Law Publications, 1987). Details on current legislation can be found in Barbara H. Kriss, *No-Fault and Uninsured Motorist Automobile Insurance* (New York: Matthew Bender, 1988 and supplements).

12. Aaron D. Twerski also notes the differences between earlier legislative strategies and the recent approaches to product liability; "Rebuilding the Citadel: The Legislative Assault on the Common Law," *Trial* 15 (November 1979): 55. See also James A. Henderson, Jr., "Products Liability: The Gathering Momentum Toward Statutory Reform," *Corporation Law Review* 1 (1978): 41–47.

13. U.S. Secretary's Commission on Medical Malpractice, *Medical Malpractice* (Washington, D.C.: Government Printing Office, 1973), pp. 25, 99–102.

14. Bernzweig, *By Accident*, p. 136.

15. Ibid., p. 134.

16. See McCafferty and Meyer, *Medical Malpractice*, chaps. 5 and 7. For an earlier survey see Kandy G. Webb, "Recent Medical Malpractice Legislation: A First Checkup," *Tulane Law Review* 50 (1976): 655–91.

17. The events are recounted in *Congressional Quarterly Almanac* 42 (1986): 287–89.

18. See testimony from insurance industry representatives in "The Liability Insurance Crisis," Hearings Before the Subcommittee on Investigations and Oversight of the House Committee on Public Works and Transportation, 99th Congress, 2nd Session (1986); "Availability and Cost of Liability Insurance," Hearing Before the Senate Committee on Commerce, Science and Transportation, 99th Congress, 2nd Session (1986).

19. For statutory documents and comprehensive citations see *American Law of Products Liability 3d*, especially §1:2. A recent survey of state legislation can be found in the 1987 "Update" of the Attorney General's Tort Policy Working Group, chaps. 4, 5. For earlier summaries see Richard K. Herrmann, "An Overview of State Statutory Product Liability Law," *Trial Lawyers' Guide* 27 (1983): 1–52; and Aaron Twerski, "National Product Liability Legislation: In Search for the Best of All Possible Worlds," *Idaho Law Review* 18 (1982): 411–508.

20. Patricia M. Danzon, *Medical Malpractice: Theory, Evidence, and Public Policy* (Cambridge, Mass.: Harvard University Press, 1985), chap. 4. According to Danzon, even the decline in 1975 was not necessarily caused by state tort reforms (p. 79). For two recent summaries by Patricia M. Danzon, see *New Evidence on the Frequence and Severity of Medical Malpractice Claims* (Santa Monica, Cal.: Rand Corporation, 1986), and "Medical Malpractice Liability" in Litan and Winston, eds., *Liability*, pp. 101–27.

21. Danzon, *Medical Malpractice*, chap. 2. Danzon has also estimated that, in 1974, only 1 out of 25 malpractice plaintiffs actually received compensation (p. 25).
22. Ibid., p. 82.
23. See 1987 "Update" of the Attorney General's Tort Policy Working Group, chap. 3.
24. See, for example, Victor E. Schwartz and Barbara H. Bares, "Federal Reform of Product Liability Law: A Solution That Will Work," *Capital University Law Review* 13 (1984): 351–86. Perhaps the tort statutes with the longest history are automobile "guest statutes" adopted by many states in the 1920s and 1930s. These laws reduced the negligence liability of drivers for injuries to passengers, in response to the patchwork tendency of courts to select standards of care from arcane common-law rules that distinguish among social guests, business "invitees," and others. See Fowler V. Harper, Fleming James, Jr., and Oscar S. Gray, *The Law of Torts*, 2nd ed. (Boston: Little, Brown, 1986), vol. 3, pp. 512–39 (§16.15). The authors note that "disagreement and confusion have marked judicial attempts to define these [statutes], even within a single jurisdiction" (p. 516). Among other pretenses for judicial independence in interpreting guest statutes, courts have invoked the principle of "strict construction of statutes in derogation of the common law" (pp. 536–37). Federal judge Richard Neely has argued that the federal courts—preferably with minimal statutory guidance from Congress—should impose a uniform regime for accident litigation. *The Product Liability Mess: How Business Can Be Rescued from State Court Politics* (New York: Free Press, 1988).
25. See the extensive analysis of open-ended judicial issues in John J. Kircher, "Federal Product Legislation and Toxic Torts: The Defense Perspective," *Villanova Law Review* 28 (1983): 1116–55.
26. Calabresi shows how the U.S. Supreme Court, professing to follow traditional negligence doctrines, gradually introduced a strict liability standard in construing the Federal Employers' Liability Act (*A Common Law*, pp. 205–9). See also Melvin L. Griffith, "The Vindication of a National Public Policy Under the Federal Employers' Liability Act," *Law and Contemporary Problems* 18 (1953): 160–87. As a further example of judicial activism applied to statutes, Calabresi relates how the Wisconsin Supreme Court "blackmailed" the legislature into changing terms in that state's comparative negligence statute (pp. 35–40).
27. See the remarks of Senator Gorton on product liability legislation that prescribes specific liability doctrines: "I continue to believe that S.100, if enacted, would have no immediate impact on uniformity, but rather would encourage additional litigation over the meaning of its

terms. . . . Because the bill would fail to provide compensation for persons currently eligible under the law of many States, result-oriented
courts would merely find inventive ways to use the language of the act to
provide recovery for plaintiffs they believe should recover" ("Product
Liability Act Amendments," Hearings on S. 100 Before the Subcommittee on the Consumer of the Senate Committee on Commerce, Science,
and Transportation, 99th Congress, 1st Session [1985], pp. 12–13).

28. Calabresi, *A Common Law*, p. 164. Grant Gilmore made similar argu-
ments in *The Ages of American Law*, p. 97. See also Robert E. Keeton,
Venturing to Do Justice: Reforming Private Law (Cambridge, Mass.:
Harvard University Press, 1969).

29. Calabresi, *A Common Law*, pp. 133, 242–43. "The current rush toward
statutorification [of product liability law] has often seemed an attempt to
freeze the law at a level that victims, as a group, cannot find tolerable"
(p. 243). Calabresi compares this development to Grant Gilmore's political analysis of the Uniform Commercial Code: "The Code, which in the
1940s had seemed much too 'liberal' to its conservative critics, had by
the 1960s become an almost nostalgic throwback to an earlier period.
The final irony of the Code project was that its eventual 'success' (that is,
its enactment) can well be taken as an attempt by the most conservative
elements in the bar to turn the clock back" (Gilmore, *The Ages of American Law*, p. 86). See also Twerski, "Rebuilding the Citadel," pp. 55–59.

30. Calabresi's theory envisions several routes to active judicial modification
of statutes: direct construction, constitutional challenges, and "dia-
logue" with legislatures, borrowing from Alexander Bickel's theory of
"passive virtues" and Henry Hart and Albert Sacks's theories of legal
process (*A Common Law*, pp. 8–43). See also Jack Davies, "A Response
to Statutory Obsolescence: The Nonprimacy of Statutes Act," *Vermont
Law Review* 4 (1979): 203–31. According to Calabresi, the need for activism would appear to become stronger over time. By contrast one of
the chief advocates of federal product liability reform believes that conflicting interpretations would arise immediately, but he expects federal
appellate review to even out those differences over time (Schwartz and
Bares, "Federal Reform," pp. 361–63).

31. Numerous witnesses in Congressional hearings on product liability reform have emphasized this problem. See, for example, Marshall S.
Shapo's comments: "The enactment of this kind of law necessarily will
place even more burdens on the judicial system than it now carries. If
the legislation is really taken as writing on a clean slate, the result will
be many years of trench warfare litigation to straighten out the meaning
of the statute without very precise guidance in the legislative history.
The more sensible alternative, I expect, would be for the courts to draw
heavily on the law as it now exists. The results then would be to add an

extra tier of decision making, and to introduce further uncertainty and confusion into a body of law which has been condemned as uncertain but has really been working itself out in a rational common-law way" (Hearings on S. 1999 Before the Subcommittee on the Consumer of the Senate Committee on Commerce, Science, and Transportation, 99th Congress, 2nd Session [1986], p. 75). As the last phrase may indicate, Shapo testified under sponsorship of the American Bar Association.

32. See Schwartz and Bares, "Federal Reform," pp. 360–61. As numerous critics of federal legislative drafts have pointed out, the statute does not create a separate federal common law of torts. Federal courts would hear cases under this law only by virtue of their diversity jurisdiction, and would thus be able to develop independent interpretations of federal statutes, even though they are bound (under the rule in Erie v. Tompkins) to follow state court interpretations of all remaining issues covered by state law. For a recent critique of the Erie doctrine, see Martha A. Field, "Sources of Law: The Scope of Federal Common Law," *Harvard Law Review* 99 (1986): 881–984. In the Senate hearings on product liability, Chief Justice Reynoldson of Iowa, on behalf of the National Conference of Chief Justices, argued, "It makes no sense to federalize a significant portion of state tort law while denying jurisdiction to the federal courts except under diversity of citizenship, when diversity jurisdiction in the view of most expert opinion, should be eliminated as a first step in reform of our dual court system. The House twice in recent years has voted to deny a federal forum to these state law cases and there is reason to believe this change ultimately will be made" ("Product Liability Act," Hearings on S. 100 Before the Subcommittee on the Consumer of the Senate Committee on Commerce, Science, and Transportation, 99th Congress, 1st Session [1985], p. 109).

33. In addition to the analysis in Chapter 6, see Deborah R. Hensler, William L. F. Felstiner, Molly Selvin, and Patricia A. Ebener, *Asbestos in the Courts: The Challenge of Mass Toxic Torts* (Santa Monica, Cal.: Rand Corporation, 1985). See Hensler's testimony in the Hearings on S. 1999, pp. 81–85.

34. In 1982 alone some twenty-four different product liability bills were pending in the Wisconsin legislature; Herrmann, "Overview," p. 3.

35. Calabresi, *A Common Law*, p. 239. Attempting to recover that uniformity for motor vehicle accidents was the apparent goal of a federal law that was ultimately defeated by a combination of trial lawyers' interest groups and constitutional arguments. See "No-Fault Insurance," Hearings before the Senate Judiciary Committee on S. 354, 93rd Congress, 2nd Session (1974); House Committee on Interstate and Foreign Commerce, "Compilation of Bills Under Consideration by the Subcommittee on Commerce and Finance on No-Fault Motor Vehicle Insurance,"

93rd Congress, 2nd Session (Committee Print, 1974). See also Herrmann: "any stability that may have finally been established in some
state courts has become unsettled by legislation that calls for either
court interpretation or raises issues of constitutionality" ("Overview,"
p. 3).

36. See Victor E. Schwartz, "The Uniform Product Liability Act—A Brief
Overview," *Vanderbilt Law Review* 33 (1980): 579–92; and Rodman
Elfin, "The Changing Philosophy of Products Liability and the Pro-
posed Model Uniform Product Liability Act," *American Business Law
Journal* 19 (1981): 267–94. For a negative review see Aaron D. Twerski
and Alvin S. Weinstein, "A Critique of the Uniform Product Liability
Law—A Rush to Judgment," *Drake Law Review* 28 (1979): 221–316.
The text of the Uniform Act was published in the *Federal Register* 43
(April 6, 1978): 14627–32.

37. Interagency Task Force on Product Liability, *Legal Study* (Washington,
D.C.: Government Printing Office, 1977), vol. 4, p. 74. See Larry A.
Ribstein, "The Model Uniform Product Liability Act: Pinning Down
Products Law," *Journal of Air Law and Commerce* 46 (1981): 349–57:
"Many of the provisions of the Act [discussed in Ribstein's article] are
drafted with the kind of open-ended language which permits courts to
continue the development of the law of products liability the Act was
intended to frustrate" (p. 356).

38. John C. Minahan, Jr., "The Eroding Uniformity of the Uniform Commercial Code," *Kentucky Law Journal* 65 (1977): 799–822; E. Hunter
Taylor, Jr., "Uniformity of Commercial Law and State-by-State Enactment: A Confluence of Contradictions," *Hastings Law Journal* 30 (1978):
337–68.

39. For federal no-fault motor vehicle standards, see congressional documents cited in note 35. A House bill that would have federalized standards for state malpractice legislation never emerged from committee.
House Bill 6100, 94th Congress, 1st Session (1975). For text and discussion see House Committee on Interstate and Foreign Commerce, "National Conference on Medical Malpractice," 94th Congress, 1st Session
(Committee Print: 1975). See also Rick J. Carlson, "A Conceptualization
of a No-Fault Compensation System for Medical Injuries," *Law and Society Review* 7 (1973): 329–69.

40. See references in notes 5 and 48.

41. Interagency Task Force, *Final Report*. Among the many articles by Victor E. Schwartz, who chaired the working task force that drafted the
report, see "Federal Action on Product Liability—What Has Occurred
and What May Occur," *Forum* 14 (1978): 287–305, and "The Federal
Government and the Product Liability Problem: From Task-Force In-

vestigation to Decisions by the Administration," *University of Cincinnati Law Review* 47 (1978): 573–90.

42. See the Interagency Task Force, *Final Report*, pp. I-24–I-26.

43. The former bill is National Product Liability Act of 1977, House Bill 6300, 95th Congress, 1st Session (1977), and the latter is National Product Liability Insurance Act, Senate Bill 403, 95th Congress, 1st Session (1977). Hearings were published only for S. 403: "Product Liability Insurance," Hearings on S. 403 Before the Subcommittee for Consumers of the Senate Committee on Commerce, Science and Transportation, 95th Congress, 1st Session (1977). For a discussion of both bills see Sheila L. Birnbaum, "Legislative Reform or Retreat? A Response to the Product Liability Crisis," *Forum* 14 (1978): 251–86.

44. A body of literature emerged challenging the argument that courts were swamped with liability suits. See, for example, Marc Galanter, "Reading the Landscape of Disputes: What We Know and Don't Know (And Think We Know) About Our Allegedly Contentious and Litigious Society," *UCLA Law Review* 31 (1983): 4–71.

45. See Chapters 4 and 5.

46. In addition to references in note 36, see Victor E. Schwartz, "The Federal Government and the Product Liability Problem," *University of Cincinnati Law Review* 47 (1978): 573–81; and Rodman Elfin, "Product Liability Law Reform: A Critique of Proposed Federal Legislation," *Southern Illinois University Law Journal* (1984): 579–617. In April 1978, along with the model statute, the task force also published an Options Paper on Product Liability and Accident Compensation Issues (*Federal Register* 43 [April 6, 1978]: 14612–32). That document recommended an executive branch study of a "practical working model" for a no-fault compensation system for consumer product liability, but no such study was ever made.

47. See O. Lee Reed and John L. Watkins, "Product Liability Tort Reform: The Case for Federal Action," *Nebraska Law Review* 63 (1984): 389–472.

48. Product Liability Act, Senate Bill 2631, 97th Congress, 2nd Session. Senate Report No. 97-670. See "Product Liability Reform," Hearings on S. 2631 Before the Subcommittee on the Consumer of the Senate Committee on Commerce, Science and Transportation, 97th Congress, 2nd Session (1982).

49. Product Liability Risk Retention Act of 1981, Pub. L. No. 97-45, 95 Stat. 949, and Risk Retention Amendments of 1986, Pub. L. No. 99-563, 100 Stat. 3170, 15 U.S.C. §§3901–3906. Congress did not pursue the more radical strategy of ending the insurance industry's exemption from federal antitrust laws, although some liberal legislators have

kept this issue alive. See *Congressional Quarterly Weekly Report* 45 (1987): 1874.

50. In addition to the 1982 hearings cited in note 48, see "Product Liability Act," Hearings on S. 44 Before the Subcommittee on the Consumer of the Senate Committee on Commerce, Science and Transportation, 98th Congress, 1st and 2nd Sessions (1983 and 1984); Senate Report No. 98-476, 98th Congress, 2nd Session (1984); "Product Liability Act" and "Product Liability Act Amendments," Hearings on S. 100 Before the Subcommittee on the Consumer of the Senate Committee on Commerce, Science and Transportation, 99th Congress, 1st Session (1985); "Product Liability Voluntary Claims and Uniform Standards Act," Hearings on S. 1999 Before the Subcommittee on the Consumer of the Senate Committee on Commerce, Science and Transportation, 99th Congress, 2nd Session (1986), Senate Report No. 99-422 [recommending as an original bill S. 2760, replacing both S. 100 and S. 1999], 99th Congress, 2nd Session (1986); House Report No. 100-748, 100th Congress, 2nd Session (1988).

51. See Marshall Shapo's remarks, "Product Liability Act Amendments," Hearings on S. 100, pp. 101–2.

52. See the discussion in Elfin, "Product Liability Law Reform."

53. S. 44, 98th Congress, 1st Session (1983), §§4–7.

54. §304(a).

55. §303(a). Manufacturers and sellers of prescription drugs would be protected from any punitive damages if they followed federal regulations.

56. §308(a).

57. On the confusion created by comparative damages under strict liability, see Elfin, "Product Liability Law Reform," p. 595.

58. S. 100, 99th Congress, 1st Session (1985), §§9(a)–(b).

59. §307(c). In addition, any plaintiff who rejects an offer of settlement under the expedited procedure is subject to the collateral source rule for economic losses, even if he or she prevails at trial.

60. Even the participants in those hearings grew weary of legalisms and began to concentrate more on compromises. After a tedious encounter over the fine points of "clear and convincing evidence," Senator Lugar pleads: "But rather than attempt to argue the principles of law that are involved, I see this as a pragmatic compromise of various forces in our economy over the course of time, that I think will promote, as I suggested, a greater fairness, probably economic growth, greater certainty for manufacturers. These at least I have seen as principles that were preeminent in the debate" ("Product Liability Act," Hearing on S. 100, p. 60).

61. S. 1999, 99th Congress, 1st Session (1985), §205(a)(2). This provision was omitted from S. 2760.

62. "For many behaviors 'effectiveness in action' is not in point, not possible, or not verifiable. This is especially characteristic of the shared social objectives that become major political issues. Such political goals depend upon perceptions and beliefs that are not, and often cannot be, based upon empirical observation. Instead, they are socially cued by others who are significant to a person, creating faith in a belief that is not susceptible to empirical disproof and at the same time creating a valued self-conception for those who believe in the goal as well as for those who reject it" (Murray Edelman, *Politics as Symbolic Action* [Chicago: Markham Publishing, 1971], p. 174). Perhaps the clearest example of symbolic action occurred in the 1988 debate before the House Energy and Commerce Committee, which was considering H.R. 1115. The right-to-life lobby argued successfully for exempting contraceptives from the bill, while women's groups had hoped to exclude products associated with birth defects; see *Congressional Quarterly Weekly Report* 46 (1988): 1599. H.R. 1115 was approved by the full committee in June 1988. See House Report No. 100-748, Sec. 207(3)(C) for the exclusion of contraceptives.

63. S. 2760, §103(b).

64. Senate Report No. 99-422, 99th Congress, 2nd Session (1986), p. 29.

65. Senator Dodd suggests that entirely different procedures should be considered for toxic illnesses ("Product Liability Act Amendments," Hearings on S. 100, p. 9). Senator Stafford was responsible for the provision added to S. 100 specifically disavowing any preemption of federal environmental laws (§3[c]). S. 2760 also permits courts to dismiss environmental suits like those filed in the aftermath of the Union Carbide accident in Bhopal, India. Under the doctrine of *forum non conveniens*, which §309 extends to all courts, judges have "discretionary power to decline jurisdiction when the convenience of the parties and the interest of justice would be better served if the action were brought and tried in another forum" (Senate Report No. 99-422, 99th Congress, 2nd Session, p. 71).

66. Robert St. Leger Goggin and Thomas A. Brophy, "Toxic Torts: Workable Defenses Available to the Corporate Defendant," *Villanova Law Review* 28 (1983): 1284.

67. Victor E. Schwartz and Thomas C. Means, "The Need for Federal Product Liability and Toxic Tort Legislation: A Current Assessment," *Villanova Law Review* 28 (1983): 1109–14. See also Schwartz's remarks in the Hearings on S. 1999, p. 145, and his article written with Liberty Mahshigian, "Failure to Identify the Defendant in Tort Law: Towards a Legislative Solution," *California Law Review* 73 (1985): 941–75.

68. See Johns-Manville Corp. v. United States, 13 Ct.Cl. 72 (1987), vacated, 855 F.2d 1571 (Fed.Cir. 1988); In re Agent Orange Product Liability

Litigation, 818 F.2d 204 (2d Cir. 1987). Lower courts have sometimes allowed indemnification in asbestos cases, but Courts of Appeals have held the line. See Eagle-Picher Industries, Inc. v. United States, 657 F.Supp. 803 (E.D.Pa. 1987), reversed, 846 F.2d 888 (3rd Cir. 1988); All Maine Asbestos Litigation, 772 F.2d 1023 (1st Cir. 1985), *cert. denied*, 476 U.S. 1126 (1986).

69. Senator Hollings gave the following warning: "Let's look at the issue of having the national Congress . . . decide the rules—I found this is a liberal crowd up here in Washington. They will spend you blind. They are spending everybody else's money that they can get their hands on right now" ("Product Liability Act," Hearing on S. 100, p. 43).

70. "Product Liability: Curse or Bulwark of Free Enterprise?" *Cleveland State Law Review* 27 (1978): 313–14.

71. S. 2760, 99th Congress, 2nd Session (1986), §§201–206.

72. See references in note 43.

73. See Interagency Task Force, *Final Report*, pp. VII-202–VII-241.

74. According to the *Product Liability Closed Claim Survey* (Washington, D.C.: Insurance Services Office, 1977), 73 percent of all personal injury claims processed by insurers were settled before a suit was filed; less than 4 percent reached a final verdict, and defendants were found liable in fewer than 1 percent (pp. 95–100). See Senator Dodd's references to this study, "Product Liability Act Amendments," Hearings on S. 100, pp. 5–6.

75. See, for example, Richard A. Posner, *Economic Analysis of Law*, 2nd ed. (Boston: Little, Brown, 1977), pp. 434–41. (In the third edition [1986], see pp. 522–33.)

76. These worries are substantiated by various statements from insurance companies on the difficulties of establishing premiums for no-fault schemes. See the passage quoted in note 101. Since product liability claims are now frequently based on strict liability rather than negligence, insurers are concerned that simple procedures for compensation would encourage fraudulent claims, or at least might amount to a system of absolute liability.

77. "Product Liability Act Amendments," Hearings on S. 100, p. 5.

78. For an empirical analysis of personal injury settlements that challenges this comfortable notion, see Hazel Genn, *Hard Bargaining: Out of Court Settlement in Personal Injury Actions* (Oxford: Clarendon Press, 1987). The conventional argument in favor of dispute settlement can be found, for example, in Robert A. Baruch Bush, "Dispute Resolution Alternatives and the Goals of Civil Justice: Jurisdictional Principles for Process Choice," *Wisconsin Law Review* (1984): 893–1034.

79. "We are concerned . . . that any attempt to balance a compensation system against the curtailment of victims' tort rights would risk produc-

ing a new class of uncompensated victims from the groups of victims who now recover under the current system" (statement of Joseph Goffman, staff attorney, Public Citizen's Congress Watch, "Product Liability Act Amendments," Hearings on S. 100, p. 148). For the other side, Victor Schwartz of the Product Liability Alliance was still resisting alternative schemes in early 1985: "S. 100 recognizes that although it is worthwhile and important to look at these problems, now is not the time to establish a compensation system" ("Product Liability Act," Hearing on S. 100, p. 68).

80. A more complicated plan was introduced as Title II of S. 1999, 99th Congress, 2nd Session (1986), and was debated in the hearings on S. 1999. Several bills before the 100th Congress contained proposals for alternatives to litigation.

81. For a recent overview see "A 'Neo-No-Fault' Contract in Lieu of Tort: Preaccident Guarantees of Postaccident Settlement Offers," *California Law Review* 73 (1985): 898–916. A sense of O'Connell's numerous proposals can be found in *Ending Insult to Injury: No-Fault Insurance for Products and Services* (Urbana: University of Illinois Press, 1975) and "An Alternative to Abandoning Tort Liability: Elective No-Fault Insurance for Many Kinds of Injuries," *Minnesota Law Review* 60 (1976): 501–65.

82. See the plan presented by Robert E. Keeton and Jeffrey O'Connell, *Basic Protection for the Traffic Victim: A Blueprint for Reforming Automobile Insurance* (Boston: Little, Brown, 1965), and also O'Connell's article, "Expanding No-Fault Beyond Auto Insurance: Some Proposals," *Virginia Law Review* 59 (1973): 749–829.

83. See the Commerce Committee's hopes for expedited settlement in Senate Report 99-422, 99th Congress, 2nd Session (1986), p. 31.

84. The New Zealand program is discussed in Chapter 11, along with other national policies on accident compensation. For an earlier survey see U.S. Department of Transportation, *Comparative Studies in Automobile Accident Compensation* (Washington, D.C.: Government Printing Office, 1970).

85. See U.S. Department of Transportation, *Constitutional Problems in Automobile Accident Compensation Reform* (Washington, D.C.: Government Printing Office, 1970). An excellent summary up to 1975 can be found in O'Connell, *Ending Insult to Injury,* pp. 204–45.

86. See cases reported in *American Law of Products Liability 3d,* among other citation sources.

87. See the discussion in Reed and Watkins, "Product Liability Tort Reform," p. 467. Relevant federal constitutional issues were discussed by the Supreme Court in upholding the Price-Anderson Act's limits on recovery in nuclear accidents; Duke Power Co. v. Carolina Environ-

mental Study Group, 438 U.S. 59 (1978). See also Susan C. Schmidt and
Andrew B. Derman, "The Constitutionality of Federal Products Liability Toxic Tort Legislation," *Journal of Product Liability* 6 (1983): 171–
84.

88. See the defiant posture of the American Trial Lawyers' Association former president, Eugene I. Pavalon, in "Fighting Back with Unity and
Success," *Trial* 23 (August 1987): 5.

89. See the survey in R. Scott Jenkins and William C. Schweinfurth,
"California's Medical Injury Compensation Reform Act: An Equal Protection Challenge," *Southern California Law Review* 52 (1979): 829–
971.

90. "Any alternative to the tort law product liability system which selects a
specific person to bear the liability burden and blame for a specific injury must, at a minimum, make a reasonable determination of causation.
Without a finding of causation the system will lack the most fundamental
element necessary to afford justice and avoid arbitrary penalties. Under
the Fifth Amendment to the Constitution the system also must afford
procedural due process—a meaningful hearing at a meaningful time"
(statement of the Chemical Manufacturers' Association, Hearings on S.
1999, p. 225).

91. See references in note 87.

92. For example, the courts have upheld the mechanism for compensating
victims of the swine flu vaccine. See Jones v. Wyeth Laboratories, Inc.,
583 F.2d 1070 (8th Cir. 1978); Ducharme v. Merrill-National Laboratories, 574 F.2d 1307 (5th Cir. 1978), *cert. denied*, 439 U.S. 1002 (1978).

93. In an early study of no-fault automobile insurance, however, O'Connell
found empirical evidence that most consumers favored some form of no-
fault plan (Jeffrey O'Connell and Wallace H. Wilson, *Car Insurance and
Consumer Desires* [Urbana: University of Illinois Press, 1969]).

94. On the perils of dispute settlement without legal representation see,
among others, Owen M. Fiss, "Against Settlement," *Yale Law Journal*
93 (1984): 1073–90.

95. "The fundamental flaw in S. 1999, and all other legislation that attempts
to separate compensation from tort law through a two-tier, exclusive
choice system, is that the two-tier approach inherently sends confusing,
contradictory signals to the parties in a personal injury dispute. Regardless of the underlying purpose . . . it is virtually impossible to prevent
considerable litigation over the liability standards in both tort and compensation" (testimony of Gene Kimmelman, representing the Consumer Federation of America, Hearings on S. 1999, p. 130). The only
way S. 2760 responds to this problem comes in §305(b), allowing courts
to impose financial sanctions on attorneys who delay court proceedings
or otherwise fail to operate in "good faith." Such sanctions were already

available under Rule 11 of the Federal Rules of Civil Procedure, which courts occasionally invoke; but clearly such sanctions have been unable to stem the tide of litigation. See Stephen B. Burbank, "Sanctions in the Proposed Amendments to the Federal Rules of Civil Procedure: Some Questions About Power," *Hofstra Law Review* 11 (1983): 997–1011.

96. S. 2760, §§201–206.

97. Jeffrey O'Connell, "Offers That Can't Be Refused," *Northwestern University Law Review* 77 (1982): 589–632.

98. Ibid., pp. 604–6. Another important provision of S. 2760 would allow courts to bar damages to plaintiffs under the influence of alcohol or drugs, when such condition was "more than 50 per centum responsible" for the injury (§311). This kind of rule is of great strategic importance to defendants seeking leverage in settlement negotiations, whatever its value from the standpoint of impersonal justice.

99. Despite decades of speculation about the proper design of settlement procedures in personal injury cases, the first comprehensive empirical study appeared in 1987. Hazel Genn's book questions two common assumptions in the debate over settlement mechanisms: "the fallacy that it is always possible to predict with any degree of certainty the likely outcome of a trial," and the notion that "the adjustment of the parties' positions and expectations occurs only, or principally, in response to legitimate legal considerations, rather than in response to a host of pressures and concerns which would have no place in court proceedings" (*Hard Bargaining*, pp. 12–13). O'Connell himself expresses doubts about the particular two-tiered plan in S. 1999: "The great problem, I think, with this bill is that it tries to give both parties the right to behave strategically, and I think that is going to create . . . much chaos" (Hearings on S. 1999, p. 78). On O'Connell's ambivalence about political compromises in statutory compensation procedures, see Richard Pierce, "Institutional Aspects of Tort Reform," *California Law Review* 73 (1985): 917–40.

100. See Genn, *Hard Bargaining*, chap. 6. Marc Galanter's well-known analysis explains the advantages of "repeat players" over "one-shotters" ("Why the Haves Come Out Ahead: Speculation on the Limits of Legal Change," *Law and Society Review* 9 [1974]: 95–160). Galanter's study covers a continuum of procedures from settlement through litigation. For a recent study testing similar factors at the appellate court level, see Stanton Wheeler et al., "Do the 'Haves' Come Out Ahead? Winning and Losing in State Supreme Courts, 1870–1970," *Law and Society Review* 21 (1987): 403–45.

101. In a statement that must have chilled every tort reformer, the American Insurance Association announced that it was worried about "proposals which would in part or in whole graft a compensation system based

upon injuries from exposure to products onto a fault-based tort liability
system. We believe that such a dual system would be distinctly more
expensive than the current system. . . . There are enough aspects of
unpredictability in the tort system to be accommodated by the under-
writer without having to anticipate that a liability system could be
scrapped entirely and a compensation system more expensive substituted in its place. . . . Also, from an insurance point of view the absence of statistical information upon which to make projections of costs
would mean that a compensation mechanism would be extremely difficult to price and would probably be uninsurable in the commercial market" ("Product Liability Act Amendments," Hearings on S. 100, p. 175).
Earlier in the same hearings, a spokesman for manufacturers had stated
the obvious point that "for any compensation system to be acceptable it
must be insurable" (statement of Joseph R. Creighton for the Coalition
for Uniform Product Liability Law, p. 126).

102. Richard J. Pierce, Jr., reaches similar conclusions about two-tiered
schemes; "Encouraging Safety: The Limits of Tort Law and Government
Regulation," *Vanderbilt Law Review* 33 (1980): 1281–331.

103. For different assessments of this tendency see Robert A. Dahl and
Charles E. Lindblom, *Politics, Economics and Welfare* (New York:
Harper & Brothers, 1953), and Theodore J. Lowi, *The End of Liberal-
ism*, 2nd ed. (New York: Norton, 1979).

104. Though far from a market ideologue, Calabresi has formulated this argument on at least two occasions: *A Common Law*, p. 243, and "Product
Liability: Curse or Bulwark?" p. 314.

105. The same point is made by David Rosenberg, who nevertheless thinks
that courts should reshape themselves to deal more expeditiously and
consistently with environmental accidents ("The Causal Connection in
Mass Exposure Cases: A 'Public Law' Vision of the Tort System," *Harvard Law Review* 97 [1984]: 849–929).

Chapter 8

1. James Huffman, *Government Liability and Disaster Mitigation* (Lan-
ham, Md.: University Press of America, 1986), p. 623.

2. For a comprehensive overview see Peter V. Saladin, *Verantwortung als
Staatsprinzip* (Bern: Verlag Paul Haupt, 1984).

3. For a historical survey of federal immunity see John M. Steadman,
David Schwartz, and Sidney B. Jacoby, *Litigation with the Federal Gov-
ernment*, 2nd ed. (Philadelphia: American Law Institute and American
Bar Association, 1983); and Floyd D. Shimomura, "The History of
Claims Against the United States: The Evolution from a Legislative To-
ward a Judicial Model of Payment," *Louisiana Law Review* 45 (1985):

625–700. For background on the Eleventh Amendment see John J. Gibbons, "The Eleventh Amendment and State Sovereign Immunity: A Reinterpretation," *Columbia Law Review* 83 (1983): 1889–2005. For a current review of both federal and state immunity see Peter H. Schuck, *Suing Government: Citizen Remedies for Official Wrongs* (New Haven, Conn.: Yale University Press, 1983).

4. Huffman supports this view in his comparative survey of government liability across varying political cultures (*Government Liability*, pp. 578–98).

5. During the 1960s and 1970s state immunity was subjected to numerous judicial and statutory assaults. See Shepard's, *Civil Actions Against State Government, Its Divisions, Agencies, and Officers* (Colorado Springs: Shepard's/McGraw-Hill, 1982). More recently, states have adopted statutory schemes for preserving sovereign immunity, but with stipulated exceptions. See, for example, Roy Kimberly Snell, "A Plea for a Comprehensive Governmental Liability Statute," *Kentucky Law Journal* 74 (1985–86): 521–79.

6. For a general discussion of doctrinal issues see Fowler V. Harper, Fleming James, Jr., and Oscar S. Gray, *The Law of Torts*, 2nd ed. (Boston: Little, Brown, 1986), vol. 5, pp. 696–736 (§§29.12–29.15). For a detailed survey of caselaw see Lester S. Jayson, *Handling Federal Tort Claims* (New York: Matthew Bender, 1964 and supplements).

7. United States v. S.A. Empresa de Viacão Aerea Rio Grandense (Varig Airlines), 467 U.S. 797, 809-14 (1984). This opinion reaffirms the Court's much-criticized decision in Dalehite v. United States, 346 U.S. 15 (1953), but leaves the contours of "discretion" rather murky. See the analysis in D. N. Zillman, "Regulatory Discretion: The Supreme Court Reexamines the Discretionary Function Exception to the FTCA," *Military Law Review* 110 (1985): 115–43. In 1988 the Supreme Court issued a unanimous decision holding that federal regulation of polio vaccine production was not entirely protected from liability claims. Berkovitz v. United States, 108 S.Ct. 1954 (1988).

8. The most comprehensive overview is Peter H. Schuck, *Agent Orange on Trial: Mass Toxic Disasters in the Courts* (Cambridge, Mass.: Belknap Press, 1986).

9. See Michael Lipsky, *Street-Level Bureaucracy*: Dilemmas of the Individual in Public Services (New York: Russell Sage, 1980).

10. The "new property" concept comes from Charles A. Reich, "The New Property," *Yale Law Journal* 73 (1964): 733–87. By focusing on discretionary acts, the civil rights tort action is on a collision course with the FTCA's exemption from liability of public regulatory policy—somewhat confusingly called the *discretionary function* exemption. See Harper, James, and Gray, *The Law of Torts*, vol. 5, pp. 716–27 (§29.14).

11. See Schuck, *Suing Government*, p. 30.

12. Ibid., pp. 85–89; Harper, James, and Gray, *The Law of Torts*, vol. 5, p. 660, n. 13 (§29.9).

13. See Schuck, *Suing Government*, pp. 119–20.

14. See Kathleen M. Sullivan, "Sins of Discrimination: Last Term's Affirmative Action Cases," *Harvard Law Review* 100 (1986): 78–98.

15. See "Developments in the Law—Section 1983 and Federalism," *Harvard Law Review* 90 (1977): 1227–50.

16. Among numerous sources, see Phillip J. Cooper, *Hard Judicial Choices: Federal District Court Judges and State and Local Officials* (New York: Oxford University Press, 1988); Donald L. Horowitz, *Courts and Social Policy* (Washington, D.C.: Brookings Institution, 1977); and Richard A. L. Gambitta, Marlynn L. May, and James C. Foster, eds., *Governing Through Courts* (Beverly Hills, Cal.: Sage Publications, 1981).

17. I have developed this argument in some detail in "Second Thoughts about Law as an Instrument of Social Change," *Law and Human Behavior* 6 (1982): 153–68.

18. For an overview of events and sharp criticisms of the program, see Richard E. Neustadt and Harvey V. Fineberg, *The Swine Flu Affair: Decision-Making on a Slippery Disease* (Washington D.C.: Department of Health, Education and Welfare, 1978).

19. *Weekly Compilation of Presidential Documents* 12 (1976): 484–85.

20. Neustadt and Fineberg, *The Swine Flu Affair*, pp. 48–62.

21. 90 Stat. 1113 (1976). This statute was briefly codified at 42 U.S.C. §§247b (j)–(l) (1976).

22. Davis v. Wyeth Laboratories, Inc., 399 F.2d 121 (9th Cir. 1968); Reyes v. Wyeth Laboratories, Inc., 498 F.2d 1264 (5th Cir. 1974), *cert. denied*, 419 U.S. 1096 (1974).

23. 42 U.S.C. §247b (k)(1)(B)(1) (1976).

24. U.S. Justice Department, Civil Division, Torts Branch, "Swine Flu Statistics as of December 1, 1986."

25. For detailed commentary on FTCA procedures see Jayson, *Handling Federal Tort Claims*.

26. 42 U.S.C. §247b (k)(2)(A)(i) (1976).

27. See Judge Gesell's Final Pretrial Order, M.D.L. Docket No. 330, Misc. No. 78-0040 (D.D.C., filed November 15, 1979).

28. See In re Swine Flu Immunization Products Liability Litigation, 446 F.Supp. 244 (J.P.M.D.L. 1978). The reporting service was the *Swine Flu Litigation Reporter*, issued by Andrews Publications, Edgemont, Pa.

29. Jones v. Wyeth Laboratories, Inc., 583 F.2d 1070 (8th Cir. 1978); Ducharme v. Merrill-National Laboratories, 574 F.2d 1307 (5th Cir. 1978), *cert. denied*, 439 U.S. 1002 (1978).

30. See Richard L. Greenstreet, "Estimation of the Probability That Guillain-Barré Syndrome Was Caused by the Swine Flu Vaccine: U.S. Experience (1976–77)," *Medicine, Science and the Law* 24 (1984): 61–67; and Alexander D. Langmuir et al., "Epidemiological and Clinical Evaluation of Guillain-Barré Syndrome Reported in Association with the Administration of Swine Influenza Vaccines," *American Journal of Epidemiology* 119 (1984): 841–79. Langmuir's model projects up to about 250 Guillain-Barré cases caused by swine flu vaccine.

31. See the Department of Health Education and Welfare press release, June 20, 1978. The statement was reported in the *New York Times* under the misleading headline "Negligence Not a Factor in Flu Compensation," June 21, 1978, p. 12.

32. Neustadt and Fineberg, *The Swine Flu Affair*, p. 51.

33. 42 U.S.C. §247b (j)(1)(F) (1976).

34. The consent forms used in the swine flu program are reprinted in General Accounting Office, *The Swine Flu Program: An Unprecedented Venture in Preventive Medicine* (Washington, D.C.: Government Printing Office, 1977), pp. 87–90.

35. The report in question was Charles Hoke, David Barry, and Michael Hattwick, "Systematic Reactions to Influenza Vaccines: Review of Current and Past Experience" (June 6, 1976, submitted to CDC Bureau of Epidemiology). It was included as part of Exhibit 2b in pretrial proceedings, note 27. See also the testimony of CDC administrator J. Donald Millar, "Review and Evaluation of the Swine Flu Immunization Program," Hearings Before the Subcommittee on Health and the Environment of the House Committee on Interstate and Foreign Commerce, 94th Congress, 2nd Session (1976), p. 349.

36. See the summary of the defense position in Judge Gesell's Final Pretrial Order, pp. 8–9.

37. Jayson, *Handling Federal Tort Claims*, provides references for cases in which judges have ruled on the causal connection with Guillain-Barré Syndrome; see §6.06a. Steve Gold has observed that these cases provide a rare opportunity to compare findings of cause-in-fact made exclusively by judges rather than juries ("Causation in Toxic Torts: Burdens of Proof, Standards of Persuasion, and Statistical Evidence," *Yale Law Journal* 96 [1986]: 387, n. 55 and 389, n. 64).

38. See the recommendations in Scott Learned, "Statutory Modification and Assumption of Private Liability: The Nuclear Energy and Flu Immunization Programs," *University of Pittsburgh Law Review* 40 (1979): 487–516.

39. For post-swine flu perspectives on government liability in immunization programs, see Office of the Assistant Secretary for Health, "Reports and

Recommendations: National Immunization Work Group on Liability"
(Washington, D.C.: Department of Health, Education and Welfare,
1977).

40. See the discussion of the FTCA legislative history in United States v.
S.A. Empresa de Viacão Aerea Rio Grandense (Varig Airlines), 467 U.S.
797, 807-14 (1984).

41. See the Supreme Court decision in Laird v. Nelms, 406 U.S. 797 (1972).

42. For a summary of this argument and Judge Gesell's response, see his
Final Pretrial Order, p. 2.

43. Resource Conservation and Recovery Act of 1976, Pub. L. No. 94-580,
90 Stat. 2795, 42 U.S.C. §§6901–6987.

44. Comprehensive Environmental Response, Compensation, and Liability
Act of 1980, Pub. L. No. 96-510, 94 Stat. 2767, 42 U.S.C. §§9601–9657.
The most important amendments were those accompanying reauthorization: Superfund Amendments and Reauthorization Act of 1986 (popularly known as SARA), Pub. L. No. 99–499, 100 Stat. 1613.

45. See Frank P. Grad, *Environmental Law*, 3rd ed. (New York: Matthew
Bender, 1985).

46. For state laws dealing with issues covered by CERCLA, see Environmental Law Reporter, *State Superfund Statutes 1984* (Washington,
D.C.: Environmental Law Institute, 1983).

47. For a useful study of this feature of American policy development, see
Robert Stevens and Rosemary Stevens, *Welfare Medicine in America: A
Case Study of Medicaid* (New York: Free Press, 1974).

48. The investigations culminated in the resignation of EPA Administrator
Anne Burford, and the conviction and incarceration of her associate administrator, Rita Lavelle. See *Congressional Quarterly Almanac* 39
(1983): 333.

49. Statement by EPA Administrator Lee M. Thomas, "Superfund Improvement Act of 1985," Hearings on S. 51 before the Senate Committee on the Judiciary, Environment and Public Works, 99th Congress,
1st Session (1985), p. 11.

50. Office of Technology Assessment, *Superfund Strategy* (Washington,
D.C.: Government Printing Office, 1985), pp. 18–21. Another influen-
tial study (and more polemical) was William Drayton, *America's Toxic
Protection Gap* (Washington, D.C.: Environmental Safety, 1984).

51. For a breakdown of revenue sources see note 55.

52. Superfund Section 301(e) Study Group, "Injuries and Damages from
Hazardous Wastes—Analysis and Improvement of Legal Remedies,"
97th Congress, 2nd Session (Committee Print, 1982).

53. See generally Barry Boyer and Errol Meidinger, "Privatizing Regulatory Enforcement: A Preliminary Assessment of Citizen Suits Under
Federal Environmental Laws," *Buffalo Law Review* 34 (1985): 833–964;

Jeannette L. Austin, "The Rise of Citizen-Suit Enforcement in Environmental Law: Reconciling Private and Public Attorneys General," *Northwestern University Law Review* 81 (1987): 220–62. Nor will we touch on another CERCLA litigation strategy: civil damage suits, brought against polluters by state and federal governments, for damage to natural resources—under §107 (a)(4)(C).

54. "Developments—Toxic Waste Litigation," *Harvard Law Review* 99 (1986): 1466.

55. Of $8.5 billion authorized by Pub. L. No. 99-499, $2.5 billion will come from a broad-based tax surcharge on all businesses, $2.75 billion from a special excise tax on crude oil, $1.4 billion from a similar tax on chemical feedstocks, and $1.25 billion from general revenues. The remaining $.6 billion is expected to come from "interest, fines, and cost recovery" from individual polluters. See *Congressional Quarterly Almanac* 42 (1986): 111–19. For comparisons with other funding proposals, see "Last-Ditch Effort to Rescue 'Superfund' Bill," *Congressional Quarterly Weekly Report* 44 (1986): 2317.

56. Besides reimbursing the Superfund for cleanup costs (§107), CERCLA also authorizes judicial enforcement to compel private parties to finance those costs on their own (§106). According to an EPA senior enforcement officer, the legal costs and burdens of §106 actions have deterred EPA from using this option very forcefully, and with increased funding under SARA that trend is likely to continue (Richard H. Mays, "Settlements with SARA: A Comprehensive Review of Settlement Procedures Under the Superfund Amendments and Reauthorization Act," *Environmental Law Reporter* 17 [1987]: 10102).

57. On the history of judicial interpretation see "Developments—Toxic Waste Litigation," pp. 1511–43.

58. George Clemon Freeman, Jr., "Tort Law Reform: Superfund/RCRA Liability as a Major Cause of the Insurance Crisis," *Tort and Insurance Law Journal* 21 (1986): 536.

59. Testimony of John C. Butler III, summarizing a study carried out on behalf of the American Insurance Association, "Insurance Issues and Superfund," Hearing before the Senate Committee on Environment and Public Works, 99th Congress, 1st Session (1985), pp. 115–37.

60. See note 55 for the breakdown on Superfund financing from 1986 to 1991.

61. EPA Administrator Thomas has variously put the figure for EPA legal expenses at 12 percent and "between 10 and 15 percent" of Superfund appropriations. See "Superfund Reauthorization: Judicial and Legal Issues," Oversight Hearings before the Subcommittee on Administrative Law and Governmental Relations of the House Committee on the Judiciary, 99th Congress, 1st Session (1985), p. 75.

62. For an overview up to 1986, see "Developments—Toxic Waste Litigation."

63. This statement applies only to EPA cost recovery actions under §107. Under this and other sections of CERCLA, private parties and state governments are also assigned special roles as plaintiffs.

64. Butler's "best estimate" is that total litigation costs to all parties for cleaning up 1,800 sites will be $5 billion. For purposes of comparison, EPA Administrator Lee M. Thomas expects, over the next five years, to recover $2.6 billion, of which only $.6 billion would represent net income to the Superfund (see Hearings on S. 51, pp. 10, 14, 85). Neither estimate includes costs of possible compensation actions brought by private parties outside the CERCLA framework.

65. This wider circle of PRPs (it becomes difficult to separate the jargon of environmental regulation from the acronyms for toxic chemicals) was acknowledged in SARA's provisions concerning settlement negotiations (§122). An economic rationale for broadening the scope of liability is found in Note, "Liability of Parent Corporations for Hazardous Waste Cleanup and Damages," *Harvard Law Review* 99 (1986): 986–1003. For some critical reactions see Joel R. Burcat, "Environmental Liability of Creditors: Open Season on Banks, Creditors, and Other Deep Pockets," *Banking Law Journal* 103 (1986): 509–41. See also, *Superfund Report: What Do Responsible Parties Do Now?* (Rockeville, Md.: Aspen Publishers, 1986).

66. Michael Dore, "Dealing with the Post-SARA Dynamics of PRP Settlements," *Environmental Law Reporter* 17 (1987): 10431–33.

67. Freeman notes that Justice Department attorneys have recently tried to circumvent the "cause-in-fact" element by relating CERCLA litigation to the common-law concept of quasi-contract. This would allow the federal government "(a) to avoid traditional tort law standards of proof of causation, (b) to increase the measure of recoverable damages and (c) to avoid the federal statute of limitations on tort actions which is shorter than the federal statute of limitations on contract" ("Tort Law Reform," pp. 532–33).

68. See "Developments—Toxic Waste Litigation," pp. 1520–24.

69. See Douglas F. Brennan, "Joint and Several Liability for Generators Under Superfund: A Federal Formula for Cost Recovery," *UCLA Journal of Environmental Law and Policy* 5 (1986): 101–35.

70. According to one attorney testifying in House oversight hearings, joint and several liability "has caused a fundamental and profound widespread inability of generators to settle cases early or late" (see "Oversight Hearings," p. 286).

71. For examples of costs involved in specific Superfund cleanups, see "Insurance Issues," pp. 134–88.

72. "Developments—Toxic Waste Litigation," pp. 1511–55; Freeman, "Tort Law Reform," pp. 530–38; William D. Ruckelshaus, "Environmental Risks and Liabilities—Identification, Assessment, and Management," *Houston Law Review* 24 (1987): 11–25.

73. One administration official suggested to a Senate committee that the federal government would use its "prosecutorial discretion" to moderate the impact of liability doctrines on defendants "marginally related to the sites" ("Superfund Improvement Act of 1985," Hearings on S. 51 before the Senate Committee on the Judiciary, 99th Congress, 1st Session [1985], p. 36, statement of Assistant Attorney General Habicht.)

74. For a caustic analysis of these inconsistent policies, see Freeman, "Tort Law Reform," pp. 517–30. The 1986 report tried to resolve the different approaches by distinguishing "the tort system" from "a legislative choice to allocate the cost of [environmental] programs among those who contributed to the problems the programs are designed to remedy" (U.S. Attorney General's Tort Policy Working Group, "Report on the Causes, Extent and Policy Implications of the Current Crisis in Insurance Availability and Affordability [Washington, D.C.: Government Printing Office, February 1986], p. 66, n. 7). But any legislative package of "tort reform" in the area of product liability would likewise represent a legislative choice; the only issue is how to operationalize the concepts of causation and accountability. The working group misleadingly suggests that we can meaningfully distinguish a system based on intrinsic fairness from one based on legislative instrumentalism. The rhetoric of tort reform tries (unpersuasively) to import the moral prestige of the former system into the intrinsically instrumental world of legislation.

75. See Mays, "Settlements with SARA." As noted above, Mays (senior enforcement attorney for the EPA) expresses some doubt that the settlement goals of Superfund can be achieved under provisions in the recent amendments.

76. See the comments of Habicht, "Insurance Issues," p. 19.

77. See the comments of Edmund B. Frost, an attorney speaking on behalf of the Chemical Manufacturers Association, indicating that post-settlement contribution suits as a method of apportioning cleanup costs among responsible parties "will double court costs" of Superfund defendants ("Oversight Hearings," p. 497).

78. The points in this paragraph are all covered by Mays, "Settlements with SARA." See also Carroll E. Dubuc and William D. Evans, Jr., "Recent Developments Under CERCLA: Toward a More Equitable Distribution of Liability," *Environmental Law Reporter* 17 (1987): 10197–204; Lauren Stiller Rikleen, "Negotiating Superfund Settlement Agreements," *Boston College Environmental Affairs Law Review* 10 (1982–83): 697–714; Ellen J. Garber, "Federal Common Law of Contribution Under the

1986 CERCLA Amendments," *Ecology Law Quarterly* 14 (1987): 365–88.

79. This conclusion is supported by Mays, "Settlements with SARA." In addition see J. William Futrell, "Hazardous Wastes and Toxic Substances: Lessons from Superfund, RCRA, and Other Environmental Laws," *Houston Law Review* 24 (1987): "Vast numbers of attorneys have been involved in Superfund settlement negotiations, leading many people to ruefully ask the question, how many people does it take to clean up a Superfund site? The answer: 500 lawyers and one bulldozer operator" (p. 140).

80. 100 Stat. 1613, §122 (e)(3)(C).

81. §122 (d)(1).

82. Dore, "Dealing with Post-SARA Dynamics," p. 10432.

83. §122 (d)(2). Richard B. Stewart has examined the fragmentation of interests resulting from third-party involvement in administrative procedures ("The Discontents of Legalism: Interest Group Relations in Administrative Regulation," *Wisconsin Law Review* [1985]: 655–86).

84. Mays, "Settlements with SARA," p. 10102.

85. §101 (b)(1). The language quoted supersedes an exclusion for government units that involuntarily acquire ownership or control of property, through bankruptcy, tax delinquency, abandonment, or other circumstances related to state sovereign authority.

86. Dubuc and Evans, "Recent Developments Under CERCLA," p. 10202.

87. Ibid., pp. 10202–04. See also Jesse Michael Feder, "Congressional Abrogation of State Sovereign Immunity," *Columbia Law Review* 86 (1986): 1436–52. In 1988 the Supreme Court agreed to hear an appeal on this issue, in a case that had previously been remanded to the appeals court for reconsideration, after the passage of SARA. United States v. Union Gas Co., 792 F.2d 372 (3rd Cir. 1986) (holding that the Eleventh Amendment preserves state immunity); remanded, 107 S.Ct. 865 (1987); 832 F.2d 1343 (3rd Cir. 1987) (holding, in light of SARA, that the Eleventh Amendment does *not* preserve state immunity); *cert. granted*, 108 S.Ct. 1219 (1988). Other inroads into the Eleventh Amendment have been made in FTCA cases, when states are later joined as parties. United States v. Hawaii, 832 F.2d 1116 (9th Cir. 1987); Barrett v. United States, 853 F.2d 124 (2nd Cir. 1988).

88. See United States v. Mottolo, 605 F.Supp. 898 (D.N.H. 1985) (permitting defendant to counterclaim against New Hampshire for "failure to adequately conduct and supervise the various clean-up operations").

89. Dubuc and Evans, "Recent Developments Under CERCLA," p. 10202.

90. Special rules regarding cleanup of federal facilities are treated by the statute at §120. See generally Barry Breen, "Federal Supremacy and Sovereign Immunity Waivers in Federal Environmental Law," *Environ-*

mental Law Reporter 15 (1985): 10326–32; Donald W. Stever, "Perspectives on the Problem of Federal Facility Liability for Environmental Contamination," *Environmental Law Reporter* 17 (1987): 10014–19; David W. Goewey, "Assuring Federal Facility Compliance with the RCRA and Other Environmental Statutes: An Administrative Proposal," *William and Mary Law Review* 28 (1987): 513–52.

91. For discussions see Frank B. Cross, "Procedural Due Process Under Superfund, *Brigham Young University Law Review* (1986): 919–55; Alfred R. Light and David O. Ledbetter, "Process Overdue: The Erosion of Judicial Review Under Superfund," *Federal Bar News and Journal* 34 (1987): 27–33.

92. See "Developments—Toxic Waste Litigation," pp. 1487–90, 1555–65. The recent amendments strengthened this position developed under case law; see §113 (j).

93. Freeman, "Tort Law Reform," p. 534

94. See Ruckelshaus, "Environmental Risks," pp. 19–21.

95. See Freeman, "Tort Law Reform," p. 525, n. 21.

96. Howard Latin has questioned the strategy of fine-tuning regulatory procedures: "'Fine-tuning' would require assessments of particularized circumstances, and would therefore usually increase decisionmaking costs, delays, inconsistencies, bureaucratic discretion, and opportunities for manipulative behavior by regulated parties" ("Ideal Versus Real Regulatory Efficiency: Implementation of Uniform Standards and 'Fine-Tuning' Regulatory Reforms," *Stanford Law Review* 37 [1985]: 1332).

97. For a thoughtful elaboration of these points, see Robert L. Rabin, "Environmental Liability and the Tort System," *Houston Law Review* 24 (1987): 27–52.

98. "The Causal Connection in Mass Exposure Cases: A 'Public Law' Vision of the Tort System," *Harvard Law Review* 97 (1984): 849–929. For a different assessment of the comparative advantages of administrative procedures over judicial enforcement, see two articles by Richard J. Pierce, Jr., "Encouraging Safety: The Limits of Tort Law and Government Regulation," *Vanderbilt Law Review* 33 (1980): 1281–331; and "Institutional Aspects of Tort Reform," *California Law Review* 73 (1985): 917–40.

99. Atomic Energy Act Amendments of 1957, Pub. L. No. 85-256, 71 Stat. 576, 42 U.S.C. §2011–2134.

100. See the discussion in *Congressional Quarterly Almanac* 43 (1987): 311. In July 1987 the House of Representatives approved by a vote of 396–71 a version of H.R. 1414, which had been recommended by three House committees. The Senate, however, was unable to resolve differences between rival bills emerging from two of its committees. In March 1988 the Senate suddenly changed course and passed the House bill by voice

vote. President Reagan signed the law in August. Pub. L. No. 100-408, 102 Stat. 1066.

101. See the position of the Environmental Policy Institute on behalf of a variety of environmental groups, in the report by the Subcommittee on Energy Research and Production of the House Committee on Science and Technology, "Legislative Inquiry on the Price-Anderson Act," 99th Congress, 2nd Session (Committee Print, 1986), pp. 214–42. Similar objectives were framed in Senator Stafford's bill, S. 1761 introduced in that same Congress.

102. These figures are contained in the Report of the House Committee on Interior and Insular Affairs, which recommended passage of H.R. 1414 (House Report No. 100-104, part 1, p. 5). See also the appendices to Senate Report No. 100-218.

103. Nuclear Waste Policy Act of 1982, Pub. L. No. 97-425, 96 Stat. 2201, 42 U.S.C. §§10101–10226.

104. For a general overview of the act and its history, see the General Accounting Office summary in the testimony of Keith O. Fultz before the Subcommittee on Energy Research and Production of the House Committee on Science and Technology, reprinted in "Legislative Inquiry on the Price-Anderson Act," pp. 94–109.

105. House Report No. 100-104, part 1, p. 4. The $500 million figure is the limit of Congress's original indemnification agreements with all licensees and contractors. For commercial facilities, that obligation was replaced by a plan for retrospective assessment of $5 million on all licensed plants, which numbered 109 in mid 1987. To this figure was added $160 million from the private insurance market. For Department of Energy contractors, the original indemnification agreements and amounts remained in use. Under the 1988 reauthorization, the retrospective assessment was raised to about $63 million per plant.

106. For details on H.R. 1414 see House Report No. 100-104, parts 1–3. Other views on statutory limits were contained in Senate Reports No. 100-70 and No. 100-218. The threshold of $7 billion would decrease with any decline in the number of licensed commercial plants.

107. See House Report No. 100-104, part 1, pp. 8–11.

108. Ibid., pp. 11–13.

109. For an overview of current issues, see Joseph P. Tomain, "Law and Policy in the Activist State: Rethinking Nuclear Regulation," *Rutgers Law Review* 38 (1986): 187–239. Also of interest is the Nuclear Regulatory Commission's report to Congress, "The Price-Anderson Act—The Third Decade" (Washington, D.C.: Government Printing Office, 1983).

110. The most ambitious commitment for congressional action was contained in the report of the Senate Committee on the Environment, Senate

Report No. 100-218, which would have required Congress to choose between creating alternative compensation procedures within six months, or leaving itself open to reimbursement of all civil liability claims, under the legislative device of a "judgment appropriation." The 1988 Congressional compromise applies no such pressures, and it essentially allows Congress and the President an indefinite period for working out a specific compensation plan.

111. House Report No. 100-104, part 1, p. 12.

112. FTCA procedures should still apply to any nuclear accident claims based on actions by federal employees. Actions by federal contractors would fall under the same Price-Anderson procedures applicable to commercial operators, with whom the federal government has indemnification agreements.

113. See Arnold W. Rietze, Jr. and Deborah J. Rowe, "The Price-Anderson Act—Limited Liability for the Nuclear Industry," *Environmental Law Reporter* 17 (1987): 10185–96; and Leslie D. Lass, "The Price-Anderson Act: If a 'Chernobyl' Occurs in the United States, Will the Victims Be Adequately Compensated?" *Glendale Law Review* 7 (1987): 200–16. Rietze and Rowe provide a summary of recent speculation on the potential costs of a major nuclear accident in the United States, estimates that vary from amounts well under the old Price-Anderson threshold all the way to $300 billion. The authors pay close attention to specific components of these estimates, such as the costs of long-term medical surveillance and specialized medical procedures. Using recent CERCLA guidelines for monitoring toxic exposures, they estimate the costs of long-term surveillance for every 100,000 persons at $40 million. Bone-marrow transplants (only 12 of which were performed following Chernobyl) now cost between $112,000 and $472,000 per operation.

114. House Report No. 100-104, part 1, p. 5.

115. This is the position taken by a consortium of public interest environmental groups, in a report prepared by the Environmental Policy Institute; see "Legislative Inquiry on the Price-Anderson Act," pp. 214–42.

116. In addition to the Environmental Policy Institute document mentioned in note 115, see John V. Buffington, "The Price-Anderson Act: Underwriting the Ultimate Tort," *Dickinson Law Review* 87 (1983): 679–704.

117. See Robert St. Leger Goggin and Thomas A. Brophy, "Toxic Torts: Workable Defenses Available to the Corporate Defendant," *Villanova Law Review* 28 (1983): 1208–85.

118. See generally Harper, James, and Gray, *The Law of Torts*, vol. 3, chaps. 11–14.

119. See House Report No. 100-104, part 1, p. 3.

120. See the Environmental Policy Institute statement cited in note 115.
121. Atomic Energy Act Amendments of 1966, Pub. L. No. 89-645, 80 Stat. 891, 42 U.S.C. §2210(n).
122. See Harper, James, and Gray, *The Law of Torts*, vol. 3, p. 206, n. 49 (§14.4).
123. See Buffington, "The Price-Anderson Act," p. 694.
124. For a detailed discussion of these burdens in the context of lawsuits against the U.S. government for exposing civilians to radioactive fallout during the course of atomic testing in the 1950s, see Howard Ball, "The Problems and Prospects of Fashioning a Remedy for Radiation Injury Plaintiffs in Federal District Court," *Utah Law Review* (1985): 267–324.
125. For a brief overview see the report by the Government Accounting Office, "Three Mile Island: The Most Studied Nuclear Accident in History" (Washington, D.C.: Government Printing Office, 1980).
126. See Rietze and Rowe, "The Price-Anderson Act," p. 10191. More than 150 separate cases were filed against various Three Mile Island defendants by more than 3,000 claimants in various state and federal courts. See Senate Report No. 100-218, p. 13.
127. House Report 100-104, part 1, p. 16.
128. Stibitz v. General Public Utilities Corp., 746 F.2d 993 (3rd Cir. 1984), *cert. denied*, 469 U.S. 1214 (1985).
129. House Report No. 100-104, part 1, p. 18. See also Senate Report No. 100-218, p. 13.
130. See *Ending Insult to Injury: No-Fault Insurance for Products and Services* (Urbana: University of Illinois Press, 1975), and other works cited in Chapter 7.
131. Another difficulty in relying on tort procedures to allocate finite compensation funds is the regulation of legal fees. Under pre-1987 law, litigation expenses would come off the top of the fund guaranteed by Price-Anderson. Both House and Senate committee sponsors of new legislation recognized the potential for serious depletion of the fund by unregulated litigation, but neither devised specific solutions; House Report No. 100-104, part 1, pp. 15–16; Senate Report No. 100-218, p. 12. Another source of pressure on limited funds will be punitive damages; both reports supported the availability of punitive damages under Price-Anderson, vindicating the Supreme Court's interpretation in Silkwood v. Kerr-McGee Corp., 464 U.S. 238 (1984).
132. See Richard Wilson, "Nuclear Liability and the Price-Anderson Act," *Forum* 12 (1977): 612–21. Wilson suggests that the same private-public collaboration should occur in other areas of potential large-scale liability.
133. See the discussion in Chapter 6 for references. A related problem is the impact of mass litigation on liability insurance cost and availability. See

Jerry Hougland Stewart, "The Pollution Liability Insurance 'Crisis': Development of a Problem, Suggestions for a Solution," *Capital University Law Review* 15 (1986): 677–97.

134. David Rosenberg, Review of Paul Brodeur's *Outrageous Misconduct, Harvard Law Review* 99 (1986): 1706.

135. Richard A. Epstein, *Takings: Private Property and the Power of Eminent Domain* (Cambridge, Mass.: Harvard University Press, 1985), pp. 36, 13. Predictably, Epstein treats the Price-Anderson Act as "taking" individuals' private common-law rights (pp. 243–44).

136. See Patrick C. McGinley, "Regulatory 'Takings': The Remarkable Resurrection of Economic Substantive Due Process Analysis in Constitutional Law," *Environmental Law Reporter* 17 (1987): 10369–76.

137. Rabin, "Environmental Liability," p. 33.

138. Ibid., p. 38.

139. Ibid., p. 41.

Chapter 9

1. Lawrence M. Friedman and Jack Ladinsky, "Social Change and the Law of Industrial Accidents," *Columbia Law Review* 67 (1967): 81.

2. For general background see Herman M. Somers and Anne R. Somers, *Workmen's Compensation* (New York: John Wiley & Sons, 1954), chap. 2; Daniel T. Doherty, Jr., "Historical Development of Workmen's Compensation," in National Commission on State Workmen's Compensation Laws, *Compendium on Workmen's Compensation* (Washington, D.C.: Government Printing Office, 1973), pp. 11–19.

3. For an overview see National Commission, *Compendium on Workmen's Compensation*, pp. 101–295. Detailed descriptions of state programs can be found in Arthur Larson, *The Law of Workmen's Compensation* (New York: Matthew Bender, 1987).

4. The new procedural framework superseded the alternative statutory strategy, used briefly by some states, of modifying tort rules governing employer liability. See Somers and Somers, *Workmen's Compensation*, pp. 21–26.

5. Many states have raised the maximum benefit rate for temporary disability to at least 100 percent of the statewide average weekly wage, but the formulae vary widely across the country. See Karen R. DeVol, *Income Replacement for Short-Term Disability: The Role of Workers' Compensation* (Cambridge, Mass.: Workers' Compensation Research Institute, 1985).

6. See Larson's treatise, *The Law of Workmen's Compensation*, for details of state programs. Some states respond indirectly to cases of permanent

impairment (like the loss of a limb) by compensating a higher proportion of a worker's lost income.

7. See references in note 28.

8. See references in notes 32 and 48.

9. See, for example, Laurence Locke, "Adapting Workers' Compensation to the Special Problems of Occupational Disease," *Harvard Environmental Law Review* 9 (1985): 249–82.

10. The phrase comes from Peter W. J. Bartrip's comprehensive review of British policy: *Workmen's Compensation in Twentieth Century Britain: Law, History and Social Policy* (Aldershot, Eng.: Gower Publishing Co., 1987), p. 1. See also Bartrip's study of nineteenth-century conditions, written with S. B. Burman, *The Wounded Soldiers of Industry: Industrial Compensation Policy, 1833–1897* (Oxford: Clarendon Press, 1983).

11. The former approach is epitomized in the phrase used by British reformers: "the wounded soldiers of industry." See Bartrip and Burman, *Wounded Soldiers*, p. 5. Evidence for the latter position was presented by Richard Posner, "A Theory of Negligence," *Journal of Legal Studies* 1 (1972): 29–96, who slyly suggests that common law trends would have promoted "optimal" investment in accident prevention more effectively than workers' compensation.

12. Deborah A. Stone, *The Disabled State* (Philadelphia: Temple University Press, 1984), p. 98. See also Friedman and Ladinsky, "Social Change."

13. The British workers' compensation scheme was converted to a system of social insurance in 1946, although it still leaves workers the option of seeking common-law damages. See Bartrip, *Workmen's Compensation in Twentieth Century Britain*, chap. 9; P. S. Atiyah and Peter Cane, *Accidents, Compensation and the Law*, 4th ed. (London: Weidenfeld & Nicolson, 1987), chaps. 14–15. Social insurance is also to be distinguished from programs requiring potential victims to purchase insurance for themselves.

14. Fowler V. Harper, Fleming James, Jr. and Oscar S. Gray, *The Law of Torts*, 2nd ed. (Boston: Little, Brown, 1986), vol. 3, p. 129 (§13.1).

15. Ibid., pp. 135–55 (§§13.3–13.5). For the British experience see Bartrip and Burman, *Wounded Soldiers*, chap. 7.

16. For a range of views comparing current product liability options and workers' compensation, see National Legal Center for the Public Interest, *Conference on Workers' Compensation and Workplace Liability* (Washington, D.C.: National Legal Center for the Public Interest, 1981), pp. 38–93f; Judith A. Schening, "Federal Products Liability Legislation: Not the Cure for Workers' Compensation Ailments," *Northern Illinois University Law Review* 6 (1986): 319–46.

17. Occupational Safety and Health Act of 1970, Pub. L. No. 91-596, 84 Stat. 1590, 29 U.S.C. §§651–678.

18. Federal Employees' Compensation Act of 1916, 39 Stat. 742, 5 U.S.C. §§8101–8149. Some state courts struck down state workers' compensation programs, based on federal constitutional theories of due process. See especially the decision of the New York Court of Appeals in Ives v. South Buffalo R.R. Co., 201 N.Y. 271, 94 N.E. 431 (1911). The U.S. Supreme Court rejected this rationale in New York Central R.R. Co. v. White, 243 U.S. 188 (1917). For a contemporary discussion of constitutional issues see Eugene Wambaugh, "Workmen's Compensation Acts: Their Theory and Their Constitutionality," *Harvard Law Review* 25 (1911): 129–39.

19. New York Central R.R. Co. v. Winfield, 244 U.S. 147 (1917). The statute in question, the Federal Employers' Liability Act of 1908 (FELA), 35 Stat. 65, 45 U.S.C. §§51–59, granted federal court jurisdiction for employee compensation actions against railroad companies, eliminated the fellow-servant rule, and changed the contributory negligence defense to the more lenient comparative negligence rule. See Clarence A. Miller, "The Quest for a Federal Workmen's Compensation Law for Railroad Employees," *Law and Contemporary Problems* 18 (1953): 188–207. Similar coverage was extended to injured seamen in 1920 under the Jones Act, and to maritime workers in 1927 under the Longshoremen's and Harbor Workers' Compensation Act. For a current discussion and critique of FELA, see Victor E. Schwartz and Liberty Mahshigian, "The Federal Employers' Liability Act: A Bane for Workers, A Bust for Railroads, A Boon for Lawyers," *San Diego Law Review* 23 (1986): 1–15.

20. Edward D. Berkowitz, *Disabled Policy: America's Programs for the Handicapped* (Cambridge: Cambridge University Press, 1987), pp. 33–35.

21. National Commission on State Workmen's Compensation Laws, *Report to Congress* (Washington, D.C.: Government Printing Office, 1972), pp. 13–27. This report was mandated by OSHA in a compromise between defenders of state workers' compensation and advocates of federalized standards.

22. The last effort in Congress is documented in "National Workers' Compensation Standards Act of 1979," Hearings Before the Subcommittee on Labor Standards of the House Committee on Education and Labor, 96th Congress, 2nd Session (1980).

23. Edward D. Berkowitz and Monroe Berkowitz, "Challenges to Workers' Compensation: An Historical Analysis," in John D. Worrall and David Appel, eds., *Workers' Compensation Benefits: Adequacy, Equity, and Efficiency* (Ithaca, N.Y.: ILR Press, 1985), p. 176.

24. See the statement of Harvey Alter and Samuel A. Roth, representing

the U.S. Chamber of Commerce, "Compensation for Occupational Diseases," Hearings Before the Subcommittee on Labor Standards of the House Committee on Education and Labor, 99th Congress, 1st Session (1985), pp. 258–91.

25. See testimony of Frederick J. Ross (Raymark Corp.) and John A. McKinney (Manville Corp. of Denver) in "Asbestos Workers' Recovery Act," Hearing on S. 1265 Before the Subcommittee on Health of the Senate Committee on Finance, 99th Congress, 1st Session (1985), pp. 13–92.

26. Before 1985 the federal government faced possible civil liability for some asbestos injuries, based on its alleged failure to warn employees of private contractors about possible health hazards. In congressional hearings both the government and asbestos companies stressed that federal legislation was necessary to save the government from ruinous liability, but eventually a federal appeals court found the failure-to-warn theory inconsistent with sovereign immunity. Shuman v. United States, 765 F.2d 283 (1st Cir. 1985).

27. Friedman and Ladinsky, "Social Change," p. 72.

28. Litigation within the formal structure of workers' compensation will be discussed below. In addition, courts have recently carved out exceptions to employers' immunity from tort liability—the original *quid pro quo* for the employers' acquiescence in no-fault, vicarious responsibility. See Sheila L. Birnbaum, "Inroads in the Immunity Shield: Employee Tort Actions Against Employers," in National Legal Center for the Public Interest, *Conference on Workers' Compensation*, pp. 115–24; Merton E. Marks, "Status of the Exclusive Workers' Compensation Remedy: Actions by Employees Against Coemployees, Employers and Carriers," *Tort and Insurance Law Journal* 22 (1987): 612–23. Employers may also be sued for reimbursement by defendants in product liability cases based on workplace injuries: see the discussion in *Conference on Workers' Compensation*, pp. 50–93f; and Michael T. Hertz, "The Tort Triangle: Contribution from Defendants Whom Plantiffs Cannot Sue," *Maine Law Review* 32 (1980): 83–145.

29. Berkowitz, *Disabled Policy*, p. 33.

30. See the recommendations of Jerry J. Phillips, in National Legal Center for the Public Interest, *Conference on Workers' Compensation*, pp. 50–56.

31. See Eli P. Bernzweig, *By Accident Not Design: The Case for Comprehensive Injury Reparations* (New York: Praeger, 1980), pp. 21–23; John H. Lewis, Richard S. Cohen, and Gary S. Klein, "Major Issues in Workmen's Compensation Law," in National Commission, *Compendium on Workmen's Compensation*, pp. 181–204.

32. According to most estimates, the overall costs to employers tripled during the period 1950–83, with approximately half that increase occurring

during 1972–78. For a comprehensive analysis see John F. Burton, Jr., and Alan B. Krueger, "Interstate Variations in the Employers' Costs of Workers' Compensation," in John R. Chelius, ed., *Current Issues in Workers' Compensation* (Kalamazoo, Mich.: Upjohn Institute, 1986), pp. 111–208.

33. "The Status and Direction of Workers' Compensation," in Chelius, *Current Issues*, p. 10.

34. Berkowitz, *Disabled Policy*, p. 24.

35. Ibid. In 1971, Merton C. Bernstein observed, "The intricacies of workmen's compensation law now rival those of property and tax law with which only the most expert or most naive feel at ease. Despite yesterday's plan for procedures simple enough to make unnecessary lawyers who earned impressive fees for Employer Liability Act cases, many union lawyers today prefer the known hazards of secondary-boycott injunction proceedings to the miasmal swamps of workmen's compensation proceedings" ("The Need for Reconsidering the Role of Workmen's Compensation," *University of Pennsylvania Law Review* 119 [1971]: 995).

36. Karen R. DeVol, *Income Replacement for Long-Term Disability: The Role of Workers' Compensation and Social Security Disability Insurance* (Cambridge, Mass.: Workers' Compensation Research Institute, 1986).

37. According to a 1980 U.S. Department of Labor study, the major sources of support for people severely disabled by occupational disease were as follows: Social Security (53 percent), pensions (21 percent), veterans' benefits (17 percent), welfare (16 percent), workers' compensation (5 percent), and private insurance (1 percent) (*An Interim Report to Congress on Occupational Disease* [Washington, D.C.: Department of Labor, 1980], p. 61). These figures are based on 1974 data collected by the Social Security Administration, and have been criticized on various grounds.

38. See Ann P. Bartel and Lacy Glenn Thomas, "The Costs and Benefits of OSHA-Induced Investments in Employee Safety and Health," in Worrall and Appel, *Workers' Compensation Benefits*, pp. 41–56. The authors attempt to account for the different results in earlier studies by W. Kip Viscusi, "The Impact of Occupational Safety and Health Regulation," *Bell Journal of Economics* 10 (1979): 117–40, and Murray L. Wiedenbaum and Robert de Fina, *The Cost of Federal Regulation of Economic Activity* (Washington, D.C.: American Enterprise Institute, 1978).

39. Robert H. Ashford and William G. Johnson, "Negligence Versus No-Fault Liability: An Analysis of the Workers' Compensation Example," *Seton Hall Law Review* 12 (1982): 766.

40. See Richard B. Victor, *Workers' Compensation and Workplace Safety*: *The Nature of Employer Financial Incentives* (Santa Monica, Cal.: Rand Corporation, 1982); "Experience Rating and Workplace Safety," in Worrall and Appel, *Workers' Compensation Benefits*, pp. 71–88.

41. Harper, James, and Gray, *The Law of Torts*, vol. 3, p. 82, n. 35 (§11.2). For a summary of insurance practices and policy issues, see C. Arthur Williams, Jr., "Workers' Compensation Insurance Rates," in Chelius, *Current Issues*, pp. 209–35. For harms related to environmental accidents, insurance faces special problems in promoting microeconomic efficiency; see Kenneth S. Abraham, *Distributing Risk: Insurance, Legal Theory, and Public Policy* (New Haven, Conn.: Yale University Press, 1986), p. 51.

42. In October 1987 the House of Representatives passed a notification bill over the strenuous objections of Republicans, who predicted a "litigation landslide" if the bill became law; "Risk-Notification Legislation Passed by House," *Congressional Quarterly Weekly Report* 45 (1987): 2513–14. For general background see Ronald Bayer, "Notifying Workers at Risk: The Politics of the Right-to-Know," *American Journal of Public Health* 76 (1986): 1352–56.

43. Terence G. Ison, "Etiological Classifications in Compensation Systems," *Adelaide Law Review* 10 (1985): 86–91. Attilio D. Renzetti, Jr., notes the "disruption in many aspects of society in coal mining communities" as medical and legal guidelines for the federal Black Lung Program led to anomalies in awards among miners, "when there is no substantial difference in their medical condition." As Renzetti concludes, "Fundamentally, there are no sound medical reasons for dealing with occupational lung diseases on a piecemeal basis." "The 'Black Lung' Act: A Pitfall?" in J. Bernard L. Gee, ed., *Occupational Lung Disease* (New York: Churchill Livingstone, 1984), p. 244.

44. Cited in Peter S. Barth and H. Allan Hunt, *Workers' Compensation and Work-Related Diseases* (Cambridge, Mass.: MIT Press, 1980), p. 147. The Department of Labor's 1980 *Interim Report to Congress* found that "only five percent of those severely disabled from an occupational disease receive workers' compensation benefits" (p. 3). See also the Labor Department's summary of other studies, pp. 67–72.

45. Peter S. Barth, "Compensation for Asbestos-Associated Disease: A Survey of Asbestos Insulation Workers in the United States and Canada," in Irving S. Selikoff, *Disability Compensation for Asbestos-Related Disease in the United States* (New York: Mt. Sinai Hospital of the City University of New York, 1982), chap. 5; Donald L. Spatz, "Issues in Asbestos Disease Compensation," in Chelius, *Current Issues*, pp. 287–311 (discussing the "best case" example of the New Jersey workers' com-

pensation system). A recent study by the Workers' Compensation Research Institute, using data from Massachusetts, explores a number of reasons why asbestos victims have failed to use workers' compensation. *Asbestos Claims in Workers' Compensation: The Decision to Use Workers' Compensation and Tort* (Cambridge, Mass.: Workers' Compensation Research Institute, 1988).

46. Barth and Hunt, *Workers' Compensation*, pp. 147–87.

47. Ibid., p. 187. See also Barth's proposal for a separate administrative system for compensating occupationally caused cancer: "A Proposal for Dealing with Compensation of Occupational Diseases," *Journal of Legal Studies* 13 (1984): 569–86.

48. Processing costs under workers' compensation are variously estimated at 40 to 52 percent of each dollar awarded in compensation, which is not far below the 60 percent rate for tort law, and well above the 5 percent rate for Social Security disability. See Bernzweig, *By Accident*, pp. 22, 178.

49. The 1973 bill was H.R. 6906, 93rd Congress, 1st Session. Among later bills see H.R. 5224, 97th Congress, 1st Session (1981) (the "Fenwick bill"); S. 1643, 97th Congress, 1st Session (1981) (the "Hart bill"); and H.R. 5735, 97th Congress, 2nd Session (1982) (the "Miller bill"). For an overview of proposals through 1982 see Eugene R. Anderson, Irene C. Warshauer, and Adrienne M. Coffin, "The Asbestos Health Hazards Compensation Act: A Legislative Solution to a Litigation Crisis," *Journal of Legislation* 10 (1983): 25–80.

50. H.R. 3090, 99th Congress, 1st Session (1985). James E. Vermeulen, testifying on behalf of the Asbestos Victims of America, no doubt spoke for other organized plaintiffs in denouncing an alternative bill preempting tort law as "a disgraceful piece of legislative garbage which merely adds insult to our injuries" (Hearing on S. 1265, p. 216).

51. In addition to references in note 42, see David S. Sundin, David H. Pederson, and Todd M. Frazier, "Occupational Hazard and Health Surveillance," *American Journal of Public Health* 76 (1986): 1083–84.

52. The major exception was the Miller bill, which would have channeled claims directly into the federal Office of Workers' Compensation. A similar approach appeared in the model statute contained in Anderson et al., "Asbestos Health Hazards."

53. The Fenwick bill included the cigarette industry as a contributor, while the Miller bill excused the federal government from all contributions to the fund.

54. The only major proposal to include presumptions was the Miller bill, to be discussed in the next section.

55. See the remarks of Frederick J. Ross (Raymark Corp.), "Occupational

Disease Compensation Act of 1983," Hearings on H.R. 3175 Before the Subcommittee on Labor Standards of the House Committee on Education and Labor, 98th Congress, 1st Session (1983), pp. 123–42.

56. In addition to references cited in the previous section, see Elinor P. Schroeder, "Legislative and Judicial Responses to the Inadequacy of Compensation for Occupational Disease," *Law and Contemporary Problems* 49 (Autumn 1986): 157.

57. H.R. 5735, §§5(b)(1)–(3).

58. See the response of Frederick J. Ross to provisions in a related bill, Hearings on H.R. 3175, pp. 142–48.

59. Anderson et al., "Asbestos Health Hazards," pp. 50–51.

60. See Schroeder, "Legislative and Judicial Responses," p. 164.

61. For some reckless comments comparing "efficiency arguments" with "political arguments," see George L. Priest, "Law and Economics and Law Reform: Comment on Barth's Cancer Compensation Proposal," *Journal of Legal Studies* 13 (1984): 587–92.

62. Federal Coal Mine Health and Safety Act of 1969, Pub. L. No. 91-173, 83 Stat. 742, 30 U.S.C. §§801–962.

63. 83 Stat. 793, Sec. 401(b) (1969); 20 C.F.R. §718.201 (1988). These separate definitions are discussed in both medical and lay terms by James L. Weeks and Gregory R. Wagner, "Compensation for Occupational Disease with Multiple Causes: The Case of Coal Miners' Respiratory Diseases," *American Journal of Public Health* 76 (1986): 58–59. See also W. Keith C. Morgan, "Coal Workers Pneumoconiosis," in W. Keith C. Morgan and Anthony Seaton, eds., *Occupational Lung Diseases*, 2nd ed. (Philadelphia: W. B. Saunders, 1984), pp. 377–448.

64. For a thorough (and somewhat polemical) review of economic and social conditions in the mining industry, see two works by Barbara Ellen Smith: "Black Lung: The Social Production of Disease," *International Journal of Health Services* 11 (1981): 343–59; and *Digging Our Own Graves: Coal Miners and the Struggle Over Black Lung Disease* (Philadelphia: Temple University Press, 1987).

65. See Peter S. Barth, *The Tragedy of Black Lung: Federal Compensation for Occupational Disease* (Kalamazoo, Mich.: Upjohn Institute, 1987), pp. 8–9. Barth's general criticisms of state workers' compensation programs in the late 1960s are reflected in various publications of the National Commission on State Workmen's Compensation Laws, of which Barth was executive director. See, for example, the commission's 1972 *Report to Congress*, which was mandated by the 1970 Occupational Safety and Health Act as a preliminary step toward federal oversight of workers' compensation; and the views collected in National Commission, *Compendium on Workers' Compensation*.

66. For analysis see John R. Nelson, Jr., *Black Lung: A Study of Disability Compensation Policy Formation* (Chicago: University of Chicago School of Social Service Administration, 1985), pp. 19–20.
67. Ibid., pp. 40–54, provides a detailed account.
68. Donald Elisburg, "Federal Occupational Disease Legislation: A Current Review," in Chelius, *Current Issues*, p. 262.
69. 83 Stat. 793, §411(c)(1) created a rebuttable presumption of occupational causation for any diagnosed case of "pneumoconiosis" in a miner employed for ten years or in more than one mine. §411(c)(2) provided that the same employment history would establish a rebuttable presumption that death from any respiratory disease was caused by "pneumoconiosis." See Barth, *The Tragedy of Black Lung*, pp. 111–14.
70. §411(c)(3).
71. §411(c)(4), added by the 1972 amendments, Black Lung Benefits Act, Pub. L. No. 92–303, 86 Stat. 154.
72. §413(b), also added by the 1972 amendments, 86 Stat. 154.
73. §402(d), added by the 1977 amendments, Black Lung Benefits Reform Act, Pub. L. No. 95-239, 92 Stat. 95 (1978). See Barth, *The Tragedy of Black Lung*, pp. 145–48.
74. Barth, *The Tragedy of Black Lung*, p. 284.
75. Black Lung Benefits Revenue Act of 1981, Pub. L. No. 97-119, 95 Stat. 1635.
76. By the mid 1980s the Black Lung Trust Fund was running a deficit of $2.5 billion, financed out of the federal treasury (*Congressional Quarterly Almanac* 42 [1986]: 521).
77. Leslie I. Boden, "Problems in Occupational Disease Compensation," in Chelius, *Current Issues*, pp. 323, 321. The Black Lung experience has become an obligatory example for commentators warning against the likely costs of any occupational disease program. See, for example, James W. Newman, Jr., *Occupational Disease* (New York: Insurance Information Institute, 1987), pp. 92–105.
78. See Nelson's conclusions, *Black Lung*, pp. 154–71. For a general theory of expansionary forces in disability programs see Deborah A. Stone, *The Disabled State* (Philadelphia: Temple University Press, 1984).
79. Boden argues that such diverse perspectives are inescapable, given that "any presumption is likely to include in its scope workers without occupational disease, and is likely as well to exclude workers with occupational disease." The scientific expert cannot judge "whether to compensate fewer occupational disease victims in order to compensate fewer 'undeserving' claimants" (Chelius, *Current Issues*, p. 320).
80. See Barth, *The Tragedy of Black Lung*, pp. 275–84. See also Renzetti, "The 'Black Lung' Act," pp. 244–45.

81. See Schroeder, "Legislative and Judicial Responses," p. 170. For an example of litigation tangles resulting from the Black Lung Program's incremental evolution, see the 1987 Supreme Court opinion in Mullins Coal Co. v. Director, Office of Workers' Compensation Programs, 108 S.Ct. 427 (1987).

82. The proposed Victim Assistance Demonstration Program appears in Senate Report No. 99-11, Committee on the Environment and Public Works, 99th Congress, 1st Session (1985), pp. 48–54.

83. Superfund Section 301(e) Study Group, "Injuries and Damages from Hazardous Wastes—Analysis and Improvement of Legal Remedies," 97th Congress, 2nd Session (Committee Print, 1982). Recommendations of the study group were incorporated in S. 946, 98th Congress, 1st Session (1983). A program for compensating toxic injuries was earlier presented by Stephen M. Soble, "A Proposal for the Administrative Compensation of Victims of Toxic Substance Pollution: A Model Act," *Harvard Journal on Legislation* 14 (1977): 683–824. Congress omitted personal-injury compensation from the scope of the 1980 Superfund law, but created the study group to research the underlying issues.

84. Superfund Study Group Report, pp. 196–205.

85. Additional draft legislation in the 98th Congress envisioned even broader use of judicial procedures. See Alfred R. Light, "A Comparison of the 301(e) Report and Some Pending Legislative Proposals," in American Bar Association, *Recovery for Exposure to Hazardous Substances: The Superfund Section 301(e) Report and Beyond* (Washington, D.C.: American Bar Association, 1984), pp. 32–38.

86. The substance of the model is spelled out in ten separate recommendations, Superfund Study Group Report, pp. 193–283.

87. Ibid., p. 290.

88. For a summary of events surrounding the compromise funding formula, see *Congressional Quarterly Weekly Report* 44 (1986): 2317.

89. See Douglas F. Brennan, "Joint and Several Liability for Generators Under Superfund: A Federal Formula for Cost Recovery," *UCLA Journal of Environmental Law and Policy* 5 (1986): 101–35, along with other references cited in Chapter 8.

90. See the discussions by Victor E. Schwartz and others, reprinted in National Legal Center for the Public Interest, *Conference on Workers' Compensation*, pp. 38–93f.

91. See the Department of Labor's 1980 *Interim Report to Congress*.

92. See Anderson et al., "Asbestos Health Hazards."

93. Ibid., p. 48.

94. See criticisms in the report sponsored by the U.S. Chamber of Commerce, *Compensation for Injury from Exposure to Hazards: Some Con-*

siderations in Evaluating and Forming Public Policy (Washington, D.C.: U.S. Chamber of Commerce, 1985), pp. 227–28.

95. For an assessment of litigation prospects under the 1986 Amendments ("SARA"), see Richard H. Mays, "Settlements with SARA: A Comprehensive Review of Settlement Procedures under the Superfund Amendments and Reauthorization Act," *Environmental Law Reporter* 17 (1987): 10101–13.

96. Superfund Study Group Report, pp. 245–51.

97. For an analysis of the federal role in vaccine programs, see Office of Technology Assessment, *A Review of Selected Federal Vaccine and Immunization Policies* (Washington, D.C.: Government Printing Office, 1979); for biomedical research see National Commission for the Protection of Human Subjects of Biomedical and Behavioral Research, *The Belmont Report* (Washington, D.C.: Government Printing Office, 1978).

98. National Childhood Vaccine Injury Compensation Act of 1986, Pub. L. No. 99-660, Title III; 100 Stat. 3755; 42 U.S.C. §300aa. See the President's statement in *Weekly Compilation of Presidential Documents* 22 (1986): 1565–67. Some details of the law were changed the following year by the Vaccine Compensation Act Amendments of 1987, Pub. L. No. 100-203, Title IV, §§4301–4307; 101 Stat. 1330-221.

99. Referring to language in a 1987 Congressional report, some courts have interpreted the new vaccine law as placing only minor restraints on plaintiffs wanting to pursue state tort remedies. See, for example, Abbot v. American Cyanamid Co., 844 F.2d 1108 (4th Cir. 1988), and Graham v. Wyeth Laboratories, 666 F.Supp. 1483, 1492 (D.Kan. 1987). House Report No. 100-391 (100th Congress, 1st Session [1987], pp. 690–712) seems to suggest that Congress was using carrots rather than sticks in trying to lead litigants away from tort law. The message in this report represents a shift from that of the previous year, as Congress became concerned about limiting overall expenditures. It thus diluted the program in various ways: by shifting the responsibility for federal administration from the regular district courts to the United States Claims Court, and by capping the number of awards that could pass through the federal system in any single year. State tort law could not be completely buried unless Congress was prepared to fund the vaccine program at a higher level. It remains to be seen, of course, whether this dual system will take any pressure off vaccine manufacturers.

100. While the statute avoids the troublesome language of presumptions, it accomplishes the same purpose by setting out a Vaccine Injury Table listing the covered vaccines, relevant side effects, and the time period within which first symptoms must be manifested. To deny payment, the

Department of Health and Human Services must show by a "preponderance of the evidence" that the facts alleged by the claimant are un-
true or do not meet the listed conditions, or that the claimant's injury
was due to other sources (100 Stat 3755, §2113[a]).

101. A funding mechanism was proposed in House Report No. 99-908, 99th
Congress, 2nd Session (1986), pp. 33–34, but was deleted from the bill
at the last minute; thus the program was delayed until Congress could
approve a new excise tax. When actuaries first calculated that the tax for
DPT vaccine would need to be $8.00 per dose, some politicians thought
the program was doomed. But House negotiators reduced the cost to
$4.50 by scaling back the coverage. Even this arrangement faced a possi-
ble presidential veto, but was saved as part of the overall budget recon-
ciliation bill for 1988. See "Vaccine Compensation Plan Cut Back by Two
House Panels," *Congressional Quarterly Weekly Report* 45 (1987): 2516.

102. §2115(a)(2)–(4).

103. §§2121–2122. In addition, §2123 sets some procedural hurdles in the
plaintiff's path toward punitive damages. These limits do not apply,
however, to persons injured before the law took effect.

104. The act also covers measles, mumps, rubella, and polio (§2114[a]).

105. The major studies on DPT are cited by Allison B. David and Ali Jalilian-
Marian, "DTP: Drug Manufacturers' Liability in Vaccine-Related Injuries," *Journal of Legal Medicine* 7 (1986): 190–203.

106. The status of childhood vaccine programs is comprehensively reviewed
in a staff report by the Subcommittee on Health and the Environment
of the House Committee on Energy and Commerce, "Childhood Immunizations," 99th Congress, 2nd Session (Committee Print, 1986).

107. See the testimony and exhibits presented by Dissatisfied Parents Together ("DPT") in "National Childhood Vaccine-Injury Compensation
Act," Hearing Before the Senate Committee on Labor and Human Resources, 98th Congress, 2nd Session (1984), pp. 46–145.

108. See the remarks of John E. Lyons (Merck & Co.), "Vaccine Injury Compensation," Hearing Before the Subcommittee on Health and the Environment of the House Committee on Energy and Commerce, 99th
Congress, 2nd Session (1986), pp. 220–30.

109. 90 Stat. 1118 (1976).

110. Department of HEW, *Liability Arising Out of Immunization Programs*:
Final Report to Congress (Washington, D.C.: DHEW, 1978). The report seems to have been heavily influenced by Calabresi's analytical
categories.

111. See the Office of Technology Assessment, *Review of Selected Federal
Vaccine and Immunization Policies*, p. 139.

112. *Liability Arising Out of Immunization Programs*, pp. 130–41.

113. National Immunization Work Group on Liability, "Reports and Recom-

mendations," reprinted in Office of the Assistant Secretary for Health, *Reports and Recommendations of the National Immunization Work Groups* (Washington, D.C.: DHEW, 1977), p. 13.

114. *Reports and Recommendations of the National Immunization Work Groups*, p. 14. The preface to this report makes it plain that the work group on liability could not reach consensus on basic principles (p. i).

115. See the Office of Technology Assessment, *Review of Selected Federal Vaccine and Immunization Policies.*

116. For a historical overview of federal involvement in the ethics of biomedical research see Albert R. Jonsen, "Public Policy and Human Research," in James M. Humber and Robert T. Almeder, eds., *Biomedical Ethics Reviews* (Clifton, N.J.: Humana Press, 1984), pp. 3–20.

117. HEW Secretary's Task Force on the Compensation of Injured Research Subjects, *Report* (Bethesda, Md.: National Institutes of Health, 1977), pp. III-2–III-3.

118. Ibid., section IV.

119. Ibid., p. III-1. The report contains veiled references to inconsistencies in litigation, but its major objection comes in a cryptic comment that "the tribulations connected with litigation and its emphasis on the adversarial process do not create the ambience which the research community should want to promote" (p. V-2).

120. Ibid., pp. VI-4–VI-5, VI-7. Engelhardt's report is reprinted in Appendix A, pp. 45–63.

121. See the background report by Frederick G. G. Barber, Jr., ibid., Appendix A, pp. 167–98.

122. See ibid., pp. VII-5–VII-11. The regulations appeared at 45 C.F.R. §46.103 (1979).

123. "If the individuals involved understand and appreciate the risks, their choices should be tolerated. One should be as tolerant of martyrs for unconventional understandings of science as one is of martyrs for what others may hold to be unconventional religious viewpoints" (*Foundations of Bioethics* [New York: Oxford University Press, 1986], p. 294; see also pp. 23–49).

124. Task Force on the Compensation of Injured Research Subjects, *Report*, p. VI-5.

125. See, for example, Paul S. Appelbaum, Charles W. Lidz, and Alan Meisel, *Informed Consent: Legal Theory and Clinical Practice* (New York: Oxford University Press, 1987), pp. 151–74.

126. See especially works by Richard Epstein discussed in Chapter 5.

127. On the performance of Institutional Review Boards see President's Commission for the Study of Ethical Problems in Medicine and Biomedical and Behavioral Research, *Implementing Human Research Regulations* (Washington, D.C.: Government Printing Office, 1983). Ethics

committees in medical settings may still face judicial oversight; see Andrew L. Merritt, "The Tort Liability of Hospital Ethics Committees,"
Southern California Law Review 60 (1987): 1239–97. The Supreme
Court's decision in Patrick v. Burget, 108 S.Ct. 1658 (1988), opened the
way to possible antitrust challenges to peer-review committees in hospital settings. Issues for further clarification are suggested by Bolt v.
Halifax Hospital Medical Center, 851 F.2d. 1273 (11th Cir. 1988).

Chapter 10

1. Gustave H. Shubert, *Some Observations on the Need for Tort Reform*
   (Santa Monica, Cal.: Rand Corporation, 1986), p. 11.
2. Izhak Englard, "The System Builders: A Critical Appraisal of Modern
   American Tort Theory," *Journal of Legal Studies* 9 (1980): 68.
3. It takes a presentation as bold as Richard Epstein's libertarian theories to
   bring these assumptions to the surface. Among the works discussed in
   Chapter 5, see "A Theory of Strict Liability," *Journal of Legal Studies* 2
   (1973): 151–204; and *Modern Products Liability Law* (Westport, Conn.:
   Quorum Books, 1980).
4. As Ison notes, a similar presumption operates most of the time in medicine as well. "The prevailing practice is that uncertainty about the etiology of a disease is deemed to warrant a negative assumption" (Terence G.
   Ison, "Etiological Classifications in Compensation Systems," *Adelaide
   Law Review* 10 [1985]: 90).
5. For a summary of legal issues see Fowler V. Harper, Fleming James, Jr.,
   and Oscar S. Gray, *The Law of Torts*, 2nd ed. (Boston: Little, Brown,
   1986), vol. 5, pp. 453–64 (§28.16).
6. This treatment of causation is related to classic definitions from academic
   sociology. "A very large percentage of our inquiries in the social sciences
   involve questions of the less and the more, between the then and the
   now, the here and the there, this group and the other group. Alike they
   call for analysis of evidences of disparate kinds, pertaining to the physical
   environment, the various circles of the social environment, and the pat-
   terning of the mental and somatic characterisics of individuals and
   groups, thus revealing conjunctures of conditions that are somehow registered in what we have ventured to name the dynamic assessment. Our
   discovery of causation is consequently always incomplete and at best progressive, always leaving room for future investigation." R. M. MacIver,
   Social Causation (1942; reprint New York: Harper & Row, 1964), p. xiii.
7. For the argument that epidemiological findings define potential preventive strategies for public policy, see Leon S. Robinson, *Injuries: Causes,*

Control Strategies, and Public Policy (Lexington, Mass.: D. C. Heath, 1983); Sol Levine and Abraham Lilienfeld, eds., *Epidemiology and Health Policy* (London: Tavistock, 1987).

8. These orientations can be understood as frameworks with some of the qualities of Thomas Kuhn's research "paradigms" or Michel Foucault's "discourses." They are not empirical hypotheses to be tested, but conceptual systems within which analytical criteria (including legal, economic, and moral criteria) take on distinctive meaning. In philosophical terms they are transcendental frameworks that make other arguments possible, and thus are not testable arguments in themselves. Rather than plunge into contemporary debate over the historical, sociological, political, or moral status of these systems, I am labeling them purely *heuristic*: their value will come from what they enable us to see differently about concrete policies and social philosophies concerning accidents. An introduction to the use of broad explanatory frameworks in social theory can be found in Quentin Skinner, ed., *The Return of Grand Theory in the Human Sciences* (Cambridge: Cambridge University Press, 1985).

9. For current perspectives on these themes see William M. Sullivan, *Reconstructing Public Philosophy* (Berkeley and Los Angeles: University of California Press, 1986); Lawrence A. Boland, *Methodology for a New Microeconomics: The Critical Foundations* (Boston: Allen & Unwin, 1986); Robert Wuthnow, *Meaning and Moral Order: Explorations in Cultural Analysis* (Berkeley and Los Angeles: University of California Press, 1987).

10. The idea of dividing these two functions of tort law between separate policies was presented by Terence G. Ison in his pioneering work, *The Forensic Lottery* (London: Staples Press, 1967). It has been elaborated in other works by Ison, P. S. Atiyah, and Donald Harris. See for example P. S. Atiyah and Peter Cane, *Accidents, Compensation and the Law*, 4th ed. (London: Weidenfeld & Nicolson, 1987); and Donald R. Harris et al., *Compensation and Support for Illness and Injury* (Oxford: Clarendon Press, 1984). For applications to Canada, see E. P. Belobaba, *Products Liability and Personal Injury Compensation in Canada: Towards Integration and Rationalization* (Ottawa: Policy Research, Analysis and Liaison Directorate, Policy Coordination Bureau, Consumer and Corporate Affairs, 1983). Stephen D. Sugarman has suggested some creative ways to implement the basic concept in the American context ("Doing Away With Tort Law," *California Law Review* 73 [1985]: 555–664).

11. Among works cited in Chapter 1, see G. Edward White, *Tort Law in America: An Intellectual History* (New York: Oxford University Press, 1985); and George L. Priest, "The Invention of Enterprise Liability: A Critical History of the Intellectual Foundations of Modern Tort Law," *Journal of Legal Studies* 14 (1985): 461–527.

12. See for example Guido Calabresi, *The Costs of Accidents* (New Haven, Conn.: Yale University Press, 1970), p. 43.

13. The kind of regulation envisioned under market theories of general or optimal deterrence requires that the market somehow quantify the prospects for future damage. Some theorists imagine that the liability system can supply this information, as an aggregate of past court decisions about the extent of damage in individual cases. For the formal argument see Calabresi, *The Costs of Accidents*, which is also discussed in Chapter 4.

14. See Atiyah and Cane, *Accidents*, p. 558.

15. National Childhood Vaccine Injury Act of 1986, Pub. L. No. 99-660, Title III; 100 Stat. 3755; 42 U.S.C. §300aa. This law is discussed in Chapter 9.

16. See, for example, Richard Epstein's arguments in *Modern Products Liability Law*, pp. 110–12.

17. The vaccine compensation program is an unusual example in several ways. The statistical association between substance and injury is much clearer than with other consumer products, in part because of the careful surveillance that accompanies mass immunization efforts, but also because of the purely physiological means by which an otherwise beneficial product turns on its user and causes serious injury. The clarity of this association invites the courts to impose liability, but the most likely judicial targets (the vaccine manufacturers) are able to retaliate against clearly defined public health objectives. Thus when Congress embraces the presumptions contained in the environmental orientation, it has specific reasons to do so. See the discussion in Chapter 9.

18. Regulations for federally sponsored research have existed since the late 1970s. For pending developments see Gregory A. Jaffe, "Inadequacies in the Federal Regulation of Biotechnology," *Harvard Environmental Law Review* 11 (1987): 491–550. See also Charles Perrow, *Normal Accidents: Living with High-Risk Technologies* (New York: Basic Books, 1984), pp. 293–303; and Diana B. Dutton, *Worse Than the Disease: Pitfalls of Medical Progress* (New York: Cambridge University Press, 1988).

19. See the study recently published by the Environmental Defense Fund, mentioned along with other research in the *New York Times*, "Even with Action Today, Ozone Loss Will Increase," March 20, 1988, p. 1. The Montreal Protocol on Substances That Deplete the Ozone Layer is scheduled to go into effect in 1989, if ratification is successful. See Senate Executive Report No. 100-14, 100th Congress, 2nd Session (1988).

20. Unlike civil litigation, criminal justice proceedings take the form of "the public" against the defendant. Under the environmental approach to accountability, criminal proceedings represent the most personalized levels of attribution under conditions where society wishes to make both symbolic and pragmatic responses. A recent trend toward bringing environmental injury cases under criminal statutes suggests an appetite on the part of the public for some kind of symbolic response to group and corpo-

rate behavior—one that an accountability policy could always indulge. Whether or not this is a healthy release of public frustrations surrounding environmental accidents, it is probably of only limited utility in controlling future accidents.

21. See Ison, *Forensic Lottery*, chap. 4; Harris et al., *Compensation and Support*, pp. 327–29; Jane Stapleton, *Disease and the Compensation Debate* (Oxford: Clarendon Press, 1986), pp. 49–51.

22. Although proximate cause has disappeared from strict liability, there remains the troublesome burden on plaintiffs to establish some "cause in fact" that ties the injury to an alleged source through something more than random association; see Harper, James, and Gray, *The Law of Torts*, vol. 4, pp. 85–130 (§20.1–20.3).

23. See Terence G. Ison, *Accident Compensation: A Commentary on the New Zealand Scheme* (London: Croom Helm, 1980), chap. 2; and Stapleton, *Disease*, pp. 147–58.

24. Ison, "Etiological Classifications," pp. 86–91; Stapleton, *Disease*.

25. As we shall see in the next section, however, causal relationships interpreted by epidemiological models still have an important part to play in accident prevention.

26. See the National Childhood Vaccine Injury Act of 1986, §2115(a)(2)–(4). For the New Zealand Accident Compensation Act, see Act No. 181, 1982 N.Z. Stat. 1552, §79.

27. For an overview see Robert H. Haveman, Victor Halberstadt, and Richard V. Burkhauser, *Public Policy Toward Disabled Workers: Cross-National Analyses of Economic Impacts* (Ithaca, N.Y.: Cornell University Press, 1984).

28. See Deborah A. Stone, *The Disabled State* (Philadelphia: Temple University Press, 1984), pp. 172–75.

29. In addition to ibid., chaps. 3–4, see Edward D. Berkowitz, *Disabled Policy: America's Programs for the Handicapped* (Cambridge: Cambridge University Press, 1987); and Saad Z. Nagi, "The Concept and Measurement of Disability," in Edward D. Berkowitz, ed., *Disability Policies and Government Programs* (New York: Praeger, 1979), pp. 1–15.

30. In addition to Haveman et al., *Public Policy*, see the earlier book by the same authors on American policy: Richard V. Burkhauser and Robert H. Haveman, *Disability and Work: The Economics of American Policy* (Baltimore: Johns Hopkins University Press, 1982).

31. Needless to say, the literature on disability programs is quite vast. In addition to general texts cited here, see International Social Security Association, *Social Security and Disability Issues in Policy Research* (Geneva: International Social Security Association, 1981).

32. For a summary of public programs see George E. Rejda, *Social Insurance and Economic Security*, 2nd ed. (Englewood Cliffs, N.J.: Prentice-Hall, 1984); and Health Insurance Association of America, "Compen-

sation Systems Available to Disabled Persons in the United States"
(Washington, D.C.: Health Insurance Association of America, 1979). See
also the useful essay by Beth Stevens on the interplay of public and private programs in American social policy: "Blurring the Boundaries: How
the Federal Government Has Influenced Welfare Benefits in the Private
Sector," in Margaret Weir, Ann Shola Orloff, and Theda Skocpol, eds.,
The Politics of Social Policy in the United States (Princeton, N.J.: Princeton University Press, 1988), pp. 123–48.

33. The conflict between tort procedures and rehabilitation has also been
studied; see Terence G. Ison, "The Therapeutic Significance of Compensation Structures," *Canadian Bar Review* 64 (1986): 605–37.

34. Jerry L. Mashaw, *Bureaucratic Justice: Managing Social Security Disability Claims* (New Haven, Conn.: Yale University Press, 1983).

35. Some relevant evidence for occupational disease was discussed in Chapter 9. As Deborah Stone points out, courts have further contributed to
expansion of disability cases by liberal construction of statutory language
in entitlement programs (*Disabled State*, pp. 152–61).

36. George Rohrlich, "Multiple Public Compensation Schemes and the
'Comprehensive Compensation' Approach," paper presented at the an-
nual meeting of the Association for Risk and Insurance, Arlington, Texas,
August 14, 1978, p. 13.

37. Ison, *Forensic Lottery*.

38. Stapleton, *Disease*.

39. A fuller discussion of comprehensive plans, with references, is presented
in Chapter 11.

40. Stapleton, *Disease*, pp. 142–58.

41. Atiyah and Cane, *Accidents*, p. 549. In the mid 1980s New Zealand reex-
amined the basic principles of the ACA, along with possible revisions in
scope and funding patterns. A study released in 1988 by the New Zealand Law Commission recommended gradual expansion of the program
to include illness and other forms of disability. *Personal Injury: Prevention and Recovery*, Report on the Accident Compensation Scheme (Wellington: New Zealand Law Commission, 1988).

42. Sugarman's 1985 proposal thus has a somewhat old-fashioned sound. In
fact, he proposes no political *quid pro quo* for the abolition of tort, and
his strategy seems limited to persuading the electorate that "the costs of
the tort system outweigh its benefits" ("Doing Away with Tort Law," p.
558). Based on our review of current political debate over tort reform
(Part III), it seems doubtful that the most active interest groups are ready
to agree with that assessment.

43. For similar reflections see Kenneth S. Abraham, "Individual Action and
Collective Responsibility: The Dilemma of Mass Tort Reform," *Virginia
Law Review* 73 (1987): 845–907.

44. Deborah R. Hensler, William L. F. Felstiner, Molly Selvin, and Patricia A. Ebener, *Asbestos in the Courts: The Challenge of Mass Toxic Torts* (Santa Monica, Cal.: Rand Corporation, 1985), pp. xxvii–xxviii.

45. These figures are taken from James S. Kakalik, Patricia A. Ebener, William L. F. Felstiner, and Michael G. Shanley, *Costs of Asbestos Litigation* (Santa Monica, Cal.: Rand Corporation, 1983), pp. 10, 37, 39, based on an estimated $40 billion in total future compensation payments. Legal costs for the defense can be projected at an additional $25 billion, while reductions from compensation awards for plaintiff legal costs should be around $15 billion.

46. In re "Agent Orange" Product Liability Litigation, 597 F.Supp. 740 (E.D.N.Y. 1984), 611 F.Supp. 1221 (E.D.N.Y. 1985), aff'd, 818 F.2d 145 (2d Cir. 1987), *cert. denied*, 108 S.Ct. 695, 2898 (1988). Among references cited in Chapter 6, the best overview is Peter H. Schuck, *Agent Orange on Trial: Mass Toxic Disasters in the Courts* (Cambridge, Mass.: Belknap Press, 1986).

47. These terms were used by the Court of Appeals, 818 F.2d 179, 182–84.

48. The death benefit was set at $3,400, and the disability benefit (which used definitions from the Social Security Act) carried a maximum of $12,400 (611 F.Supp. 1396, 1417–27). As Schuck observes, this approach relies on causation to define the outer boundaries of eligibility—Vietnam veterans exposed to Agent Orange—but abandons it for purposes of equity within the class (*Agent Orange on Trial*, p. 220). The extraordinary degree of judicial discretion exercised by Judge Weinstein in this distribution plan was upheld by the Court of Appeals, 818 F.2d 179, 181–82.

49. Schuck, *Agent Orange on Trial*, p. 223.

50. For 1986 figures see "Social Security Programs in the United States," *Social Security Bulletin* 50, no. 4 (1987): 44. The 1983 figures come from the Veterans Administration Office of Information Management and Statistics, "Data on Vietnam Era Veterans" (Washington, D.C.: Veterans Administration, 1983), p. 30. Congress continues to debate new benefits for Agent Orange veterans. In 1988 the Senate Veterans Affairs Committee approved S. 2011, which would have extended disability benefits to all Vietnam veterans suffering from certain forms of cancer.

51. Schuck, *Agent Orange on Trial*, p. 5.

52. Atomic Energy Act Amendments of 1966, 80 Stat. 891, Sec. 3, 42 U.S.C. §2210(n).

53. For background on the litigation see Stibitz v. General Public Utilities Corp., 746 F.2d 993 (3rd Cir. 1984), *cert. denied*, 469 U.S. 1214 (1985).

54. See the discussion in House Report 100-104, part 1, p. 16.

55. "Developing Social Policy in Conditions of Rapid Change: the Role of Social Welfare" (1972), in Brian Abel-Smith and Kay Titmuss, eds., *The*

Philosophy of Welfare: Selected Writings of Richard M. Titmuss (London: Allen & Unwin, 1987), p. 264.

56. It seems pointless to worry about the precise boundaries of the concept of disability, at least until disability policy moves substantially further down the road. Once causal categories have been abandoned, it is up to each society to decide which "diswelfares" it will recognize, and how it will respond to psychological, economic, and spiritual deficits. In legal commentary on the New Zealand scheme, there appears to be something of a contest to see who can envision the "broadest" compensation policy. See, for example, Sugarman, "Doing Away with Tort Law," p. 643 (he includes unemployment and retirement); and David G. Owen, "Deterrence and Desert in Tort: A Comment," *California Law Review* 73 (1985): 665–76 (he includes laziness and stupidity).

57. Advocates of market-based deterrence frequently allude to empirical evidence supporting their position that no-fault compensation invites careless behavior, which in turn transgresses the favored norm of optimal deterrence. See for example William M. Landes and Richard A. Posner, *The Economic Structure of Tort Law* (Cambridge, Mass.: Harvard University Press, 1987), pp. 10–11. In their enthusiasm, they sometimes overstate the results, ignoring the inevitable limitations of statistical arguments construing complex events. For example, "Swan's study of New Zealand's no-fault law found that the law had caused a 20 percent increase in automobile accident deaths" (Landes and Posner, p. 11, n. 32). Whatever Swan's study actually says, it seems to contradict the conclusion of Craig Brown, whose data show a "predominantly downward trend in the number of accidents, deaths, and injuries," which "continued and even accelerated after New Zealand adopted the Accident Compensation Act" ("Deterrence in Tort and No-Fault: The New Zealand Experience," *California Law Review* 73 [1985]: 1002). For other rejoinders see Sugarman, "Doing Away with Tort Law," pp. 587–90; and Mark Kelman, "Comment on Hoffman and Spitzer," *Columbia Law Review* 85 (1985): 1037–47.

58. A good summary of these arguments can be found in Norman Furniss and Timothy Tilton, *The Case for the Welfare State: From Social Security to Social Equality* (Bloomington: Indiana University Press, 1977), chap. 4.

59. See Stone, *Disabled State*, chap. 6.

60. In the past two decades, retributive goals have regained some of their earlier prominence in discussions of criminal justice; see Francis A. Allen, *The Decline of the Rehabilitative Ideal: Penal Policy and Social Purpose* (New Haven, Conn.: Yale University Press, 1981).

61. See Calabresi, *The Costs of Accidents*.

62. This is the impression one gets from David Rosenberg's article, which would restructure the judicial process around the goal of limiting aggre-

gate compensation awards to the economically optimal level of liability ("The Causal Connection in Mass Exposure Cases: A 'Public Law' Vision of the Tort System," *Harvard Law Review* 97 [1984]: 849–929). See also Guido Calabresi and Alvin K. Klevorick, "Four Tests for Liability in Torts," *Journal of Legal Studies* 14 (1985): 585–627.

63. The main issues in the regulation debate are summarized in Stephen Breyer, *Regulation and Its Reform* (Cambridge, Mass.: Harvard University Press, 1982), part I.

64. William Haddon, Jr., "Advances in the Epidemiology of Injuries as a Basis for Public Policy," *Public Health Reports* 95 (1980): 418.

65. Ibid. The functional approach to regulation can be illustrated by efforts to produce a safer pertussis vaccine, now being undertaken by joint public-private ventures ("What's New in Vaccines," *New York Times*, May 15, 1988, p. 13). Before the recent federal law removing DPT vaccine injuries from the tort system, the courts had attempted to stimulate safety efforts by holding manufacturers causally (and therefore financially) responsible. The result, as we saw in Chapter 9, was to endanger vaccine supply by scaring manufacturers out of the market.

66. For a classic analysis of multiple regulatory techniques, see the seminal text by Robert A. Dahl and Charles E. Lindblom, *Politics, Economics, and Welfare: Planning and Politico-Economic Systems Resolved into Basic Social Processes* (New York: Harper & Brothers, 1953).

67. For a concise summary of this period see Congressional Quarterly, Inc., *Environment and Health* (Washington, D.C.: Congressional Quarterly, 1981).

68. Because of the structure of litigation, of course, the basic elements of the prevention strategy were individual court decisions awarding compensation to particular plaintiffs. For an overview see (among other sources cited in Chapter 1) Harper, James, and Gray, *The Law of Torts*, vol. 5, pp. 573–92 (§28.32A).

69. For a representative statement see Leon Green, "Tort Law Public Law in Disguise," *Texas Law Review* 38 (1959 and 1960): 1–13, 257–69.

70. The exception is Richard Epstein, whose version of strict liability tried to limit redistribution even more than the old negligence regime; see "A Theory of Strict Liability."

71. See Breyer, *Regulation*, part I.

72. Richard B. Stewart, "Regulation and the Crisis of Legalisation in the United States," in Terence Daintith, ed., *Law as an Instrument of Economic Policy: Comparative and Critical Approaches* (Berlin: Walter de Gruyter, 1988), p. 112.

73. The actual impact of product liability trends on corporate decision making, to the limited extent it has been studied, seems to deviate considerably from the presumptive ideal; see George Eads and Peter Reuter, *Designing Safer Products: Corporate Responses to Product Liability Law and Regulation* (Santa Monica, Cal.: Rand Corporation, 1983).

74. On the priority of political and economic systems, see John G. Cullis and Philip R. Jones, *Microeconomics and the Public Economy: A Defense of Leviathan* (Oxford: Basil Blackwell, 1987).

75. For more general arguments along similar lines, see Charles E. Lindblom, *Politics and Markets* (New York: Basic Books, 1977); and Claus Offe, "The Divergent Rationalities of Administrative Action," in *Disorganized Capitalism* (Cambridge, Mass.: MIT Press, 1985), pp. 300–16.

76. Robert E. Lane has offered some social-psychological hypotheses on the conditions favoring political control over economic systems ("Market Thinking and Political Thinking," in Adrian Ellis and Krishan Kumar, eds., *Dilemmas of Liberal Democracies* [London: Tavistock, 1983], pp. 122–47).

77. Harper, James, and Gray explore this thesis and find historical evidence that even the "golden age" of negligence managed to shift accident costs, in a variety of cases (*The Law of Torts*, vol. 3, pp. 103–14 [§§12.1–12.3]).

78. For the breakdown of $8.5 billion authorized in 1986, see *Congressional Quarterly Almanac* 42 (1986): 111–19.

79. For reasons transcending the debate over accident policy, a variety of revenue sources other than excise taxes could be used to fund compensation and regulation costs. For a general survey of issues see Joseph A. Pechman, *Federal Tax Policy*, 5th ed. (Washington, D.C.: Brookings Institution, 1987).

80. Calabresi's analytical description of this model remains the clearest (*The Costs of Accidents*).

81. This position is eloquently stated by Perrow, *Normal Accidents*.

82. The expectation that tort law will simply fade away, rather than be dramatically abolished, is shared by most of our European allies, as we will see in the following chapter. See especially the *Report* of the British Royal Commission on Civil Liability and Compensation for Personal Injury (London: HMSO, 1978).

83. Shubert, *Some Observations*, p. 11.

84. John Dunn, *Rethinking Modern Political Theory* (Cambridge: Cambridge University Press, 1985), p. 189.

Chapter 11

1. George H. Gates (President of Grinnell College) in a letter to the American progressive Henry Demarest Lloyd, October 11, 1900, cited in Peter J. Coleman, *Progressivism and the World of Reform: New Zealand and the Origins of the American Welfare State* (Lawrence: University of Kansas Press, 1987), p. 51.

2. See Deborah A. Stone, *The Disabled State* (Philadelphia: Temple University Press, 1984), chaps. 2–3. For the impact of New Zealand industrial policies on the American progressive movement, see Coleman, *Progressivism*.

3. For the most recent reprint of the statute see Act No. 181, 1982 N.Z. Stat. 1552.

4. The most influential works for spreading the New Zealand story were Geoffrey W. R. Palmer, "Compensation for Personal Injury: A Requiem for the Common Law in New Zealand," *American Journal of Comparative Law* 21 (1973): 1–44; Donald R. Harris, "Accident Compensation in New Zealand," *Modern Law Review* 37 (1974): 361–76; and P. S. Atiyah, *Accidents, Compensation and the Law*, 2nd ed. (London: Weidenfeld & Nicolson, 1975).

5. For a study of the social, economic, and political context in which the ACA evolved, see Jane C. Kronick, ed., "The New Zealand Accident Compensation Act as a Value Response to Technological Development," Final Report to the National Science Foundation, Grant No. OSS76-14794 (1978). For an analysis by one of the key developers of the scheme, see Geoffrey Palmer, *Compensation for Incapacity: A Study of Law and Social Change in New Zealand and Australia* (Wellington: Oxford University Press, 1979).

6. Frank Parsons, *The Story of New Zealand* (Philadelphia: C. F. Taylor, 1904), p. 713 (citations from Coleman, *Progressivism*, pp. 16, 55).

7. The leading analysis of the ACA is Terence G. Ison, *Accident Compensation* (London: Croom Helm, 1980). For another commentary, written by an administrative judge whose decisions helped shape the legislation after passage, see A. P. Blair, *Accident Compensation in New Zealand* (Wellington: Butterworths, 1978). George Rohrlich's report provides a candid view of operational problems encountered by the scheme. *A Study of Comprehensive Compensation Approaches*, Report to the Department of Health, Education and Welfare, Grant No. 10-P-98048-3-01 (1981). Miriam Vosburgh has outlined an implementation analysis of the New Zealand plan; see "Implementation Analysis: The Case of Accident Compensation in New Zealand," *Evaluation and Program Planning* 9 (1986): 49–59.

8. A contemporary inquiry into the Social Security system, however, defended the existing pattern of selective, means-tested, flat-rate benefits against the benefit philosophy espoused by the ACA (*Social Security in New Zealand*, Report of the Royal Commission of Inquiry [Wellington: Government Printer, 1972]). For a discussion of the ACA in the context of New Zealand social security policy, see Jane C. Kronick, Miriam G. Vosburgh, and William W. Vosburgh, "Changing Principles for Disability in New Zealand," paper delivered at the IX World Congress of Sociology,

Uppsala, Sweden, August 1978; and Richard Gaskins, Jane C. Kronick, and William W. Vosburgh, "Community Responsibility for Accident Victims: Changes in the New Zealand Welfare State," *Social Service Review* 51 (1979): 261–74.

9. Elsewhere I have made a detailed analysis of how the ACA evolved during the drafting process, in response to conflicting pressure from social welfare and common law traditions ("Tort Reform in the Welfare State: The New Zealand Accident Compensation Act," *Osgoode Hall Law Journal* 18 (1980): 238–79.

10. The initial report is generally referred to as the "Woodhouse Report" (*Compensation for Personal Injury in New Zealand*, Report of the Royal Commission of Inquiry [Wellington: Government Printer, 1967]). Other reports influential in shaping the final form of the ACA include a government White Paper, "Personal Injury—A Commentary on the Report of the Royal Commission into Compensation for Personal Injury in New Zealand" (Wellington: Government Printer, 1969); and a parliamentary report, "Report of the Select Committee on Compensation for Personal Injury in New Zealand" (also known as the "Gair report") (Wellington: Government Printer, 1970).

11. Woodhouse Report, part 6.

12. Ibid., part 7. New Zealand began a comprehensive review of the ACA in the mid 1980s, dealing with questions of future scope and funding. One committee of government officials laid out a range of options for public debate. *Review by Officials Committee of the Accident Compensation Scheme* (Wellington: Accident Compensation Corporation of New Zealand, 1986). In addition, a special study conducted by the New Zealand Law Commission, chaired by Sir Owen Woodhouse, called for gradual expansion of the program to include illness and other forms of disability. *Personal Injury: Prevention and Recovery*, Report on the Accident Compensation Scheme (Wellington: New Zealand Law Commission, 1988).

13. The report was published in three volumes; *Compensation and Rehabilitation in Australia*, Report of the National Committee of Inquiry (Canberra: Australian Government Publishing Service, 1974). For background and a concise commentary on the proposed bill, see Harold Luntz, *Compensation and Rehabilitation* (Melbourne: Butterworths, 1975).

14. These objections are summarized in "Clauses of the National Compensation Bill 1974," Report of the Senate Standing Committee on Constitutional and Legal Affairs (Canberra: Australian Government Publishing Service, 1975).

15. See Terry Carney and Peter Hanks, *Australian Social Security Law, Policy and Administration* (Melbourne: Oxford University Press, 1986), pp. 33–36 (n.b. the statement of Brian Howe, Minister for Social Security, on

the review projected for 1986–88, p. xi). Another figure in the Hawke Labour government, Attorney-General Gareth Evans, noted that the Labour Party platform contained a commitment to "a national compensation scheme on a no-fault basis, with universal coverage for all injury and for work-related injury and disease" (Attorney-General's Department, *Personal Compensation for Injury: Proceedings of a Seminar* [Canberra: Australian Government Publishing Service, 1985], p. 142). In 1984 the New South Wales Law Reform Commission issued a lengthy report proposing a no-fault scheme for automobile accidents (*Report on a Transport Accidents Scheme for New South Wales* [Sydney: New South Wales Law Reform Commission, 1984]). This impressive study reviews current no-fault policies in the Australian states, and foresees gradual progress toward comprehensive no-fault within Australia's federal structure.

16. See Luntz, *Compensation and Rehabilitation*, chap. 4.

17. Report of the National Committee of Inquiry, §254.

18. In the 4th edition of *Accidents, Compensation and the Law* (London: Weidenfeld & Nicolson, 1987), P. S. Atiyah acknowledges this assumption (p. 619), and he concedes that new evidence on the environmental sources of disease undermines the distinction.

19. See Ison, *Accident Compensation*, p. 19. For a critique of the distinction in light of more recent epidemiological research, see Jane Stapleton, *Disease and the Compensation Debate* (Oxford: Clarendon Press, 1986).

20. Report of the National Committee of Inquiry, §351(d).

21. Ibid., §347(e). The shift in argument was also cleverly framed to reflect the Committee's official terms of reference, which originally covered only the personal injury scheme, but was later amended to include possible extension to illness and congenital disabilities (§§22–23, 347[b]). See also Luntz, *Compensation and Rehabilitation*, pp. 4–6.

22. In 1963 a committee chaired by the New Zealand Solicitor-General, Sir Richard Wild, had reviewed the performance of the tort system in handling automobile accident claims. The committee made no major recommendations for change, despite data suggesting defects in the tort system; but Wild authored a spirited minority report that used those data to recommend sweeping legislative reforms. See "Report of the Committee on Absolute Liability" (Wellington: Government Printer, 1963), discussed in the Woodhouse Report, §§137–41.

23. Terence G. Ison, *The Forensic Lottery* (London: Staples Press, 1967).

24. Woodhouse Report, §97.

25. See, for example, Walter J. Blum and Harry Kalven, Jr., *Public Law Perspectives on a Private Law Problem: Auto Compensation Plans* (Boston: Little, Brown, 1965); Robert E. Keeton and Jeffrey O'Connell, *Basic Protection for the Traffic Victim* (Boston: Little, Brown, 1965); Jeffrey O'Connell, "Expanding No-Fault Beyond Auto Insurance: Some

Proposals," *Virginia Law Review* 59 (1973): 749–829; and Jeffrey O'Connell, *Ending Insult to Injury: No-Fault Insurance for Products and Services* (Urbana: University of Illinois Press, 1975) (referring to the New Zealand plan as a "blind alley," pp. 73–76).

26. "It is wrong that comparable needs should be graded to produce incompatible results. . . . [A] failure to define and act upon a comprehensive social strategy is a failure to develop a social conscience" (Report of the National Committee of Inquiry, §238).

27. Woodhouse Report. §485.

28. The Pearson Commission's *Report* was printed in three volumes (London: HMSO, 1978).

29. Atiyah, *Accidents, Compensation and the Law*, 2nd ed.

30. Pearson Report, §§2, 241, 907, 1414–1422. The report on "Safety and Health at Work" (London: HMSO, 1972) was known as the "Robens Report." For background on the thalidomide episode, see Harvey Teff and Colin R. Munro, *Thalidomide: The Legal Aftermath* (Westmead, Eng.: Saxon House, 1976).

31. John G. Fleming, "The Pearson Report: Its Strategy," *Modern Law Review* 42 (1979): 253.

32. Ibid., p. 249. See the Motor Accidents Act 1973 (Vic.) and Motor Accidents (Liabilities and Compensation) Act 1973 (Tas.).

33. Fleming, "The Pearson Report," p. 267.

34. Pearson Report, §1732, p. 367, §§1721–22.

35. Ibid., §1717.

36. An important collection of critical essays was edited by D. K. Allen, C. J. Bourn, and J. H. Holyoak, *Accident Compensation after Pearson* (London: Sweet & Maxwell, 1979).

37. See primarily Stapleton, *Disease*, and Donald R. Harris et al., *Compensation and Support for Illness and Injury* (Oxford: Clarendon Press, 1984). Sugarman, however, relies on the general economic argument that "the costs of the tort system outweigh its benefits" ("Doing Away with Tort Law," *California Law Review* 73 [1985]: 555–664).

38. For representative views see Adalbert Evers, Helga Nowotny, and Helmut Wintersberger, *The Changing Face of Welfare* (London: Gower, 1987). A cautious plea for reconsidering no-fault automobile legislation appeared in a recent survey of possible changes in the civil judicial system. *Civil Justice Review*, Report of the Review Body on Civil Justice (London: HMSO, 1988), §§455–456.

39. "Developing Social Policy in Conditions of Rapid Change," in Brian Abel-Smith and Kay Titmuss, eds., *The Philosophy of Welfare: Selected Writings of Richard M. Titmuss* (London: Allen & Unwin, 1987), pp. 254–68.

40. Ibid., pp. 263–64.

41. Woodhouse Report, §59.

42. Ibid., §56.
43. See the citation to the 4th edition, *Accidents*.
44. Claus Offe, "Democracy Against the Welfare State?" *Political Theory* 15 (1987): 523.
45. Woodhouse Report, §1.
46. For recent attempts to state similar ideas in the idiom of contemporary philosophy, see W. Curtiss Priest, *Risks, Concerns, and Social Legislation* (Boulder, Colo.: Westview Press, 1988), pp. 103–68; and Robert E. Goodin, *Protecting the Vulnerable: A Reanalysis of Our Social Responsibilities* (Chicago: University of Chicago Press, 1985), especially chap. 5. Goodin relies heavily on analogies with civil liability, and in the end he seems to locate "group responsibility" within a framework of stolid individualism. "Ultimately, all group responsibilities must be analyzed in terms of responsibilities of the individuals comprising the group" (p. 138).
47. Woodhouse Report, §2.
48. See Ison, *Accident Compensation*, chap. 8.
49. Woodhouse Report, §§9, 433.
50. This topic is discussed in greater detail in my article "Tort Reform in the Welfare State," pp. 269–79.
51. See Ison, *Accident Compensation*, chap. 6.
52. In the *International Encyclopedia of Comparative Law*, vol. 11, part 2 (Tübingen: J. C. B. Mohr, 1986), Tunc's survey is given the title "Traffic Accident Compensation: Law and Proposals" (chap. 14). By contrast, Hans-Leo Weyers's nearly contemporary survey explores additional areas of possible tort reform (*Unfallschäden: Praxis und Ziele von Haftpflicht- und Vorsorgesystemen* [Frankfurt a.M.: Athenäum Verlag, 1971]).
53. *International Encyclopedia of Comparative Law*, §14–92.
54. See also the more limited survey in Keeton and O'Connell, *Basic Protection for the Traffic Victim*.
55. See Weyers, *Unfallschäden*.
56. Pearson Report, vol. 3.
57. Ibid., §§533–35; see also Robert H. Haveman, Victor Halberstadt, and Richard V. Burkhauser, *Public Policy Toward Disabled Workers: Cross-National Analyses of Economic Impacts* (Ithaca, N.Y.: Cornell University Press, 1984), chap. 13.
58. The study in question appeared in 1965. See Pearson Report, vol. 3, §§946–50. In 1975 Israel approved a separate law for road accidents.
59. International Colloquium on Compensation for Personal Injury, June 16–19, 1986, Uppsala, Sweden. The conference was sponsored by the Folksam Insurance Co. and Skandia Insurance Co., Ltd. I am indebted to Donald Harris for sharing his copies of the approximately twenty separate national reports.
60. As will be explained herein, these programs are not voluntary for specific

individuals, but only for labor unions, local medical care advisory councils, and drug manufacturers.

61. For a description of the Traffic Damage Act, see Erland Strömbäck, "The Swedish System: Insurance in Favour of the Victims of Motor Traffic," International Colloquium, Report no. 2, pp. 20–23.

62. Jan Hellner, "Compensation for Personal Injury: The Swedish Alternative in an International Perspective," International Colloquium, Report no. 1, p. 2. Hellner's views were published in "Compensation for Personal Injury: The Swedish Alternative," *American Journal of Comparative Law* 34 (1986): 613–33.

63. For an overview and references to standard literature, see Norman Furniss and Timothy Tilton, *The Case for the Welfare State* (Bloomington: Indiana University Press, 1977), chap. 6.

64. Carl Oldertz, "The Swedish Security Insurance for Work Related Injuries, the Patient Insurance and the Pharmaceutical Insurance: Descriptive Report," International Colloquium, Report no. 3, pp. 5, 34. For a study based on 1982–83 research data, see Marilyn M. Rosenthal, *Dealing with Medical Malpractice: The British and Swedish Experience* (Durham, N.C.: Duke University Press, 1988).

65. "There are other objects of compensation for personal injuries than covering basic needs; in a welfare state any person who may suffer an injury will want protection which enables him to retain his standard of living even if he is injured." Hellner, "Compensation . . . The Swedish Alternative," pp. 7–8.

66. See, for example, George L. Priest, "The Current Insurance Crisis and Modern Tort Law," *Yale Law Journal* 96 (1987): 1521–90.

67. For a recent version of O'Connell's durable proposal, see "A 'Neo No-Fault' Contract in Lieu of Tort: Preaccident Guarantees of Postaccident Settlement Offers," *California Law Review* 73 (1985): 898–916.

68. Hellner, "Compensation . . . The Swedish Alternative," pp. 10–11.

69. For meditations on these themes, see the report of the Swedish Secretariat for Future Studies, *Time to Care* (Elmsford, N.Y.: Pergamon Press, 1984).

70. Hans-Leo Weyers, "Compensation of Personal Injuries in the Federal Republic of Germany," International Colloquium, Report no. 6, pp. 5–6.

71. Ibid., p. 6.

72. Izhak Englard, "Traffic Accident Victim Compensation in Israel: A Decade Experience with No-Fault," International Colloquium, Report no. 14, p. 14.

73. For a discussion of similar pressures in Japan see Alfred A. Marcus, "Compensating Victims for Harms Caused by Pollution and Other Hazardous Substances: A Comparison of American and Japanese Policies," *Law and Policy* 8 (1986): 189–211.

74. "Haftungsersetzung durch Versicherungsschutz—Rechtsvergleichendes Generalreferat," in John Fleming, Jan Hellner, and Eike von Hippel, *Haftungsersetzung durch Versicherungsschutz* (Frankfurt a. M.: Metzner Verlag, 1980), pp. 74–75.

75. Offe, "Democracy Against the Welfare State?" p. 530.

76. Ibid., pp. 528, 524–25.

77. Ibid., pp. 523–24.

Index

Accidents: definition of, 3, 5–6, 15–18, 353 n.6; paradigm (accidents), 18–25. *See also* Environmental accidents

Accidents and disease: epidemiological approach to, 49–52, 121–24, 293, 301–2; and policy issues, 4, 9, 16, 299, 332, 445 n.19

Accountability policy: compensation policy, in relation to, 295–98; deterrence concepts in, 119–24, 139, 317–21; and epidemiological issues, 297, 311–14, 317; and political system, 80–81, 99–100, 265–66, 296–97, 311; and public responsibility, 309–21; and Superfund funding model, 231, 275–78. *See also* Regulatory policy

Administrative compensation plans: and biomedical injuries, 278–86, 293; and causal criteria, 254, 263, 266, 274, 280, 296, 298–99; and federal responsibility, 258; and financing, 272, 276–78, 442 n.79; and litigation, 260–61; and occupa-

tional disease, 262–72; presumptions of, 266, 270–72, 274, 280, 429 n.79; social-welfare programs, in relation to, 268, 271–72, 278, 326, 330, 332–34; and workers' compensation, 253–62, 264, 275. *See also* Comprehensive accident policies

Agent Orange, health effects of, 182–83

Agent Orange litigation: causation issues of, 55; costs of, 306–7; criticism of, 186; description of, 181–86; and governmental immunity, 182; and judicial strategies, 184–86

AIDS, liability issues of, 163

Alternative dispute resolution: and asbestos claims, 175–77; and liability legislation, 94, 194, 201, 207, 209–13, 224–26, 246; and Superfund, 236–37

Analytic philosophy, 42, 130–31, 132, 363 n.54, 381 n.30

Aristotle, 147

Asbestos: federal role concerning, 266; health effects of, 4, 16, 90,